AMERICA AND WESTERN EUROPE

Studies of the Research Institute
of the German Society
for Foreign Affairs, Bonn

This study was supported through a grant
by the Fritz Thyssen Stiftung

Typeset by CCC at William Clowes & Sons Limited,
London and Beccles

AMERICA AND WESTERN EUROPE

Problems and Prospects

Edited by
Karl Kaiser and Hans-Peter Schwarz

Lexington Books
D.C. Heath and Company
Lexington, Massachusetts
Toronto

Library of Congress Cataloging in Publication Data
Main entry under title:

America and Western Europe.
Problems and Prospects.
Translation of Amerika und Westeuropa.
Includes bibliographical references and indexes.
1. Europe—Foreign relations—United States—Addresses, essays, lectures.
2. United States—Foreign relations—Europe—Addresses, essays, lectures.
3. United States—Foreign economic relations—Europe—Addresses, essays,
lectures. 4. Europe—Foreign economic relations—United States—Ad-
dresses, essays, lectures. 5. United States—Foreign relations—1977-
—Addresses, essays, lectures.
I. Kaiser, Karl, 1934-   II. Schwarz, Hans Peter.
D1065.U5A8613   1978   327.73'04   78-19242
ISBN 0-669-02450-3

Second printing, August 1979

Published simultaneously in Canada

Printed in the United States of America

International Standard Book Number: 0-669-02450-3

Library of Congress Catalog Card Number: 78-19242

LIST OF CONTENTS

PART THREE
DIMENSIONS OF SECURITY

PART FOUR
STRUCTURAL PROBLEMS IN THE WEST

PREFACE

by John J. McCloy

To contribute an adequate preface to a book which combines a comprehensive resume of Western European and North American postwar relationships and a dedication to such an old friend and collaborator as Kurt Birrenbach is not a simple task. I find it very difficult to separate in my mind the subject from the individual.

In thinking back over the events and the individuals that typify the postwar relationships across the North Atlantic, it becomes clearer to me than ever how vitally the welfare and indeed the survival of the liberal democracies have depended upon the closeness of those relationships.

The defeat of Hitler's aggressions in Europe was, of course, itself in large part the result of a joint Atlantic effort and when the encroachments from the East at the close of the war began to crowd in on the disaster-stricken areas of West Europe, it was only a joint effort on both sides of the Atlantic which enabled a reasonable standard of living and the full preservation of Western freedoms to prevail. The almost miraculous rehabilitation programs which were put into operation after the war constituted a critical and spectacular joint effort.

Likewise the new moves toward a Common Market and the elimination of restrictive trade practices and procedures within Europe were the result of a common objective conceived of and stimulated from both sides of the Atlantic. The Soviet Union's ambitions to extend its dictatorial hegemony into Western from Eastern Europe were repelled only through joint efforts and the display of common determination and common strength. The threat was not, as some revisionists would have it, merely an irrational fear of Soviet aggression instigated by American intransigence. The threat was real and it was the deep-seated and prevailing sense of common purpose and common destiny across the Atlantic which rose to meet it. The joint actions taken during this period following the catastrophe of a great war with its concomitant totalitarian expansion caused the period to become looked upon as a striking example of imaginative and courageous statesmanship. It was a period during which the liberal democracies regained strength, preserved their freedoms and secured the peace.

But today we find new circumstances and new forces at work and again the liberal democracies have to face new problems. Again we have an economic threat. This time it is more complex than the one which was faced in the 1940's and 1950's. North-South issues have arisen to complicate the East-West ones and no longer can things be put in order by having one predominantly strong country provide the money and raw materials to assist in the restoration of a stable economic order. Totalitarian regimes have proliferated rather than subsided since the 1940's and 1950's. The arms race continues fundamentally unrestrained with ultimate or nearly ultimate weapons lying triggered for instant use in silos or other launchers around the world. The strength and prestige of the United States has been compromised by its loss of a not so minor war and because of these developments the credibility of the American deterrent is being raised. There has appeared the arguable assertion that military superiority, nuclear, conventional and naval, once resposing in the democracies, has passed over into the hands of Communist powers. Whether the indisputable Soviet buildup in arms is motivated by a desire to have a "win" in the event of war or primarily to achieve a certain political leverage in peacetime, the fact remains that an element of uncertainty and disquiet in respect to the future has arisen. The threat of Communist Party control over some governments in the NATO Alliance does not decrease the uncertainty or instill confidence in the vigor of the Alliance.

The quality of Western leadership will again be measured by continued adherence to principle and by courageous common action. At this stage in history it might be arguable what Soviet intentions and capabilities may be, but what is not arguable is the continued need for a strong and combined will and capacity on the part of the free democracies to maintain their integrity and common faith. Again a common purpose and a sense of common destiny constitutes the best clear chance for the preservation of their freedoms and the peace of the world.

In an earlier period statesmen of stature and courage came forward to resolve the issues. They include such names as Acheson, Marshall, Monnet, Bevin, Clay, Schuman and Adenauer. If the new figures are not yet identified, they will emerge provided the network of contacts between the Western democracies is strong and is constantly kept up to date. The security of the liberal democracies can be maintained and advanced in the face of all new threats, but it requires more than merely noting the facts of change and acting as if the strengths displayed in the past might no longer have meaning or utility.

A suitable appraisal of the energy and imagination which Kurt Birrenbach devoted over a period of approximately twenty years to the maintenance of constructive relationships between Western Europe and North America cannot very well be condensed into this preface. It is in large part due to him and his sustained efforts that the depth of the texture of those relationships have been built up and improved. Earlier I have listed some of the outstanding names which have been associated with the subject of this book and the name of Birrenbach ranks with them for his interests and energies have contributed to almost every aspect of the Atlantic relationship. Birrenbach's engaging personality, together with his capacity for penetrating appraisals, opened doors to him in the Atlantic ministries whenever he sought information or cooperation. His judgments, always respected, were frequently reflected in constructive action taken by his own and other governments within the Alliance.

Many of his friends say he is a worrier, and a worrier he certainly is and has been over what he considers to be the pressing need for the closest understanding between Europe and North America. He becomes worried whenever he feels that a good understanding may not be in operation. His worries, however, never lead him to despair. They never cause him to lose his enthusiasm for the full employment of his talents on behalf of the cause to which so much of his life has been devoted.

John J. McCloy

INTRODUCTION

For many years the central importance of the relationship between America and Western Europe was undisputed for both sides. However, the radical changes that took place in world politics in the early seventies, including the breakdown of the Bretton Woods system, the October War with the ensuing oil crisis, and an aggravation of the conflict between North and South, created new problems and raised doubts as to whether the Atlantic relationship still retained the same degree of importance, not to mention its ability to function, compared with the earlier postwar period. Pentagonal chimeras and the neo-Bismarckian style of the Nixon years aided in strengthening these doubts.

Things have changed in the European part of the Atlantic world as well. The oil crisis and global recession have left deep scars. The entire southern periphery of NATO underwent change as a result of the Cyprus conflict, internal tensions in Greece and Portugal, and the political ascendancy of communist parties. These developments were accompanied by domestic crises, the inability to act in the area of foreign policy, and, often enough, tensions in relations with the United States.

After Gerald Ford's presidency had already led to a noticeable revival of American and European partnership, the election of President Carter enabled a school of thought to establish itself which sees in the industrial democracies the primary and most natural point of orientation for American foreign policy, and as partners for coordinating policy.

Thus, it seemed time to convene a group of American and Western European analysts to test the feasibility of this issue. Can the concept of coordinated American-Western European foreign policies be reconciled with present and future variables in domestic politics and the international system? What are the major points of conflict among the industrial democracies? How can cooperation be organized both conceptually and practically?

The authors of this volume, whose contributions were presented and discussed at a conference in November 1976 and then finalized in the winter of 1976/1977 in the light of these discussions, belong to different schools of thought and certainly have different views on a number of problems. Nevertheless, they all belong to that group of American and European foreign policy experts which is fortunately large and does not approach the subject from the start with the gloomy question: "Atlantis lost?" Instead they bring the conviction with them from different national and professional areas of experience that a concerted policy for the industrial democracies not only offers the only sensible answer to the challenges of the present and the future but that such a policy also has a chance of succeeding.

Of course they are aware that the best intentions are no substitute for realistic analysis and appropriate political action. An examination of the conditions, interests, and trends in the relevant areas very clearly shows the great difficulties that must be taken into account. This is true both of the relations between the democracies of North America and Western Europe, as well as of the future of the European Community.

Western Europe is, without a doubt[1], a group of states that for many reasons is committed to pursuing a common foreign policy and harmonizing large areas of domestic policy. It is evident, on the other hand, that the centrifugal forces influencing this economic, cultural, and security community have a considerable effect. This will doubtless be one of the central issues in the years to come. The increased complications in the Western European area will, as a matter of course, profoundly influence relations with North America. Conversely, the United States is still able to cautiously but effectively bring its influence to bear on these developments, if its will is strong enough and if the intensive contact at all levels with Western Europe, characteristic of the period after the Second World War, is maintained.

A comparatively small number of problems and issues were chosen from the multitude of possible questions and tasks that seem to be of central importance for the course of further developments. This selection from the universe of problems is, in any case, just as subjective as the essays by the authors which are, however, thematically coordinated. Our intention was not to produce a compendium, but rather a thought provoking, lively, politically oriented book.

The essays in section I are meant to illuminate a few basic preconditions for a partnership in foreign policy which are often overlooked when only economists or security experts analyze such problems: our respective basic philosophies and the images we have of each other on either side of the Atlantic, the development of cooperation among elite groups; the important problem of academic exchange and mutual cultural influence. Further studies (particularly concerning domestic developments) were intended, but could not be implemented in the given time frame.

The studies in section II are devoted to the problems of the Western economic system. The first two analyses examine the future of the market economy from the viewpoint of types of economic order and demonstrate to what extent economists from different schools of thought evaluate problems the same way, and where they arrive at different conclusions and solutions. The following study on the reform of the international economic system shows particularly how much economic relations between the industrial democracies have to involve the developing countries. The essay on the role of multinational enterprises uses an important example to examine what interdependence and loss of sovereignty means in practice. The paper on trade unions gives a survey of the political functions these organizations have in the important countries of the Atlantic area. At least in the Western European area they have assumed a key role in both a positive and negative sense.

In section III basic questions of present security policy are discussed from various points of view and, in part, with different evaluations. Security, here, is broadly defined, and thus it seemed appropriate to include a detailed discussion of "Eurocommunism"[2] in this section.

Section IV centers on the structural problems of the international system. Several studies here show that the concept of "American and Western Europe" is too narrow; Japan must be included in the solution of important problems, and in North America not just the United States but also Canada must be considered. The trilateral philosophy that also strongly influences Washington's view of things is certainly visible here. The other papers in this section examine the European Community as a regional system in the larger context of global relations as well as the relations between the United States and the European Community. Since the book is the result of a German initiative, it seemed fitting to analyze the special problem of German-American relations (which is important for the whole area) in the context of Washington's European policy.

In their conclusion the editors examine a few of the many problems and tasks discussed here that they consider to be particularly important for an agenda of political action.

The editors wish to take this opportunity to express their thanks to the authors who created this book patiently, cooperatively, and with impressive punctuality. The reader will recognize that there are no basic differences between the viewpoints of the Americans and the Europeans. Different emphases, where they are present, do not follow a national or regional pattern. This too is a sign of the community of common problems and political outlook that has developed in the postwar period.

Particular thanks go to Franz J. Klein who organized the conference on the papers, presented and handled the editing. We would also like to thank the translators and the American and German publishers for their contributions.

As John J. McCloy mentions in the preface, this book is intended to honor Kurt Birrenbach on his 70th birthday. From the German side the editors are only too happy to affirm this impressive laudation of his political activity. As co-founder of the German Society for Foreign Affairs, as its loyal promoter, and as the Society's present president, Kurt Birrenbach has made an exceptional contribution to a tradition of non-partisan cooperation in the analysis of problems of foreign policy as well as to the development of the systematic study of foreign security, and foreign economic policies, always stressing the link between practice and theory. Thus, with the presentation and dedication of this volume the editors at the same time express the thanks of a group of persons that extends beyond the sphere of activity of the German Society for Foreign Affairs.

Karl Kaiser   Hans-Peter Schwarz

Notes

[1] As evidenced by most of the studies in this volume.

[2] Because of various developments in this field, the contribution was entirely rewritten for the English edition in order to take into account events until December 1977.

PART ONE

OPINIONS, CULTURE AND ELITE RELATIONS

The Europeans' Image of America

by WOLFGANG WAGNER

I

There is of course, no such thing as *the* Europeans' image of America. America is a world in itself, a commonwealth of various peoples, a mixed assortment of colors, a conglomerate of industrial cities, immense agricultural areas and nearly unpopulated regions. Someone who first sets foot on this continent in one of the great metropolises of the East – usually the Europeans' first exposure to America – has an entirely different impression of the United States than someone else who is first introduced to America in the friendly southern atmosphere of California and is submerged in the gay easy-going life style of San Francisco. To make the picture-puzzle complete one would have to ask which America is meant: the America of Thomas Jefferson or of Watergate, the America of Wall Street or of the fervent piety of a black parish singing spirituals, the America of the "multis" or the slums, the America of the farmer or of the army of nameless office workers.

By the same token, the Europeans themselves are much too heterogeneous to have a homogeneous image of America. Not only does each nation have its own specific historical experience with the United States; images also vary according to generation and social strata. What still seems like paradise to the poor Sicilian, fills the Swede, intellectually oriented toward the ideal of a classless society, with disgust. The Irishman living in poor surroundings envies the uncle in New York who has attained modest prosperity; the cultivated Frenchman pities the friend forced to live in the Mid-West far from the theatre, concerts, and literary circles.

Not only can there be no consistent image of America amongst Europeans; it can also not be expected that the varied images and impressions Europeans have of the United States bear any relationship to reality. Nations have never gone to the trouble of forming a correct image of other countries, but instead have always preferred a few handy clichés. Such clichés have the advantage of explaining everything with ease; moreover, they can easily be employed for political ends. In praising the virtues of the Germanic tribes, Tacitus hoped to combat the decline in moral standards amongst his Roman countrymen. During the war, Hitler's denunciation of the "complete lack of culture" of the Americans[1] was aimed at reinforcing opposition to the West.

Clichés change from period to period following the ebb and flow of historical currents; but since the selection of stereotypes is limited, the same views return again and again, pleasantly familiar, regardless of changes that take place.

Anyone wanting to understand the image the Europeans have of America cannot avoid examining the colorful collection of labels which Europe has attributed to America in the course of history. The fact that such images emphasize, almost without exception, the differences between America and Europe not only stems from the human tendency to differentiate, but in this specific case more directly from the fact that since the eighteenth century American society has developed, despite all kinship, in conscious opposition to Europe: that which in America was felt to be liberation from an outmoded world of narrowness, conventions, and subjugation appeared to the Europeans as a break with universally binding precepts. The more America sought new alternatives, the stronger the Europeans perceived a challenge which forced them either to justify their own way of life and thus condemn America or to accept America as a model and hence to paint America in glowing colors.

From the very beginning three characteristics peculiar to America struck the Europeans as a strong contrast to their accustomed surroundings. The first aspect was the size, vastness and (apparent) virginity of the country. For the pilgrim fathers and their descendents this endless, sparsely populated continent to which they could flee from afflictions of all kinds in Europe – be they political, religious or social – was like a gift of God, "God's own country," created by some miraculous providence for his chosen children. To the European, on the other hand, accustomed for centuries to a limited space which forced people to manage frugally and to respect strict rules, this surplus of land seemed either a senseless waste or a magnificent freedom, and the untamed will to subject oneself to this vastness seemed like sinful presumptuousness or the invitation to unprecedented adventures. Later the American mania for making and breaking records aroused similar feelings: the Europeans were confronted with skyscrapers, and felt awestruck or aghast at a hypertrophy which defies human dimensions. The size of American companies – some of which have budgets as large as those of smaller European states – evoked either respect or fear. "The world is small; only America is large." This advertising slogan of an American shipping line sums up in a nutshell America's provocation of Europe.

A second characteristic, the freedom and license of the new world, reinforced such feelings. The Europeans, accustomed for generations to living in hierarchical structures which set narrow limits to the development of the individual, lacked the imagination to fully comprehend a political community which, well into this century, possessed almost none of the attributes of a state as it is understood and accepted in Europe as a matter of course, but which instead presented itself merely as a society. Whether the absence of state authority manifested itself in the lawlessness of the "Wild West" or in the gangster milieu of Chicago, whether in freedom of religion or in the reign of the dollar, in any case the European was faced with a world which questioned all his standards. This world could attract or repel him, depending upon his temperament and inclination; but whenever it touched him he was forced to measure his familiar rules against it: the alternative demanded comparison.

This comparison was finally forced upon the Europeans – and this is the third characteristic peculiar to America: the consciousness of being "chosen" which inspired the first Americans and which has persisted to this day through all the vicissitudes of history. When a nation or another social group claims to be elevated through God's grace above all others, then the others have the alternative of accepting this alleged judgment, and hence their own inferiority, or of rebelling and contesting this claim. These two attitudes have always vied with one another in Europe; but since passionate admirers of America were almost always free to move to the promised land, the critics of American arrogance have almost always dominated. This objection to the American self-evaluation was promoted well into our century by the proud awareness of the Europeans, developed over their long history, that their continent deservedly occupies the center of the world, as the refuge of Christianity and as the cradle of culture, as the stronghold of science and the point of departure for the great discoveries. What did America have – itself a country discovered by Europe – as a society without tradition, to offer in comparison?

Thus from the very beginning America did not allow for any indifference or complacency, but instead demanded a clear judgment of either full approval or complete damnation.[2] The alternatives posed have always allowed only a simple choice: *pour ou contre*? The answers were, of course, equally severe. At the end of the eighteenth century when Europe rediscovered America, first as a society and later also as a state, opinions were so contradictory that it is often difficult to envisage the same country as being behind them. Turgot's extolling of America as the "hope of the human race" stands side by side with the brusque condemnation by the Abbé Corneille de Pauw in 1769 of the conquest of the New World as the "greatest misfortune which ever happened to mankind." Another Abbé, Ferdinando Galiani, wrote at the same time: "Everything here in Europe is decaying, religion, the laws, the arts and sciences, and everything strives toward renovation in America." He advised Madame d'Epinay: "Don't buy a house in the Chaussée d'Antin, but in Philadelphia!"

II

A more detailed analysis would probably show that the opinions of Europeans on America have fluctuated greatly over the past 200 years. At times when Europeans were enthused by freedom, such as during the period of the French Revolution, in the years around 1830 and 1848 the United States stood in high esteem. At other times the traditionally negative prejudices were revived. There were and are to this day, marked differences between the various nations and social strata. It is striking that well into the twentieth century prejudices against America were less pronounced amongst the poor in Europe than amongst the bourgeoisie and the intelligentsia; for the proletariat and the poorer members of the bourgeoisie, America was always a refuge in time of need, a land of promise offering a chance even to the destitute, while the educated tended to look down upon this country as supposedly lacking in intellect and culture. Today the situation is reversed: in particular since World War II America has become a mecca for scientists and artists, while it now repels great segments of the working class, under the influence of Marxist thought and exasperated by feelings of jealousy.

Considering that the opinions and feelings of the lower social strata, including the millions of European emigrants, generally do not find expression in literature, it is not surprising that the negative view outweighed the positive in written comment on America. Such commentary was, in general, dominated by three recurrent themes: America as a continent without culture, America as the country of idolatry of money, and America as the Babylon of licentiousness.

"These Americans are a nation of shopkeepers who stink to high heaven. Dead to all intellectual life, dead as a door nail." Nikolaus Niembsch, Edler von Strehlenau, better known under his pen name, Nikolaus Lenau, was certainly anything but unbiased when he stated this summary verdict after the failure of his romantic effort at farming in the virgin forests of America, which he had undertaken in the hope of "getting rich quick." He found it characteristic of America that there were no nightingales there. America was constantly the object of "bon mots" that betrayed more desire for ridicule than concern for the truth. Even such a cynical, hardboiled man as George Bernard Shaw asserted: "The 100 percent American is 99 percent idiot."

And after a visit to the United States, Sigmund Freud, who was later to find his largest following in America, pronounced a verdict which would suggest that he had travelled through America with blinkers on: the conscious exists everywhere in the world except in the USA.

The emigration of many American artists to Europe in search of a new homeland was pleasant corroboration of the cultural prejudices of many Europeans. When, after long sojourns in Rome and Paris, the cultivated Henry James finally established himself in London and took English citizenship, was this not striking proof that the intellect no longer felt at home in America? How else could one interpret the mass exile of American artists (and would-be artists) in Paris, or the obligatory "educational tour" through Europe for the sons and daughters of the rich, not only to become acquainted with the cultural treasures but also to be initiated in the mysteries of the finer ways of life? It was obvious that the United States could surpass the Old World in terms of wealth, but without roots of their own the American would always have to return to the source of European culture. The capacity for Americans to achieve independent intellectual and artistic achievement was disputed from the outset. In the arrogant words of George Clemenceau: "America? That is the development from barbarity to decadence without the detour through culture."

Whether it was still in the stage of barbarity or already decadent remained unclear. What repelled the Europeans was not only the lack of intellectuality but the uncouth manners as well. With a shudder, Rudyard Kipling observed: "The American. . . knows no meals. He stuffs himself three times daily for ten minutes." In the nineteenth century chewing tobacco and spitting became the symbols of the American lack of cultivation, and were replaced in the twentieth century by chewing gum. Henryk Sienkiewicz reported "that most (Americans) move their jaws constantly as if they belonged to the family of ruminants and every now and then were to spit out a disgusting tobacco sauce". And Heinrich Heine lyricized: "Yet a country makes me fear, where the people chew tobacco, where they bowl without kingpin, where they spit without spitoons."

To the Europeans, chewing clearly seemed to be not only an expression of the American character but a substitute for intellectual activity as well, leading Ernst Ludwig von Wolzogen to conclude that: "If Cartesius had been born a Yankee he would have modified his famous 'cognito ergo sum' to read: 'I chew therefore I am!'"

The relationship between the sexes in America was a source of particular irritation to European visitors. It seemed to them to be characterized at one moment by incomprehensible prudery, at the next by coarse sexuality – in any case devoid of charm and lacking the refined art of love which especially the romantic peoples of Europe regarded so highly. Usually the American women were blamed for the situation. Kurt Tucholsky's drastic assertion that "below the waist they are made entirely of celluloid" bordered on flattery; for the current cliché saw them as mere dolls, that is, celluloid right up to the hairline. "An American lady," so stated by France Trollope, "scowls; even the youngest and prettiest can purse their lips and wrinkle their brows and look as hard and uninviting as their own grandmothers." No wonder that Ferdinand Nürnberger, in his widely read book with the telling title "The America-Weary," judged that of all the stupid moves that a German in America can make, the stupidest and most unforgivable, would be to marry an American woman.

The lack of culture, and here all critics of the New World are in agreement, was closely related to the materialism of American society which in turn expressed itself most graphically in the all pervading race for the dollar. This characteristic of the Americans was observed as early as the first half of the nineteenth century before the period of industrialization. When Fabrizio (in Stendhal's *La Chartreuse de Parme*) says that he wants to go to New York and become a soldier of the Republic the Duchess warns that he will see "what cult is practised before their idol the dollar."[3] Without ever having been there, Heine similarly concluded that: "Worldly utility is their true religion and money is their God, their one all-powerful God."[4] In his *Fröhliche Wissenschaft* Nietzsche asserts in a most unscientific manner (also judging from afar) that an "Indian-like coldness, characteristic of Indian blood, lies in the American way of striving for gold."[5] In the same context he describes the "breathless haste of work" as "the true vice of the New World," thus closing the circle: constant work as the means to the end of earning money, a plebeian attitude towards life which does not, of course, allow for a state of leisure in which alone true culture can thrive.

But what else can be expected of a country "where the most despicable of all tyrants, the mob, asserts its full dominance," as Heine ill-humoredly put it?[6] Even the European who, like Heine, yearned for freedom in Europe was repelled by the egalitarianism of American democracy. As Heine expressed it in his famous lines:

"Sometimes I have a mind to sail to America to the great freedom stable inhabited by egalitarian boors."

To be sure, most educated Europeans suspected that humanity was making a great experiment in America with its free society, but the manner in which freedom was practiced there appeared reprehensibly excessive to most of them. Far from giving the United States proper credit for having given refuge to millions of European immigrants, they, on the contrary, accused it of offering "asylum to the rabble of Europe."[7]

The Europeans were, indeed, less inclined to be impressed by the civil rights and political freedom in America than to focus on and stigmatize the misuse of this freedom. Since F. Vulpius first expressed the view in 1847 that America was "the country of freedom for all thieves, rogues and swindlers" this cliché has appeared again and again up to the present. In 1946 Hermann Hesse informed Thomas Mann with great satisfaction that "in Germany the dangerous criminals and racketeers, the sadists and gangsters are no longer Nazis nor do they speak German; they are Americans."[8] No one ever considered that perhaps these excesses were not too high a price to pay for freedom – a freedom which had never been experienced in Europe. The European, brought up to revere order, saw in America a boundless freedom which seemed to him like anarchy and as a rule preferred the good old order at home to this freedom which did not really seem to him to deserve the title. In 1933 George Bernard Shaw scoffed: "I am held to be a master of irony. But not even I would have had the idea of erecting a statue of Liberty in New York."[9]

Opinions vary as to whether America is a young or an old country, that is, still barbarian or already decadent. When Goethe wrote "America, you're better off than our Continent, the old. . ." he assumed that a young society, unencumbered by "ruined castles" had an advantage – although he hoped in vain that America would, therefore, be spared "legends of knights and robbers and ghost stories" (in America: Westerns and E. A. Poe). This feeling that Europe had turned to stone, that it was barren, whereas America still offered the chance to throw the ballast of the past overboard and to begin anew, dominated in the nineteenth century. Voices such as Lenau's which described America as the "true homeland of decline" were the exception. But this description referred primarily to life in the New World and less to the political conditions there. For a while the American Republic was for most people no more than an experiment which bode uncertain results. Hegel went so far as to maintain that "America had not yet progressed far enough to have need of a kingdom."[10] Alexis de Tocqueville, usually cited today as the principal witness for the defense, was the first great political writer who, based on his own observations, came to the conclusion that Europe's future was anticipated in the United States. He was not alone. In Germany, Friedrich List saw the United States as a model for the future.

III

A new approach only became possible when, in the course of this century, a change occurred in the kind of European who spent longer periods of time or who settled in America. Here we must differentiate between two large groups: immigrants[11] who turned their backs on Europe above all as a result of the persecution of the Jews and Hitler's campaign of conquest during World War II, some of whom later returned, for example Max Horkheimer and Theodor Adorno, Ernst Fraenkel and Golo Mann; and the immense throng of scientists, artists, writers, politicians, and journalists who after the war felt themselves pressured into undertaking an "educational trip" – at least once in their lives – to the United States, to Harvard or Princeton, Columbia or Berkeley; a reversal, so to speak, of the previous flow of Americans to Europe.

For the first group, as for the immigrants in the nineteenth century, America was a place of refuge; but in contrast to those who, above all, sought the chance of a new life, the new immigrants primarily welcomed the spiritual freedom in America. America offered the second group a scope of scientific research and artistic activity far surpassing that of the rest of the world and a center to which the Europeans must go on a pilgrimage just as previously the Americans went to Paris and Rome.

In addition, through their decisive intervention in two European wars, the United States and its citizens appeared to the Europeans in a new light. The young American boys who appeared in Flanders in 1917 and in 1944 in Normandy were seen as messengers from another world, a world full of vitality and inexhaustible reserves. By contrast, the Europeans saw themselves as old and effete. Nor could the nations of Western Europe, crushed by Hitler (and after 1945 many Germans as well), ignore the fact that Europe had not been capable of defending itself against totalitarianism by its own power but had to thank the United States for its salvation. As the USA with its great initiative, the Marshall Plan, had helped both the winners and the losers back onto their feet, it would have been the height of ingratitude not to have accorded this country and its citizens the recognition which was their due.

In those years, Europe, shaken in its self-confidence, saw itself squeezed between the two new world powers and confronted with the choice between the two ways of life as represented by the Soviet Union and the United States. For the great majority of Europeans the choice was easy; Soviet Communism in its Stalinist form had revealed its most abhorrent side during the war and in the following years had shown much too brutal a disregard of the will of the peoples in Eastern Europe which it had brought under its dominance. By contrast, the American way of life appeared much more familiar; the freedom which America preached satisfied one of the Europeans' fundamental needs after years of suppression, and to the extent that American politics and behavior appeared strange, these peculiarities were graciously overlooked in favor of the material advantages which they brought in their wake. In short, whereas Europeans had earlier believed that it would do the American barbarians a world of good to take a lesson from Europe, the United States was now accepted in many if not all respects as a model. When one of the returning emigrés, Golo Mann, described the rise of America as "the most astonishingly 'fortunate' event in the last 150 years,"[12] he probably expressed the feeling of many Europeans – that, had it not been for this lucky event, as Europeans were universally aware, Europe would have suffered a similar fate to that of Poland, Hungary, Czechoslovakia, and other countries.

The change of attitude can be demonstrated in any number of ways; suffice it here to illustrate this point with two typical quotations. In 1948 Carl Zuckmayer described how ten years earlier, he and Franz Werfel had resisted the temptation to go to America (which was later to become their second homeland) and in the process compiled the best of all collections of anti-American clichés: "I had never been there and Werfel had only been there once for a short visit in New York. But we knew everything there was to know about what was there or was not there from bad food to psychic and erotic frigidity... A country of fantastic standardization, one-dimensional materialism, of soulless mechanics. A country without tradition, without culture, without craving for beauty or form, without metaphysics, without fine wines, a country of chemical fertilizers and can-openers, without grace, without manure heaps, without class and without sloppiness, without Melos, without Apollo, without Dionysos. Should we escape the slavery of European mass dictatorship only to submit ourselves to the tyranny of the dollar, of business, advertising and brutal indiscretion?"[13]

But Zuckmayer did go to the United States after all and when he returned after the war and wrote about America, his description threatened to become such a eulogy that he cut himself short: "Far be it from me to praise America at the expense of or to the detriment of Europe. For I myself am an inveterate European, born and bred. And America gave me the chance to remain European, indeed German, in my profession, in my thinking and activity, in my potential and my work and at the same time with all my heart to be a citizen of America – a neighbor in a neighboring country, in a country whose passion and adventure is the future, in a country full of clear, clean, simple humanity, in whose language yes means yes and no means no, in a country which can no longer be excluded in visions of our European future, not as our master but as our travelling companion with whose free people we hope to strive together for a free and brotherly world."[14]

Was this an exception? By no means. It was typical of the majority of Europeans who came into closer contact with America in those years that they, often reluctantly, discovered in America virtues which had been lost or buried in Europe. Sometimes merely coming in contact with Americans in Europe was sufficient. Curzio Mâlaparte, one of the most widely read authors in that time period, wrote the following declaration of love for America and the Americans: "I like Americans no matter what their color . . . white or black, their soul is much brighter than ours. I like the Americans, because they are good Christians, upright Christians . . . because they believe that they alone are men of honor and that all the peoples of Europe are more or less dishonest. Their sense of humanity, their generosity, their honesty, and the pure simplicity of their ideas, their feelings, the sincerity of their behavior . . . gave me hope in a better humanity, the certainty that only the goodness— the goodness and innocence of these magnificent boys from across the Atlantic who landed here in Europe to punish the bad and to reward the good – could redeem both the people as a whole and the individual from their sins."[15] To be sure, a whole range of clichés are presented in this case; but it was not by chance that they appeared in one of the most successful novels in those years. Once again the United States appeared in a transfigured light as the great hope of the world, a country of unbroken strength which was determined to employ its strength so that good might triumph; in Greece as in Berlin, in Turkey as in Korea.

But it was not only America's commitment to freedom throughout the world that improved its reputation in the eyes of the Europeans. As in the twenties and thirties, a powerful impulse from American culture in the form of jazz came to Europe and filled the young in particular with enthusiasm; after the war current American literature was zealously consumed: Ernest Hemingway, John Steinbeck, and William Faulkner were admired as representatives of a new, fascinating literature. European theaters pounced upon the works of Tennessee Williams, Thornton Wilder, and Eugene O'Neill. In a wave that came somewhat later, American painters conquered the European art scene. The great orchestras, conductors and soloists demonstrated America's position as a nation of culture. American films took over a dominant position. The United States showed itself not only as the militarily most powerful and economically strongest country in the world but simultaneously as the leading nation in many realms of culture. The previous disdain, the slightly deprecatory, somewhat arrogant condescension towards America had somehow been eliminated.

Nonetheless, critical voices continued to be heard. But the new anti-Americanism which took shape in these years differed fundamentally from previous criticism of America. It was characteristically divided into criticism from the "left" and from the "right." The leftist critique was closely related to the new global opposition between the United States and the Soviet Union. Here, admiration for the Soviet Union and communism as well as an aversion to the predominance of the United States and the capitalist system it represented all came into play. Amongst the more important spokesmen that should be mentioned are Jean-Paul Sartre and Simone de Beauvoir, for both had experienced America firsthand and the niveau of their criticism by far surpassed that of the vulgar anti-Americanism as propagated by the Communist parties, for example, or in the "Ami go home" period. In Germany Leo L. Matthias's book *Die Entdeckung Amerikas anno 1953* (Hamburg: Rowohlt 1953) which did its best not to accord America a single redeeming feature, remained for years the only striking example of anti-Americanism.

The criticism from the "right" was kindled by the fear that the individuality of Europe was threatened by the domination of the United States. What was termed "Americanization"[16] was, indeed, an incontestable phenomenon in many areas, from management in industry to the mechanization of the kitchen, from automization of production processes to the conversion of eating habits to canned goods. It took a considerable time for the insight gradually to take hold that, although it indeed was no accident that the phenomenon arose in America, it had its roots in the nature of modern society and its trend towards increasing rationalization; so that, as Golo Mann put it, "America was only a few steps ahead of the general development."[17] In his widely read book, the *American Challenge*, Jean-Jacques Servan-Schreiber later made it clear to the Europeans that in order to assert themselves they should not evade the methods coming from America but must, on the contrary, do everything in their power to make these methods their own.

Towards the end of the sixties, leftist anti-Americanism experienced such an enormous revival that for several years it threatened to dominate the mood in Europe. The point of focus was racial unrest and the Vietnam War, but also the student movement in America which quickly spread to Europe.[18] It was suddenly discovered that American society was not as ideal as it had appeared after the war. Unequal treatment of the blacks, crimes of violence, the slums and the discrepancy between the external power of the United

States and the poverty among sections of the American population were rediscovered: the European societies which had in the meantime further developed their welfare systems which provide for everyone, appeared to many to be more "progressive." The Watergate scandal and the confusion during the final phase of the Vietnam War and of Nixon's presidency radically undermined the respect and trust which the United States had won in the two previous decades. But this phase passed with the end of the Vietnam War, student unrest, with Nixon's replacement, and the ensuing process of moral cleansing. In fact, the manner in which the United States came to terms with the problems of the turbulent phase evoked new respect. Europeans were impressed by the fact that the United States was able to cope with the "oil crisis" of 1973 better than most European countries. They again became conscious of the size and power of America.

IV

The Europeans' image of America is both unsettled and, at the same time, established. Clichés of the past are maintained with surprising tenacity through turbently changing times. However, which ones are dragged out at any one time depends on the predominant climate. For 200 years America's friends have been hoping that the friendly view of the United States will finally prevail and disperse the shadows obscuring the picture. But her opponents have been waiting just as long for what they consider the great illusion of America to be destroyed and the naked, repulsive figure of the New World to reveal itself. Instead we experience a constant struggle between the two views of the nature of America and the Americans, in which alternately the positive, and the negative aspects predominate. Since this struggle has already been going on for so long, it would hardly be too audacious to predict that these two views of America will continue to compete with one another in the future.

This prospect may disappoint the Americans and their European friends, but they should console themselves with the thought that it could be worse, as a glance at another continent shows. For centuries, Latin-American literature has been dominated by anti-Americanism that often borders on open hatred. That which in Europe is the exception is the rule here. Important writers such as Pablo Neruda and Miguel Angel Asturias, to name but two Nobel Prize winners, contributed to a poisoning of the intellectual atmosphere in relations with the United States that may not be remediable for generations.

The example of Latin America may, at the same time, offer an indication as to what factors influence the American image. It seems to be just as dependent on the degree of self-confidence of the peoples in question and how they approach America, as it is on the behavior of the United States, its large corporations and its citizens. Nothing is as detrimental to a relationship as a feeling of inferiority and dependency. When companies such as the United Fruit Company or ITT behaved like colonial powers in Latin-American countries, they may have been serving short or medium term business interests but they did nothing to enhance the image of the United States. And again, the United States cannot complain when it maintains friendly relations with a dictator for an extended period of time and the oppressed people, once the regime has been overthrown, emotionally rejects that regime's former friends.

Power evokes respect, but not love. The more clearly power is demonstrated the greater the respect may be, but the less will be the inclination towards love. That is the experience other world powers had in the past and it is the burden of the United States today.

The fundamental difficulty in the European-American relationship consists in the fact that the United States has to demonstrate power to protect its European allies, but these demonstrations, which are intended to deter Soviet expansionist desires, inevitably evoke feelings of inferiority in those protected. A similar situation can be observed in the economic sector. Without the active interest of large American firms in the European market during the past decades, the Western European economy could not have recovered as rapidly from the effects of the war. However, in many cases, this interest is considered disturbing. Europe and America will have to live with these facts in the future.

The more America avoids giving Europeans the impression that it wants to force something on them, and the more every European nation or Europe as a whole develops self-confidence with which to endure American supremacy more calmly, the easier it will be to live with the situation. The Europeans will probably not be able to realize the other possible alternative within the foreseeable future, that alternative being the formation of a European federation which would be an equivalent partner to the United States.

Notes

[1] cf. Henry Picker, *Hitlers Tischgespräche im Führerhauptquartier 1941–1942*, Stuttgart: Seewald 1963, p. 220.

[2] The latest study on this subject is by Manfred Henningsen, *Der Fall Amerika*, Munich: List 1974. A collection of quotations is contained in Gert Raeithel, (ed.), *Citronen für Onkel Sam*, Munich: Kindler 1975. Many of the following examples have been taken from these two studies, which also contain additional bibliographic references.

[3] Stendhal, *Werke*, Munich: Desch 1965, p. 739.

[4] Heinrich Heine, *Sämtliche Schriften*, Munich: Hanser 1971, Vol. 4, p. 39.

[5] Friedrich Nietzsche, *Die fröhliche Wissenschaft*, Leipzig: Kröner 1917, Nr. 329.

[6] Heine, op. cit., p. 39.

[7] Henningsen, op. cit., p. 11.

[8] Hermann Hesse/Thomas Mann, *Briefwechsel*, Frankfurt a.M.: S. Fischer 1968, p. 112.

[9] George Bernard Shaw, *The Political Madhouse in America and Nearer Home*, London: Constable 1933, p. 32.

[10] Georg Wilhelm Friedrich Hegel, *Die Vernunft in der Geschichte*, quoted in: Henningsen, op. cit., p. 95.

[11] A few names are mentioned in the contribution by François Bondy.

[12] Golo Mann, *Vom Geist Amerikas*, Stuttgart: Deutsche Verlags-Anstalt 1954, 3rd edition, 1961, p. 28.

[13] Carl Zuckmayer, *Als Emigrant in Amerika*, in: Egon Schwarz/Matthias Wegner, (ed.), *Verbannung, Aufzeichnungen deutscher Schriftsteller im Exil*, Hamburg: Wegner 1964, pp. 149 f.

[14] Ibid., p. 154.

[15] Curzio Malaparte, *Die Haut*, Karlsruhe: Stahlberg 1950, pp. 18 f.

[16] cf. Jürgen Gebhardt, *Ursprünge und Elemente des Amerikanismus*, Munich 1969, unpublished manuscript; cf. Henningsen, op. cit., (footnote 2), pp. 210, 234 f.

[17] Golo Mann, op. cit., p. 11.

[18] cf. Klaus Mehnert, *Jugend im Zeitbruch*, Stuttgart: Deutsche Verlags-Anstalt 1976. The best known examples are: Rolf Hochhuth, *Guerillas*, Hamburg: Rowohlt 1970; Reinhard Lettau, (ed.), *Täglicher Faschismus*, Munich: Hanser 1971.

The Americans' Image of Europe

by J. ROBERT SCHAETZEL

Assessment of American attitudes toward Western Europe must begin with reference to the general mood of the country regarding both domestic and international issues. Given the uncertainty and ambiguity of public opinion an appreciation of these general views may be of even greater value than attempts to isolate more specific American attitudes with respect to Europe. A further caveat: it would be vainglorious to dare, in these days of confusion and contradiction, to offer confidently "The American Image of Europe," a presumed summary of the vagrant moods of 200 million odd – in several senses of the word – citizens. Hence, despite use of public opinion polls and studies, discussion with foreign and American experts, this must be one man's personal analysis and conclusion.

I

In this murky area one thing is clear: after years of decline the nadir of American interest in international affairs was hit in 1974. The most comprehensive study of this subject has been done by Potomac Associates.[1] Their current analyses noted that there had been "an enormous change in priorities . . . Twelve years ago the top five items all related to international and defense matters; now the ten leading items all have to do with domestic problems. Only in eleventh place do 'Keeping our military and defense forces strong' and 'The growing dependence of this country on foreign nations for supplies of oil and other natural resources' emerge, the latter tied at that ranking with 'The problems of our elderly senior citizens.' Ranked 22 is 'Maintaining close relations with our allies'"; "Communist leaders becoming members of the cabinet and sharing executive power in such countries as France and Italy" ranks 25th. Potomac Associates found a slight increase in public interest in foreign issues in 1976 over 1974. A substantial improvement in the economy could reverse what for a time seemed to be a long-term trend of declining attention.

Needless to say, polls provide at best only one clue to American attitudes.

They give a dimension, state a problem, but are far from definitive. They necessarily understate leadership thinking and influence and cannot anticipate the impact of elite groups in altering general public opinion. The polls, nonetheless, are an important point of departure.

The shift in national priorities is evident; why this came about is less clear. In the post-World War II period America's taste for simple, tidy solutions, quickly arrived at, was fed by a series of policies designed to cope with world problems as perceived in the heady atmosphere of victory. America's taste for institutional action and reaction was nourished by the United Nations and Bretton Woods systems, and the stillborn ITO; technical assistance was accepted as the magic cure to the needs of the poor nations; when Stalin shattered illusions that wartime collaboration would continue, NATO and regional security pacts were the response. All of these policies were conceived within an action-oriented society, by leaders committed to advocacy, and aided by the atmosphere of traditional American optimism.

That these institutions and programs did not bring us to the promised land is less important to this analysis than the impact of unsuccess on American attitudes toward international relations. Failure and dashed hopes coincided with other negative factors. To a degree America's buoyant expectations relied on international cooperation. These hopes faded in the face of cold Russian hostility, and bitterness was to be added later as de Gaulle both obstructed common programs and attacked American motives.

As the Cold War intensified, Stalin's unpaid allies in the United States – Senator McCarthy and the China Lobby – elaborated the theme of a two-dimensional world. They played on Americans' unsophistication and persuaded many that an insecure world, communist success in Eastern Europe and Mao's conquest of the mainland were essentially functions of official American incompetence or duplicity – probably both.

The gross self-mutilation of the McCarthy era subsided – in such dramatic form that one of its high priests would become President and initiate the openings of 1972 to Moscow and China – but confusion and disenchantment remained. Furthermore, during this tumultuous quarter of a century too many domestic economic and social issues had been ignored – civil rights, campus unrest, damage to the environment, urban decay, law and order. General public concern with these internal problems, intense debate over alternative responses, and growing worry about costs have had the effect of pushing international issues to one side.

Then there was that Typhoid Mary, Vietnam, which spread a host of evil side effects across the land – youth set against established institutions; the national ignominy of failure; a sense of American guilt, with an undercurrent of anger at allies who denied support but were handy with criticism. A latent antipathy to foreign entanglements was encouraged. Subsequent disclosures about the excesses of CIA and Lockheed intensified a cynicism which had become a new part of the national ego.

A more subtle point is the degree to which Nixon and Kissinger contributed to this process of American disengagement. For an America that had just lost its innocence Kissinger's diplomatic method offered the escape of foreign theater and allowed the citizenry to slide into the role of passive spectators. Aside from Vietnam, where the problem was how to escape, little was demanded of Americans other than to observe a colorful drama. Nixon's 1972 opening to China, made possible by Mao's reassessment of China's strategic interests, intrigued rather than involved the American public. This mood of detachment allowed Americans to accept the Nixon-Kissinger obsession with US-USSR relations.

II

This is the general background against which more specific American attitudes must be seen. If Americans still assign a relatively low priority to international matters it is probable that the views expressed are suggestive rather than definitive, subject to modification if there is strong leadership.

In addition to the factors cited above, the media – press and television – contribute to or reflect (probably both) the great shift in American priorities. The evidence is discouraging: newspapers eliminate staffs of foreign correspondents; minimal coverage of international news in other than major metropolitan papers; television treatment reduced to one and a quarter minutes on the 22-minute nightly network news shows.

The currents of opinion detected by the Potomac Associates studies suggest that today the American attitude toward international affairs has these major components: the nation is clearly more security conscious, more concerned about the possibility of another war, determined to maintain strong military forces, increasingly suspicious of the Soviet Union, more nationalistic and inclined to act unilaterally. Americans' sense of a greater need for allies is entirely consistent with this mood. Furthermore, there has been a dramatic surge in the willingness to "come to the defense of its major European allies with military force if any of them are attacked by the Soviet Union." In 1974 only 48% agreed with this proposition: in 1976 56 percent agreed.[2]

Americans continue to look on Western Europe as vital to their security; as a region which shares its democratic values. Thus beneath all the changes noted above, continuity with the past exists – containment of Soviet ambitions, a sense of Europe's indispensability to a secure, prospering world. But within the context of lowered expectations and domestic preoccupations, Americans are less sanguine about the role Europe will in fact play, or indeed, of Europe's will.

The combination of continuity in basic perceptions of America's interests abroad and reordered priorities suggests the possibility of spasmodic, emotional, public reactions to specific European developments. One example was the highly adverse repercussion from Ford's rebuff of Solzhenitsyn. Americans accepted his bald definition of the differences between the communist and democratic systems and fell into gloomy agreement with his predictions about the decline of the West. Oversold by Nixon and Kissinger on the virtues and advantages of detente, Solzhenitsyn confirmed the suspicion that detente was serving Soviet rather than American purposes. He told Americans what they suspected: idealism and morality had been leached out of American diplomacy. An articulate, neo-conservative, anti-communist group has been growing within the American intellectual community. With its moralistic flavor, antipathy towards the established, "long-haired" left, and with commitment to Israel, such a movement, although still that of a minority, has a potentially strong appeal to American labor and perhaps to the media. Adverse reactions to Helsinki and the attacks on detente are further examples of the tendency to leap to quick, simple and traditional responses to issues within the framework of familiar patterns.

III

Despite revived conservative strength in Germany, France, Britain and Sweden, the American public senses a Europe drifting to the left – helped by the evidence of the Labor government in Britain, the Social Democratic and Liberal Coalition in Germany but principally by the success of the Communist Party in Italy, active communist parties in Portugal, Spain and Greece, and enhanced prospects for the Mitterand coalition in France. Semantical difficulties influence this perception. For example, there is no social democratic party in America; hence Americans have no rule of thumb in judging the nature and probable behavior of these unfamiliar European political groupings. "Labor" and "trade union" are not scare words in America. Consequently, public opinion in the United States is little exercised by the militants of the British Labor Party or those in the Trade Union Congress. Yet Italian communists, in current word and deed more moderate than the British extremists, create real anxieties. "Communism" is a word that still frightens Americans.

The prospect of communist participation in one or two major Western governments attracts growing American attention. In June a Gallup poll asked this question: "Which of these things (respondents were shown a card) should the United States do if the Communists came to power in Italy and France." The card listed the following:

"A. Use military force.
 B. Apply economic and political pressure.
 C. Get out of NATO.
 D. Cooperate with the Communists."

The poll indicated that "About half (49 percent) of all persons interviewed think that economic and political pressure should be applied if the Communists came to power. About one in every five (22 percent) favors the use of military force with more younger than of the older people favoring this action. Only about one person in ten (9 percent) favors cooperation with the Communists." If one adds to this the 13 percent who advocate getting out of NATO a total of 84 percent took an exceedingly hard line. However, Potomac Associates found in their survey that the public put this issue near the bottom of the list of priorities, number 25. The apparent contradiction can be resolved by noting that while the question seems the same, two quite different reactions were sought. Potomac Associates wanted to find what priority the public assigned the issues; Gallup asked what the United States should do. The answers correspond to the national mood: slight interest in foreign problems; but when, pressed to recommend a course of action, and in the absence of strong leadership, a preference for the tough, belligerent response is indicated.

These reactions suggest other currents of American opinion. First, Eurocommunism is a new phenomenon which does not fit into the familiar patterns of the past. Declining interest in foreign affairs and limited information generally can lead to volatile, and, at least initially, aggressive reactions.

The more general image of Western Europe, again within the context of other American preoccupations, is of an increasingly confused and disunited continent, politically unstable, caught in serious economic difficulties. This impression is hardly surprising in view of the general lack of knowledge, interest and inability of the media to analyze intelligently, if at all, extremely complex European political-economic developments. The magnitude of the problem can be appreciated by reflecting on how to explain to Americans the nature of the German government coalition – the alliance of SPD with the FDP, of CDU support of co-determination, of opposing positions on Eastern policy.

One of the most striking developments in American attitudes has been sharpened concern about national security. The interlocking factors include apprehension about the decline of American importance and power in the world relative to the USSR and China; the sense of a dangerous world and a ruthless, unpredictable adversary; a remarkable degree of "trust and confidence . . . in the leadership of our armed forces" – up to 68 percent, to be contrasted with a sharp drop from 67 percent in 1974 to 53 percent in 1976 of confidence in the federal government's handling of foreign policy.[3] Potomac Associates concludes, "They want to feel certain that our military strength places the United States clearly and unequivocally beyond the danger of challenge by force. We want to be – and be seen by others to be – number one in the world of total military power."[4]

This emphasis has several implications for American-European relations. The commitment to NATO is implicitly strengthened as contention over the troops in Europe issue is dissipated. The contentiousness of this latter problem has also been mitigated by the collapse of the fixed exchange rate system and thus of American fixation with balance of payments statistics. There is a further, somewhat cynical explanation for the national enthusiasm for national security programs. At a time of recession and high unemployment, labor, business and political interest groups become natural allies in combating proposals to reduce defense expenditures.

No substantial body of opinion argues, as has been the case in the past, that Europe should by now assume responsibility for its own defense, or that America carries a disproportionate share of a common security task. There is resignation in this view, however; a sense that no matter what might have been hoped in the past, Western Europe, for the foreseeable future, will be unable to organize its political, general economic and defense resources so as to assure its own security. Only a few American voices argue from demographic and crude economic data (George Kennan for one) that there is no objective reason why 300 million Western Europeans cannot mount their own defenses – other than a lack of will. But continued economic stagnation might well bring adherents to this view.

The nuclear issue – power plants, reprocessing facilities, waste disposal, weapon proliferation and seizure by terrorists – has caught public attention and concern and will certainly grow. Americans are puzzled by the apparent inability of Europeans to appreciate the dimensions of the problem, are frustrated over the prospective sale of plants and technology to such nations as Brazil, South Korea and Pakistan. This is perceived as blind European governmental support of crass business interests. Senatorial proposals for harsh retaliatory action against nations that pursue such policies are harbingers of the future.

American business and economic opinion is bearish about Europe. With the exception of Germany it sees countries unable to reconcile public demands for governmental services with national product. These observers would agree with Carli that in substantial part this is less an economic than a political problem. They fear a growing pattern of political, and in some cases, doctrinaire, interference with the market economy – for example, the proposals of the TUC and members of the Labor Party to nationalize the banks, to shore-up inefficient and marginal enterprises. Laws which preclude reduction of labor forces introduce a rigidity, as many Americans see it, which has caused American companies to curtail European investment and operations and to look to their domestic facilities to meet future growth of demand. This American retreat has been encouraged by Europe's persistent high inflation, high unit costs, unimpressive productivity and low profits. The spread of co-determination or worker participation in Europe, somewhat surprisingly, has not frightened America management.

The apprehensions of American farm interests, despite their enormous European sales, have not been assuaged by the continued growth of this market. The attitudes of the agricultural bloc seem made up of: "No matter how good it is it might get worse; and it could be better," and, "If we don't complain who knows what new restrictions those Europeans will think up." The farmers' attitude is highly egocentric – they are preoccupied with problems of survival, of escalating costs, and have little interest in or curiosity about the similar but greater difficulties of fellow farmers in Europe. They see no inconsistency with American quotas on European cheeses and American outrage that there should be European proposals for taxes on margarine.

One of the persistent beliefs is that Europe is the artful protectionist, declaring its liberality, denouncing American behavior, but cleverly manipulating imports through government regulation and under-the-table restrictions. The myriad devices whereby European governments insure that national procurement remains the providence of local concerns is cited as a notorious example. A primordial American conviction is most clearly evident with respect to international trade, the notion that American negotiators always come in second, that the simple, good-hearted American will inevitably be done in by the cleverer, more determined European. It is an article of faith that the United States was the big loser to the Europeans in the Kennedy Round negotiations. The notion of incompetent American innocents abroad was furthered by the Soviet wheat deal.

The attitude of organized labor is a special and discouraging case. Nationalism and protectionism have replaced labor's impressive post-war record of constructive involvement in international affairs. Its current approach mirrors with only slight distortion one side of the national mood: protectionism; general suspicions of multinational companies and the conviction that corporate investment in Europe mean the loss of American jobs. The labor movement is also an example of the manner in which a minority in the United States establishes a policy. A handful of AFL/CIO executives lay down "labor's views" with little interest or dissent from locals around the country. For George Meany and his associates the dangers of this world have not changed, only our insight is less acute. The seminal evil is communism. Anger is mixed with contempt over the failure of European unions to recognize the charade of Soviet and Eastern European government-sponsored "unions." Meany expresses contempt for those European unions that largely ignore what he sees as the primary responsibility of a labor union – wages and conditions of work – and concentrate on ideological and political issues. The category "Manual" in the following table from Potomac Associates' study of attitudes toward international affairs indicates that American labor is more anti-internationalist today than any of the other identified groups:

	National	Professional	White Collar	Manual	Non-labor (retired)
Internationalist	44	49	48	36	48
Mixed	33	38	28	31	31
Isolationist	23	13	24	31	20

IV

The utter complexity of contemporary attitudes toward Europe can be brought into focus by examining the evolution of American views of the European Community: from post-war optimism, belief in quick solutions, active involvement; then, as European unity lost momentum, to a substantial loss of interest, skepticism and uneasy apprehension. The reaction is disillusion. The excitement of the 1950's and '60's in a bold and exciting adventure has been lost as the Community flounders in bewildering detail, endless national wrangling and shows little evidence of becoming the "United States of Europe."

Yet this negative attitude reflects more drift of attention than basic change of attitude, or new hostility. American interest in a United Europe is latent and could be aroused. That small, reasonably informed and interested band of supporters is discouraged over the failure of Europe to organize itself so that it can speak with one voice, to rally its great human and material resources so that Europe can play a world role commensurate with its basic interests. This judgment applies especially to the crises in the Middle East and southern Africa. They overlook forthright Community action with respect to Portugal and concentrate on the failure of Europe collectively to cope with critical situations close to home – Italy, Greece, Turkey and Cyprus. Stagnation in the Community brings sour satisfaction to a tiny group of skeptics who never believed the effort would succeed. They now relish their authority as vindicated prophets.

American diplomacy both matches and shapes the national mood: nationalism; preference for relations with several of the principal European governments and leaders rather than the difficult labor of working through Brussels or attempting to encourage collective European action. An inward-looking America has lost sight of the advantages to it of a more united Europe. Furthermore, it has neither the inclination nor the generosity of spirit to appreciate the difficulties, to applaud the substantial success of the European movement and to understand the magnitude of the enterprise.

V

This review suggests a maze of paths and byways which lead in every direction. This may be its value, if the impression left is confusion, ambiguity and paradox. The shock of the oil embargo, the unprecedented dependence on others for essential raw materials have forced Americans to face the uncomfortable reality of a much more complex world. Moreover, those responsible for the conduct of Atlantic relations and those interested in this aspect of international affairs must accept the premise of American preoccupation with domestic economic and social problems. This ordering of priorities is fixed for the discernible future. This is not a peculiarly American phenomenon. A glance at the leaders of opposition parties demonstrates that they sense that the road to political power lies through attention to public discontent with domestic ills. Kohl, Thatcher and Mitterand are hardly notable as thinkers or innovators in the field of foreign affairs.

A probe of the apparent contradiction whereby heads of government devote so much time to a subject of manifest popular unconcern has some relevance to this analysis. Incessant bilateral meetings, protestations of competence in foreign affairs, devotion to the cause of world peace all seem less a matter of conviction that the politicians see their activities as crucial to the well-being of their subjects, or a response to insistent popular demand, than as an escape from almost insoluble domestic problems. Diplomacy as a game is therapy, especially among Americans and Europeans, for the harried politician. The Puerto Rico meeting was a depressing example of a conference designed to distract if not beguile the public, to manufacture an aura of serious international discourse, and thus to escape for a moment intractable domestic problems. This diversionary tactic neither deals with the heart of American-European relations nor the pressing economic problems of the world. The public was not amused or bemused. If this seductive device becomes endemic it will only strengthen public cynicism.

Nixon-Kissinger-Ford diplomacy has aggravated the general mood described above. By ignoring or underestimating the importance of economic and social factors there has been little serious and no sustained American leadership in this area. Sensitivity to the fundamental significance of economic phenomena to an ordered world would have led to an understanding that these problems can only be dealt with through American-Western European collaboration. Rather than a strategy, random suggestions and ideas have been thrown out as conjurer's tricks, programs launched but then allowed to drift as Washington's attention wandered.

Because of Kissinger's "grand strategy," with Soviet-American relations dominant, the American public's subliminal perception is of a less important Europe. Thus American interest stirs only over such issues as Eurocommunism or damage presumed to have resulted from detente. Intuitively many Americans have absorbed Kissinger's conception of Europeans as pawns in the great game among the superpowers. The American predilection for intimate, self-serving relations with a few major European political figures has not left the impression of serious and constructive Atlantic relations. Those Americans paying attention sense that Schmidt is cultivated because of German economic power; Giscard due to the hard-learned lesson of French capacity to obstruct; Callaghan for reasons of nostalgia and British readiness to serve as America's errand boys.

It should not be overlooked that the Europeans are more than willing partners in this game. They have eagerly developed and maintained these personal, bilateral relationships. When charged with a lack of attention to the Community or collective European action, Washington's defense is to point out the evident lack of European interest. It is hard to avoid the conclusion that if Europeans are content with this peculiar relationship of relatively small European nation states willingly providing their proxies, then why should the American public have a larger view of Europe and its role?

VI

An unpleasant brew is simmering: Americans as uninterested spectators; bilateralism routinized; nationalistic, unilateralist behavior prevalent; plus a manifest uninterest in institutions – the latter point made more difficult by the general public's disenchantment with the United Nations. As a result, American opinion has retrogressed from its immediate post-war interest in developing an international regime of enforceable rules and effective organizations. Jean Monnet, in his recent memoire, indirectly spoke to this point when addressing the dangers inherent in nationalism: "It is not a question of political problems which, as in the past, oppose forces which are seeking domination or superiority. It is a question of causing civilization to make new progress, by beginning to change the forms of relations between countries and by applying the principle of equality amongst peoples and of relations between countries. The people no longer wish to have their future linked to the skills and ambitions of their governments. They do not want any temporary settlements, and therefore they want an organization, a procedure for discussion and joint decisions to be set up in our countries."

American indifference to the European Community is thus partly due to Washington's mere pro forma acknowledgement of its existence. Similarly, neglect of the OECD has stultified this potentially useful organization. Indeed, the habitual use of ad hoc arrangements flies in the face of the principles Monnet describes. Inevitably America's disposition toward nationalistic, unilateral behavior is encouraged.

The ambivalence of the United States regarding world affairs is clear, as is its ambivalence about Europe. The litany is hackneyed: "We want a strong, united Europe prepared to assume its proper place in international affairs." The question is how much this is old rhetoric and to what degree these words reflect firmly held American views. The emphasis on superpower politics and maneuver, the revived consciousness of a Soviet menace, the immediate political boiler-plate that "we will be satisfied with no status other than military superiority" transfer to Americans generally the notion of the lonely, self-reliant and tough cowboy. The Mayaguez episode was a disturbing example of how this attitude can be translated into action and be rewarded by popular acclaim.

It would be prudent for Europe to regard the United States as a difficult partner. The extensive Potomac Associates polls and analyses support this conclusion. Aside from the relative importance the public attaches to national defense, an objective which is in fact a nationalistic priority, relations with Western Europe are not reached, even implicitly, until priority number 16: "Maintaining respect for the US in other countries." One can only speculate why this is a matter of such importance to the public: Wounded ego? Apprehension and embarrassment about the loss of status due to Vietnam? Watergate and Angola? But only at priority 22, "Maintaining close relations with allies," is there a direct link identified between the United States and Europe. It might be pointed out that number 19, several points higher in the American consciousness, is: "Collecting and disposing of garbage, trash and other solid wastes."

Fortunately the picture is not exclusively negative. As the Potomac Associates point out: "The essential stability since 1974 of the relative internationalist-isolationist balance, after several years of steady decline in the former and growth in the latter, should be viewed in the context of a revitalized concern for some of our principal allies. And the sober realism of the public assessment of current and future relations with major adversaries is noteworthy; at the least, there are no unwarranted expectations to be easily violated, and so to bring disillusionment and cynicism. Future negotiations can be conducted with the domestic support of a people tired of being fooled, whether by their own government or by their enemies, and prepared to have their leaders bargain hard from a position of strength."[5]

VII

Nonetheless there is a disturbing bias built into American attitudes which, although not aimed at Europe, has profound implications for Atlantic relations. Where economic interdependence is for the expert the central fact, for the public the preference is for unilateralism and for the aggressive pursuit of national interests. The country has become largely insensitive to the plight of the poor countries; more precisely, sympathy is expressed along with reluctance to support rhetorical compassion with real resources. Certainly an inner-oriented society is less prepared and willing to recognize the political, economic and psychological problems of its European allies. Finally, the aura of self-reliance contains the potential for a dramatic change in attitude toward the Atlantic Alliance. Should NATO show signs of serious weakness, then a Fortress America sentiment could take command.

As has been seen, with respect to security matters enhanced popular support is remarkable. But here, too, there are disconcerting implications. Interest in allied relations does not necessarily mean support for sophisticated collective security. There is little enthusiasm, for instance, for equitable sharing of military research and development, procurement and production. The pro-defense, anti-detente and anti-USSR thrust of opinion creates a major hurdle for future arms limitation negotiations.

An extraordinary challenge is posed to American leadership. Opinion is not set in concrete. Ambivalence and preoccupation are hardly the most desirable public attitudes, but they are better than strongly held wrong views. An optimistic reading of the current state of public opinion suggests an America that has shaken off the guilt and suspicion generated by Vietnam, again fearful of Soviet capacity and intentions, and ready for firm executive leadership. It could be a nation willing once again to allow its government considerable foreign policy latitude.

If American leadership is to move the country along positive lines much depends on Western Europe itself. If European governments have become addicted to the glamor and self-service of German, French or British-American relations and fail to make progress in collective European enterprises then Americans will intuitively sense that their allies across the Atlantic are not serious. The Community is a testimony of European imagination. Europe has shown the gift for initiative and the capacity for effective collective action in its relations with the developing countries, notably with the Lomé convention (one can only deplore the failure of Americans to recognize this achievement), as it has shown reluctance to face the issue and to develop a common approach to the danger of the proliferation of nuclear materials and technology.

It is hard to predict the direction the United States will take in 1977. A pessimist can find much support for his gloom in the evidence of an inward-looking America, its nationalistic spirit and preference for unilateral action, its heavy emphasis on defense and military hardware.

The optimists have a good deal going for them. The worst now seems behind America in terms of attitudes towards international affairs. A President and Congress from the same party set the stage for a government working in greater harmony which in turn is likely to produce a mood of public support. While the area of maneuver available to the President is substantial, he must navigate around certain definite obstacles. There is little generosity of spirit or even open-mindedness toward the North-South problem. It will not be easy to get Americans to accept the policy of military equivalence with Soviet Union, for national security is construed as requiring superiority to the Russians, being "number one." The lessons Americans drew from Vietnam mean aversion to anything that looks like military engagements in places where the nation's vital interests are not clearly self-evident. While Americans will respond to firm leadership they expect to be informed; they particularly expect the Congress to be consulted.

It would appear, in sum, that the new Administration need not be seriously inhibited by general American opinion or its more specific image of Europe. The few issues where opinion may constrain the President need not stand in the way of close, mutually beneficial relations with Europe. Success or failure of American policy will turn primarily on the imagination and skill the new Administration brings to the task.

Notes

[1] I am indebted to Potomac Associates (Washington, D.C.) for the coincidental release in September 1976, of three excellent studies: William Watts and Lloyd A. Free, *America's Hopes and Fears – 1976*, (Policy Perspectives, 1/1976); Robert W. Tucker, William Watts, Lloyd A. Free: *The United States in the World: New Directions for the Post-Vietnam Era?* (Policy Perspectives, 2/1976); Walter Slocombe, Lloyd A. Free, Ronald R. Lesh et. al., *The Pursuit of National Security: Defense and the Military Balance*, (Policy Perspectives, 3/1976).

[2] Tucker, Watts, Free, op. cit., p. 29.

[3] Slocombe, Free, Lesh, Watts, op. cit., p. 32.

[4] Ibid., p. 42.

[5] Tucker, Watts, Free, op. cit., p. 40.

The Bases for Postwar Cooperation

by ROBERT R. BOWIE

For the Atlantic nations, the postwar period has been shaped by the extent of their cooperation, especially in the two fields most central for the modern state – security and economic well-being. Such cooperation has had its ups and downs; doubtless it has fallen short of the needs, especially in the more recent years. Yet it is unique in its scope and depth and is in striking contrast to the relations before World War II.

That notable achievement was not inevitable. It has been, as Acheson said, created by the dedicated effort of political leaders and elites[1] in these nations. What were the factors and conditions which contributed to this achievement? This essay explores that question, especially for the period when the foundations were laid and the framework created. Then it briefly considers the differences in current conditions which affect the prospects for future cooperation. It is useful to start by recalling the sequence of events which prompted and molded postwar cooperation.

I

The building of the specifically Atlantic structures did not begin until 1947. During World War II, the planning for postwar collaboration had been based on wider foundations. As early as August, 1941, Roosevelt and Churchill set out, in the Atlantic Charter, goals for global cooperation for postwar security, economic progress and access to trade and raw materials on equal terms for all nations. A few months later, the Charter was endorsed by the "United Nations," which included, among others, the European governments in exile, members of the British Commonwealth, the Soviet Union and China, and many Latin American states.

In the economic field, the postwar objectives were further defined in the 1942 lend-lease Agreement (Article VII) between the United States and the UK which committed them to seek with others "the expansion by appropriate international and domestic measures, of production, employment, and the exchange and consumption of goods, . . . the elimination of all forms of discriminatory treatment in international commerce, ... the reduction of tariffs and other trade barriers; and in general to the attainment of all the economic objectives" of the Atlantic Charter.

These aims were given concrete form in the 1944 Bretton Woods agreements, setting up the International Monetary Fund (IMF) for monetary matters, and the World Bank (IBRD) to finance reconstruction and development; they were later complemented by the GATT to handle trade. These economic institutions were designed, of course, to establish a global system with world-wide participants. The lead in creating them, however, was taken by the United States and Great Britain. While the USSR and several East European nations signed the agreements, they did not take part in the organizations. More temporary was UNRRA, formed in 1943 to provide relief and aid for liberated areas.

In the field of security, the postwar planning, which was initiated at the Moscow Conference of October, 1943, took two forms. One was the formation of the United Nations, which sought to provide for collective security on a global basis, drawing on the League experience. The United States, Britain and France plus the Soviet Union and China were to be permanent members of the Security Council.

The other plans for security were for the occupation regime for Germany (and Japan). The plan for Germany, worked out by the United States, Great Britain, and the Soviet Union, largely through the European Advisory Commission and the wartime summit conferences, was confirmed at the Potsdam Conference in August, 1945. It divided Germany into four zones (US, Soviet, British, and French) and provided for joint administration of Germany through the Allied Control Council composed of the four powers. (France, though allotted a Zone, was not at Potsdam.) In essence, the aim was to keep Germany disarmed, economically weak, and under joint control.

The initiatives for strictly Atlantic cooperation were a second stage, provoked by the postwar events. The wartime plans had assumed: (1) that the wartime allies would continue to cooperate "for the organization and maintenance of peace and security" as agreed at the Moscow Conference and elsewhere; and (2) that the war-torn economies would revive, within the environment created by Bretton Woods and the trade organizations, after temporary assistance from UNRRA following liberation.

As time passed, it became clear that these key assumptions underlying the earlier planning were not valid. The European economies were not recovering as had been expected from the devastation and disruption of the war. And the Soviet Union was not cooperating either in occupied Germany or in the Foreign Ministers conferences; instead, it was pursuing its own purposes as

Churchill warned in his "Iron Curtain" speech in March, 1946, and Kennan in his famous cable from Moscow in February, 1946. The USSR now began to seem more menacing than the defeated enemies. Nearly a year of debate and reappraisal led to a new consensus in the United States and the European nations. The result was a drastic reorientation of their policies.

The economic stagnation in Europe prompted the Marshall Plan, initiated in June, 1947. This program was limited to Western Europe when the Soviet Union, Poland, and Czechoslovakia, though originally invited, withdrew in the initial phase. While the initiative came from the United States, the recovery effort was managed as a joint activity, mainly through OEEC, based on cooperation within Europe and between Europe and the United States.

Measures for security went in parallel. First came the Truman doctrine for aid to Greece and Turkey in March, 1947. Then the Brussels pact of early 1948 among the West Europeans was followed by the Vandenburg resolution (June, 1948) which led to the North Atlantic Treaty (1949) for the collective defense of the Atlantic area against the Soviet threat. By late 1950, NATO was organized in order to reinforce the Treaty guarantee by machinery for planning strategy and a unified command in the event of aggression.

These events radically modified the position of Germany. Economically, it had become apparent that Europe was too interdependent to be able to prosper with Germany stagnant. Faced with the French and Soviet refusal to treat Germany as a whole, as had been agreed at Potsdam, the United States and Britain combined their occupation zones, and the French soon joined. Under the Marshall Plan, Germany became a participant in the recovery effort and the OEEC. In rapid steps, a Constitution (Basic Law) was adopted creating the Federal Republic; elections were held and a government formed under Adenauer; and the occupation regime was sharply curtailed.

More radical was the Schuman proposal of May, 1950, for the Coal and Steel Community, as a first step toward a United States of Europe. It was both political and economic in purpose. It reflected the view that Europe's prosperity depended on the creation of a wider market, free from tariffs and other restraints, and that politically, Europe's states, especially France and Germany, must bury past rivalries to move toward a peaceful destiny together. Schuman's bold idea was to seek to reconcile France and Germany, as well as the other European states, by meshing their interests and subjecting all of them to common rules and institutions. The Coal and Steel Community was in effect by 1952. After the defeat of the European Defense Community in 1954 by the French Assembly came the creation of Euratom and the European Economic Community.

Meanwhile, in September, 1950, the United States, convinced that the

Federal Republic was a needed partner in the defense of Europe, made this a condition for sending more forces to Europe and appointing General Eisenhower to head the NATO forces. While the mode of German participation was not settled until 1954, the corollary was clear: the ending of the occupation and the return of Germany to the European family as a full member.

In retrospect, this decade remains remarkable in many ways. In a few years, the Atlantic nations rapidly revised the premises for the initial post-war policies where they proved mistaken. They developed a new set of relations among themselves for cooperation on security and economic welfare. The United States radically modified its view of its role in the world. The Federal Republic became a full partner in the West. The European nations launched the European Community, including Germany. And to make their cooperation effective, the Atlantic states created new institutions and procedures in OEEC, NATO, the European Community, and other agencies.

What were the factors which made possible such bold and rapid innovations?

II

One factor surely was the outstanding calibre of the leaders in the Atlantic area in that period. By any standard, the roster is impressive: Truman, Churchill, Bevin, Adenauer, Spaak, de Gasperi, Schuman, Lange, Pearson; and assisting them were men like Acheson, Marshall, McCloy, Clay, Harriman, Bruce, Eden, Franks, Keynes, Cripps, Monnet, Hallstein, Marjolin, and many, many more.

These were men of unusual vision and courage. Many had been drawn into public life by the war. They assumed that their task was to lead public opinion, not to follow it. And most of them had strong convictions about what needed to be done and how to do it.

The public was receptive to such leadership. In many countries, people were inevitably disillusioned with the past and ready for changes. They were prepared to give confidence and support to leaders who offered a better prospect for security and prosperity for the future. On the Continent at least, the nation-state was widely discredited and bureaucracies or special interest groups were not yet well enough organized to oppose initiatives.

Yet the fact that the various leaders and their associates were able and courageous did not guarantee that they would agree on what needed to be done or how. The extensive collaboration achieved during this creative period required: (1) common definitions of the tasks; (2) consensus on practical measures; (3) compatible priorities in carrying them out. When one takes account of the major changes in assumptions, the novelty of the problems, the adjustments in priorities, and the extent of cooperation needed, it is not easy to explain how a group of 15 or more states was able to meet these requirements in so short a time.

III

How far was it due to earlier transnational friendships or acquaintance among the various elites? In general, the leaders and elites had not known one another before the war.

Some, of course, had had experience or training on the other side of the Atlantic. Jean Monnet, for example, had been in banking in New York. Some of the Americans had been Rhodes Scholars, including such men as Dean Rusk; General Charles H. Bonesteel; W. Walton Butterworth: Harlan Cleveland; Colonel George Lincoln; Lincoln Gordon; George McGhee; J. Burke Knapp; and Charles Saltzman to name a few.

Conversely, some Europeans had studied in the United States under Rockefeller Foundation fellowships: Henri Bonnet, French Ambassador to the United States (1944–1954); Edvard Hambro, at the UN for Norway; Pieter Lieftinck, one-time Dutch finance minister; Robert Marjolin, the first OECD Secretary-General and later vice-president of the EEC Commission; Andre Philip, a French finance minister; Eric Roll, at the OEEC and NATO for the UK; and Arne Skaug, at OEEC and NATO for Norway.

And, of course, members of the United States Foreign Service, who had studied and served in Europe in the inter-war years, came to occupy key positions in the postwar period. Some examples include: H. Freeman Matthews; William R. Tyler and Walter Stoessel; Jacob D. Beam; David Popper; Leo Pasvolsky; Ernest Gross; and Van Buren Cleveland. And the same was true of foreign service officers of the European states. Some of the Europeans had lived and worked in other European countries. The exodus from Germany under Hitler had, of course, brought many able people to the United States, Britain and other European countries.

Most of the initial contacts among the elites dated from the war itself. The many combined wartime boards and agencies for conducting the war and for postwar preparation brought together American, British, and other experts and officials. And with the German conquest of the Continent, many leading figures, including those in the governments in exile, had come to live and work in the United Kingdom and the United States during the wartime period. But, in large part, the linkages among the elites in the postwar period were the product of working together in devising and operating the common programs and the new institutions. The reasons for their success in working together lay deeper.

IV

The critical links among the elites who forged the postwar cooperation were not personal but intellectual: they came to the tasks with important shared premises and convictions. For most of them the late 1920's and 1930's and the wartime period itself had been the formative stage in their lives and largely shaped their outlooks. From the shattering events of those years, they had derived similar "lessons" to guide postwar policies.

One such event was the Great Depression. All of the industrial countries had suffered grievously from this traumatic experience, with its unemployment, bankruptcies, and general economic stagnation. Most of them had followed unilateral policies of "beggar thy neighbor" with disastrous consequences all around. Many of these countries, at the outbreak of the war, still had large pools of jobless and slack economies. Many people were convinced that Hitler could never have come to power in Germany without the disruption of the depression, which made fertile soil for his appeal. But even in other countries which had weathered the storm, such as the United States and the UK, the depression had left deep social scars.

One of the lessons which was widely drawn from this experience was the vital necessity for cooperation among the industrial countries in creating and maintaining an open international economic system and in managing their interdependent economies. They could not afford the heavy costs of another deep depression or unilateral action in trying to cope with their economic problems. Thus, almost all of the elites in the United States, the United Kingdom, and on the Continent, started from the premise that joint action was necessary to avoid a repetition of such an economic disaster and to devise a better monetary and open trading system.

That shared conviction underlay the initial steps to create the Bretton Woods system. And when it became clear by 1946–1947 that more was needed to revive the European economies, that conviction underlay the US proposal of the Marshall Plan and the readiness of the European countries to work closely with one another in trying to achieve recovery. Finally, that conviction created the climate in which the measures for reintegrating Germany into the Western economic system were accepted, even so soon after the war. That Western Europe could not recover and prosper with Germany stagnant was widely understood. This premise was certainly one of the major factors in the Schuman proposal in 1950 and in the later working out of the European Economic Community.

At least as important in creating common premises was the second shared historical experience, namely, the rise of Hitler and its consequences. In the prewar period, the various countries had played quite different roles; and they had paid in quite different ways for the failure to deal with Hitler earlier. But, in the end, all had suffered tragically. And the Atlantic nations all reached one common conclusion: that it was essential to deal promptly with any similar menace in the future by collective means. It would be fatal for each country, once more, to go its own way. The Atlantic nations were convinced of the necessity for common action in order to achieve security and to deter aggression before it could be mounted effectively.

The United Nations and the allied occupation regime in Germany (and Japan) were the first efforts to put these principles into effect. But both assumed and depended on continuing cooperation among the wartime allies. Thus the United Nations, with its veto for each of the five "Great Powers", was bound to be ineffective against a Soviet threat. Hence, when Stalin appeared to pose such a threat in Iran, Greece and Turkey, Berlin, Czechoslovakia and, finally, Korea, he evoked vivid memories of the failure to deal with Hitler. Having drawn the same lessons from the past, the leaders of the Atlantic nations naturally reacted in a similar way: since the UN was clearly inadequate, they sought collective security through an alliance to deter the possibility of Soviet aggression.

Finally, even on the issue of Germany, there were "common lessons" from earlier experience, but they were drawn into two stages. While Germany was considered the potential danger, as after World War I, the unconditional surrender and the occupation regime were intended to avoid some of the "mistakes" of the Versailles Treaty, which Hitler so skillfully exploited. So was the provision for reparations from dismantling plants instead of from current output which had been a running sore after World War I.

But the passage of time and the conditions after World War II led to deeper "lessons". Before long, a good many began to worry about the reliance on holding Germany down. An economically weak Germany was clearly a heavy drag on European recovery and prosperity. That linkage was highlighted by the analyses for the Marshall Plan, which suggested the necessity of loosening the economic restrictions on Germany in Europe's own interest. Hence the controls might not succeed, but only breed resentment once more. Thus the Schuman proposal for the Coal and Steel Community was a basic reversal in policy. In the first stage of the occupation, France had sought to dismember Germany and blocked even treating it as an economic unit as agreed at Potsdam. Yet the Schuman Plan was based on a more fundamental "lesson" from the past: that the European states could end their rivalries and achieve stable peace only within a system which imposed common rules without discrimination and brought the Germans back into the European family. That this conception was put forward and accepted only five years after World War II, with all its brutalities, devastation and hatred, is still unprecedented. It can be explained only by the common experience on the Continent of the tragic costs of the historic rivalries.

Thus, the shared historical experience and the common lessons and outlook derived from it provided the foundations for cooperation, both Atlantic and European. It meant that the various leaders and elites started from similar premises in identifying and analyzing the problems and in devising solutions. In general, they had compatible criteria as to what was important to do and to avoid, and as to what would work.

Undoubtedly, the fear of the Soviet Union after 1946–1947 was a major factor in enabling the Atlantic nations to work together effectively. That fear assured that cooperation for economic recovery and security would enjoy high priority even at the expense of competing interests. In consequence, the Atlantic nations could maintain their cooperation in these fields, despite deep differences on other issues, like colonialism or the Suez crisis in 1956.

It was notable, however, that the Atlantic leaders and their citizens were able to recognize by 1947 that important assumptions underlying the original postwar regime had been ill-founded and achieved a broad new consensus.

On the economic front, that is less surprising. The Europeans, of course, experienced at first hand the breakdown of their economic system. The shortages of food, coal and other necessities underscored their interdependence. For the United States, the evidence of the European situation came from many sources. The occupation regime under General Clay faced directly the dire conditions in Germany which required heavy appropriations for relief and food. Reports from Europe were confirmed by the visits of trusted officials like Will Clayton; and General Marshall returning from the Conferences of Foreign Ministers became keenly aware of the deteriorating situation. Finally, Congress sent abroad its own special committees which made comprehensive studies and reports which carried great weight. The destruction of cities, factories, mines and transport had, of course, been visible from the start. But as Marshall stressed in his Harvard speech of 1947, even more serious was the "dislocation of the entire fabric of European economy . . . the complete breakdown of the business structure of Europe." That had taken longer to recognize. Restoring it would "require a much longer time and greater effort than had been foreseen." This diagnosis inevitably recalled the conditions in the Great Depression and provided a ready basis for consensus, both in Europe and across the Atlantic, on the necessity to act rapidly to remedy the situation.

The reappraisal of Soviet purposes was a gradual process and more controversial. Some had been suspicious of the USSR even before the end of the war; others began to have doubts as a result of Soviet actions in Eastern Europe, Iran, and Greece, in occupied Germany and the Council of Foreign Ministers, and in the rejection of the Baruch Plan in the Fall of 1946. Yet there was dispute about how to interpret the successive pieces of evidence and about the proper response. The Churchill speech on the Iron Curtain and the Kennan cable from Moscow early in 1946 saw the Soviet Union as an expansionist power which must be contained. Secretary Wallace and others sought to explain and justify Soviet conduct and resisted a stronger policy toward the USSR.

The consensus on the Soviet threat and the necessity to resist it crystallized rapidly after the decision to support Greece and Turkey in March, 1947. By July, 1947, when Kennan's "X" article in *Foreign Affairs* laid out the revised appraisal and strategy it seems to have been widely accepted by Congress and the public. The Czech coup and the Berlin blockade in 1948 reinforced and confirmed this consensus. Apparently, attitudes and judgments in Europe followed a similar course. To repeat, the parallel to the 1930's inevitably shaped both the assessment and the response.

V

General consensus on the need to cooperate for economic progress and collective security, however, was not enough to achieve those purposes. That required agreement on a wide variety of specific and practical measures. And, despite the complexity and novelty of the problems, the Atlantic nations were able to reach such agreement to a remarkable degree.

Their success was due to many factors. The fact that the tasks – recovery and security – seemed definite and clear, though extremely difficult, was a tremendous asset in focussing effort and priorities in finding solutions. The credit for devising the concrete programs of action goes mainly to the institutions which were created, to the way the governments used them, and to the men who made them work effectively.

In developing the habits and practice of cooperation, the OEEC and its committees and agencies and the NATO civilian and military agencies were critically important as was the Allied High Commission for Germany during the early years.[2]

While intergovernmental, these agencies had substantial impact on national policies. The OEEC, for example, "developed a most remarkable corporate quality, with far-reaching influence on major policies of the member governments and with considerable creative initiative which helped give shape to the pattern of European economic recovery."[3] The NATO Council and its various agencies performed something of the same function in the security and political field. And so did the Allied High Commission, especially during the period when the Federal Republic was being brought into the Western Community and the occupation phased out.

This impact was derived from several strengths. First, the governments saw these institutions as forums for examining problems together and finding common solutions. Accordingly, they were manned by individuals who were not only able, but had standing at home. As those confronting the problems at first hand, they expected to make a major input into the decision-making in Washington, London, Paris, and other capitals, and to be consulted before actions were taken. And they were. The United States, for example, was represented in Europe, especially in the initial period from 1946–1955, by men of independent stature – General Clay, Averell Harriman, David Bruce, John J. McCloy, Lewis Douglas, General Eisenhower and many more. And the other countries had delegations of comparable ability and standing. They and their colleagues had the opportunity to analyze the problems together, and to understand the special concerns and interests of the various members.

Second was the contribution of able Secretariats. The initial Secretaries-General of OEEC (Robert Marjolin from 1947 to 1955) and of NATO (Lord Ismay and Paul Henri Spaak) and their staffs contributed substantially to the effectiveness of these organizations and processes. While their nominal authority was limited, their actual influence on the process of discussion, innovation, and compromise was enormous and highly constructive. Through informal discussions, they and their staffs were able to clarify differences among the members, to keep negotiations going, and to submit proposals to bridge differences.

Often such formal and informal consultation would produce a joint proposal which might diverge from the initial instructions of the various delegations, but which offered a practical solution which the governments were willing to accept. This process, which went on in OEEC, in the NATO agencies and in the Allied High Commission, created an *esprit de corps* which contributed greatly to overcoming differences and producing effective cooperation.

Paralleling these procedures were the consultations through embassies and in endless bilateral and multilateral discussions. The openness of the bureaucracies in providing information and receiving ideas and data also meant that allies had informal channels both for providing their inputs during the course of national decision-making and in keeping informed of the considerations affecting it. This give-and-take was important both in providing a sense of participation and in avoiding sudden surprises.

Under postwar conditions, US leadership was welcomed, with little friction about relative roles. The Europeans recognized their need for US support. Economically, they required resources from the United States and its help in getting trade and industry started again. And once the Soviet danger was recognized, US military power was the indispensable component for a deterrent or for defense. The Europeans were relieved that the United States recognized its interest in a prosperous and secure Europe and was prepared to use its power for these purposes. But the Europeans did not passively follow the lead of the United States. On the contrary, they were active partners in analyzing the needs and in devising solutions. Thus, the building of the Atlantic relations and institutions was a genuinely joint endeavor from the beginning.

There were, of course, divergencies, mainly about means. But these exceptions illuminate the basic point as to the significance of the historical experience. One example was the British resistance to transfers of authority to international agencies. Thus, in the formation of the Council of Europe, Britain insisted on unanimous agreement among ministers for taking any action. Similarly, when OEEC was set up, the British insisted it must be inter-governmental, only with decisions taken by unanimity, and with a "weak" Secretariat. Finally, when Schuman made his Coal and Steel proposal, the British rejected any scheme based on the kind of "supra-national" institutional structure which Schuman outlined.

In each case, the British perspective differed from that on the Continent. For many continental nations, the past had discredited nationalism and the nation state. (France was a special case.) Britain, proud of its wartime accomplishments, still saw itself as a major power with links to the United States, the Commonwealth, and Europe. Thus, while accepting the need for cooperation, Britain was not ready to impair its independence by any sort of supra-national or external controls.

Time brought changes both ways. Its postwar difficulties and the loosening of Commonwealth ties ultimately forced Britain to revise its view of its role and to seek to join the European Community. And revival eroded the readiness of France and, to some degree, Germany, to sacrifice autonomy. Indeed, after 1958 under de Gaulle, France outdid the earlier British attitude. In the name of French independence, he blocked all efforts to move the European Community toward political integration and even rejected the limited degree of "integration" involved in NATO.

But these were exceptions. Most of the other European leaders and elites accepted that such independence was no longer feasible. With its greater size and power, however, the United States could retain more freedom of action, although it recognized the necessity for Atlantic cooperation and the conditions for achieving it.

By about 1960, however, conditions were changing. Economic and political recovery in Europe and the emergence of the European Community opened up questions about roles and influence. And the agenda of issues also broadened. The conversion of OEEC into OECD, with the United States and Canada (and later Japan and others) as members, the greater focus on economic coordination among the advanced countries, and the creation of the DAC (Development Assistance Committee) for coordinating aid to the developing countries partly symbolized some of the changes.

It is not necessary, however, to trace the later history for our purposes. The preceding analysis illuminates the basis for the cooperation in the postwar years. It highlights how much the creative collaboration of that period was facilitated (1) by the consensus among the elites as to the problems, the necessities and the priorities based on shared "lessons" drawn from the earlier catastrophes, and (2) by institutions and methods of policy-making well-suited to convert that general consensus into concrete actions which could be jointly pursued.

VI

In the light of the postwar experience, what are the prospects for future cooperation among the advanced countries of Europe, North America, and Japan?

Certainly the need is greater than ever before. Interdependence has become a catchword, but it sums up the reality. Its depth and extent were dramatized by the ramifications of the OPEC price jump. That action had its impact not only on the energy equation, but on the world monetary system, global inflation and recovery, the plight of the poorest LDCs, as well as on the spread of nuclear power and of proliferation, the Arab-Israeli dispute and stability in the Middle East.

Obstacles to Cooperation

Cooperation to cope with interdependence now and in the future will be much more difficult than in the postwar period.

1. The problems are far more numerous and complex:

(a) As their economies and societies steadily become more closely linked, the advanced countries must concert their policies to achieve prosperity, stability, and growth and to cope with inflation, recession or balance of payments.

(b) The growth of Soviet military power, and its greater reach, the Sino-Soviet split, the divergences in Eastern Europe, and detente have made relations with these nations much more complicated and opened up a host of issues regarding arms control, trade, technology, human rights, access etc.

(c) The emergence of 80 or more new states, many weak and poor, demanding a larger share in decision-making and in the benefits from the global system, creates new problems and greater difficulty in agreeing on joint action.

(d) Food and population, energy and resources, the environment, and the oceans have emerged as global problems requiring wide cooperation for handling.

2. For many issues there is no consensus about premises, diagnoses, and solutions. Many of them are novel; the concepts and knowledge for solving them are lacking or inadequate. Often the issues are closely linked together and cannot be handled one at a time.

Achieving the necessary agreement will not be easy. Even the advanced countries differ widely on their appraisals, priorities, and proposals. The LDCs often approach the problems from very different perspectives, with more stress on equity and participation. Finally, communist states bring divergent attitudes and priorities to relations generally.

3. International issues are deeply enmeshed in domestic politics today. Managing the welfare state frequently requires coordinated or common action which may entail choices or actions harmful to specific domestic interests. And handling many global issues or LDC demands, such as market access, will affect the structure of industry and commerce in advanced countries.

Yet in democratic welfare states, the influence of special interest groups often impedes or delays the making and carrying out of decisions for the wider needs. Many governments, in both advanced and developing states, are politically weak. In Western Europe and Japan, many depend on narrow majorities or even minority support, which is hardly adequate for making hard choices and decisions. And the climate of detente reduces the pressure to subordinate parochial interests as in the earlier period.

4. Leadership is also more ambiguous. With their own revival and the relative decline in US power, Western Europe and Japan have become somewhat less inclined to accept US leadership. And since Vietnam, the United States is somewhat less disposed to take on the burdens of leadership. Questions of roles and relative authority are divisive among the advanced countries, and are highly sensitive for the LDCs which deeply resent their limited influence. Yet the European Community lacks the cohesion to provide leadership and will be slow to achieve that capacity, even if it resumes progress toward unity. Japan shows no desire to take the lead. And aside from OPEC, the LDC weakness is apparent.

Thus the task of achieving the requisite cooperation for handling the issues now confronting the advanced nations and many others is much more difficult than in the initial postwar period.

Assets

In the effort to cooperate on these problems, however, the advanced nations still have very large assets.

1. In tackling these new issues, they at least can build on the habits, practices, and institutions which they have developed in thirty years of working together. This is an invaluable advantage, in sharp contrast to the postwar situation when such habits and institutions had to be created.

2. Moreover, the Atlantic nations (and to a lesser degree, Japan) now have a large pool of leaders and elites who have a solid foundation for working together. Three decades of education, travel, conferences and cooperation among the advanced countries have developed a remarkable amount of shared knowledge, experience, and understanding, not only among the elites, but among much of the informed public. Such transnational linkages now extend to professional, business, academic and other private groups as well as officials of all sorts and parliamentarians.

3. The European Community can also facilitate cooperation, even though it has thus far fallen short of its aims. The members of the Community

recognize their mutual dependence, act together for many purposes, seem determined to maintain the Community, and will probably move further in the future.

4. Finally, there is the element of time. In the postwar era, the necessity to respond to the Soviet threat and European stagnation required a rapid and unforeseen shift in direction. In the current period, while the problems are extremely complex, many of them are also long-term in character. That does not mean that efforts to cope with them can be put off, as democratic states are inclined to do. (The energy problem shows some of the costs of doing so.) But the fact that they are long-term does allow an opportunity to learn how to deal with them and to develop agencies and methods of cooperation over a period of time. In adapting attitudes and relations and achieving collaboration, time can be a priceless resource, if wisely used.

Clearly, it will be an arduous and protracted task to build the consensus as to conditions, theories, goals, and means needed for common action to resolve these many problems. In doing so, the Atlantic states (and Japan) have substantial advantages both for coping with their own problems and with the wider global issues. But this consensus cannot be based on "lessons" from the past in the way that was done in the postwar period. No doubt experience since the war will be valuable in devising specific reforms, as in reshaping the monetary system or rules for trade. And the experience with the postwar institutions and methods of policy-making do have lessons for effective cooperation which are still relevant for the new problems. But new analysis and debate, both public and private, will be needed to develop compatible premises and frameworks for confronting and resolving the wide range of problems that lie ahead.

References

For this interpretive essay, there seemed no need for supporting footnotes. Section III on the extent of prewar contacts was based on research done for me by Dr. Wayne R. Strasbaugh, who examined an extensive range of materials for this purpose.

For understanding the attitudes, interpretations and judgments of the time, the memoirs of key postwar figures were an indispensable source.

Other useful works include the following:

Aron, Raymond: *The Imperial Republic*, Englewood Cliffs: Prentice-Hall 1974.

Aubrey, Henry G.: *Atlantic Economic Cooperation*, New York: Praeger 1967.

Ellis, Howard S.: *The Economics of Freedom*, New York: Harper 1950.

Gimbel, John: *The American Occupation of Germany*, Stanford: Stanford UP 1968.

Horie, Shigeo: *The International Monetary Fund*, New York: St. Martin's Press 1964.

Jones, Joseph M.: *The Fifteen Weeks*, New York: Viking 1955.

Jordan, Robert S.: *The NATO International Staff/Secretariat, 1952–1957*, London: Oxford UP 1967.

May, Ernest R.: *Lessons of the Past*, New York: Oxford UP 1973.

Price, Harry B.: *The Marshall Plan and Its Meaning*, Ithaca: Cornell UP 1955.

Reitzel, William/Morton A. Kaplan/C. G. Coblentz: *United States Foreign Policy, 1945–1955*, Washington, D.C.: The Brookings-Institution 1956.

Ulam, Adam B.: *The Rivals: America and Russia Since World War II*, New York: Viking 1971.

A Decade of American Foreign Policy, Basic Documents, 1941–1949, Senate Committee on Foreign Relations, Washington, D.C.: U.S.G.P.O. 1950.

American Foreign Policy, 1950–1955, 2 Vols., Department of State, Ed. Washington, D.C.: U.S.G.P.O. 1957.

Notes

[1] The term "elites" is used as shorthand for those who have significant roles or influence in the making and conduct of policy, including politicians, officials, and outsiders.

[2] The IMF and the GATT and the institutions of the European Community also made major contributions in developing cooperation among their respective members. It is not feasible, however, to discuss their roles in this essay.

[3] Lincoln Gordon, *International Organization*, Vol. 10, 1956, No. 1, p. 3.

Academic Exchange and its Impact

Ulrich Littmann

Close ties between Europe and the United States in the area of higher education are an integral part of American intellectual history. Ample documentation of such experience in both countries can be found in various publications on this subject.[1] But it was only in the twentieth century that structures evolved to incorporate transatlantic academic exchanges into social and political relations. Such mutual exchanges began after World War I;[2] the expulsion and flight of European scholars to the US marked the period between 1933 and 1945 – and its impact can still be felt today.

In focussing upon the development in academic exchanges since the end of World War II the following paragraphs will present an area which has found little attention in social research; we realize that space imposes a geographic and topical limitation.

Only few differentiating or comprehensive studies are available on the subject of exchanges and their effects.[3] The main reason may be that cultural relations have been recognized and accepted only in recent decades as the "third pillar of foreign policy" (although not everywhere to the same degree); it is certainly no mere coincidence that, almost simultaneously in 1975/76, the Parliamentary Commission of the German Bundestag referred to cultural relations as a part of world politics and the American Assistant Secretary of State John Richardson spoke of an "emerging planetary consciousness" in this context.[4] In addition: it must be taken into consideration that in economic and social spheres new forms of cooperation have arisen and that international exchange has been, and still is, extending to segments of the population which were previously neglected.

In order to facilitate the understanding of the context of this study, which by necessity is short and superficial, we shall first clarify the terms and then describe the extent, structures and effects of academic exchanges; for, to borrow from genetic terminology, common phenotypes are to be examined with respect to their genotypic structures.

Clarification of Terms

For a better understanding of this paper it is first necessary to describe the range of our topic. Statistical data requires a differentiation which we shall attempt by using only a few rough grids. Questions as to the value and impact of transatlantic exchanges and answers to them are occasionally expressed under quite different assumptions.

First of all, there are widely varying groups of persons participating in what is referred to as academic exchange:

– Short-term visitors such as participants in conferences, lecture tours or guest programs ("look-see programs"). These account for a large share of transatlantic traffic, but in terms of our subject they live, so to speak, "out of a suitcase."

– Participants in language courses and practical trainees; university graduates in exchanges arranged by international companies.[5] Language courses (vacation courses at universities, language training at Goethe Institutes or American centers) certainly have their merits within the framework of cultural policy efforts, but they lack the learning and teaching situation typical of higher education in the host country. If understood as an introduction to or as a supplement of experience abroad, language courses are an indispensable orientation instrument and refresher courses are a valuable addition.

– Long-term visitors, i.e., scholars and students who establish a temporary but continuous residence of at least one regular academic term (usually a semester or academic year) at a university or research center in the host country. This is the only category which is included in the statistics, and it is with this group that this paper will deal primarily. Even within this group we have to distinguish among two types of students: resident or long-term students who pursue their entire higher education abroad and assess their stay abroad mainly in terms of successfully completing a degree program; and exchange students (usually one year) who wish to complement or to broaden their domestic curricula by studying abroad but whose primary educational goals are to complete degrees in their home country. In a similar manner this distinction also applies to scholars.

For the interpretation of overall statistics it should be noted that while between Europe and the US the exchange situation prevails, third-world countries mostly send resident students.

In discussing educational exchanges it is often overlooked that the objectives of cultural foreign policy often differ and, therefore, also need to be examined.[6] Even if we disregard the areas of information policy (media), national schools abroad, tourism and development aid (these are less significant in European-American *academic* exchanges), we can still distinguish three approaches:

– *Objectives determined by Science Policy*: The promotion of particular research projects, research teams or research-oriented teaching and training programs. For these, as a rule, scholars are sought whose expertise in the subject or methodology is considered particularly valuable for a specific project or for institutional cooperation; nationality frequently is more incidental to than decisive for participation in the exchange (an exception is the "Awards Program" of the Alexander von Humboldt Foundation with its limitation to American nationals of exceptional scholarly qualifications).

However, it is an inconsistent practice that grant-giving agencies send only those scholars abroad who are nationals of their respective countries – often to the detriment of those national institutions which have appointed alien residents to tenured positions.

– *Objectives determined by Educational Policy*: The promotion of projects, programs or measures aiming, within a wide spectrum, at the structure and content of the educational systems of the countries involved. Although this approach is more typical for the relations between industrialized and developing nations, there are also remarkable examples in transatlantic exchanges: large portions of general student exchanges (German Academic Exchange Service – DAAD, Fulbright), the program for future teachers of English conducted by DAAD, the various experimental programs of Fulbright Commissions all over Europe, as well as the discussions about a "Big Lift" of German high school graduates to obtain a full college and university education in the US (Schwarz-Schilling Plan and Butler Plan).

– *Objectives determined by Cultural Policy*: Based on an expanded and liberalized "culture" concept as defined by the German Parliamentary Commission, and referring to the phrase, as used in American legislation, of "mutual understanding" (which at first glance may look shallow and misleading), the promotion and integration of exchanges into social and political relations between nations and peoples. Such objectives include both academic and non-academic aspects. To give a few examples: consideration of less known or predominantly minority-oriented institutions; area studies as a substitute for reduced foreign language requirements; the exchange of artists[7] and art and music students; the inclusion of trade union officers and youth leaders. In this context we should also mention the personal and social experience of participants which has become part of the established goals in several exchange programs.

This schematic listing does not mean that there are any strict dividing lines; in most cases – especially outside of "organized" exchanges – the objectives will overlap. Nevertheless, in order to carry out efficiency analyses and success controls it may be necessary to be able to distinguish groups of participants as well as the objectives; this also helps to explain why national interests of the various European countries take priority over European commonness when it comes to the implementation of exchanges. The statistics and the comments on the structure of exchanges throw more light on this aspect.

Statistical Information

It is generally known that by far the largest part of (individual) academic mobility in the free world occurs with no or very little government reglementation. This, however, does by no means imply that such world-wide encounters of scholars or students have no political or politico-cultural significance – on the contrary: it forces governments to concern themselves with this topic. But as long as aspects of cultural policy are activated as the "third pillar of foreign policy" analyses will have to relate overall figures with government measures in intercultural relations.

With appropriate reservations concerning the completeness and consistency of the available statistics[8] it is still appropriate to show the scope and geographic relations.

Figures are available for student exchanges from and to the United States; they include, with a high degree of probability, 90 percent of the exchangees:

	Foreign Students in the US (rounded)		American Students Abroad (rounded)	
	1955	1974	1959	1972
	34,000	150,000	15,000	34,000
	from		in	
(Western) Europe	15%	10%	69%	52%
Far East	30%	35%	4%	7%
Latin America/Mexico	25%	20%	11%	15%
North America/Canada	13%	6%	13%	19%
Near and Middle East	13%	15%		6%
Africa	4%	9%		1%

With regard to exchange of scholars (lecturers and researchers) statistical coverage is even more difficult; according to the information supplied by many research institutions and promotional programs the nationalities of their staff are neither taken into consideration nor registered. However, the available figures point to the scope and size of such relations:

	Foreign Scholars in the US (rounded)		American Scholars Abroad (rounded)	
	1960	1973	1959	1972
	3,000	10,800	2,200	6,600
	from		in	
(Western) Europe	43%	42%	54%	60%
Far East	29%	30%	17%	10%
Latin America	6%	7%	10%	11%
North America/Canada	5%	6%		1%
Near and Middle East	7%	7%	9%	5%
Africa		4%		6%

Actually, the only surprising item in these tables is the relatively modest number of European students in the US. It should be added, however, that a liberal interpretation of the term "student" shifts the accents somewhat; the high degree of selectivity among European students corresponds more closely to American research-oriented universities.

The question now arises as to whether common characteristics of exchange figures exist in the European area. To the extent that the available statistical material can be broken down, a number of considerable country-specific differences become evident. The comprehensive international UNESCO statistics for the academic year 1972 offer following information:

– In France 39 percent of the 35,000 foreign students are Africans, 21 percent Europeans, 7.6 percent US Americans; of the 9,400 French students abroad over 20 percent are in Africa, slightly under 20 percent in the US, smaller groups are in Germany (16 percent) and Switzerland (13 percent).

– In the United Kingdom the Asians form the largest contingent with 36 percent of a total of 27,000 foreign students, followed by Africans (21 percent), Central Americans/Caribbeans (15 percent), Europeans (14 percent) and US Americans (4 percent); of the 13,000 Britons studying abroad, the largest European group, we find more than 6,000 in Canada (46 percent), 3,000 (28 percent) in the US, around 9 percent in France and 5 percent in the Federal Republic of Germany.

– In the Federal Republic 40 percent of the 34,000 foreign students come from Europe, 33 percent from Asia, 6.7 percent from the US; of the slightly under 9,000 German students abroad, a great number are registered at universities of German-speaking neighbors: 26 percent in Austria and 16 percent in Switzerland; around 1,900 (21 percent) study in the US.

The scholarship statistics of the US Department of State confirm the limitations of government activity on the one hand, but they also show the priority accorded to Europe on the other hand.

A more extensive interpretation of the statistics, which has been deleted here for reasons of space, would show even more clearly the different points of departure for internal and intergovernmental cultural policy. As a result, the following sections of this paper will concentrate upon German-American exchanges as a kind of case study.

The following figures characterize German-American exchanges:

	German Students in US		American Students in the Federal Republic
1955–56	778		778
1962–63	1,003		1,406
1967–68	2,309		2,431
1969–70	2,634		2,182
1972–73	1,927	(1971–72)	2,176

	German Scholars in US		American Scholars in the Federal Republic
1961–62	254	1960–61	123
1972–73	722	1971–72	432
1973–74	635	1972–73	454

These figures do not include teacher exchanges; since 1954 between 20 and 30 German and American teachers have participated each year in governmental exchange programs; in addition, about 300 American teachers were employed by German school authorities in 1972 under limited contracts[9] (but their number has decreased drastically in recent years).

Unfortunately, no exact breakdown as to academic fields is available for the various groups. However, from the reports of institutions and organizations which handle German-American exchanges the following rough estimates may be drawn: among the senior scholars natural scientists and engineers predominate (about half of the total); the humanities and social sciences follow with about one fourth each. In student exchanges the humanities (language/literature) account for the bulk of participants while social sciences and natural/engineering sciences are represented by about 20 percent; among American students barely 15 percent come from science disciplines (steady increase since 1972).

Structures and Planning in Academic Exchanges

While it is self-evident to the continental European that governmental regulations prevail in planning, funding and coordination, it must be emphasized that the American tradition is built upon the pragmatic cooperation of public and private institutions/organizations. These different approaches (which, after all, reflect domestic conditions in the educational systems on both sides of the Atlantic) explain why the United States, as a rule, does not conclude general cultural agreements with other countries.

It would be beyond the scope of this article to describe in detail the development of country-specific structures. The following examples will, therefore, be symptomatic for the prevalence or absence of ways in which set objectives and their implementation interact.

The Council of Europe has appointed a Committee for Cultural Cooperation to facilitate coordination between the member countries; but thus far hardly any steps have been taken towards a common exchange with the US. Basically the individual European countries establish their own priorities; each of them pursues its own cultural policy vis-à-vis the US with differing objectives and different financial, political and administrative means. The Federal Republic of Germany has given high priority to academic cooperation with the US both in absolute and relative terms. As teaching and research in Germany are embedded in the system of public and constitutional law, the participation of the state in the form of funding, representation in committees, advisory or coordinating functions is accepted as a way of life; the cooperation of large foundations supplements and expands the activities of a cultural policy outlined by the state.

The structure in the US is different: much greater importance is attached to the private sector. The institutions of higher learning, the agencies of academic self-administration (including scholarly associations) and, of course, the foundations operate with a degree of autonomy and with financial means which are alien to most European countries. Even more: countless individual decisions are made entirely outside of government influence; admission of foreign students or invitations to guest professors are arranged locally, frequently on the basis of economic rather than politico-cultural considerations; occasionally private foundations award scholarships by criteria which are in no way coordinated. Just because this is the case and because the pragmatic operations in the various institutions have, all in all, produced acceptable results, the possibilities of state influence have remained much more limited than in Europe. The structure of the educational system and of its international components thus explain the reservations shown by the US Congress in appropriating government funds for such purposes.

An almost classic example for the dilemma of American cultural foreign policy between politico-cultural planning and the failure of its implementation is the International Education Act of 1966: it was initiated by President Johnson and prepared by a prominent task force of politicians, educators, scientists and foundation officers;[10] both houses of Congress passed the bill, but left without budget appropriations, the Act was doomed to an existence as a politico-cultural ruin.

On the other hand, American legislation on international educational exchange also demonstrates how social forces in education may be drawn into cooperation with the government and with Congress – and how far the relatively narrow leeway for cultural foreign relations can effectively be used. The Mutual Educational and Cultural Exchange Act of 1961 (better known as the Fulbright-Hays Act) which is based on earlier legislation, offers a broadly defined political concept aiming at bilateral cooperation with foreign governments on the one hand and the participation of societal groups on the other hand. Two boards whose members are appointed directly by the American President are assigned to develop and evaluate principles and guidelines (US Advisory Commission) and to implement and supervise programs as well as to select grantees (Board of Foreign Scholarships). "The members [of these boards] . . . shall represent the public interest and shall be selected from a cross section of educational, cultural, scientific, technical and public service backgrounds."[11] Bilateral planning and implementation of exchanges with the participating countries takes place in the so-called Fulbright Commissions (presently 44 world-wide, of these 16 in Europe); however, procedures have proven so successful that other government programs have been adjusted to them. In this manner, a surprising number of areas of educational and cultural policies as well as of science policy – these, however, with considerable country-specific deviations – can be coordinated, funded and directed, especially since American and foreign ministries are directly involved in the decision-making process.

Problems as well as advantages of these confusing points of departure can be shown by a few typical examples:

– The DAAD (German Academic Exchange Service) as the German exchange agency (or "contract agency" in American terminology) for

world-wide student exchanges receives 94 percent of its budget from
various government appropriations;[12] its US counterpart, the Institute of
International Education (IIE) receives only 34.8 percent.[13] The discrepancy
becomes even larger if one takes into account that the American
government funds for IIE are spent for contractually arranged special
assignments and that the program volume of IIE is considerably larger
than the budget figures indicate, due to contributions in kind (scholarships
and tuition waivers of US institutions) which are administered or arranged
under government programs but cannot be expressed in actual budget
figures.

– The bilateral German Fulbright-Kommission receives DM 5,900,000
($2,565,000) p.a. in government appropriations (German government
about 77 percent, US government about 23 percent); due to additional
scholarships, salaries and private funds the actual program volume is
increased by another DM 3,655,000 (16 percent from German, 84 percent
from American sources) which add to the politico-cultural effect.[14]

– The German Marshall Fund of the United States receives DM 10,000,000
($4,350,000) p.a. from the German government as its sole financial source;
however, it administers and awards this money as an American private,
non-profit foundation "without any influence by German authorities." Of
course, this foundation is primarily project-oriented and less active in
traditional academic exchanges (and, incidentally, is one of the few
examples of common European approaches).[15]

Obviously, the conditions under which transatlantic academic exchanges
take place have an impact upon planning operations and the results of
programs and projects. If, for example, the German government is able to
allocate, on short notice, substantial funding for a special program to make
possible a training session at English-speaking universities for Germans who
are to become English teachers (DAAD Anglistics Program), questions of
particular significance for educational and cultural relations arise: How
should the students in such a program be distributed between the US, Canada
and Great Britain?; how will this program affect attitudes in the host
countries? Although, in a *formal* manner, the exchange/contract agency
operates quite independently, it is dependent upon the cooperation with the
funding ministry. In this sense and in relation to other exchanges between
European countries and the US, it cannot be overlooked that in this
combination of government and private activities and many personal efforts,
shortcomings are bound to develop which bear on cultural or political
relations but for which exchange agencies cannot assume responsibility.

The diversity and variety of interest and planning put national and multinational – or at least bilateral – priorities side by side, at times even in opposition to one another. This results in two consequences; agreement between national agencies and governments on desiderata, funds and measures on the one hand and bilateral coordination on the other. With regard to the first complex, agreement in the Federal Republic is achieved by voluntary cooperation and representation in boards and, to a considerable degree, through government pressure in the appropriation of funds. In working committees at the Conference of West German University Rectors (WRK) or at retreats such as the Arera Conference (1972) program and budget planning are harmonized and coordinated far beyond government-sponsored exchanges. The core of intergovernmental arrangements is attained at the annual "cultural talks" between the heads of the cultural divisions of both foreign ministries. The results of these talks reach far beyond traditional academic exchanges, as demonstrated by the Harrison House Conference (1975) where, for the first time, the expanded definition of the culture concept was not just discussed but rather incorporated into actual program planning.

Impact of Exchanges[16]

"Success" of government-sponsored or private exchanges belongs to the natural expectations of funding sponsors and the public at large. After all, and rightly so, American "accountability" and its German counterpart "efficiency control", form the basis for decisions in cultural foreign policy. In the following comments – and with a view restricted to US-European exchanges – the private sector will largely be disregarded; for, frequently enough, private exchange arrangements are made quite without the consideration of general principles: e.g., an applicant for a competitive public exchange program is rejected for lack of qualification, but is accepted and financed anyway by a well-known university in the host country – the anticipated failure of the student then causes embarrassment for which, however, the official exchange cannot be held responsible.

Important in official exchanges is the original objective under which a project is initiated. In this regard, the annual reports of exchange/contract agencies provide ample insights.

Obviously it is simple to document success and benefits in exchanges of research policy orientation. A glance at the annual reports of the German Research Association (DFG) or the Alexander von Humboldt Foundation with their abstracts, lists of publications, professional appointments or lectures, easily evidence which results have been achieved and how these relate to previous planning. It must be kept in mind, however, that scholarly qualification alone determines the selection of a researcher. Of course, it should be added that quite often eminent scholars exercise influence as "multipliers" on administrations and planning beyond their own academic disciplines.

Assessment of impact is much more difficult in other areas of cultural policy objectives since effects as a rule become visible only after a period of years. This applies not only to students but also to professional groups such as teachers, lawyers or economists.

It is a mistake to assume that the "success" of studies abroad can best be proved by academic degrees:[17] apart from the fact that the definition of the exchange student establishes a relation to the education at home, recent admission and examination regulations generally exclude American exchange students from acquiring an academic degree in Europe; that this happens occasionally anyway speaks for the high level of the selection mechanism. The American system of higher education is, indeed, much more flexible in this regard, and the structure of certain degree programs (e.g., in comparative law or business administration) offers remarkable incentives to the foreign student and post-graduate. In DAAD's normal program, which is primarily designed for post-graduate applicants (or those just short of their final examinations) matriculation in a graduate degree program is the rule rather than the exception, even though participation may not be intended to lead to completion. It should also be emphasized that the exchange of young lawyers or law graduates has gained in attraction through the availability of Master's degrees (LL.M. or MCL.) as an additional examination which does not exist at home.

Objectives of education-policy orientation have frequently created false expectations and led to misunderstandings.[18] The difference between a kind of "educational tourism" and real exchange becomes apparent in such situations, as could be demonstrated by a number of examples.

Some of the results of transatlantic exchanges which are relevant educational policy are listed below incompletely and just for the sake illustration: curricular and examination reforms at medical school groups grated internships and tests); training of teachers for specific lectures in (rather than for types of schools); new planning and personnel training in university administration; expansion of foreign language te and Germanistics methodology and area studies (DAAD Anglistics Program of Fachhochs- programs of DAAD and Fulbright-Kommission); in sion of Fachhoch- chulen – career-oriented colleges – into educational xchange (pilot program of Fulbright-Kommission); standardization in computer science training (DAAD special program); institutional partnerships with individual and project support; continuing education for middle strata of university teachers and for faculty at teachers colleges and career-oriented colleges (here at the initiation stage).

In the borderline area between educational and cultural policy we find an abundance of examples from which again only a few will be cited:

- The promotion of "area studies", that is, of American Studies in Europe, including cooperation in the European Association for American Studies, as well as of European Studies in the US. Particularly in view of the unfortunate reduction of foreign language requirements and their substitution through general courses ("humanities alternatives") at American high schools and colleges, regional or area studies gain special significance. It is no surprise, however, that in this field cultural competition among European countries persists despite some pan-European beginnings: not only American foreign language teachers associations (e.g. AATG – American Association for Teachers of German) but likewise the various European diplomats and cultural posts in the US pursue their own legitimate interests. In establishing German Studies visiting professorships at US institutions (to be filled by German scholars) the federal government, the large foundations and the exchange/contract agencies maintain close cooperation. The special seminar courses in German area studies, conducted for American professors of German by the Fulbright-Kommission in conjunction with Bonn University, prove as well how closely area studies and cultural policy may be linked with a specifically American educational problem.

- The promotion of international education for law students and law graduates (DAAD and Fulbright programs, also Max Rheinstein fellowship of the Alexander von Humboldt Foundation).

- The promotion of innovations in adult education: expansion of exchanges to include museum and library experts (Fulbright-Kommission); it is ~markable in this context that, for example, a considerable amount of frĝstions for use of museums for educational purposes have been adopted have'ę US, while scientific concentration and methodology in Europe

- Compara found to be attractive for American experts.
introduced ṟresearch in vocational education; this area is just being Europe and in ᵪchanges, but it will grow with the structural reforms in Looking at the ou US.
considered in the conteᵪtives determined by cultural policy, which we have of social and general politics, it becomes clear that

it is extremely difficult to assess the impact of transatlantic academic exchanges. For we are dealing with the sum of individual as well as institutional expectations and experiences – viewed from both the outside (society, sponsors) and the inside (participants). Moreover, the approach is most important: obviously, in fields such as climate research, and space technology or in research concerning problems of industrial societies, scientific results may have an enormous political effect or even measurable economic value; conversely, it cannot be denied that to many scientists knowledge of the host country is (at least initially) a matter of indifference. But even in structured programs the weights have shifted in the post-war generation of academic exchangees, as evidenced by a few examples:

Although – or precisely because – German-American academic exchanges after World War II were from the very beginning excluded from re-education operations, the American experience of exchangees in the 1950's gained in political significance: integration, acceptance, free personal development as well as equality in the US, on the one hand; and participation in the difficult phase of reconstruction in Germany, on the other hand, conveyed to German and American exchange students and professors a consciousness for "mutual understanding" and mutual respect.

– During the period of anti-Americanism in Europe, that is, the late 1960s and early 1970s, academic exchange programs and supporting agencies remained remarkably free from any repudiation through the universities or the public. Large numbers of grantee reports (and from both sides of the Atlantic) during those years have proven, in addition, how essential two characteristics of exchanges have become: selection by qualification and integration in the host country. For the credibility of a foreigner who at the same time is a personal (and in many cases esteemed) acquaintance is often greater and sometimes more significant than the impressions of another country as conveyed by the press, radio and television. It is evident in the final reports from grantees during those years – and at other times, as well – that almost without exception the correction of their own or someone else's prejudices is held to be as important as the academic experience; frequently this non-academic aspect was a "by-product", also among those whose main interest had been in pure research.

– Looking at one's own country from abroad is among the most impressive experiences of exchanges:

"... above all, this experience has given me the chance to consider my country objectively in examining her responsibilities within the world community. Moreso it has caused me to examine the role of Americans in Europe, and especially in Germany, in the past as well as the present, and has caused me to reconsider my responsibilities and purposes in the future."

This (real) quotation could be found in similar wording in most final reports of American grantees.

In this context it is particularly instructive to consider that the present German student generation of grantees (born between 1949 and 1954) is confronted with German problems, often for the first time in their lives, in the United States. Such problems include: the Third Reich, the Jewish question, the division of Germany, Germany's relations with Eastern Europe (Oder-Neiße) etc. In conversations with American fellow-students, in the discussion of TV programs or press reports German students suddenly discover that they cannot dodge such issues as unconcerned, innocent juveniles. At the suggestion of its grantees the Fulbright-Kommission has re-introduced the topic "Contemporary German History" into the orientation conferences for departing Germans. Similarly remarkable is the frequent comment, made not only by young Germans, that in the US one felt more like a European than a German (French, Dutch, Belgian); this, too, shows a new kind of consciousness among the young generation.

– Several special programs for groups of persons who had up until now been excluded from academic exchanges have been generated through the expanded culture concept: the Harvard Trade Union Program (for non-academics; Fulbright program in conjunction with the German Federation of Trade Unions/DGB and AFL-CIO), the Iowa Writers' Program, or the Council of International Programs for Youth Leaders and Social Workers (CIP-Cleveland in conjunction with the Federal Ministry for Youth, Family and Health, the Fulbright-Kommission and several American universities). Additional endeavors, such as the artists' program of the DAAD or the special efforts directed towards accommodation of minority students (Fulbright) aim in the same direction.

– Study-abroad programs – although widely differing in scope and character – conducted by American universities and colleges in Europe should be assessed primarily on the basis of their politico-cultural dimension; about one third of all American students attending German universities are enrolled in such programs. This may explain some of the recent regulations for the admission of foreign students (from which presumably such American programs are deriving the most benefit).

The examples presented thus far have been basically of a bilateral nature and should be supplemented by a glance at the European dimension of cooperation in terms of the overall theme of this book.

Again, it is self-evident that purely research oriented exchanges have a broader base, however, they can be evaluated only in that context. Joint research in the areas of the "big sciences" or environmental studies leads to contacts of shorter or longer duration between institutes and scientists, but it remains a matter of fortuity beyond all considerations of traditional cultural policy as to where and how research projects are carried out; whether an American scholar joins a European or international cooperative research project in France, Belgium or Germany has little to do with a personal preference for a particular country – the choice is determined instead by the existing structures of research or personnel on the basis of international arrangements.

The Alexander von Humboldt Foundation is an exception in this area as it offers its grantees the opportunity to spend three months in another (usually European) country. An attempt is made to broaden both the scientific and the personal experience.

The fundamental impulses leading to cooperation, as regards to the objectives of educational and cultural policy concerning European-American academic exchanges, originated in the United States. Not only is the field of "European Studies" itself a reflection of geographic, cultural and historic dimensions as viewed by Americans; the regional approach has also been adopted in exchange programs of private as well as scholarly agencies (e.g. Ford and Rockefeller Foundations, the American Council of Learned Societies) and in government-sponsored programs.

Many study-abroad programs of American colleges and universities operate across national boundaries all over Europe. Through publications and services the Institute of International Education and the Council on International Educational Exchange help to facilitate this movement.

The US Department of State and the Board of Foreign Scholarships have become particularly skilled at promoting cooperation with Europe as a whole, especially since the structure of bilateral participation by the various European governments involves them directly in the decision-making processes: the 16 directors of the binational Fulbright Commissions in Europe (plus those of Yugoslavia and Israel) form a continuous task force in which country-specific and regional programs are coordinated and common issues of implementation are discussed. In this manner, the Department of State, as well as the various national governments and binational commissions, are actively engaged in regional cooperation beyond merely bilateral objectives. Through the so-called "Interfoundation Lectureship Program," American Fulbright professors may be invited to guest lecture in any of the participating European countries while holding fellowships in only one European country. By splitting grants and through special programs it has been possible to present projects of common European concern in a transatlantic dialogue: in 1973 a Fulbright seminar on educational reforms in Europe and in the US took place in Salzburg; in 1975 a Fulbright symposium was held in Rome on the topic of urban renewal; in both cases American Fulbright professors working in Europe, and European experts and politicians (up to the cabinet level) took part in the conferences. That this form of cooperation is by no means organized by the US alone is demonstrated, for example, by the Berlin Meeting of American Fulbright grantees (students, professors, teachers) to which, as suggested by the German government, Americans who received their awards in other European countries are invited as well. This meeting is characterized by the encounter with the political, economic and cultural realities not just of Berlin, but also with those of the Federal Republic, of Europe and their relations with the United States. If the 300 participants regard the Berlin Week as a highlight of their entire grant period, then this underlines once again the significance of non-academic impressions in the exchange.

Although the European dimension is taken seriously in the US, neither side cares to view "North America" in its totality, that is, as a combination of the United States and Canada. In this respect an important and interesting perspective has, thus far, received little attention; it should be examined in Europe and be drawn closer into politico-cultural planning.

There is no doubt, of course, that exchanges do not only produce positive results. Aside from the many unsuccessful applicants (up to 80 percent in certain grant programs) whose disappointment may often turn against the envisaged host country and against the idea of exchanges itself, and apart from the endless administrative complexities of the different bureaucracies, academic exchanges simply cannot live up to all of the individual and official expectations placed on them:

– Academic exchange does not bring the world closer to peace, as Harold Isaacs recently observed:[19] and "mutual understanding" does not mean the acceptance of foreign patterns of government or life style, as a study of Eisenhower scholars has shown;[20] such expectations exceed the capabilities of exchanges.

– It is impossible to conceive of European-American academic exchanges as elitist programs and at the same time to conduct them on a broad and democratic basis – unless the different objectives among the agencies or institutions are more clearly defined.

– The success of academic pursuits abroad cannot always be measured in terms of publications completed or academic degrees obtained; the preparation of a course as a grant activity abroad (e.g. for a community college teacher) may well be accepted within the framework of traditional academic exchange.

- In view of the poor arrangements concerning equivalences of degrees and academic credits the formal benefit for the individual exchangee may be marginal. However, it is significant that, for example, in German-American relations talks on this topic could be introduced only by way of government-sponsored exchanges.
- The "brain-drain" problem has been an impediment for exchanges for many years, especially with the US and above all in exchanges of science-policy orientation. Without denying the negative impact on national research (and also not ignoring the European practice with respect to other countries) it would be worth our while to investigate the resulting paradox, that is, to what positive extent this phenomenon may have facilitated institutional and inter-country cooperation.
- Finally, academic exchange has not met the expectations, voiced by several European governments, that the use of national languages (French, German, Italian etc.) in scientific publications should correspond to the national proportion of authors in any particular volume: among exchange scholars English has become a kind of lingua franca; they, indeed, consider this development as a positive contribution to international cooperation (this would be different in programs stressing "mutual understanding").

A Glance at the Future

At this time it is impossible to describe accurately the trends and developments in academic exchanges between the US and Europe. It is evident that the conditions have changed considerably from those when transatlantic exchanges began after World War II. Concepts have evolved out of accidental historical circumstances and humanitarian actions, and the social and economic reconstruction phases of the early postwar years; such concepts have, of course, not always been congruous in the US and in Europe. We cannot expect – it may not even be desirable – to regulate the variety of transatlantic encounters in a comprehensive manner. But that will make it all the more necessary to develop strategies and priorities in the different areas of objectives and with a view towards national, bilateral and multilateral principles.

Several discernible factors in the US and in Europe will certainly bear upon the future of exchanges.

One definite tendency is that cooperation with research-policy orientation will continue on a bilateral as well as a continental scale. The natural and engineering sciences will continue to form a solid basis in this area. Technology transfer issues also result in a transatlantic community of interests vis-à-vis Third World countries despite occasional economic competition.

In the United States, a growing concentration of foreign cultural relation measures directed towards non-European areas is becoming evident.[21] During the early postwar years – until about the late 1950's – governmental or government coordinated programs documented the priority of exchanges with Europe, be it for reasons of tradition or available funds (from war surplus) or because of political and humanitarian considerations; however, by the mid-60's different tendencies were shifting the focus of American exchanges efforts: new programs following the "sputnik shock" (e.g. NDEA since 1958) directed educational opportunities towards other continents; the civil rights movement, both in the expansion of the educational system to accommodate "mass education" or, later "universal education" and in its recognition of ethnic pluralism, resulted in more concern for domestic problems (as opposed to internationalism) and in the competition for funds; the Vietnam War and US involvement in development programs for Third World countries shifted emphasis, too; in addition there is an impact from special programs in which the government has little direct influence (such as the so-called "oil country programs"). It is realistic to assume that the economic situation in the US and concomitant (relative) reductions in Congressional and foundation appropriations will affect the priorities of the government as well as the institutions. A few random illustrations of the present situation – as it relates to educational exchange – can be listed here, such as reduced foreign language requirements at many colleges and high schools and the ensuing job insecurity of language teachers; concentration, almost imposed on agencies (and government offices), upon services for foreign sponsored and non-sponsored students mainly from developing countries; decreasing interest in many study-abroad programs.

On the other hand, the official cultural foreign policy of the US (State Department, US Office of Education) has been particularly instrumental in major efforts towards establishing regional or program emphases and in the coordination or guidance of exchanges with a view towards principles of cultural and general foreign relations. The organization of the State Department by regional subdivisions (e.g. Cultural Unit/Western Europe) as well as its initiatives to cooperate with the private sector depend largely on officers and diplomats, but all these aspects prove how closely cultural relations have been integrated into foreign policy itself. Therefore, proposals as discussed in 1977 with a view towards separating cultural relations from general foreign policy (and adding those to information services) will be scrutinized abroad – and especially in Europe – in terms of political significance rather than as a mere administrative procedure.

European developments at this time still point in several directions.[22] Apart from exchanges under science-policy orientation and aside from cooperative analysis and planning in the OECD (which affect changes only indirectly) there are mainly country-specific conditions which determine trends, some of these, of course, parallel throughout Europe. The pattern in the Federal Republic as one example also includes factors common to all of Europe. The expansion of post-secondary education (Fachhochschule in Germany, polytechs in Great Britain, instituts universitaires de technologie in France) accompanied by restricted access to higher education (numerus clausus) and by curricular reforms (intermediate examinations, standardized duration of curricula) are changing the traditional pattern of academic exchanges, particularly with regard to objectives under educational and cultural policies. Substantial problems are arising in the area of equivalences; in contrast to the American system of academic and professional admission tests, the German system is still marked by a principle of admission determined through terminal examinations; there are wide gaps in European regulations concerning professional licencing as well as in curricula and examinations, and even wider gaps appear in such relations with third countries (in which American degrees frequently form a kind of "standard currency"). The cost of a stay in the US is an important factor especially if prices are rising. Inadequate information on American education as well as some aftereffects of anti-Americanism may influence individual decisions. This list of factors – though incomplete – does not only affect exchanges in a negative way; e.g. while many German students abstain from any form of studying abroad in order to complete their examinations in familiar surroundings in the shortest period of time and with the best grades possible and thus hope to be successful in professional competition, other students try to acquire additional qualifications by going abroad, and to the US in particular. The legal framework of the German educational system, in the form of the federal financial support program or the expected regulations on the standard length of studies, prove how thoroughly inner-German decisions may affect exchanges.

On the other hand, the German federal government has, regardless of the coalition combination, never left a doubt as to the importance of academic cooperation with the US. It lends support not only by planning and co-funding binational programs such as the Fulbright-Kommission, but also by promoting cooperation among exchange agencies.

Considering the short span of time that cultural foreign policy has been pursued, the results are impressive. But much remains to be done. Perhaps it is no coincidence that a German politician, speaking as a European, set a long-range objective for exchanges with the US:

> We must get to know each other better, still more: we must learn to live with each other. More young Europeans must have the opportunity of exploring the social landscape of America, of discovering America's outlook on life, of becoming familiar with its history, and the process must be reciprocal.

Notes

[1] cf. John S. Brubacher and Willis Rudy, Higher education in transition, New York: Harper 1958, chapt. 9; Erich Marcks, Männer und Zeiten, Leipzig: Quelle & Meyer 1922, Vol. 2, pp. 47–74.

[2] cf. Anniversary Report of DAAD: *Der Deutsche Akademische Austauschdienst 1925–1975*, DAAD-Forum 7, Bonn: DAAD 1975.

[3] Lily von Klemperer, *International Education: A Directory of Resource Materials . . .*, Garrett Park, Md.: Garrett Park Press, 1974. Monographs on exchange programs often contain valuable but mostly program-related information, e.g. Walter Johnson and Francis J. Colligan, *The Fulbright Program – A History*, Chicago: University of Chicago Press 1965. The results of the research groups under the auspices of Prof. Otto Klineberg, Paris: (cooperation with Cologne University: Heine von Alemann, *Educational Exchange in the Federal Republic of Germany*, Köln: Institut für Vergleichende Sozialforschung, Universität Köln, Dec. 1973, mimeogr.), and Gerd Gerken, Berlin and Dr. Hannelore Gerstein, DAAD Bonn, are either not pertaining to the present topic or cannot yet be used.

[4] German Bundestag, Drucksache 7/4121 (7 Oct. 1975), p. 8; for an excellent account of the reforms in Germany cf. Richard Straus, *Notes on a German Debate*, in: *Exchange*, No. 3, Winter 1977. John Richardson, Jr., *Preparing for a Human Community*, in: *The Department of State Bulletin*, No. 1929, 14 June 1976, p. 757.

[5] Susan S. Holland, *Exchange of People Among International Companies: Problems and Benefits*, in: *The Annals of the American Academy of Political and Social Science*, Vol. 424, March 1976.

[6] cf. *Zeitschrift für Kulturaustausch*, No. 3, 1975; also illustrative are the different approaches of the German Parliamentary Commission and the American "Stanton Panel".

[7] Joan H. Joshi, *International Exchange in the Arts, Annals*, op. cit.

[8] The tables are based on: *UNESCO, Statistical Yearbook 1974*, Paris 1975; Institute of International Education, *Open Doors*, New York: IIE, annual editions since 1955; Board of Foreign Scholarships, *Reports on Exchanges*, Washington, D.C., Dec. 1974. Cf. Also Wallace B. Edgerton, *Who Participates in Educational Exchange?*, in: *Annals*, op. cit. Several national compilations differ considerably from the UNESCO statistics which are established by largely uniform principles: British Council figures (Statistics of overseas students in Britain 1974–1975) include more (e.g. vocational) institutions. Some American statistics register 6,300 American students in France while the UNESCO reports merely 2,300; a check of the *Guide to American Academic Programs*, Paris: USIS, suggests that the American figures include programs that are not completely integrated into French universities.

[9] Ulrich Littmann, *Perspectives from Bonn*, in: *Exchange*, No. 2, 1974, p. 26.

[10] Allan A. Michie, ed., *Diversity and Interdependence Through International Education*, New York: Education and World Affairs 1967.

[11] P.L. 87–256, Sec. 106 (b)(3); Johnson and Colligan, op. cit., p. 337.

[12] German Bundestag, Drucksache 7/4121, p. 118.

[13] Letter dated 18 August 1976 from IIE President Edgerton to the author.

[14] Auditor's Report of Treuhand-Kommandit-Gesellschaft to the Contracting Governments.

[15] Report on current activities, May 1976.

[16] The evaluation is based on annual reports of German exchange/contract agencies, especially Deutsche Forschungsgemeinschaft, Alexander von Humboldt Stiftung, Deutscher Akademischer Austauschdienst, as well as reports of binational Fulbright commissions in Europe and of American agencies and organizations. Also John T. and Jeanne E. Gullahorn, *International Educational Exchange: An Assessment of Professional and Social Contributions by American Fulbright and Smith-Mundt Grantees, 1947–1957*, East Lansing: Michigan State University 1960, mimeogr.; *A German Appraisal of the Fulbright Program: A Study Among German Participants of the Cultural Exchange Between the Federal Republik* [sic] *and the USA*, Frankfurt/M.: DIVO 1961, mimeogr.; William H. Sewell and Oluf M. Davidsen, *Scandinavian Students on an American Campus*, Minneapolis: University of Minnesota Press 1961; George P. Springer, *A Report on the Fulbright-Hays Student Exchange Program Seminar*, New York: Institute for International Education 1968, mimeogr.; Johnson and Colligan, op. cit.; finally, grantee reports as well as correspondence with and on European exchanges from 1953 through 1976.

[17] For discussion of methods and contents of such evaluations cf. Hannelore Gerstein, *Ausländische Stipendiaten in der Bundesrepublik Deutschland: eine empirische Erhebung* ... DAAD-Forum 1, Bonn: DAAD, pp. 11 ff.

[18] Steven Muller, *Deutsche Einflüsse auf die amerikanische Hochschulentwicklung*, and Theodor Heidhues, *Amerikanische Einflüsse auf Ausbildung, Forschung und Hochschulstruktur in der Bundesrepublik Deutschland*, Bonn: Deutsche Forschungsgemeinschaft etc., 1976, mimeogr.; Ulrich Littmann, *Universal education: Eigenarten des amerikanischen Bildungssystems, Das Parlament*, No. 22–23, 1976.

[19] *Chronicle of Higher Education*, No. 14, 31 May 1976, p. 3.

[20] *Time*, European Edition, 31 May 1976, p. 18.

[21] *Education for Global Interdependence: A Report with Recommendations to the Government/Academic Interface Committee*, Washington, D.C.: American Council on Education [1975].

[22] Positive initiatives for European cooperation in this area are contained in the report by Jean Capelle, *Special Project Mobility*, Strasbourg: Council of Europe, 14 June 1976, CCC/ESR/PSM [76] 2.

Culture as a Bridge

by FRANÇOIS BONDY

The history of the "images" – whether frightening or idealized – which are shared by Europeans about America, or, to a lesser extent, by Americans about Europe, has acquired increasing importance for research in the field of European-American relations and is closely connected with the cultural aspects of these relations. Studies of these "images" in novels, poetry, and works of art, as well as in everyday attitudes and stereotypes, represent a vast body of work. In this book Wolfgang Wagner correctly observes that the Europeans are themselves far too heterogeneous a people to have a homogeneous image of America ("America" in this context, significantly enough, implies merely the United States).

Actual cultural relations between America and Europe are distinct from such "images," but not in every respect. Real experiences cannot be completely separated from imagination any more than our daily lives can be separated from our dreams, fantasies and myths, as Sigmund Freud discovered some time ago.

The Cleveland Museum of Art's Bicentennial Exhibition, organized by Hugh Honour, presented a rich collection of material illustrating the development of the European image of America. The exhibition catalog as well as Honour's work, "The New Golden Land," describe the many changes in this image in admirable detail.

One must distinguish between two periods of development: The first begins with the discovery of America and ends toward the middle of the nineteenth century – a period when few people had an opportunity actually to see the country, and images were therefore largely based on fantasy; the second is our era, in which mass immigration to America, travel, and various other contacts made possible through new means of communication and expression (telegraph, telephone, radio, photography, films, and television) have turned both direct and vicarious experience into a mass phenomenon. The fantasy with which Burgkmair the Elder, in his "Triumph of Emperor Maximilian," depicted the Indians as people of Calcutta, and with which other painters surrounded American natives with Asiatic flora and fauna differs substantially from the fantasies of modern Europeans dreaming of "their" America. They differ as much as modern science fiction writers differ from Paracelsus, who "proved" that the Indians had no soul. The America we know through fiction is by no means a completely fictitious America. A European who is acquainted with American films, who has had contact with American subcultures and life styles through music, clothing, consumer habits, and various customs will already feel familiar with many aspects of America during his first visit, a result of preconceptions which were partial but by no means false. This European will not experience the shock of confronting the totally new, as did those before him.

I previously hinted at a reservation concerning the reciprocity of images. Since its inception the United States has viewed itself as an "idea" – as a draft of a work or as a finished masterpiece – just as Europe has viewed it as a real refuge or an ideal future. Europe, however, is seen by the Americans as representing the past, a history of an acknowledged or rejected dependence, and is something "forgotten" by immigrants. It is only a small number of American intellectuals who value Europe as a place where they can live better, more meaningful lives. This lack of reciprocity, however, in no way diminishes the presence of real mutual influences.

These actual cultural relationships are rooted in institutions, established by the Europeans long before the days of independence and the formation of the Union. Those Europeans brought with them their religion, their traditions, their democracy. Certainly the concept of newness, a new beginning, a "new Adam," dominated the American consciousness. This is, indeed, an essentially American cultural peculiarity.[1] How this sense of newness – humanity begins again with each generation – has been combined with an almost rigid political and legal traditionalism strikes Europeans as one of the strangest and most persistent contradictions about America.

The immigration of millions of Europeans since 1840, first from Northern Europe, then from the South and the East, has deeply transformed the United States. Prior to these immigrations "imported" blacks made up one third of the population, compared with only one tenth thereafter. For the last hundred years, and in particular since 1933, the immigration of scientists, scholars and artists has had a profound influence on various areas of American culture ranging from architecture to political theory; one need only think of the "Bauhaus," psychoanalysis, art history, Gestalt psychology or nuclear physics. The catalog of the exhibition "The Golden Door. Artist-immigrants of America 1876–1976" in the Hirschhorn Museum[2] is an amazing documentation of this European influence. It includes documents on Albers, Richter, Mondrian, Rothko, Duchamp, Steinberg, Gropius, Mies van der Rohe, Moholy Nagy and de Kooning. As the catalog puts it:

"Modern art is inconceivable without the contribution of such giants as Josef Albers, Marcel Duchamp, Mark Rothko, Jacques Lipchitz, Mies van der Rohe and Hans Hofmann, all of whom were born abroad and immigrated to the United States." (Abram Lerner) "In no other period in American history were our thought and art and culture more deeply stirred or more grandly shaped by currents from abroad." (Daniel J. Boorstin).

Certainly one cannot ignore the contribution of immigrants to American culture when evaluating the relationship between Americans and Europeans. There are many studies which examine their contribution; among the most informative are the biographical histories written by Leo Szilard and Laura Fermi. What Europeans saw as a "brain drain" (including one fourth of all Central European Nobel Prize winners) was seen by Americans as a welcome "brain gain," and this in a period of extremely limited immigration such as had never occurred before or after. The list in the book "Two Hundred Years of German-American Relations"[3] of all writers, artists, and scientists who came as refugees to the USA between 1933 and 1941, is impressive. In 1935: the physicists Hans A. Bethge, Wolfgang Pauli, Edward Teller, the philosopher Rudolph Carnap, the composer Kurt Weill; in 1938: the stage director Max Reinhardt, the architect Mies van der Rohe, the philosopher Ernst Bloch, writers Thomas Mann and Hermann Broch, social scientists Karl W. Deutsch, Leo Strauss, Erich Vögelin; in 1940: the psychologists Charlotte and Paul Bühler, writers Heinrich Mann and Alfred Döblin, the composer Paul Hindemith, the historian Paul Rothfels; in 1941: Max Ernst, Bertolt Brecht, Hannah Arendt. These are only a few of the hundreds of names listed.

Originally (particularly between 1880 and 1914) immigration was the goal mainly of the lower classes, mostly from Southern and Eastern Europe, and thus a mass phenomenon; during the Third Reich it was the rescue of an intellectual elite, made possible through special operations.

The immigration limitations, based on implicit racial principles, were only abrogated under President Johnson. This abrogation had a positive effect on non-white, non-European immigrants, not only for Latin American rural workers, whose illegal entry was already tolerated, but also for thousands of medical doctors from developing countries, in particular the Philippines, who helped fill a critical demand for doctors in the United States. In this case one can view immigration as a contribution by poor countries, who carried the costs of education and training, to the well-being of the world's richest nation. This problem is now being recognized and widely discussed. One must, however, also consider that in the United States, in contrast to Europe, the stages from immigration to citizenship are predictable and certain.

The melting pot: Today this term is often used critically. Attention is directed to origins, cohesiveness, the special traditions of individual groups and peoples, to the so-called ethnics. Over half a century ago Louis Adamić, himself a Southern Slav, described the United States as a "nation of nations," an expression coined by Walt Whitman. Since the sixties the ethnics have become a key cultural and political concept.

Unlike the aspirations of the European minorities such as the Basques or the Bretons, the problems of the ethnics have not led to a series of separatist movements or to demands for independent statehood. For several years, blacks have considered the idea but this was primarily to strengthen their own sense of identity, a positive valuation of a particularity previously seen as a stigma: "Black is beautiful." In the bestseller "Roots," Haley, the black author, traces the history of his family back to its African origins. The Jewish sense of a special cultural heritage may have set the precedent. Today the values and way of life of the Indians are also seen in a new light. Even in the realm of language – Spanish is becoming dominant in several parts of the country – assimilation and homogeneity are no longer seen as the marks of true Americanism.

This pluralism is new, developing from the growing ethnic awareness of Southern and Eastern Europeans; the working class is moulded more by this ethnic awareness than by class-consciousness. Patrick Moynihan and Nathan Glazer have shown that the growth of the ethnic movement has not merely meant a renunciation of the concept of a melting pot. Ethnic customs and values are being organized and cultivated, but even this is a part of Americanism: adaptation. The ethnics fight for respect, influence, representation on election committees, admission to universities, etc. They form powerful pressure groups. For this very reason a "Balkanization" of the ethnics is not to be expected; geographic dispersion, social mobility and the real claims and hopes of the minorities, all these work against such a disruptive process. In fact, the "ethnics" aim at integration and participation, at helping to overcome discrimination. Yet this new awareness of ethnic identity is significant for American culture, in particular in the field of education.[4]

Great Britain, a country beset with the problem of integrating large numbers of Blacks and Asians, is now trying to learn from the American experience.[5]

The "Wasps," once a model for other Americans, have become only one minority among many. At the same time the universally applied new immigration practices render obsolete the discussion of immigration as a unique link between Europe and America.

Is there, nevertheless, a cultural community based on traditional affinities and a special partnership in which strategic considerations, intellectual affinity to Europe, and Europe's importance as an economically highly developed region, support one another? Certainly, there is a "Europe" in America which we on our continent do not perceive the same way as Americans do. Who has not observed how Europeans from many nationalities – from Roman Jakobson to Victor Weisskopf – come together in American universities or "think tanks," just as they once might have in Göttingen. But this tradition has disappeared from our continent. This is so not only because the United States has attracted so many scholars, but also because Europe has no truly European academic institutions, with the exception of CERN in Geneva, which is only for nuclear physicists and lacks the interdisciplinary stimulus. The ethnologist Claude Lévi-Strauss has told what his encounter with Jakobson, whose structural methods he transposed into his own field, had meant to him. Where else but in America could such an encounter have taken place at that time?

The European intellectuals represented a great enrichment and a stimulus for America, while America itself represented a chance for these intellectuals. But has their influence had only positive effects? Here, one must differentiate. Their contributions to the development of American economic and military power are generally recognized. However, this is not the case in those areas where opinions, doctrines, ideologies are at stake. Protest has been growing over the infiltration of political thought by the revolutionary, the doctrinaire, or the pessimistic spirit which is associated with Central Europe of the twenties and thirties. This criticism has been popularized by the satirical humor of Tom Wolfe. He holds up to ridicule "the attitude of the European artist and thinker as the lonely genius facing the rubble of a declining world." He mocks Americans who fall for all these foreign and pretentious notions – from "Bauhaus" to psychoanalysis to Herbert Marcuse. Not only Wolfe, but also journals of high intellectual standards warn against applying the "Weimar" syndrome to the American situation and against prophecies of fascism in America. An ideological phase has come to an end during this decade (in this time of such short-lived changes we should, however, avoid declaring the "end of an era"). Yet, it is precisely in this non-ideological period that criticism of imported doctrines and schools of thought is being articulated. This can take place at the level of intellectual debate, as for example in criticism in the "Review of Politics" and in "Commentary", on Hannah Arendt's fascinating but sometimes bewildering mixture of conservative and anarchical thought. But the criticism can also become part of a primitive revolt against intellectualism as such.

We can say, almost without paradox, that Americanization was able to produce, if not the most desirable, the only truly complete community of European intellectuals – aside from a few isolated instances which, by comparison, hardly count quantitatively.

If we consider the extent to which Europeans are involved in the creation of American culture – not only artists (École de Paris) but also writers (Vladimir Nabokov, Jerzy Kosinski, etc.) – then we can assert that only Americanization could provide European intellectuals with something they all share. In the fields of natural science, technology, and the social sciences – history, sociology, psychology, comparative literature, etc. – each European nation has, at present, closer relations with the US than with any other European nation. All attempts to create a Franco-German partnership have not altered the fact that in these neighboring nations English, because of America, remains the leading second language, just as it remains the *lingua franca* of science and scholarship. Many a German and Frenchman who have spoken out for a united Europe have done so – as Raymond Aron once observed – in English. The situation is somewhat different in the field of literature, since many Eastern and Northern European authors, who are seldom introduced to America, are read in German-speaking areas – authors like Sweden's Lars Gustafsson or Poland's Zbigniew Herbert. In general, however, the influence of American styles and works on Europeans is greater than any corresponding influence coming from European countries. Which young European artist is as well-known throughout Europe as Rauschenberg or Warhol? We are now the "receivers," just as previously we were the "givers."

Similar stimuli and impulses, however, can have different impacts. Let us consider the striking example of the American novel. For German-speaking areas, in particular the Federal Republic, it has been claimed: "After 1945, American novels found a receptive climate in West Germany which cannot be compared with any other constellation in the history of literary influence ... Not only were the material, organizational, and political variables optimal, but the German reader was also psychologically well prepared to receive American epic prose."[6]

During the same years in France, however, one could notice a strong anti-Americanism among traditionalists and left-wing intellectuals alike, fuelled by a strong desire to radiate rather than absorb literary and artistic influence. The American novel, nevertheless, had a greater impact in France than in German-speaking countries. In the thirties, William Faulkner was extolled first by André Malraux, then by Jean-Paul Sartre, and, after 1945, became the subject of many critical evaluations. These critiques themselves in turn became increasingly influential (for example Claude-Edmonde Magny, with "Le roman américain") and had considerable impact on the French novel, just as Edgar Allan Poe had once impressed Baudelaire and Mallarmé. Relations developed in this case were more profound than others which had been consciously cultivated. This is not meant as a criticism of welcome efforts, but it is important, and indeed gratifying, to realize that nothing can replace spontaneous choice and the joy of discovery.

What about that sector of American literature, so important of late, whose authors are Jews and second-generation Eastern Europeans? These authors, including Philip Roth, Bernard Malamud, Norman Mailer, and above all Saul Bellow, are problem-conscious urbanites, predecessors of other Americans who only later became urbanized. They express a special ironic, intellectually articulated attitude to life with which other Americans from different backgrounds have come to identify. Their rise to prominence brought international recognition in the form of the 1976 Nobel Prize for Saul Bellow – an award which came as no surprise to any American intellectual or, for that matter, to any reader. With their cosmopolitanism and their understandably often horrified interest in Europe, these authors have become descendants of the early philosophical New England novelists from Hawthorne to Melville, rather than imitators of the expatriates like Henry James, Ezra Pound, and T. S. Eliot, who remained in Europe. Saul Bellow, born in Canada three years after his parents had emigrated from Petersburg, has lived in Chicago since he was nine years old. More than any other, Bellow has introduced ideas into the novel, and not just Hemingway's "instinct," the "gut feeling" which makes a fight worth fighting. The novel as the ironic literature of ideas, as it was once for Voltaire, could now once again become a link between America and Europe. Yet, these novelists, who, despite a common background, should not be taken as a literary group, found less resonance in Europe than did Sinclair Lewis, Upton Sinclair, Thomas Wolfe, Hemingway, or Steinbeck. But why? The literary treatment of ideas, the description of a watchful, cautious intellectual instead of a man of action could not evoke much curiosity. After Thomas Mann and Marcel Proust no American novelist of ideas could convey to the European reader the shock of the unfamiliar. Similarity of motives is less exciting than contrast. Moreover, misunderstandings usually arise precisely where we think we understand each other best.

In any case, the American intelligentsia includes a considerable European component. One need only think of that Harvard historian and political scientist who immigrated as an adult and later became the second most important man in the government, addressee of Nixon's letter of resignation.

Now that Henry Kissinger is no longer in office we may look at him from a historical perspective. What did it mean to American-European links that a European intellectual played such a prominent role in the US? First, we should keep in mind that since World War II two other Secretaries of State, General Marshall and Dean Acheson, have meant even more to the relationship between the United States and Europe. For Marshall, Europe had become an "object" which needed help to once again become a "subject." For Acheson, the partnership was closely linked to an awareness of common traditions and interests. The situation was different for John Foster Dulles, who witnessed with bitterness the failure of the European Defense Community as an end to hopes for a United States of Europe. Kissinger sometimes seemed very "German" to the Americans, with his tendency to lecture, to philosophize on history, and to refer to Spengler. In American rhetoric secret diplomacy is often rejected as something evil. America perhaps needed an expert from the continent to develop the disreputable but, unfortunately, necessary art of diplomacy. Were not the Medici, Concini, Mazarin necessary to France at a time when only Italians had mastered that art? During his term of office Henry Kissinger did not seem as sympathetic to Europeans or to American Jews as both groups had expected him to be. One speculated about his complexes or need to over-compensate. Since Roosevelt, however, intellectuals have been entrusted with important administrative responsibilities not because of their opinions, moral values, or special loyalties, but on the basis of their competence. This was particularly true for Presidents Kennedy and Nixon, who looked for men of intellectual competence but did not expect them to contribute to better international understanding.

Emigration and return. This is a particularly important aspect of cultural links. Case studies are needed on the extent to which teachers returning from the US have helped to relax the traditionally rigid university structures in Europe. During the Weimar Republic there was still a gap between the professors and "Bohemian intellectuals." After 1945, however, there was no difference between professors like Walter Höllerer or Walter Jens and writers such as Günter Grass or Uwe Johnson. Even before the rise of the student movement, German universities had become less ceremonial institutions, in part due to the influence of these professors returning from the US.

The student movement itself began with a spark which flew from Berkeley to West Berlin. Political anti-Americanism – with its sit-ins, teach-ins, and demonstrations against the Vietnam War – reflected the ideas and moods of American youth. The important role temporarily played by Herbert Marcuse confirmed the existence of this American-European link.

Here we are dealing with two kinds of protagonists and two types of influence. The protagonists were, on the one hand, the emigrants who left for America (from Germany alone 234 scholars in the economic and social sciences[7]) and later returned to Europe permanently or at least at regular intervals; and, on the other hand, the students and young academics who came to the United States and absorbed its academic style and way of life. Ralf Dahrendorf, for example, was a student in the US and, later, brought back to Germany the new trends and methods of American sociology. In Paris, Raymond Aron, who had once introduced German sociology to France, began popularizing American methods. Sociologists and historians (Michel Crozier, François Furet) went for months, sometimes years, to work in American institutes. These experiences not only had scientific repercussions in Europe but also led to a new generation of academics more critical of any ideology.

These two groups – the older re-emigrants and the young academics – who became acquainted with America have had a complementary effect on the development of mutual understanding.

Finally, there are the two forms of Americanization: First, the life style with its consumer habits and its subcultures; second, the world of research, literature and art. Certainly the boundaries cannot be fixed: Where, for instance, do we place the comics, or jazz? The subcultures have a particularly strong attraction for young people in Eastern Europe and the Soviet Union. They appeal to the non-conformism and generation-consciousness of these young people – the ode to "blue jeans" in a play by the GDR author Plenzdorf is one example. The influence of Americanization in European academic culture is evident; some European universities, for example, require the use of Samuelson's textbook on economics – in English.

Are the American-European ties contributing to a political partnership? They do not aim to eradicate all differences; America's political and institutional particularities – from Watergate to Carter's rise to power to the creative socio-political role of the judges – cannot be forced into the European mould and this fact has become quite obvious in recent years.

We must aim at a better understanding of these differences as well as of the common ground in language, tradition or concept of freedom which persists or which is developing. Can this common ground be defined as a community? We must first understand the differences and similarities, the attractions and repulsions, in view of basic values and common problems.

The expression "culture" has been used here in its broadest sense: systems, works, traditions, life style, everyday values. We could neither take a complete inventory nor conduct a thorough examination of its relationship to the European-American sense of community and, at best, outline a few trends. It is our hypothesis that a partnership based only on mutual interests without a certain affinity in life styles and patterns of thought, that is in cultural ties, cannot last. Even the closest of ties are, however, no guarantee – they are a necessary but insufficient prerequisite. The fact, however, that culture can be helpful does not mean that it can be burdened with specific tasks, particularly in the field of creative arts. Culture is never just an instrument; this is no reason, however, to underrate its role, its potential in fostering European-American solidarity.

Notes

[1] See R. W. B. Lewis, *The American Adam*, Chicago: University of Chicago Press 1955.

[2] Washington, D.C.: Smithsonian Institution Press 1976.

[3] München: Heinz Moss Verlag 1975, p. 103.

[4] For a discussion of the ethnic-cultural pluralism of the metropolis, see Sabina Lietzmann, *New York*, Hamburg: Hoffmann und Campe 1976.

[5] See Walter H. G. Armytage, *The Expansion of Higher Education: the American Exemplar*, Birmingham 1962.

[6] Rudolf Haass in: *Nordamerikanische Literatur im deutschen Sprachraum seit 1945*, München: Winkler 1975.

[7] René König, *Studien zur Soziologie*, Frankfurt: Fischer-Bücherei 1971, pp. 103 ff.

PART TWO

THE WESTERN ECONOMIC SYSTEM

The Future of the Free Market Economy

by NORBERT KLOTEN and WILHELM RALL

The Topicality of the Problem

The free market system of economic activity in the Atlantic countries need not be the system of the future, not even in places where free coordination mechanisms geared to the decisions of autonomous economic agents are generally accepted. It is not impossible – indeed, some facts imply – that there will be a lasting change in the forms of free market coordination (also) in that part of the world which has reached by far the highest level of social welfare (i.e., the strictly "Atlantic" industrial nations of Western Europe and North America plus Japan, Australia and New Zealand).

The uncertainty is for some a cause for resigned concern and for others a reason to remain flexible in the field of regulatory policy – both in the internal organization of national economies and in international economic relations. The uncertainty is not only a sign of the unreliability of all forecasts, it is also fostered by developments observable today.

Such developments are drawn to everyone's attention by spectacular political disagreements. The last event of this kind at the international level was the fourth session of UNCTAD in Nairobi in the early summer of 1976. The industrial nations of the Atlantic world, which in principle, albeit with a deplorable lack of unity, favored free market solutions to the problems of world trade, found themselves forced by the majority of countries of the Third World and the Socialist bloc into the role of the outsider, indeed of the accused.

The traditional forms of external relations as practised by them were rated as the main cause of the present (and for the developing countries so unsatisfactory) distribution of wealth in the world. The decisions taken by the Conference set signals that point to the stricter regulation of external relations and more intervention in world trade. Quite a number of observers felt obliged to predict the demise of the liberalization of economic exchanges which the western industrial countries had arranged after the Second World War, especially since relations between the industrial countries themselves could certainly be better. Even those who are not prepared to detect, in such phases of mounting economic difficulties, initial signs of a trade war between Europe and the United States (or between the United States and Japan) will not be able to deny that considerable potential strains exist between the partner countries. On top of this ample measure of regulatory problems comes the further problem of East-West trade, which has expanded strongly in the last decade. Between 1965 and 1975 its share in the foreign trade of the European OECD countries rose from 3.5 percent to 5.2 percent.[1] Because of the non-free market system in the Socialist countries, the traditional pattern of the free (as far as possible) exchange of goods has been replaced in this case by specific solutions such as compensation and cooperation agreements, which are not, or not readily, comparable in conditions and results to the exchange between two free market economies. (This is true notwithstanding the heavy stress placed by the CMEA countries on such elements of liberalization as the most-favored-nation clause).

National economic systems are also showing signs of change which strengthen doubts as to the future primacy of the free market system. Criticism of the free market economy is as old as the concept itself and developments since the war have shown that in many countries faith in the capabilities of the free market mechanism has not always been very strong, but the proposition that the traditional regulatory mechanisms are no longer able to cope with the countries' future problems is now gaining support everywhere. The advocates of this view point above all to examples of concentration and monopolization, to the inflexibility of prices and wages, to the advance of government incomes policies and government failures when faced with the demands of social groups, and to the failures in the field of international cooperation.

Some Remarks on Methodology

The significance attached to regulatory arguments in the political debate varies considerably from country to country in the western world. Those who have grown up in the German tradition of regulatory policy tend to rate the importance of this question very high – indeed, in the view of other countries, to overrate it. Nevertheless, it should be beyond dispute that the question of the basic regulatory principles of our economies must rank high in political discussion; otherwise one would be subscribing to an aimless agnosticism or a blind faith in the mechanical operation of historical laws.

Any involvement in the argument about the future form of economic systems is fraught with risks. The firm ground of proven scientific knowledge is left all too soon and the area of speculation, backed only by professional experience, is ventured into. A succession of luckless forecasts has accompanied economics since its earliest days. The complexity of the subject, inadequate knowledge of the processes involved, and methodological problems make it particularly difficult to predict changes in social and economic systems. This is partly because the scientific methods of regulatory policy are not as developed as those of quantitative economic policy; moreover, they are in dispute. Types of systems are normally described in terms of general principles (and not, as Walter Eucken has suggested, by reference to the constitutive elements of ideal economic systems). The vagueness of the concepts of systems that are current today makes them appear applicable to a large number of existing economic forms of organization. Thus, free market/capitalist or Socialist economies are distinguished without agreement having been reached on the criteria underlying the distinction. This is not generally considered important, not even if visionary interpretations of, say, a "third approach" make analytical strictness seem desirable. Such strictness, if one wishes to practice it, may go to the extent of embodying certain regulatory principles in formal models, as Enrico Barone showed as long ago as 1907 for a centrally planned economy. For the free market economy such formal models, either as simultaneous systems of equations or as structures composed of market forms, market behavior and market results, are almost commonplace. A regulatory approach that is raised to the status of a quantitative calculation in this way sharpens the capacity to think in functional categories and to assess economic interdependences and regulatory compatibilities. The weakness of such an approach is the very high, but indispensable, degree of abstraction. Model structures are not, after all, concrete reproductions of reality. If greater realism is required, this can only be achieved at the expense of formal strictness, which is replaced by more general descriptions, the analytical value of which depends entirely on the selection of the phenomena constituting the system and on the level of argumentation.

A comparison of economic systems and an attempt to record the changes within a particular economic system may be based on

- the coordination mechanisms employed, the corresponding processes for formulating objectives and their effectiveness from the point of view of allocation policy,
- the pattern of distribution, with reference to both incomes and wealth, and
- social welfare, as determined by economic growth, the structure of the real national product, the distribution of national income, and also the forms of participation in decision-making.

An index of social welfare, if there were such a thing, would enable economic systems and changes in them to be rated from the standpoint of welfare economics and thus would permit the quantification of the effect of such changes on welfare. Do changes in social and economic systems result in welfare gains or welfare losses? Some people appear to know the answer to this question although all existing concepts of welfare theory lack operationality even with respect to simpler questions. Judgments in the field of welfare policy do not have to be cogently substantiated.

The same applies to the distribution of incomes and wealth as a comparative criterion; this criterion would be usable only if there were precise data, translatable into welfare calculations, on what society (and the groups it contains) regards as being in line with distributional requirements; in this connection functional distribution is less important than personal distribution (inclusive of indirect government transfers). There are no such data.

The only approach to be based on much firmer (though likewise not absolutely safe) ground is that of the coordination mechanisms and the corresponding processes for formulating objectives, and thus indirectly of the effectiveness of factor allocation – unless virtually all the results of microeconomics are (to be) rejected. This comparative criterion involves the characteristic coordination mechanisms of the system, i.e., the extent to which coordination between the economic plans of the public sector and the private sector, of producers and consumers, of capital investors and savers is effected through markets (coordination centers) and through prices (coordination media) – that is, the extent to which individual planning holds its own. It is the primacy of market coordination and hence in principle also of the private ownership of the means of production that constitutes the free market system; however, this excludes neither a large government share nor government economic activity nor even public ownership of the means of production. A free market system in the modern sense is compatible with government guidelines and a redistribution of incomes, for instance through taxation and transfer payments; from the neo-liberal point of view, too, a government policy of defining a framework is typical of the system. Those who nevertheless analyse free market coordination processes with the analytical line of reasoning customary today are by no means subscribing to early liberal models of the domestic economy or the structures of pure foreign trade theory (which, it may be noted in parentheses, were already used by the classical economists to clarify certain processes); instead, they are merely confining themselves in their choice of criteria to a few organizational principles characteristic of the system. By referring to these principles the change in the system can be recorded more easily and the area in which quantity presumably turns into quality can be defined.

For the analysis and prognosis of changes in the internal organization of individual economies and in world economic relations, evolutionary processes within the common link (primacy of decentralized planning and predominance of private ownership of the means of production) are no less interesting than radical upheavals. The category "free market economy" (like any other system) must be interpreted dynamically, i.e., as a system that is adaptable to changing social objectives and new technological and social conditions. This is important, for it rules out work with a rigid, inflexible criterion. What is necessary is to demonstrate the continued existence or divergent development of those regulatory principles which have formed the industrial countries of the free market type and marked their mutual trade relations. In this context, the term "free market economy" embraces all the economies of the Atlantic community regardless of their disparity in particular respects, e.g., the United States with its very small welfare state component or Sweden with its large one, Germany with its concept of the social market economy, France where economic activity is to a high degree government planned, the United Kingdom and Italy where a large proportion of the means of production are nationalized, Japan with its traditional close ties between the business and government sectors, etc. The economic coordination mechanisms of many countries of the Third World are also basically conceived along free market lines. Thus the question of the future of the free market economy in the Atlantic nations sets a task of an analytical and prognostic nature; it does not call for comparative consideration of, say, whether the conditions for workable decentralized trade mechanisms were better in the past than they will be in the future, or which alternative systems are likely to provide better or worse solutions to future problems. Hence it is not a matter of what would be desirable from a given point of view, much less of a comparison of economic policy concepts.

But even an attempted prognosis must necessarily be modest in scope; all we can do is examine factors that are discernible today and might determine future developments. For this purpose we must first glance at past developments. We may recognize trends that can give us guidance for the future.

Analysis and prognosis would be easier if they could be based on relatively immutable historical laws. If one assumes – like Marxists of every kind or (in attenuated form) Schumpeter as well – an inevitable historical sequence of processes and systems, this reduces the problem to the identification of the correct temporal dimension. If, on the other hand, one accepts the position adopted by, say, the neo-liberals – which is that within certain limits (e.g., those set by social and technological conditions) the system can be freely selected, i.e., that systems can and must be shaped – one has not only to understand the processes that affect the basis of the decision but also to consider the changes in social preferences that determine the objectives of regulatory policy.

In our retrospective survey we distinguish between regulatory tendencies within national economies and regulatory tendencies in international economic relations. This distinction is justified only on heuristic grounds as the operation and adequacy of any system are dependent on the structure of the other systems. This is particularly true of external economic relations. The organization of international trade along free market lines is likely to produce the results usually ascribed to this coordination mechanism only if the national economies involved are organized along the same lines. The dependence between international and national systems is less pronounced in the opposite direction. Protectionist strategies which permit decentralized decision-making in a national economy are quite practicable; they will of course affect the result, if not the form, of the economic process.

The Development and Trend of the World Economic System

In the period between the two world wars, the international division of labor retrogressed considerably, compared with the situation before the First World War, because of the tendency of national governments to combat economic difficulties by dirigiste intervention and external protectionism. The world economy was increasingly threatened by decay. The lessons then learned were to be taken into account in the period after the Second World War. Signs of a reorientation became visible during that war, in the shape of the Atlantic Charter of 1941 in which Roosevelt and Churchill declared their intention of promoting the free access of all countries to the goods and raw materials markets. The decisive step towards implementing this programme of the liberalization of world trade was the Havana Charter of 1947. It contained provisions on the reduction of tariffs and quotas, but also admitted the possibility of slowing down liberalization for reasons of employment or economic growth. An international trade organization was to be set up to supervise the observance of these resolutions. However, the Havana Charter never entered into force; its ratification in the United States was first delayed and then, in 1950, blocked altogether by irreconcilable differences. To ensure that progress in world trade arrangements should not be dependent on the ratification of a still incomplete international treaty, a provisional agreement was signed in 1947. This was the General Agreement on Tariffs and Trade

(GATT), which was put into effect as an interim agreement. This provisional agreement, which was subsequently modified on a number of occasions, has proved extremely durable, and it still provides a basic framework for world trade, particularly trade between the industrial nations.

The general object of the agreement was to enhance the economic welfare of all member states "by the conclusion of agreements . . . which on the basis of reciprocity and for mutual benefit aim at a considerable reduction of tariffs and other trade barriers as well as the elimination of discrimination in international trade." By 1963 five tariff rounds had been completed in the course of which tariff and non-tariff trade barriers, especially between the industrial nations, were removed. The largest single step towards a further reduction of tariffs was taken in the Kennedy Round. It followed the 1962 Trade Expansion Act of the US Congress, which empowered the President to conclude between 30 June 1962 and 1 July 1967 trade agreements with other countries involving a considerable lowering of tariffs. As the size of the agreed tariff reductions differed from one group of goods to another, most of the headway in liberalizing trade was made in trade between the industrial nations.

If nothing but the results of the GATT tariff rounds were considered, however, an incomplete or even misleading picture of the state of liberalization in the Atlantic countries would be gained. In the European part of the Atlantic community there was a trend towards limited integration after the Second World War, and the consequences of this for foreign trade went well beyond the provisions of the GATT agreement. The most significant products of this trend were the European Economic Community (EEC) and the European Free Trade Association (EFTA). The EEC, which was established under the Treaties of Rome of 25 March 1957, had as its primary object from the outset the comprehensive economic and political integration of its six member states. During a transitional period, a common market was to be created for industrial and agricultural goods (the latter by means of special market organizations) by abolishing domestic tariffs and quantitative restrictions in stages, while standardizing external tariffs at the same time (customs union), by guaranteeing the free movement of labor and capital, and by liberalizing payments. This in turn was intended as a major element in a broader concept of integration, namely – in today's terminology – a European economic and monetary union. The seven member countries of EFTA confined themselves to the progressive reduction of tariffs and quantitative restrictions among themselves, i.e., to the development of a free trade area, with no intentions of further unification. In both areas the envisaged degree of liberalization had been reached by the end of the sixties

(EFTA had excluded agricultural produce). On 1 January 1973 the United Kingdom, Denmark and Ireland joined the European Communities. A transitional period ending in 1977 was agreed upon for the removal of existing barriers. In the same period the status of a European free trade area is to be reached with the other four EFTA countries and Norway. In Europe the full liberalization of trade (except for agricultural produce) has thus largely been completed. (On the other hand, it can hardly be said that convincing progress has been made towards economic and monetary union.)

The regulation of trade relations between the United States and Europe has not kept pace with these developments. The Kennedy Round resulted in a tariff reduction of about 35 percent; even so, substantial tariff barriers still exist. In the case of industrial goods, where liberalization has proceeded furthest, about 50 percent of imports are duty-free in the European Community and little more than a quarter in the United States. The average tariff level for these goods is between 6.2 percent and 10.9 percent, depending on the method of calculation, in the United States, and between 3.9 percent and 6.9 percent in the Community.[2] These average figures obscure the fact that in both areas there are still peak tariffs of up to 30 percent. Today, however, attention is focused not so much on tariffs as on the non-tariff barriers to transatlantic trade. Agriculture is of outstanding importance in both areas. The United States imposes numerous restrictions on imports and exports (the latter, however, only for limited periods). The protectionist nature of the Community agricultural sector, which works with import levies, is obvious. But in trade in industrial goods as well as in the agricultural sector there are a number of elusive non-tariff trade barriers whose quantitative significance can hardly be assessed. A constant point of dispute is the US tariff fixing, particularly the application of the American Selling Price system. The European countries remain critical of the discriminatory procurement policies of the US government (although European governments cannot claim to be completely innocent of such practices themselves). The United States, in turn, accuses the European Communities of granting illegal export subsidies, in particular; this criticism is mainly levelled at the arrangements for granting VAT refunds at the Community borders. But the problem of export subsidies is not restricted to the field of border taxation, which is fairly easy to define. The whole practice of the subsidizing of certain industries or types of production by national governments ultimately tends to distort the pattern of trade. National economic policy, especially structural policy, thus has effects that cross over national frontiers.

If one tries to assess the present state and future prospects of liberalization in the Atlantic countries, one is forced to diagnose, for the moment at least, the danger of stagnation. In some respects there may even be retrogression. It is hard to decide whether the importance of non-tariff barriers has in fact increased, as might be inferred from their growing prominence in discussions. The growth of non-tariff barriers is often less the result of new legislation than a problem of the practical regulation of external relations. Whether more use is being made today of this possible means of hampering international trade, i.e., whether non-tariff barriers have partly replaced tariffs in function, can only be established by a more detailed analysis covering a longer period of time.

If this frequently expressed opinion were to be borne out, this would set back the implementation of free market principles more than tariffs do. From the regulatory point of view it might even be necessary to diagnose a step backwards behind the status quo ante. Tariff barriers constitute a framework of conditions that distort international price relationships in a particular way determined by the tariff rate; as a result, the international division of labor does not reach the level of free trade. Within this framework, however, trade can develop freely. The same applies to some non-tariff barriers, such as open or concealed export subsidies; but the great majority of such barriers, e.g., quotas of all kinds, act like interventions, that is, they are much more dirigiste in character than tariffs are.

Thus it cannot be said that the process of liberalization is running smoothly. Resistance has been evident from the very beginning, such as that which blocked the Havana Charter. Moreover, dirigiste regulations were in force, especially in the monetary field, for a relatively long period after the signing of the GATT agreement, and their effects obscured those of the liberalization of trade. The conflict of aims between this liberalization, with its favorable impact on the living standard of all the countries involved, and national objectives whose attainment seems endangered by the structural adjustments required by free trade, has always been acute; the breakdown of the 1973 Geneva negotiations in the context of the Tokyo Round is one of the most recent indications of this. Hence trade barriers have mainly been dismantled in areas where resistance has been smallest and the problems easiest to solve. It is not surprising that liberalization is making little headway as it is increasingly running into difficulties.

The fact that GATT has exerted its strongest effect on trade between industrial countries of the free market type is a further outcome of the strategy of selective tariff reductions. It is true that the tariffs on all groups of goods were lowered in the Kennedy Round and that solutions that take special account of the situation of developing countries (such as the non-application of the GATT reciprocity clause vis-à-vis such countries) were found, but the average tariff reductions for the goods traded mainly between industrial nations were higher than those for the groups of goods that make up the bulk of the developing countries' exports. This applies even to raw materials and agricultural products (except those of tropical origin), but much more to the industrial goods in respect of which developing countries are at a competitive advantage because of their relatively lower costs. Textiles are an outstanding example of this. The differences in the treatment of the various groups of goods reflect the traditionally protectionist attitudes of the western economies and their fear of radical structural adjustments. The dissatisfaction with tariff developments in the GATT area, which the Third World countries have felt since decolonization, still persists. It has been joined by increasing doubts about the principle of liberalization in world trade. The argument is that the free play of economic forces always tends to confirm an existing imbalance of power (i.e. the dominant position of the western industrial countries) and to keep the international division of labor in its present state, which is unsatisfactory to the developing countries because it assigns to them the role of commodity suppliers. Seen from this point of view, free market systems are an instrument for exploiting the Third World and free trade is an ideology for consolidating power.

In their assessment of GATT the developing countries concur with the Socialist nations, even if their motives differ. The inception of the United Nations Conference on Trade and Development (UNCTAD) in 1962 was not to a small degree the result of this convergence of interests. From the start it was intended as a counterbalance to the GATT system. The resolutions of the Conference have no direct binding legal consequences for external relations, but because of the increasing political weight of the Third World and its proven solidarity, especially in the confrontation with the western industrial nations, these resolutions can be expected to have considerable influence in the long term.

But if the state of relations between the developing countries and the western industrial nations were judged solely on the basis of the GATT agreements and UNCTAD resolutions, an incomplete picture would again be obtained. The external relations of the Atlantic countries include much more comprehensive arrangements, especially those embodied in the Lomé Agreement of February 1975 between the European Communities and 46 developing countries of the African, Caribbean and Pacific areas. It superseded the agreements of Jaunde and Arusha and, at the same time went far beyond these in content. With the exception of some farm products for which there are agricultural market regulations, the products of the signatory states were granted free access to the markets of the Community countries while reciprocity was not insisted upon. In addition, the stabilization of export receipts by means of compensatory financing was adopted for a number of goods, and for three major products (bananas, sugar, rum) special arrangements were agreed upon.

The points of the agreement that go beyond "unilateral" liberalization foreshadow the structure of future relations between the developed industrial nations of the west and the countries of the Third World; they were a key issue at the UNCTAD meeting in Nairobi in the early summer of 1976, which was marked by sharp confrontations. The growing support for measures to regulate the market was the dominant feature of the meeting; its main demands were for an integrated raw materials programme, an import receipts stabilization agreement for specific raw materials (e.g., by indexation), the establishment and financing of buffer stocks and the creation of a common fund.

The external relations of the industrial countries with the Third World are already exhibiting a trend towards dirigiste arrangements, towards measures to regulate broad areas of the raw materials market. In the wake of the oil crisis, in particular, one group of developing countries increased considerably in political significance; the prospects of their successfully asserting their interests have grown, especially as the Western nations have conceded that new solutions have to be sought.

It is to be expected that the external relations of the Atlantic countries will have repercussions on relations between the industrial nations themselves. The world trade system is, after all, a unit. If a tendency towards the reversal of liberalization emerges in one area of world trade, it is likely that it will spread to other areas unless more comprehensive integration can be initiated for the affected group of Atlantic countries. This would mean the beginning at the Atlantic level of a development such as we experienced in Europe after the Second World War. In view of the different political situation nowadays, an Atlantic free trade area would seem most probable. However, from the standpoint of the world economy the formation of such blocs may lead to de facto disintegration (though it need not do so). The more intensively regional integration is practised, the greater the danger of such a development seems to be. It is often claimed that the growth of the European Communities has created additional barriers to trade between the developed industrial countries. But there is, for example, no way of knowing what regulations the agricultural sectors of the individual European countries would be subject to if there were no European agricultural market organizations.

Some Reflections on the Internal Development of Free Market Economies

So far we have only spoken of progress in and barriers to the implementation of free market mechanisms in relations between national economies. Yet at least as important are regulatory developments in the Atlantic countries, especially since, as we have seen, international regulatory structures cannot be judged in isolation from national systems. As there has not, since the war, been a changeover from a free market economic system to a non-free market system in any of the countries considered here, and as there has not been a changeover in the opposite direction either (apart from the dismantling of wartime controls, which lasted varying lengths of time), an analysis must ask whether there have been shifts within the free market system that amount to a trend. This primarily means tendencies that indicate a qualitative change in the free market economy or would lead to such a change if they persisted. The possible existence of such trends must be investigated with respect to three key elements of our economic system:
– the competitive system (here the scale and intensity of market coordination must be examined)
– private ownership of the means of production (both the scale of private ownership and the relative freedom to exercise control are of interest)
– government economic policy (above all the orientation of regulatory and process policies towards free market conditions is relevant here).

It must be admitted from the outset that a clear picture cannot be obtained in any of these three areas. As far as competition is concerned, a process of concentration among enterprises is taking place in all countries, and in major industries such as iron and steel, chemicals, automobile production, electrical engineering and a number of others, it has led almost everywhere to higher degrees of concentration which – looked at from a purely national point of view – may well endanger the viability of competition, even if a broad oligopoly, rather than multiple competition, is considered the guiding principle in competition policy. This increasing concentration at the national level contrasts, however, with a fact that rules out the conclusion that we are faced with a general reduction in competition. This is the expansion of the market across national frontiers. The liberalization of trade in industrial goods has lowered the barriers to the market for foreign enterprises and increased the number of potential suppliers. Of course, the process of concentration has also crossed national frontiers in the meantime and in some cases led to closely-knit oligopolies even at the supranational level. In Europe this applies, for instance, to petroleum, steel, passenger cars, certain kinds of glass and synthetic fibres. Then there are the problems connected with multinational corporations, with conglomerate concentration (which is hard to define in terms of competition policy), with the general increase in corporate size in many industries, which will probably result in changed behavior in the field of competition as well. All these factors imply at least a qualitative change in the nature of competition, or even an increase in competitive restrictions in particular industries. It is not possible to make a general statement – i.e., one that is valid for all countries and all industries – about the viability of competition.

Things are similarly unclear in the case of the private ownership of the means of production. Developments in this field have varied considerably from country to country: in Italy state holding companies have increased in significance; in the United Kingdom the degree of nationalization fluctuates with the political persuasion of the government; in the Federal Republic of Germany there has been a relative decline in direct public ownership as a result of the denationalization of major concerns such as VW and VEBA, while the freedom to exercise control associated with private ownership has been modified by a number of new laws, especially in the field of worker participation. The German case shows that power to exercise control may be more important than a comparison of the relative proportions of government and private property. In general it can be said that entrepreneurial freedom in the traditional sense has decreased, albeit to varying degrees and for varying reasons. While the tendency to enhance employees' participation in corporate decision-making seems (at the moment) to be only a northern and central European phenomenon, environmental protection appears to be a factor limiting the freedom to exercise control almost everywhere. Limitations of this kind are likely to increase in future and spread to other areas of society; here, though not in the question of pure ownership, a relatively clear trend is discernible.

In the question of the orientation of government regulatory and process policy, the frequency and intensity of dirigiste measures in the various economies must be examined. Once again, however, the results are not unequivocal. It seems that dirigiste interventions follow a cyclical pattern. In economic crises many governments tend to intervene massively in economic activity with dirigiste measures, but observation over a longer period does not suggest that there has been an increase, a concentration of government intervention; instead, it implies an alternation between different types of instruments. For example, the debate on the general planning of the economy reached its peak in most Western countries in the late fifties and early sixties (in this respect Germany lagged conspicuously behind). It was during this period that planning institutions and mechanisms were established and expanded in the United Kingdom, or in the form of the "planification française." Although most of these institutions still exist today, it cannot be said that planning has been intensified in these economies; on the contrary, a kind of resignation about planability and an increasing aimlessness in the planning processes are evident.

Let us take, as our second example, dirigiste intervention in wage and price formation in the shape of incomes policy, as practised primarily under conditions of accelerating inflation. Except in a few countries where incomes policy has long been an integral part of economic policy, this instrument has been employed only in crises. In retrospect, periods of concentrated use of this instrument can be seen. The peak lay around the end of the sixties and the beginning of the seventies; thereafter the frequency of wage and price controls diminished sharply. Since then another type of government intervention in the economy has been attracting more and more public attention: the influencing of private capital spending by means of deliberate short- to medium-term structural policy. But apart from numerous rather aimless interventions in capital spending in most Atlantic countries, and apart from attempts by France, for example, to pursue a growth policy involving selective structural intervention as part of its "planification," this instrument has not yet been employed.

Nor is any clear trend to be seen in the overall orientation of government economic policy. There is, however, no mistaking the fact that political bodies are increasingly setting basic conditions, for instance in the fields of environmental protection, regional planning, labor market policy and social policy. In the aggregate these entail a limitation of the private freedom of decision, and may also affect the coordination process, but without changing its free market basis.

Does the Free Market Economy have a Future?

If in conclusion we ask whether past developments exhibit tendencies which may be expected to continue in the future, the answer is:
– As far as industrial goods are concerned, relations between the Atlantic countries are highly liberalized. Any further progress in this direction will increasingly have to concentrate on critical areas. Conflicts are particularly likely to arise between national economic targets and the objective of further liberalization of world trade. The most obvious example of this is the regulation of the agricultural market, a sector where the basic protectionist attitudes are not likely to be given up, even in the future. But

quite apart from this traditionally protected sector, the debate on the further benefits of a liberalization of world trade is becoming more animated. It is no accident that, particularly in France, intellectual interest in neo-mercantile strategies is increasing. One of the chief stimuli has been the proposition that the large number of agents and the profusion of interactions have made the international economic system so complex that it is threatening to escape the control of the responsible policy-makers. Reduced liberalization, it has been claimed, would be a solution to the almost uncontrollable world-wide instability. Plans for a fundamental restructuring of economic relations in western countries are still only at the theoretical stage; the signs do not as yet point to any change in real conditions, stagnation is not, however, out of the question.

– In the relations of the Atlantic countries with Third World countries there is an unmistakable tendency to move away from free market principles in international trade. Although past experience of stabilization agreements covering specific agricultural or mineral commodities and designed to allow for the special features of economic areas and commodity markets hardly warrants much hope, far more comprehensive commodity agreements of one kind or another and of unpredictable size seem to be imminent, unless the political signs are deceptive. In business with the Socialist countries forms of trade and financing that conform to the given internal organization principles have evolved and will probably continue to leave their mark on this field of economic relations in the future.

– It seems to be symptomatic of the internal regulatory development of the various economies that countries are unable to put up sufficient resistance to the tendency for competition to be eliminated by increasing concentration. There is thus a danger that, without a change in the legal and institutional regulatory framework of these economies, the free market system will be modified in such a way that the results of economic activity will no longer correspond to what is socially desirable. A development of this kind, together with growing demands by the social groups, might enhance the inclination of some governments to resort more than ever to dirigiste instruments in economic policy, so that they themselves help to undermine the free market coordination mechanisms.

The search for alternatives is in full swing everywhere. This may indicate a trend that with some justification can be extrapolated into the future. The occurrence of such a trend is all the more probable the more difficult it proves to bring the major economic and social problems of the present and the foreseeable future under political control. To a varying extent but with depressing qualitative uniformity, the Western industrial nations have to grapple today with slackening growth, with rising or at least persistently high unemployment and, despite the recession, with only a slightly slower fall in the value of money. Any prolonged lack of success in this fight is likely increasingly to discredit the socio-economic system itself. There are also some signs that political decision-making is undergoing a change in the direction of the inclusion of more plebiscitary elements – a change which could drastically modify the conditions of economic coordination processes.

Nevertheless, we abide by our contention that a radical departure from the principle of free market organization has not been proved either in national or in international relations. There is no evidence that the free market economy as a coordination system will disappear from the regulatory scene in the foreseeable future. It will no doubt be modified further; whether or not the result is called a "third approach" is of no importance. In any case, present-day free market economies have very little in common with the capitalist system of traditional stamp. What counts, now as in the past, is the basic decision for or against coordination via markets and prices, and thus for or against the primacy of private ownership of the means of production. The free market system is capable of surviving provided that it shows itself to be flexible. Whether it will last in its fundamental features depends on political objectives and is not pre-determined by forces inherent in it. The flexible adjustment of free market principles to changes in society includes the integration of, say, the tendency to enhance the participation of employees in corporate decision-making and of new forms of personal asset formation, and also the acceptance of the fact that problems of agglomeration, environmental risk and the ecological balance in general will cause the framework set by the government to be more restrictive in future than it has been in the past.

The pressure to adjust and modify exerted by social forces may well reach the point at which quantity turns into quality, e.g., through the nationalization of key industries accompanied by a large measure of state control over corporate decisions or through the de facto nullification of essential elements of the free market coordination process at the national or international level. Hence, the future of the free market economy will to no small degree depend on whether the Western industrial nations succeed in presenting the countries of the Third World with a convincing alternative to the dirigiste solutions which they still prefer at present. The attitude of these countries will largely be determined by the manner in which gains from the international division of labor are in future apportioned among the various countries and groups of countries.

Notes

[1] In 1965 59.1 percent of the aggregate trade of the European OECD countries was accounted for by trade between these countries themselves, 11.7 percent by trade with North America and 25.7 percent by trade with other countries. By 1975 the proportion of intra-OECD trade had risen to 64.1 percent, while that of trade with North America had fallen to 8.2 percent and that of trade with other countries to 22.9 percent.

[2] See: Hajo Hasenpflug, Dietrich Kebschull, *Handelshemmnisse beim transatlantischen Warenaustausch,* in: Wirtschaftsdienst, No. 3, 1976, pp. 729–738.

The Trend toward a Mixed Economy

by ANDREW SHONFIELD

The prevailing mood of the late "70's" in the Western industrial countries is notably more sceptical about the ability of governments as economic managers. Specifically, there is a widespread question about whether they have it in their power to manipulate the levers in a way which will ensure that the economy keeps expanding at the steady pace which was enjoyed, with only a few interruptions, during the first quarter of a century following the Second World War. And the governments themselves are not encouraging; the politicians in charge seem to be suffering from a certain loss of nerve. The high point of confidence in the effectiveness of government economic power was probably in the early and middle "60's" – during the successful US experiments of the Kennedy years with a "full employment budget" and the British Labor government's launching of its National Economic Plan. The coincident, though very diverse, failures of American and British economic policies in the late "60's" and early "70's" contributed largely to the reaction against "fine tuning" in the economic profession. It so happens that the cultural dominance of Anglo-American economics had been a potent force in setting the more optimistic expectations of governments in the earlier postwar period. The accident of the debacle occurring in these two particular countries was therefore all the more influential.

It was to some extent the exaggerations of some of the exponents of "fine tuning" at the earlier stage which subsequently brought Keynesian techniques of short-term demand management into poor repute. The reaction helped to give currency to an extreme anti-interventionist school of economic policy. This school argued that since the behavior of the economy was in fact determined by other factors, predominantly monetary, than those under the control of the fiscal policies of governments, intervention by government designed to achieve short-term changes of direction was almost bound to be ineffective in the long term and very likely to be damaging, too. On the other hand changes in the money supply, which do affect economic performance, would, unless they were very infrequent, be harmful. The policy prescriptions emerging from this school of economists who came into prominence in the "70's" amounted, in political terms, to a general exhortation to governments to keep their hands off – and let markets, unhindered, do their beneficent work!

Very few, if any, were willing in the event to obey this precept to the letter. But the new doctrines, and even more the political rhetoric which went with them, did undoubtedly help to reinforce an inclination widely evinced in Western industrial countries to reduce the *ambit* of government economic intervention. Typical consequences of this mood were first the general departure from fixed currency parities in the early "70's" and the adoption of floating exchange rates. Secondly, there was a tendency to accord greater independence of action to central banks in their dealings with ministries of finance and other departments of government. In this matter Germany and the United States have set the tone. And their influence has been considerably reinforced by the fact that these two leading exponents of the doctrine of "separation of powers" in financial management are *also* the most powerful members of the international financial system of the "70's" – at a time when other nations have become far more dependent on their goodwill to secure the external financial support which they need more frequently and on a larger scale than in the past to sustain their domestic economic policies.

It is typical of the politics of economic policy-making in the late "70's" that there is a heavy emphasis on the commitment of governments, often very reluctantly given, to money-supply targets. It is a cult in which the Americans and the Germans have, again, played a leading part. The political significance of this kind of target is that achieving it is primarily the responsibility of the central bank operating through the money market. A government can of course by its fiscal actions affect the outcome. But if a central bank disapproves of, or dislikes, some aspects of government policy, it has at its disposal – after the adoption of a money-supply target – an additional and powerful means of influence. It may, in the extreme case, see itself as having a licence to use the money market to frustrate the government.

It is noteworthy that an influential current of opinion has emerged in Western countries which argues in favor of an even more drastic separation of financial powers, through the establishment of an autonomous agency of exceptional authority to act as the overseer of Government financial policy. This is in fact a program for the institutionalized distrust of government.

There are a number of reasons why governments in the "70's" have become vulnerable to this kind of attack. For one thing, certain scientific deficiencies have become apparent in the theories underlying the short-term management of the economy. In particular, there are uncertainties about the extent of the time-lags affecting measures aimed at inducing an economic expansion or contraction. What is clear is that the time taken for such measures to work their way through the system varies with different circumstances. But the uncertainties led many governments to argue, during the later stages of the great slump of 1974–75, against intervention to stimulate visibly flagging economies, on the ground that by the time the proposed stimuli took effect, the recovery of world demand would already be in progress. Thus inadequate understanding of time lags made governments cautious and justified a policy of abstention, at a time when vigorous intervention was required to help the economic recovery along.

Another factor was the evidence of a built-in tendency for rising price expectations to accelerate sharply during periods of high pressure of demand, with no corresponding mechanism to secure an automatic reversal of the process in periods of slack demand. On the contrary, the momentum of the earlier price expectations continued, in certain circumstances, even after the economy had turned sharply downwards. Again, the effect has been to make governments more hesitant to intervene with measures of pump-priming in a recession than they would have been in the "50's" and "60's".

To some extent the failures of government intervention reflect a wider phenomenon: the blunting of the traditional instruments of economic policy with the emergence of mass affluence and large-scale public welfare from the early "60's" onwards. The responses to the old style pressures of unemployment and reduced economic activity proved to be different when a substantial floor of real income (with welfare payments indexed against price rises in many countries) had been guaranteed to the great majority of the population. It is to be observed moreover that the economy is not only less responsive to downward pressures; governments have found during the latest business cycle that people who have acquired personal assets and have the habit of saving do not react so readily to the encouragement to spend more – cuts in consumer taxes, easier credit and the various attempts pursued in different countries to induce the mass of consumers to spend the economy out of the slump must be judged a flop. The new class of affluent consumers, it emerged, had other matters on their minds, which lent themselves less readily to manipulation by technicians in ministries of finance and central banks.

Finally, national governments operate nowadays under the constraints of a much more obtrusive international environment. Apparently rational acts of policy which make good sense in purely domestic terms, like changing an exchange rate or moving the rate of interest up or down, are regularly swamped, and often frustrated, by their effects on the movement of funds through the international financial market. The consequence is that the room for maneuver of an individual country, even a big and important country, acting on its own is considerably reduced.

Anti-Government Backlash

The call for the limitation of public power, through the political elevation of the central bank or some other independent agency to impose discipline on the politicians, is part of a more general anti-government pro-market polemic. Professor Milton Friedman, who is probably its leading exponent, has deployed the argument with great vigor in a recent essay ("The line we dare not cross," *Encounter,* November 1976) and this usefully serves as a text to elucidate the underlying thinking of this movement which has come to prominence in the "70's". Its first characteristic, to which Friedman's oratorical gifts are highly attuned, is a penchant for categorical simplification. Thus he starts out by refusing to allow any distinction at all between an economic transaction between a buyer and a seller in a market place and a political transaction involving a citizen and some person or organization, actually or potentially, wielding public power. All that he can see is a competition for votes by politicians, corresponding exactly to the competition for custom among *entrepreneurs* in the commercial market, and after an election is over, the employment of such control over public goods as has been acquired by the successful politicians for the purposes of their own self-aggrandizement.

No allowance is made for the fact that it is by common consent wrong to sell one's vote and generally regarded as a crime for a candidate to buy a vote as part of a personal bargain, i.e., that the whole process is intended to be radically different from a market transaction. The underlying assumption of democratic politics is that a voter is motivated by something besides the aim of maximising his personal advantage through a deal with a candidate. Friedman seems to think that this is impossible. At any rate, all that he perceives in the political relationship is an inferior kind of economic transaction – a species of long-term service contract without a break clause.

It is little wonder that with these premises, he arrives at the conclusion that the average citizen who depends on the political process to provide him with the public goods that he desires is inevitably duped. He sets out to be a consumer and succeeds in being a victim. That is because "the fundamental difference between the political market and the economic market is that in the political market there is very little relationship between what you vote for and what you get. In the economic market you get what you vote for." This is partly because the men engaged in purveying public goods are driven entirely by "their private interest in seeking to extend the scope of their power, importance and influence." More fundamentally, the great advantage of the economic market is that transactions are taken one at a time and,

Friedman avers, are individually subject to the buyer's free and untrammelled acceptance or rejection.

Now the latter assertion seems to be based on a strangely unrealistic view of the common run of transactions in a society in which most of us are involved in a great variety of service contracts, which can only be broken suddenly at considerable inconvenience; in which many goods are provided in a small number of standard forms, designed to meet the putative tastes of large and homogeneous blocks of consumers; and in which the services, on which we spend an increasing proportion of our incomes, are frequently offered to the consumer with very little effective choice at all. It is small consolation that if one does not like the bus on which one is invited to travel, one is free to walk or to hire a taxi; nor is one much comforted in a moment of deep dissatisfaction with the telephone service by the knowledge that one can, after all, send a telegram instead. The general point is that oligopolistic modes of economic conduct are deeply embedded in advanced capitalist societies; they are not an incidental aberration of an otherwise fully functioning competitive market system.

There are so many forces making for a severe restriction in the number of producers in any given market and for a strong effort by each of them to carve out some privileged piece of terrain where it has a built-in advantage as a seller. These forces are most evident wherever there are increasing economies of scale in production or where the process is constricted by the physical limitations of an increasingly crowded society. Beyond that there are the conveniences on the side of the customer which he derives from having a continuing relationship with a big and well-equipped enterprise for the supply of services on which his comfort depends. What most of us want when we make a choice in these matters is the assurance of regular, reliable service, if possible with a responsiveness on the part of the supplier to modest variations in our needs. The supplier for his part is eager to enter into a long-term engagement with his customers, because that allows him to plan his business more efficiently. Predictability is a benefit sought by both sides. Moreover, the service element is often an important component of the package which a consumer chooses to buy when he acquires a costly durable consumer good, like a car or a central heating system for the home.

Ignoring the fact that much of what we actually buy as consumers comes in packages, rather than as individual items, Friedman enlarges on the contrast with the political process which, as he sees it, consists of one enormous package delivered once every so many years – whenever elections take place. Now this is an extraordinarily narrow view of what politics is about. It is also misleading as a guide to economic transactions. Albert

Hirschmann[1] has contrasted the uses of making an "exit," i.e., a refusal to buy or to sell something, with the persuasive function of "voice," (which is essentially the use of *political* methods to change the character of a proposed transaction or relationship) and concludes that "voice" is much more persuasive in economic bargaining than the conventional analyses of economics would lead us to suppose. Indeed he remarks that "exit" is in much of our economic behavior regarded as an extreme measure, which we normally contemplate only after we have tried other means of securing our wants and have found that they fail. He adds: "Since voice is an entirely new category for economists, our thought processes are not properly attuned to it and it will take some time to uncover all the situations in which the importance of voice has been underrated."[2]

The gross underestimate of the prevalence of the political mode in business life, together with the misunderstanding of the character of political transactions, provide the basis on which the argument is mounted for a drastic reduction in the supply of "public goods," with the aim of forcing the public sector back into something like the modest role which it occupied before the advent of the welfare society. Friedman concedes that there are certain things – his example is the conduct of war – which must be a government rather than a private decision. But "the problem is that we have extended the political market beyond things of that kind and to the kind of things where it is possible for each person to get what he votes for . . ." This raises a question of fact. Is the purchase of a necktie from an existing range in a shop – Friedman's ideal-type of economic transaction: the personal vote reflected in the one-off purchase – characteristic of the likely demands to be made on the market economy now and in the future? Or is it rather the case, as the evidence of the last quarter of a century strongly suggests, that the areas of exceptionally dynamic growth of demand are precisely for those services, like education, public transport and hospitals, which can only be efficiently provided in our circumstances by a series of collective acts of will? I see no indication of a prospective change of trend in consumer demand which is likely to halt the advance in collective provision. As I shall show later, this still leaves scope for the competitive process. But there is a widespread sentiment that most services of this kind ought to be subjected to close public supervision and control, i.e., that there must be accountability by the management to some other court besides the market.

The Changed Context of Economic Planning

There are, in addition, a growing number of economic decisions with implications of a long-term character which need to be subjected to deliberately coordinated, rather than competitive, processes. In these the public authorities will unavoidably play a leading part. Such decisions are typically those which involve high uncertainty and risk with social implications. The most obvious are risks to the natural environment (pollution, etc.) or to the man-made environment (requiring regional policies, urban redevelopment, etc.).

The third type of risk in which the public interest is involved is implicit in almost any very large-scale commitment of resources to an investment project which is both indivisible and has a long lead-time from commencement to the stage of production. The social significance of this kind of enterprise is partly a matter of "opportunity costs": if this is done, then something else has to be given a miss. Future jobs and living standards will, if the project is large enough, be significantly affected by whether the investment risk is well-judged or not. It should be understood that the expression of the public interest in cases of this sort is not going to be viewed as an unwelcome intrusion by government into a domain which by rights belongs exclusively to private enterprise. Indeed, already in many European countries the private sector is anxious to share some of the big risks with the public sector. Large-scale private enterprise has found, especially during the period of rapid advance in social welfare provision since the late "60's", that it is subjected to rising costs for social and environmental purposes. At the same time the risks associated with investment in projects involving advanced technology, requiring often a long wait before returns on investment are realized, and the commitment of big blocks of capital, are on the increase. As one manager in the chemical industry put it recently, the "entrance fee" for introducing new technology has escalated alarmingly.[3]

If the costs of innovative projects rise at the same time as the returns on capital tend to be reduced by the need to meet additional social and environmental expenses out of profits, then this could be a deterrent to certain kinds of expenditure which on other grounds may be judged to be advantageous to the community. This points to a more general consideration about the relationship between private sector investment and the public interest. It sometimes happens that the commercial judgment on an investment of high social or political importance is based on the market rate of discount of certain risks, which make the proposition relatively unattractive. This has been notoriously the case in the exploitation of energy resources in the United States. The Congressional Budget Office in considering the future of the energy programme in 1976, applied itself to this difficulty. The higher levels of energy output required might be dangerously delayed, if, as it put it, "near term technical and economic risks will be such as to inhibit private investment . . . in time to increase domestic production." Its conclusion was that securing the extra output would involve "considerable budgetary costs," in the form of subsidies ("commercialisation incentives") to cover the difference between the rate of discount applied to the commercial risk and to the political risk.[4] The proposal illustrates a trend which will, I believe, induce even those governments, like that of the United States, which have an ideological preference for the strict separation of the private and public spheres, to engage in the future in a more active and systematic collaboration with business management.

All this implies that the techniques of "indicative planning" far from being an irrelevant or anachronistic technique, as some critics have asserted, are of the essence of the management of contemporary economic problems. By economic planning I mean a systematic effort to coordinate the decisions on investment in the public and the private sectors, and to do so on the basis of explicitly stated objectives set some years into the future. The content of such economic planning has been changing in recent years: it is much less concerned with the earlier ideal of comprehensive economic management, the manipulation of all the large aggregates of economic activity. Instead, it concentrates on a limited number of priority functions, normally involving some measure of public financial involvement, which are to be pushed through because of their long-term significance for society or for future economic growth. The Seventh French Plan (for 1976–1980) clearly expresses this new approach, with the government committing itself formally by means of a legislative act to a series of priority programmes (Programmes d'Action Prioritaires), which will, however, account for only some 10–15 percent of public expenditure. Michel Albert, the Deputy Commissioner General of the French plan, explained in presenting the new scheme in an article in *Le Monde* that it represented a "methodological break" with the past. This was not only because the plan no longer aimed at comprehensiveness but also because instead of being merely "indicative," it introduced an "imperative" element into the commitment of public finance for the purposes specified in the Plan document.

It is noteworthy that throughout the preparatory phase of the most recent French planning exercise, the public sector's role has been much more important than in the past – indeed to such an extent that spokesmen for the private business community were complaining at one stage that the discussions were going forward within the government departments and the public agencies before they were being given the opportunity to make an input from the private sector into the national plan. In fact, the emphasis on securing a high degree of consistency in the plan targets and expenditures *inside* the government was entirely appropriate. Some of the outstanding failures of French planning in recent years have occurred precisely in the public sector, where insufficient attention had been paid to the serious political problem of achieving mutual consistency between the aims of often competing agencies of government.

When the latest French plan is examined in this light, it is seen to bear an interesting family resemblance to a major administrative innovation of the "70's" in the United States. This is the new Congressional budget exercise, which had its first run on the 1976–77 budget, and most especially, the institutional innovation of the Congressional Budget Office, established at the start of 1975 under the direction of Alice Rivlin. It is a new effort to bring coherence into the often conflicting objectives of the US legislature. Moreover, as Dr. Rivlin put it in explaining the long-term purpose of her agency which has been lavishly equipped with professional expertise:

"I see one of our major missions as getting the Congress to look at the multi-year implications of what it is doing, and to think five to ten years ahead about where it wants the country to go and then translate this back into immediate budget decisions."

And she added:

"If national planning means that the Congress and the Executive are seriously looking at alternative futures for the federal government and alternative futures for the country as a whole, then obviously we need to do that and the CBO seems a step in that direction."

(*Challenge,* July-August 1975, p. 30)

In fact the making of such long-term projections is laid down in the Congressional Budget Reform Act of 1974 as one of the functions of the Congressional Budget Office which it authorized to be established. So far Congressmen have not been much interested in this aspect of the new procedures which they have established. But the officials concerned expect that they will be, when the bargaining for national resources grows more intense and develops into an argument about the competing priorities for the future of the nation.

There are other examples of the changed approach to the problems of economic planning. In Britain the so-called "Industrial Strategy" launched in 1975–76 – a conscious change of nomenclature from the ambitious National Economic Plan issued with great fanfare, and negligible subsequent results, in 1965 – aims to identify a number of selected targets for priority industrial investment which are likely to serve the purposes of accelerated economic growth over a stated period of years. The government's strategy is then to work out with each industrial sector a means of financial leverage and the adaptation of individual enterprises to secure the resources required for the selective expansion of output. This is a far cry from the comprehensive five-year plan of the Labor government of the mid-1960's.

The general point which emerges from these various initiatives is that the changed circumstances of the economic environment have made some of the old style rhetoric of the struggle between business and government something of an anachronism. Of course the relationship continues to have large elements of conflict. But the picture of government constantly pushing out the confines of its power at the expense of private business which is longing to make its own decisions for itself but is not allowed to do so, is a diverting rather than an illuminating one. The instrument of economic planning in its most modern manifestation is not a way of transferring comprehensive responsibility from the market to the government. It is rather a device for supplementing the signals coming from the marketplace, which generally serve well as a guide to short-term decisions, by other decisions which have had to be made centrally on the basis of a careful analysis of the best data available. This is because the signals coming from the market on these particular matters are either too weak or positively misleading. They may be misleading simply because the market's rate of discount of the return on certain long-term investments is too high to permit them to be embarked upon in time. The state then intervenes to alter the terms of the bargain in such a way as to provide the necessary incentive for the realization of the investment which it judges to be necessary.

This has become a commonplace activity in such fields as energy, the environment and in the provision of social needs. Why has it proliferated in this way? The answer in its most general sense is, I believe, that our situation has become more *crowded,* and is likely to become much more so. There is a simple sense in which resources like air and space, and water have to be deliberately protected by collective decisions and public power, if private demands on them are to be met. Things previously regarded as available in practically unlimited quantities now have to be deliberately conserved. In economic jargon the "externalities," i.e., the costs incurred by those who are not involved in a given economic transaction, have been greatly enlarged. Once a collective decision has been made to protect a resource, i.e., to deny it to the private use of the would-be purchaser, its allocation is, in the logic of democratic politics, expected to become a public function too. The state is the guardian of "externalities."

But there is a deeper sense in which life grows more crowded and the scope for independent entrepreneurial decision becomes more constricted. It is not only the physical reach of the average person which has grown with mass affluence – our capacity to fill space and to eat up natural resources. At the same time our requirements for personal ease and for a greater measure of predictability in our own lives have increased; we object to being grossly disturbed by innovations and expect that these will be introduced in organized ways which minimize the discomfort to ourselves. There is generally a more exacting standard of what constitutes socially tolerable adjustment to abrupt change. In this sense the would-be innovator finds the place crowded, because people are sticky.

These are more of the "externalities" which the businessman has to bear closely in mind; and the terms on which he has to meet their cost are set by public decisions rather than by private bargains. Part of the planning activity of government is to anticipate them in such a way as to reduce the strains and personal discomforts caused by changes in jobs and the life styles that go with them.

In sum we have the seeming paradox that the modern state which has been discovering the limitations of its capacity for short-term management of the economy is called upon increasingly to take charge of its long-term management. The two things are however entirely different functions and, as the examples we have considered clearly indicate, involve quite different administrative techniques. The pretensions of the omnicompetent state have been shown up as hollow; but the interventionist state is more necessary than ever.

Markets and Public Goods

It is characteristic of the interventionist state, which appears to be in prospect in the next phase of development of the mixed economy, that it intervenes further back along the line of public decision-making. It does so, for example, by changing the distribution of wealth, by determining the rate of change of economic and human aggregates in the pursuit of higher levels of production, by setting limits to the pace of exploitation of natural resources. Given the limitations on material and human resources which are likely to operate in the future, governments – whether they are national or international in the range of their authority – are likely to establish a framework of rather closer constraints than at present within which economic transactions will take place.

It follows, if this view is correct, that many of the old polemics between the left-wing and right-wing parties, which have provided much of the stuff of political debate in the democratic societies of the Western World, about the respective roles of the market and of the state in the mixed economy, will have little relevance for the future. There may be differences about the appropriate instruments of public intervention that are by common consent required to give a strategic direction to one or another sector of the economy. But in the state's day to day business a common logic of government is likely to assert itself, pointing to the maximum decentralization of authority consistent with some broad measure of economic efficiency. The latter-day evolution of the welfare society, with its characteristic demand for consumer participation in the making of all public decisions affecting the lives of identifiable individuals or groups of people, imposes a formula of this kind. Some of the consequences are already visible. It is striking how the European Social Democrats, the extreme centralizers who were also the pioneers of welfare-state politics, have been learning, at different rates admittedly – Britain rather more slowly, Scandinavia and Germany faster – the wisdom of delegating responsibility for detailed economic decisions about what is to be produced, at what price, and how it is to be sold, to other mechanisms than the central apparatus of government.

The best mechanism of all, it is becoming clear even to those who started with a strong ideological preference against the recognition of the fact, is one which approximates to the market process – in the sense that consumers signal their needs directly to suppliers who are in turn motivated to respond to them by the pursuit of their own interests. The earlier argument has shown why in modern conditions where there is a built-in tendency towards oligopoly, this process of market signalling and response cannot reliably be left to the spontaneous forces of competition. There must be regulation to secure the public interest. The argument applies more obviously and more powerfully to the provision of public goods, which will almost certainly absorb a rising proportion of economic effort in Western society.

However, public regulation can take a variety of forms, and the texture of a society is deeply affected by the form that is chosen. We may continue to depend mainly on what Charles Schultze in his recent discussion of the problem calls "command-and-control techniques" – the direct exercise of bureaucratic power – or we may opt for the increasing employment of incentives which make use of the normal pursuit of private gain with a systematic shift in its direction to serve the aims of public policy. Of course, prohibitions and direct orders by the state cannot be avoided altogether in the regulation of certain economic activities. But Schultze has presented a powerfully argued case, in his recent Godkin lectures, for a set of arrangements under which people are ordered about less and much more use is made of what he terms "market-like" mechanisms. As he puts it:

"Precisely because the legitimate occasions for social intervention will continue to grow, as society becomes more complex, congested, and technologically sophisticated, we ought to treat the collective coercion component of intervention as a scarce resource. . . . And when intervening we ought to maximize the use of techniques which modify the structure of private incentives rather than those which rely on the command-and-control approach of centralized bureaucracies."[5]

As regards the regulation of private enterprise, there are a variety of ways in which the public interest can be effectively asserted without either a direct takeover of business or the imposition of a detailed set of rules subject to legal penalties. In some cases it will suffice to establish effective "price transparency," with a detailed breakdown of costs and earnings, subject to regular publicity, under the surveillance of an independent public agency. In other cases, the public authorities may set maximum rates of profit for certain goods and services, and tax the excess on an ascending scale. Similar arrangements for steeply progressive taxes could be applied to industrial pollutors of the environment or businesses which threaten to make excessive use of scarce natural resources. The point is that this type of arrangement which avoids detailed regulation of the industrial process itself but applies financial disincentives to certain kinds of industrial activity is likely to be both more efficient and less obnoxious in political terms.

In the sphere of public goods, Schultze has shown how what he calls "buy-sell relationships" could be extended to a wide range of welfare services, essentially by equipping the consumers with appropriate amounts of purchasing power (or insurance) for each service and then inviting suppliers to compete for their custom. The detailed management of such welfare service enterprises would be left to licensed entrepreneurs – subject naturally to public inspection of standards – and the citizen with his vouchers for health, education, and other services, would choose between them. Plainly the feasibility of such methods will vary from one public service to another. In some spheres, for example children's schooling, the scope for a very wide extension of private entrepreneurship, depending exclusively on payment by results, is probably not very great. This is because there are some institutions whose productive efficiency depends so much on the active participation of consumers or their representatives; in the management of its operations that what is required is some high degree of *commitment* to the enterprise. This cuts across the "buy-sell relationship," which implies that producers and consumers are different species bargaining at arms' length from one another. In a public service like a school the formula for a successful operation depends precisely on breaking down that sharp division. Again, using Hirschman's terms of analysis, a degree of "loyalty" to the institution is a condition for exercising "voice," rather than the immediate threat of "exit," as a means of pressure on the supplier.[6] Nevertheless, even within these limitations there is scope for the more positive assertion of consumer choice by converting the citizen into a buyer who has options about the use of the purchasing power with which he has been equipped.

One condition for this kind of reform is that there is no effective geographical, or other, monopoly for a school or hospital, in the sense that it is altogether too inconvenient for pupils or patients to go elsewhere. This is only to say that the consumer option must be a real one. That in turn means that profits from the supply of such services must be large enough to elicit the creation of some surplus capacity. Otherwise there will always be a tendency for a reversion to rationing. It is indeed probable that this is one of the ways in which the demand for higher quality of public services, which is surely going to be one of the features of increasing consumer affluence, will assert itself during the coming decades. It will undoubtedly be more expensive than the rationed, or quasi-rationed, type of public service which most Western societies have today.

The picture of the future which this suggests is one of a market economy which is more regulated than today but which may well be wider in its extent, since it is likely to encompass, in some modified form, considerable areas of the public sector. If one were looking for some analog to these markets of the future, one might find it today in the highly regulated money markets of Western Europe. There is still quite a lot of room for initiative, but it operates under very close surveillance and those who are successful have to have a very close understanding of the rules. It is worth observing finally that this situation does not deter recruits to the profession of banking.

Notes

[1] *Exit, Voice and Loyalty,* Cambridge, Mass.: Harvard University Press 1970.

[2] *Social Science Information,* No. 1, 1973, p. 80.

[3] The Technical Director of Imperial Chemicals Industries, quoted in the *Financial Times,* 28 January 1977.

[4] See *Budget Options for Fiscal Year 1977,* Washington, D.C.: Congressional Budget Office 1976, p. 287.

[5] *Godkin Lecture* No. 1, 1976 (N.B. mimeographed version so far only available) p. 8.

[6] *Exit, Voice and Loyalty,* op. cit.

Western Europe, the United States and Canada Facing the Problem of Reforming the International Economic System

by WILLIAM DIEBOLD, Jr.

A Perspective

We were charged, in the invitation to this conference, with "reviewing the postwar period" for the purpose of looking ahead. That is not so difficult for those who lived through that time and perhaps even helped a bit to shape it. There is an obvious risk of being too defensive or apologetic at a time when some rather respectable past accomplishments are being deprecated, depreciated, misunderstood, or even ignored. But who has criticized the postwar international economy more than those who helped shape it, who knows how far it fell short of what it might have been or what compromises made it so? And there are others who will be quick to refute arguments based on nothing more solid than fond memories.

The other part of our assignment is to "identify the new challenges facing the Atlantic world . . .." The danger here is to make the task seem too easy. One more crisis, one more prescription, is a familiar sequence for specialists in international affairs. But if we combine the two instructions might we not establish a perspective suggesting what ought to be done about the world economy in the late "70's" and "80's" in the light of what was done (or not done) from the mid "40's" to the late "60's"? After all, a new international economic order was created in that earlier period. Does the experience help this time? If another new order is to be created, what is to be its relation to the old one which has neither vanished nor come entirely to a halt? What do the answers to these two questions tell us about how the countries of North America and Western Europe – and we should not forget to add Japan – should, together and separately, try to deal with the reshaping of the world economy?

My effort to think about those questions has not produced a set of closely reasoned answers, nor is it intended to do so. Rather, this is essentially an interpretative essay covering familiar ground, not analysis based on new material or carefully documented history. It makes clear-cut arguments in some matters, suggests a range of possibilities in others and in some cases simply points direction.

Are There Any Lessons of Last Time?

One of the clearest motives of those who tried to shape the postwar world economy was to avoid the mistakes of the Versailles peace settlement and the conduct of public affairs in the "20's" and the "30's". While there were some important differences of opinion as to just what the right lessons were (Etienne Mantoux v. Keynes about the treatment of Germany; isolation v. intervention in the US; collective security v. spheres of influence, etc.), a fairly strong consensus prevailed in key quarters regarding major economic issues. Hence came the emphasis on fixed exchange rates, commitments on specific trade barriers and not just principles, freedom of capital movements unless abridged by national controls, the provision of international financing for adjustment, reconstruction and development, and so on. Above all was the emphasis on cooperation – agreement among sovereigns embodying rules, procedures, principles, and usually organizations to handle international economic issues. Naturally enough, the accomplishment fell far short of aspirations.[1] That was partly because of disagreements about what was desirable (or feasible), but there is no doubt that the "lessons of last time" left their mark on what may conveniently be called the Bretton Woods world.

It would seem natural to suppose that living memory would continue to perform its natural functions and that the remaking of the international economic order that is now under way should be guided once again – at least in part – by the "lessons of last time" so as to avoid the mistakes of the postwar activity that created the Bretton Woods world. At a few points that is undoubtedly the case. The abandonment of the old monetary system is the clearest example. The effort to "do something" about raw materials is another. But they are different kinds of examples. The first is a conclusion drawn from how the system worked over the years, not from its conception. The second concerns an effort that was seriously made but allowed to lapse. Still other examples would point to activities to which the Bretton Woods order did not give enough emphasis judged by today's values; the whole complex of measures connected with development would fit that description. The longer we make the list, the more questions will arise as to what the lessons of last time truly are. Was there too little attention to equity and participation or is this entirely a matter of the increase in number and power of the relevant claimants? Perhaps more important than the multiplication of states and even of shifts in power is a broadening of the idea of what kinds of activities and issues have to be dealt with in international economic understandings.

The disagreements within the consensus were numerous and they were dealt with in a variety of ways.[2] A key factor in that process and in the far more remarkable fact that so much of the intellectual consensus was translated into action was the special position of the United States in the late "40's" and early "50's". While avoiding logomachy about "hegemony" and "leadership," I think it is essential for an understanding of "last time" to realize that, whatever word one uses, the United States was not in a position to impose the kind of international order the intellectual consensus called for. At last, the Americans involved in the process did not think they could do so and that more or less determined what happened. To be sure, the United States could veto any kind of order it did not want. If Washington had decreed that the proper course for the world was to leave every country free all of the time to pursue whatever its current government thought were its immediate national interests, such a "system" could in a sense have been imposed on the world by the United States (and it is not too hard to imagine what the cost of that course might have been to poorer and weaker countries for some period of time). But if the international system was to be used in cooperation among many countries over the long run, then there had to be a large element of assent and commitment in the process of creating the system as well as operating it later on, and that could only be obtained on any lasting basis by persuasion and compromise.

To be sure, the ability of the United States to put resources into the activities it approved and deny them to other activities was a powerful persuader and the veto power played its part in that process, especially in a formulation that must have been particularly offensive to other democracies: "Congress will never agree to . . ." (As the phrase itself reminds us, neither the United States nor almost any other country was single-minded in these matters, so the contours of consensus and the process by which much of it became policy and some did not are more interesting than my generalizations may suggest.) Nevertheless, for a complex of reasons, perhaps not all of them are as closely correlated with the intellectual consensus and the "plain facts" of the situation as we thought at the time, the United States did guide a key group of countries into the formation of the Bretton Woods world.

One does not have to linger long over the analysis of these two salient factors in the making of the postwar world: the intellectual consensus and the dominant position of the United States. Neither exists today and so, one might reasonably suppose, there are no "lessons of last time" that are relevant to the problems the world faces in the "70's" and "80's". That may well be the right conclusion, but before committing ourselves to it let us try to be a little more precise about what the differences are between the old situation and the new one.

Disagreement about what kind of world economy would be desirable is not just international; it exists within every country as well. Within the United States, there is no broad agreement on any reasonably well defined objectives toward which the country should guide the world if it could. There is no contemporary equivalent of the picture of the world economy that resulted in the Bretton Woods system. It is not impossible that one should grow up or be formed under wise leadership. While the economic nationalism of 1970–1972 and its dangerous half truth that the United States is "like every other country" is no longer dominant, it would be wiser to act as if this possibility were just below the surface rather than that it was gone beyond recall.

There is no doubt that the power of the United States relative to other countries is greatly reduced compared to what it once was. But that statement is not a complete description of the situation. There can be little doubt that the United States still has a veto power over any global system. While the ability to persuade or induce others to take part in agreeing on new cooperative arrangements is no doubt reduced, it was always limited. No other country has greater power in that regard but the number of countries whose assent is required for significant agreements has grown larger. How large is a key question which does not have as obvious an answer as is sometimes thought. Similarly it is not clear just how much power and influence is required to produce what amount of international agreement. To come a little nearer a conclusion, it is necessary to look a little more closely at the broad changes in the world.

Western Europe's place in the American picture of a Bretton Woods world was never in doubt. Britain was seen as more important than it turned out to be. The division of Europe into east and west proved less disastrous to the international economy than might have been expected – partly thanks to the subsequent concentration on the problems and potential of the West German economy. It came to be thought that only an integrated Western Europe (which formed no part of the original picture) could play its full part in the world economy. If that is true, as many would still argue, it is no longer obvious, but it is clear that whether the Community acts as an economic unit over a wider range of matters than it does now will make a considerable difference to both the way the new questions of the international economic order are addressed and the future handling of major economic relations among the industrial countries with largely market-oriented economies (not to mention the security and political pattern of the world). It will surely also make a difference to how great an influence the European nations have in the rest of the world. But what are we to expect about integration in the future? Will its progress, at whatever pace, usually strengthen Europe in dealing with the difficulties of re-ordering the world economy? Or will the difficulties of integration – whether manifested in disputes, delay or diversion from other issues – prove a source of weakness?

Other papers deal with these crucial questions; here it is only possible to caution against accepting categorical answers, for several reasons.

(1) The course of events in Western European economic integration has rarely followed the most sophisticated and well-informed predictions for very long. The most widely accepted analyses of the dynamics and compulsions of the process have not stood up very well. The "musts" of integration have often not come to pass and yet substantial progress has been made in integration and it is hard to imagine the world without the Community.

(2) The least well understood aspect of the process of Western European integration is the one most important to the reshaping of the world economy: the conditions in which external economic pressure or challenges become major factors making for integration (and when they are ineffective or divisive).

(3) Little of significance can be derived from analysis based on the supposition that US-Community relations should be marked by something like a complete harmony of interests and that therefore division and disagreement represent the failure of a vision and require a basic rethinking of the relation. Only a handful of people whose views were to be taken seriously can have expected such homogeneity and then probably at a level of considerable abstraction. The dominant informed American view, long predating the Community, was that the United States was better off with a Europe strong enough to be independent (and therefore criticizing and disagreeing on some matters) than with a weak and dependent Europe whose support could always be counted on. The idea of countervailing power is not uncongenial to Americans. (Paul Douglas voiced it before Kenneth Galbraith; it is built into the US system itself.) Few Americans who concern themselves with national policy imagine that insulation from outside criticism or from the need to take account of foreign reactions would lead to better American policies. To be sure, it is one thing for a group of analysts and intellectuals to accept these principles and something else again for American officials to cope with a de Gaulle (if the indefinite article is permitted). Some weight must also be given the fact that unless great changes come about in ways of looking at the world, Americans are unlikely to restrain unfavorable reactions to European measures merely because they are thought to promote integration (or result from the difficulties of acting as a Community).

(4) A continuing difficulty lies in the discrepancy between the economic

and the military power of the Community. In historical terms the situation seems unnatural. The troubling effects on European–American relations are well known (but may it be easier to live with them than accept the implications of altering them?) Can one see a way out in the Community's becoming what François Duchêne called "a force for the international diffusion of civilian and democratic standards . . .?"[3]

Japan's place in the American picture of the postwar world economy was vaguer than Europe's but its importance in the actual postwar economy soon became clear. The transformation from weakness to strength was even more dramatic than Europe's and changed the world picture instead of filling in the original design, so to speak. At the same time, the process of fitting Japan into the cooperative arrangements and the special set of relations that characterize the connections between North America and Western Europe remains troublesome. Again, there is a problem about the discrepancy of economic and military power which probably affects Japan's relations with the United States and Europe differently.

Among the many things that may be said about Canada's changed position in the world, I will make only two points.

(1) The close parallelism of Canadian and American attitudes and policies in the making of the Bretton Woods system reflected not only the consensus referred to above and the shared geography but Canada's growing wish to play a part in the world that was not only independent but "distinctive" (to use a term Mitchell Sharp employed in supporting the "third option" in 1972). The contemporary version of the same pursuit favors a greater distance between Ottawa and Washington, but this does not necessarily mean divergence in basic ideas about the character of the world economy. However, it clearly makes for a Canadian preference for multilateral cooperation with numerous participants rather than the development of blocs (or trilateralism?).

(2) As in the case of Australia, Canada's weight in the world economy increases with the importance of raw materials issues. The possibilities of these countries' position somewhere between the other OECD countries and third world commodity producers deserve even more discussion.

So much for the changed relations among the democratic industrial countries on whose cooperation the conduct of the Bretton Woods international economy depended. The changes in the position of the Third World between the "40's" and the "70's" do not need even so superficial a summary – but we shall have to return to this matter later.

As we shall not be considering the place of the communist countries in the world economy in any detail, a few points are in order.

(1) The fact that these countries played no significant part in the Bretton Woods system had only a minor influence (though it was important to a few countries, notably the smaller ones in eastern Europe and possibly China).

(2) In remaking the international economic system, a new effort seems in order to work out cooperative arrangements with the communist countries. Systemic differences continue to create difficulties for some kinds of cooperation. This is particularly true in just those fields where the Western countries have made the most progress: the removal of barriers to trade and payments and the opening up of economies to one another. The situation is potentially quite different in dealing with matters – including food, energy and raw materials – where the main governmental commitment is to what might be called "positive" action. The question here is whether the Chinese or Soviet authorities are willing to enter into serious multilateral negotiations on these matters. While leaving doors open, the West ought to avoid situations in which delay in Moscow and Peking could hold up all progress.

(3) Changes in the economic practices of socialist countries and differentiation in systems and methods among them sometimes provide new though usually limited opportunities for international cooperation. These should be pursued but in a realistic and experimental manner, not as harbingers of drastic change.

Perhaps the largest question about East–West relations and the reforms of the international economic system is of a different order. The cold war played a part in shaping the Bretton Woods system but just what that part was is not always clear.[4] The main concepts of that system predated the break with the USSR and were not much altered by it. No doubt the Cold War increased the willingness of Western countries to cooperate and raised the material contribution of the United States to the process. How much difference this made is hard to judge, but it certainly affected the speed with which Germany and Japan were brought fully into the international community. It also had a bearing on Western European integration. Massive rearmament has to be added to the mix, counting as both a burden and a stimulus and coming to be a major asymmetry within the West.

Is the "lesson" that détente is bound to be divisive where the Cold War was cohesive? Or that we need a more sophisticated view of the world? In searching for a new outside stimulus to help the West overcome its natural divisions, some people find it in confrontation with the Third World – or at least parts of it, such as OPEC. There may be some marginal value in the approach so far as particular activities are concerned but it can hardly make sense to try to build a new world economy by treating a party to the system as the enemy.

It is also not possible to envisage a satisfactory reform of the international economic system that leaves the countries of the Third World in the same position they have had in the Bretton Woods system. But it does not follow that the only test of satisfactory reform is to deal adequately with the needs of the Third World. That common misconception is put in a different perspective in the next section.

The Old Order and the New

It is a major mistake to think of the "New International Economic Order" as something distinct from the rest of the international economic system or as simply an addition to what exists. One cannot prescribe sensibly for the transfer of resources, transmission of technology, commodities, development financing, etc. except in relation to the international monetary system and broad trading and investment relations. Those who are concerned primarily to make the system fairer or more just are unlikely to be able to do that by simply adding new features to the "old", and thereby reformed, system.

Unless the economies of the rich industrial nations are functioning well, they cannot play an adequate part in a new order even if its primary concern is the welfare of the developing countries. That is true whether the emphasis is on the transfer of resources, access to the markets of the industrial countries, or the introduction of major changes in the structure of the world economy. Since the welfare of the economies of the advanced industrial nations depends heavily on international economic cooperation, the breakdown of any major part of the old system is likely to jeopardize the possibilities of achieving a new international economic order.

This sequence of obvious propositions leads to a cluster of the most difficult questions confronting us. How far should the OECD countries carry cooperation among themselves even when they are dealing with issues that are of major importance to other countries? If it is desirable or inevitable to involve new countries in this process, how is this to be done and which other countries are most important? How can the two intersecting processes of cooperation – among the OECD countries and between them and developing countries – be kept from frustrating one another or made to enhance one another?

We are once again hearing about the unacceptibility of having a rich man's club try to manage the world, in terms that were common when the OECD was formed. But there is very little in the sins of commission of that group that can in fact be attributed to their working together (the sins of omission are something else again). Most of the things that the rich countries have done in cooperation have probably benefited the rest of the world economy at least in the sense that damage would have resulted from conflicts among the OECD countries. Nevertheless it cannot be taken for granted that this will always be so nor can we expect those who are outside this select group to believe that it will always act in a benign fashion. Thus, three activities have to be carried on simultaneously:

(a) The OECD countries have to take the steps necessary to deal with the problems that arise primarily among them and which, if left unsolved, would damage both them and the world as a whole. They should try to handle these matters so as to avoid or minimize damage to outsiders, but not let that concern paralyze them.

(b) In approaching global problems – on which they are likely to have a veto but not necessarily the power to impose a solution – they should do what they can to engage the responsibility of other countries in formulating measures but may well have to prepare something like a common approach; here what has been called the antechamber function is important.[5]

(c) In dealing with issues which depend essentially on bargains between themselves and the developing world, the OECD countries have to minimize the risks that each will make his own bargain at the expense of another so that both intra-OECD cooperation and the benefits of acting together in global issues are seriously jeopardized.

The approaches to this triad laid out by Miriam Camps seem to me just right.[6] But as her paper shows, the subject does not lend itself to many clear-cut prescriptions. Much depends on the characteristics of each issue and the time at which it is taken up. For example, in monetary matters the increased importance of a number of newly-rich countries is significant but has not seriously challenged the dominance of the traditional partners so far as determining the nature of the system. A quite different case exists in trade where the focus on special treatment for developing countries – preferences on the one hand and freedom to protect infant industries on the other – has tended to obscure the very large interest that developing countries have in the extension of traditional liberalization to their products, something that is not likely to take place so long as the key trade negotiations are only among OECD countries.

The difficulties of the situation are increased by the fact that the kinds of issues that now arise among the OECD countries are harder to deal with than the initial set of issues that dominated the Bretton Woods arrangements. This is because the new subjects require the acceptance of some degree of international commitment about and surveillance over what have traditionally been domestic affairs. The openness of economies means that measures aimed at domestic issues are likely to affect foreign interests and become international issues.[7]

These circumstances create intellectual difficulties, pose problems in the formulation of economic policy and threaten to "overload the political circuits," to borrow a phrase from Francis Bator. The same problems are posed by efforts to address the claims of the developing countries and to make the adjustments required to accept a substantial increase in exports from them. The resulting double overload may endanger both processes of cooperation.

A further difficulty results from the fact that the new kinds of cooperation involve groups in each country beyond those used to dealing with the rest of the world. Governmental bureaus that have been primarily concerned with domestic affairs are increasingly involved in international matters for which they are not well equipped. In countries with a division of power, there may be further problems. Federal-provincial relations in Canada provide one example. The special form this problem takes in the United States lies in the efforts of Congress to increase its influence over foreign economic policy. This political impetus is strengthened by the fact that foreign economic policy is broadening to deal with more issues that have to come before Congress. The system of the last 25 years of largely delegating authority over trade policy to the President will not suffice. In monetary affairs Congress is also likely to assert itself more than in the past.

A frequent theme of the discussion of the new international economic order is that in the world of the future there needs to be more emphasis on equitable (meaning more egalitarian) distribution. Some say this should be achieved even at the expense of "efficiency" or purely "economic" considerations while others make no connection or seem to take it for granted that "efficiency" can be maintained under any system of distribution.

Obviously, distribution affects production and productivity. No doubt the pattern of political acceptability and economic rationality will look different in the new international economic order from the way it did in the Bretton Woods system. But it would be extraordinarily misleading to let a proper concern with distributive values lead to a neglect or conscious writing down of the values of efficiency. If a major purpose of creating a new international economic order is to improve the material welfare of the majority of the people in the world, the creation of the wherewithal to do that is a central problem. Efficiency and the economic allocation of resources are more rather than less important.

How efficiency in production and equity in distribution are to be balanced is hardly a new issue; familiar formulas include rugged individualism, *Soziale Marktwirtschaft* and Babeuvisme. Naturally the problem manifests itself somewhat differently when there is a sovereign to make the decisions than when the process has to play itself out in the international arena.[8] The issue was not absent in the Bretton Woods system but a heightened awareness of it seems likely to introduce new factors into international negotiations.

One source of this awareness is the controversy about growth. The subject is too complex to be dealt with properly here, but several points are relevant to our main themes. (a) Without substantial growth there is no serious possibility of progress towards a new international economic order that brings major improvements in the economic condition of most people. (b) Growth is not automatic, but depends on the right governmental policies, which will not always be obvious or acceptable. (c) Growth of the sort and at the rates we have known can hardly be sustained in the richest and the most productive parts of the world without bringing consequences which are better avoided. (d) One of the best ways of approaching these problems is to give more attention than in the past to the composition of material growth and to the sense in which a growth of satisfaction can be achieved without an equal growth of material production. However, there can be no improvement in the "quality of life" for the majority of the world without an equivalent increase in the quality of goods and services the world produces. (e) A difference in emphasis in different parts of the world on the importance of growth and the conception of it is entirely compatible with both an efficient international division of labor and an improved distribution of productivity and consumption as well. Indeed in an ideal world the two things might dovetail nicely. However, the difference in emphasis may be sufficiently great to create serious conflicts in values which will affect the willingness of people to work closely together and thus the ability of governments to cooperate internationally. There may also be problems concerning the acceptability of substantial change in existing patterns of economy and society. Is job security, or even the "right" to the job one has always done, less of an element in the "quality of life" than more green spaces in cities? (f) If the net result of all this is slower growth than in the past – or even simply growth that does not keep up with rising expectations – the struggle over distribution may become far more acute than in the past. This is an issue with domestic implications in many countries and obvious international ones as well.

Another set of issues that plagues the reform of the international economic system concerns the proper place of market forces. Here, true differences of opinion about real issues are thoroughly mixed up with unnecessary misunderstandings that give rise to avoidable conflicts. As a subject, "the market" has given rise to some of the greatest nonsense of recent times, pro and con. Since generalization is the source of a good deal of the troubles, it seems foolhardly to comment in just a few paragraphs, but perhaps a word of warning is justified even though one cannot hope to get matters straight.[9]

There are no significant advocates of completely free markets. Any democratic government will restrict the play of market forces to meet political demands and may intervene in private economic activities to make markets more truly open and competitive. Authoritarian governments may or may not find more room for the play of market forces but naturally guide the economy to serve their view of the public purpose. Communist countries and developing countries that frequently condemn reliance on the market are happy to take advantage of the very unregulated Euro-currency market. Even in countries that extol the virtues of letting demand and supply determine the course of events, the monetary authorities often find the hardest part of their task to be offsetting market forces.[10]

Nevertheless, there are real differences. Countries with centrally planned economies can only cooperate in limited ways with those that allow a large play of market forces. Common ends can only sometimes be sought by divergent means. In one society it may be possible to redress the inequities of distribution resulting from the play of market forces by altering the distribution of purchasing power or taxing away high profits, while in another only the regulations of the market can yield comparable results.

Even those who believe that markets have to be regulated more than they are left free can see the value of two kinds of market forces. One is the long run play of supply and demand which exercises something like a force of nature on economic processes. Like most forces of nature it can be modified and resisted but sometimes only at an unacceptable cost or for a limited period of time. The other factor is the presence of some form of competition, the surest source of efficiency. It can also do much to improve distribution and increase consumption. Moreover, the adjustment in patterns of production which is fundamental to the creation of a new international economic order will rarely be brought about without the pressure of competition. It is freedom to compete that producers in developing countries ask for when they complain of European, American and Japanese restrictions on imports.

Still another source of difficulty for the New International Economic Order lies in one of its key phrases: "the transfer of resources." To many people that term translates into "foreign aid" and immediately a whole series of well-established reactions are set in motion, favorable and some just the opposite. Neither is a good starting place for building a new international economic order. Not even the issue of "discretionary" versus "automatic" transfer—or whatever pair of terms one likes – is that central. What is central is the creation of conditions in which the majority of the people in the world can live better than they do. That is an unending task which can only be achieved by making it possible for them to earn more. Both production and distribution are involved but the essence of the matter is that there should be a wider distribution of the means of production.

The requisites for development hardly need recital here. They entail the organization and mobilization of resources within developing countries and the increase in opportunities to profit from international exchanges. Obviously foreign aid has a part to play in this process – call it development financing, in all its forms – but only if it is intelligently inserted as one instrument in a complex process. All this was well known even at the height of reliance on foreign aid, but is too easily forgotten.[11]

The difference in emphasis has important implications for the international economic system. Part of this is obvious, in terms of shifts in the structure of production, trade and investment that go with a redistribution of the means of production, the opening of markets, etc. In a somewhat different perspective one can see that there is a sense in which over-reliance on foreign aid somehow treats the developing countries as if they were outside the system through which the rich countries generate the wealth for a sort of payoff. In contrast, the other approach makes it obvious that serious and lasting development for most countries requires fuller integration in the international system. There can be no doubt which is the correct formula for a new international economic order.

Once that is said one can see a further and quite different place for foreign aid. This is as the redistribution of income. The function is the international equivalent on a very limited basis, of the transfer payments that take place within all advanced societies (and most others as well). These flows from the richer to the poorer, or from the producers to non-producers, are part of what community means. There is no reason why some international flows of the same sort should not be recognized and acknowledged for what they are (though the resistance to any suggestions of obligation are great). In fact, such payments exist, more could be managed. They are not just national, i.e., flows from country to country. Some are plain charity, others the "humanitarian" element in foreign aid that many Americans have come to say is its sole justification. A proper caution is the legitimate claim that there is no justice in taxing the poor in rich countries if the benefits flow to the rich in poor countries. Still, it remains true that only the most extreme nationalists or racists can find it possible to believe that community and human solidarity are confined to smaller units than mankind. It is not just a matter of money; the means to nutrition and health can be provided in kind. What is likely to be done is probably small compared to needs, but there is no reason to let that limitation stand in the way of acknowledging the importance of endorsing the aim.

What Then Must We Do?

Our survey has been incomplete, but it is enough to show that it will be a good deal harder to shape a satisfactory international economic system now than it was at the end of the Second World War. Indeed, there is no good reason to suppose it will be possible. If there is any "lesson of last time" in this matter, it is that the hardest thing to explain is why so many good ideas were translated, however imperfectly, into practice. Allow for the added difficulties and reduced compulsions of "this time" and the most likely conclusion is that events will move the other way. It is not difficult to envisage a period, perhaps a long one, in which groups of people (mostly called nations but sometimes clustering in other combinations) will see no point in acting in any other way than seems to them to be in "their interests" – whatever that all-but-meaningless expression may suggest at the time.

Still, who can doubt that it would be desirable to find a lasting cooperative arrangement for dealing with contemporary problems? Thus, we must, in some sense, look for a latter day equivalent of the Bretton Woods system, necessarily involving more countries in significant ways and covering far more economic activities. If this proves impossible because too many countries are involved or there is too little willingness to compromise, the results are likely to be worst for the weaker and poorer countries who, in a disorganized world, will be at a considerable disadvantage compared to the richer, stronger, and more developed.

By almost any standards, the leading industrial countries would be remiss if they did not make a major effort to reform the international economic system. Much of what Western Europe, North America and Japan should do has been suggested in what was said about the OECD. A few additional points about how they can do things are worth bearing in mind.

Because the OECD countries should act together in major matters it does not follow that they all need to do everything in just the same way. There is some room for a division of labor among them which cannot always be formally organized.[12] The balance may become delicate, however, especially if the specialization takes on a geographical tinge. (In my opinion, it is not a good idea for the Community to "take care" of a certain group of developing countries, the United States another, Japan a third, etc.) Other factors affecting the balance are the asymmetries between the United States and the others referred to above and the uncertainties about the kind of action the Community can take as a unit.

Up to a point it is reasonable to think of the accommodation of LDC interests as a form of burden-sharing among the OECD countries. Certainly contributions to financial aid have to follow some rough rule of proportionality and the same might be true of the opening of markets to competitive imports from LDCs. However, we will not get very far toward building a durable new world order if the industrial countries see the process as only one of taking on burdens, however equitably shared. What is needed is a concept of international economic reform that is seen to bring advantages to all.

Perhaps the greatest difficulty will stem from the intersection of two processes of adjustment. The changing international division of labor resulting from the development of the developing countries will call for substantial changes in the structure of production in the OECD countries. At the same time, there will also be important pressures for structural change coming from within the OECD group. Conflicts may arise as to priorities, which patterns of production to favor, and the amount of change that each country can cope with in a given period of time. International mechanisms for facilitating adjustment and cushioning societies against the impact of change are easier to imagine among OECD countries but may be needed even more on a North-South basis. A good deal of attention may have to be given to keeping these two processes in balance.

As to *what* the industrial countries should propose and work towards, we can give only the barest outline although, again, much has been said or implied in the earlier discussion of the "lessons of last time" and the difficulties of the present situation.

Repair and improvement of cooperation among themselves is one of the first things the OECD countries have to do in helping remake the international economic system. The agenda on macroeconomic policy and capital flows is familiar. The new exchange rate system both fits that pattern and increases the need. The kinds of complex issues that will be encountered in the multilateral trade negotiations in Geneva should be taken as opportunities to open a continuing process of negotiating about trade practices, adjustment mechanisms, and long-run industrial policy.

Those trade negotiations may also present the best opportunity of getting away from the unconstructive division of the world into developed countries and others. The stake of many developing countries in reduced trade barriers is substantial; the amount they will be given freely with no obligations on their part is limited; many of them are quite capable of participating on a more or less reciprocal basis in international trading arrangements and would, indeed, benefit from having obligations not to raise import barriers indiscriminately. A double approach seems called for. First, the inclusion of those developing countries that are interested in some of the new trading arrangements that may be negotiated at Geneva, especially with regard to certain nontariff barriers, trade distorting practices, and adjustment measures.[13] Second, there needs to be built up – it will take time – a body of trade policy practices and obligations better suited to the needs of developing countries than anything that now exists. (Neither GATT rules nor blanket exceptions to them do very much good.) One way of getting at this set of issues would be to start remodeling the general system of preferences so that the main emphasis was not on discrimination but on freer access to markets.

As these points about trade suggest, we can envisage a pattern of cooperation in which somewhat different sets of obligations apply to countries according to degrees of development and perhaps other character-istics as well. This multi-tiered concept is not incompatible with what was said earlier about the need to integrate developing countries into a global system of cooperation. Indeed it provides a better means of doing that than to persist in drawing a line that divides the world's countries into two categories.

So far as commodities are concerned, the widely accepted view that agreements must differ according to products is sound. There is no reason, however, why a certain number of common principles should not apply to all agreements (as was provided in the Charter for an International Trade Organization drawn up in the late "40's" but never put into effect). While it is true that what might be accomplished by commodity agreements of the sort usually discussed is rather limited, there is enough concern with supply, cost, and marketing problems throughout the world to suggest that machinery to increase the transparency of the world's raw materials economy by throwing light on the scope of private agreements, the impact of government policies, etc., might be desirable.

The debate now going on about development strategies – growth v. distribution, industry v. agriculture, employment v. GNP, incentives v. equality, self-reliance v. interdependence, etc. – is very healthy. I draw two conclusions from it. First, no prescription is always best for all countries or even all countries of a certain type. Second, the choice ought to be made by the people involved. It follows that the experts from the developed countries (and I would guess the international institutions themselves) should be doing less prescribing and more consulting than has often been the case in the past. It is, to be sure, difficult to devise development assistance machinery that does not reflect preferences among types of development strategies, but there seems more to be learned from a diversity of choices than from tilting toward preferred models. Some of the largest differences resulting from different choices may well be in the attitudes of private investors and private lenders and in the ability to sell on world markets.

While the industrial countries should leave the initiative in development strategies to the developing countries, they should, as suggested above, take the initiative in a range of humanitarian activities designed to mitigate disease, hunger, and poverty. While hardheaded calculation may show that the contribution of such activities can only be marginal and that sound or unsound choices of development strategies or failures to perform economic functions efficiently are far more important to the welfare of more people, it would be a denial of the values of the OECD world to accept a new international economic order that did nothing about these matters.

There is also a series of what I have called global economic issues – food, energy, oceans, environment – which it is also in order for the OECD countries to take in hand so far as they can. It is in the nature of these issues that they cannot be dealt with adequately except through wide participation, but it is also true that to wait until there is sufficient agreement to act globally may be to put matters off to the Greek Kalends. An easy verbal prescription is that the OECD countries should devise measures that they can press ahead with on their own but that will be open to others who may come along later. It goes without saying that to find actions to fit these words is extremely difficult and sometimes impossible. But that is true of many other issues raised in this paper.

Notes

[1] As good a rendering of the consensus of liberal international opinion as exists – and thus a benchmark from which to measure the desirable – is the series of reports published by the League of Nations Secretariat when it was based in Princeton.

[2] For example, (a) long-run desiderata were reconciled with short run exigencies by specifying the conditions under which exceptions could be made to the long-run rules (the fine print of GATT and the IMF agreement),
(b) Some issues were postponed or evaded (the Final Agreement did not work as

expected for some years: the application of the scarce currency clause to the dollar was avoided by Marshall aid; reciprocity in trade barrier reductions was only formal for some period of time);

(c) Some matters were dealt with loosely or ambiguously or by arrangements so complex as to mean different things to different people (the JTO Charter's provisions on restrictive business practices and the relation of national full employment measures to trade policy obligations);

(d) Some were not dealt with at all (private investment);

(e) and some objections were supply overruled.

[3] In: Max Kohnstamm and Wolfgang Hager, eds., *A Nation Writ Large?*, London: Macmillan 1973, p. 20.

[4] Part of the responsibility for distortion lies with the people who were trying to create the system. To "sell" policies to Congress, many things that were in fact devised for economic purposes were described in exaggerated anti-communist terms. Perhaps the results – in the British loan, the Marshall Plan, etc. – justify the means but there was a price, maybe in Soviet policy, certainly in history, and perhaps in our long run understanding of the nature of the issues of the time. So far as the writing of history goes, there seems to be some improvement. The phase of revisionism that attributed most of the Cold War to the kinds of long run economic aims the United States was pursuing seems to be giving way to more balanced and fully rounded assessments that take into account the revisionist arguments but make more use of archives and weigh contemporary evidence differently. See, for instance, John Lewis Gaddis, *The United States and the Origins of the Cold War, 1941–1947*, New York: Columbia University Press 1972, and George C. Herring Jr.: *Aid to Russia 1941– 1946*, New York: Columbia University Press 1973.

[5] Henry G. Aubrey, *Atlantic Economic Cooperation: The Case of the OECD*, New York: Praeger for the Council on Foreign Relations 1967, pp. 90, 91.

[6] Miriam Camps, *"First World" Relationships: The Role of the OECD*, Paris: The Atlantic Institute for International Affairs; New York: The Council on Foreign Relations 1975.

[7] This point has been more fully explained in my book *The United States and the Industrial World*, New York: Praeger 1972, and in my article: *U.S. Trade Policy: The New Political Dimensions*, in: Foreign Affairs, April 1974, p. 472. Some other aspects are pursued in work on "Industrial Policy as an International Issue" which I am doing for the 1980s project of the Council on Foreign Relations, Inc.

[8] On the national side see Arthur M. Okun: *Equality and Efficiency: The Big Trade Off*, Washington: The Brookings Institution 1975; and Lester Thurow, *Generating Inequality: Mechanism of Distribution in the U.S. Economy*, New York: Basic Books 1975. On the problem of making the international society more of a community in these matters see some interesting passages towards the end of Barbara Ward's, *The Home of Man*, New York: Norton 1976. Please note that the distribution – efficiency trade off is a different one from the efficiency – participation trade-off, as Miriam Camps called it in *The Management of Interdependence: A Preliminary View*, New York: Council on Foreign Relations 1974. The latter was touched on without being

named in my passages on what countries are relevant. The two trade-offs tend to come together to the extent that participation affects the range of distributive patterns that are acceptable, enforceable, etc.

[9] In his paper in this volume, Andrew Shonfield has neatly demonstrated some of the shifts in attitude and practice in the treatment of markets among capitalists and socialists.

[10] In some vivid passages in Charles Coombs' *The Arena of International Finance*, New York: Wiley 1976, one sees some of the most astute central bankers in the world putting all their talents into efforts based on the belief that "the market" is the enemy to be bested or outwitted.

[11] It is worth noting in passing that a number of the main items on the agenda of the new international economic order were on the agenda of the old order, too. "Access to markets" recalls "trade not aid"; the commodity issue was high on the agenda of the "40's" (but never actually acted on); indexation is a lineal descendant of the alleged secular decline of terms of trade of raw material producing countries; "technology transfer" is what President Truman's Point 4 was all about; within the last weeks I have again heard that favorite of the Peace Corps (and the missionaries of Point 4, too); if you give a man a fish you help him for a day while if you teach him to fish you help him for life. Perhaps it is true that the story comes from Confucius.

[12] Needs and possibilities differ in economic activity, but there are political and diplomatic factors as well. See, for example, the interesting suggestion by Beate Lindemann, in her Article *Das westliche Europa und die Dritte Welt*, in Europa-Archiv No. 13, 1976, p. 435, that US negativism about the UN suggests that the Community has an enhanced role there in dealing with developing countries. Of course, one cannot assume these moods will last for ever, so a good deal of flexibility is needed to be sure that the division of labor keeps abreast of the time.

[13] Some interesting suggestions along these lines are provided in the report of the American Society of International Law's Panel on International Trade Policy and Institutions, *Re-making the System of World Trade: A Proposal for Institutional Reform*, Washington: ASJL 1976. My comments do not apply to the report's proposal for a World Trade Organization which raises other questions.

The Multinational Enterprise in Transatlantic Relations[1]

by RAYMOND VERNON

While the states of Europe and North America have been groping toward some new basis to govern their military, political and economic relationships, the leading enterprises headquartered in these states have been marching to a music of their own in restructuring their interest in foreign countries. Most leading enterprises, whatever their home base might be, have been establishing subsidiaries and affiliates in the other states of the Atlantic area, as well as in Asia, Africa, and Latin America. A tendency that only a decade or two ago was regarded as mainly American rapidly has become universal. To be sure, occasional setbacks and withdrawals on the part of individual firms have raised questions as to the durability of the trend. But as numerous studies suggest, the underlying forces that have generated the multinationalizing trend have been exceedingly strong. And those forces show no signs of diminishing in power.

The multinationalization of enterprise, however, has not reduced the role and responsibilities of the nation states of North America and Europe. On the contrary; electorates in practically all countries have continued to demand of their national governments that they should perform according to the goals of any modern welfare state, by struggling against unemployment, battling inflation, reducing gross inequalities in income, delivering health and education services, and controlling the environment against degradation. At the same time, leaders in the field of politics, labor, and education, if not in business, have continued to look mainly to the nation state for their status, their power, and their opportunities for creative expression.

Predictions have a habit of mirroring the preferences of the oracle who pronounces them. So the wistful predictions of those who would like to see the nation state melt away have clashed head on with the wishful forecasts of those who would like to see the multinational enterprise disappear. Either could happen; but on the evidence, neither seems very likely. Despite the incompatibilities that seem inherent in the simultaneous strengthening of the two institutions, both the states and the multinational enterprises of North America and Europe seem to be enlarging their powers and their responsibilities. For those concerned with the future relations of the states of

North America and Europe, the implications of that tendency strike with particular force in four key areas: the behavior of markets in critical commodities; the national capacity for planning; the technological capabilities of the economy; and the conduct of foreign relations.

The Behavior of Markets

In the numerous post-mortems that followed the extraordinary events of 1973 and 1974 in the international oil market, various changes in the structure of industry have been noted which seem of enduring importance for international relations between Europe and North America.[2]

One of these is obvious to the point of being trite. The sources of supply and the channels of distribution of critical materials no longer follow national lines. Up to World War I, the Hobson-Leninist image of a series of imperial powers, each drawing its raw materials from a cluster of satellite colonies, was not wholly unrelated to reality. But colonies and quasi-colonies, operating as controlled and predictable sources of raw materials for industrial nations, no longer are common. And the principal enterprises that are the developers, processors, and purveyors of such products no longer concentrate their activities in particular geographical areas. Whereas the Anglo-Persian Oil Company produced oil mainly in the Ottoman Empire for distribution mainly in the British Commonwealth, its lineal descendant, British Petroleum, produces oil everywhere for sale anywhere. So too with the oil companies that once could have been dubbed unmistakably American or French or Italian. This tendency, highlighted by the special events in international oil, is just as visible in aluminium, copper, chemicals, pulp and paper, and most of the other basic materials of an industrial civilization.

The reasons behind the multinationalizing trend in these basic industries have by now been thoroughly documented.[3] Many of them can be traced to a problem that has dogged producers in these industries for nearly a century. For the most part, these are activities in which plants tend to be large and capital intensive, in which the distribution network is specialized according to the product line, and in which the management staff is built up by a long process of in-house acculturation and training. In such cases, the leading firms generally are saddled with relatively high fixed costs and relatively low variable costs. This means that the leading firms see themselves constantly confronting the special risk that goes with high fixed costs, namely, the risk that one of them may temporarily cut its prices drastically as a way of increasing its share of the market. A considerable part of the strategy of the leaders in these industries consists of trying to hedge against that pervasive threat.

From the late nineteenth century until World War II, the leading firms of the various European and North American states tried to keep their latent rivalry in check by a system of geographical cartels – cartels that divided up markets on the basis of national boundaries and of recognized spheres of interest. But in the decade or two following World War II, while European firms were absorbed in rebuilding their damaged facilities and of filling pent-up local demand, American firms speeded up their push into European markets, and into the colonial areas that had once been the special preserves of the European firms. By the end of the "50's", cartel agreements could no longer serve to separate the leading firms of different nationalities and contain them in different geographical areas.

The speed-up in the geographical spread of leading firms in the basic products could be seen largely as a response to the new situation of threatened competition. To mitigate the threat, the leading firms developed a number of different practices. One was to enter into partnerships with one another in subsidiaries devoted to the development of raw materials. Partnerships of this sort commonly bracketed enterprises of different national origins. In Australia, for instance, Queensland Aluminum coupled multinational enterprises of US, British, French, Canadian and Australian origin and in Spain, Norway, and Italy, similar aluminum partnerships existed. Arrangements of a comparable sort also were common in oil and chemicals.

Such partnerships served several purposes at once. They allowed each of the partners to diversify its gambles in searching for such materials; they placed each partner in a larger number of source countries, thereby reducing its vulnerability to political threats from the governments of those countries; and they established a common cost base, as well as common production programs, for firms that otherwise would be arm's length rivals.

In order to mitigate the threat of competition, the leaders also found themselves pursuing a policy of mutual imitation. When one leader set up a subsidiary to serve a local market or exploit a raw material, others were prone to follow.[4] That policy had the effect of exposing leaders and followers to the same errors and failures, but it also reduced the likelihood that any would steal a march on the others.

Finally, the same principle of imitation could be seen at times in a so-called exchange-of-threat strategy. European and Japanese firms tended to set up subsidiaries in the US market, in those industries whose US leaders had earlier ventured into European and Japanese markets.[5] Irrespective of origin, the big firms in chemicals, automobiles, electronics, machinery, and metalworking showed an especially strong propensity for spreading into foreign areas. That tendency ensured that the European and Japanese firms would be facing the same markets as their foreign rivals, giving them exposure to similar technological stimuli and similar market demands.

The surge in the overseas interests of European and Japanese firms that developed in the "60's" and "70's", therefore, was not some ephemeral and aberrant tendency, likely to be reversed by the next adverse movement in exchange rates. Changes in the costs of international communication and transportation provided some of the necessary conditions for the response. The decline in the relative value of the dollar in the latter "60's" acted as a trigger that accelerated the response. But the driving factor was a search for the reattainment of some means of stability that the earlier American invasion had dissipated.

One of the consequences of these developments, as I suggested earlier, was that the geographical interests of the leading firms in industries such as oil, non-ferrous metals, automobiles, and basic chemicals, no longer corresponded to the limits of their national markets. Accordingly, the governments of North America and Europe could no longer assume that "their" firms were principally committed to the national market, nor, conversely, that the national market was principally in the hands of "their" firms.

The implications of that new condition for international relations have varied according to the nation, the industry, and the situation. In the case of oil, as the crisis of 1973–1974 demonstrated, it meant among other things that most individual nations were not in a position to mobilize and command the distributing organizations that served their markets. The US government, it is true, might still have made a serious effort in that direction if it had wished; but it apparently had the good sense not to attempt the maneuver, which might have destroyed what was left of its good relations with Europe. The British and French governments, according to various sources, made abortive attempts in that direction, but soon recognized their own limitations; and the Germans, Italians and Japanese governments were aware of these limitations from the very beginning. The Dutch, who were the most vulnerable target of all in the embargo, actually profited from the international structure of the oil industry and from the commitment of most leading firms, regardless of nationality, to come to the aid of their Rotterdam connections.

There are various implications to be drawn from the fact that national governments in North America and Europe seem to have lost their ability individually to command the facilities to deal with a national emergency. Since key facilities are organized on lines that straddle national borders to a greater extent than in the past, mobilization by one country would require an increased measure of passivity or acquiescence of the others. Pechiney and CFP cannot be quite as responsive to the commands of the French government, nor BP and ICI quite as responsive to British authorities, given the interests of all of these firms in neighboring countries. Even the United States, despite its lesser vulnerability, must take account of the fact that a considerable part of the interests of its basic industries lie in other leading countries. Accordingly, while each government is brought closer to a stalemate by that fact, each also is somewhat less vulnerable to the possibility that it may be the victim of the hostile, self-centered, or careless policies of its neighbors.

At the same time that the multinationalizing trend has weakened the ability of nation states to maintain some sort of effective control over their national markets, it has also weakened the capacity of the leading firms to maintain a collective scheme of their own for control of world markets. In the days before World War II, when geographical cartels prevailed, private regulation of that sort could more easily be envisaged; by mutual agreement among the leaders, each could be delegated to call the tune in its own major market. With the leading enterprises developing a multinational structure, however, an effective system of control does not seem to have been nearly as easy to achieve, at least for a sustained period. Brief periods of control have still been possible, as the various oil crises of the 1950's, 1960's, and 1970's demonstrated. But long-term agreements, after the fashion of the standstill Achnacarry accord of 1928 which set the rules of the game for oil over the succeeding decade, are no longer practicable.

As was suggested earlier, the leaders have never lost sight of the need for stability. But their ability to bring stability about has been handicapped by at least two factors.

One has been the heterogeneity in the structure and interests of the business firms involved in any of these markets, such as the markets for copper, aluminum, and chemicals. Some firms are long-established, with substantial shares of the market; others are comparatively new, with ambitions to improve their relative standing. Some are vertically integrated, from raw materials to final markets; others are simply moving in that direction. Some have large home markets in which they are well entrenched; others are obliged to rely mainly on foreign markets. Problems such as these had of course existed during the period of dominance of the geographical cartels; but as long as geography provided an effective basis of division, the problem could be held in bounds. With geographical divisions much more difficult, the problem of structural variety of the leading firms has made effective agreements a good deal more difficult.

The second factor that has added to the difficulties of effective agreement has been the increase in the sheer number of firms. For most basic materials in most of the national markets of North America and Europe, the number of firms effectively offering supplies to prospective buyers has increased substantially over the past few decades. In most national markets, for instance, the buyer of oil or aluminum or chemicals or automobiles can tap an increasing number of sources. Sometimes this has come about simply through the mounting efficiency and increasing volumes of international trade in such products; but more often, it has been a result of the fact that foreign-owned subsidiaries, backed up by the financial, technical, and supplying capabilities of their distant parent, have set up in business inside the country.[6]

On first impact, this observation may appear flatly at odds with another well-known fact. In many basic industries, such as automobiles and chemicals, national firms have been merging and consolidating at a rapid rate. The merger and consolidation process has reduced the number of leading firms that are headquartered in any given state in Europe, creating an initial impression of increased industrial concentration in these markets.

But that initial impression is misleading. In most products and most national markets, the number of firms capable of effective competition, whether by way of imports or of local production, has considerably increased. As a result, the regulatory power of leading industrial firms has been constrained, and restrictive private agreements have not played anything like the role that they had in the period before World War II. Here and there, the antitrust authorities of the European Economic Community, Germany, Britain, and the United States, have been able to detect and ferret out a case reminiscent of that period, but the scope and extent of such agreements appear considerably reduced.

The propensity for cooperation among the leading firms of North America and Europe in the basic industries, however, has not altogether evaporated. It has sometimes taken more subtle forms, being based mainly upon a recognition of mutuality of interest, and being manifested through partnerships, bulk supply contracts, and imitative strategies.[7] In periods of stress, as the oil crisis of 1973–1974 graphically demonstrated, the leaders continued to respond to long-standing mutual cooperation and forebearance, at least for the six months or so in which crisis conditions prevailed, so that the needed adjustments among them in channels of supply and distribution were handled with a minimum of visible pain. If analogous situations of crisis could be pictured in aluminum or copper or nonspecialty chemicals, my guess is that the industry leaders also could be expected – for some time and in some measure – to tailor their behavior toward one another in ways that served their collective interests. That tendency would have the effect of muffling the ability of individual states effectively to command the enterprises in their jurisdiction, and hence would have the incidental effect of reducing the capacity of the most powerful, careless, or rapacious states to harm the others by their uninhibited efforts to save themselves.

The oil crisis also serves to illustrate some of the implications that seem to be flowing from the steady increase in the number of firms engaged in the basic industries of North America and Europe. The increase had had the effect of diluting the power of any single firm or small group of firms, not only when measured by their ability to control the markets in the rich industrialized countries but also when gauged by their capacity to bargain with individual states. From the early "50's" on, the signs of waning power on the part of the old leaders in the oil industry were fairly clear. As the so-called independent oil companies bargained for concessions in foreign countries and pushed their way into international markets, their efforts progressively strengthened the hands of the governments of the oil countries and helped them to hold out for better terms. The Organization of Petroleum Exporting Countries, OPEC, accelerated the tendency a little. But the history of the negotiations between the leading oil companies and the oil-exporting countries suggests that OPEC's ambitions and achievements would have been much more modest in the face of an industry more effectively dominated by the leaders.[8]

The progressive diffusion in the structure of the basic industries of North America and Europe may mean that the leaders in those industries will have greater and greater difficulty organizing themselves in the face of a common threat. Not that the collective welfare of North America and Europe is necessarily served by such a collective capability. The common interests of the industry leaders in dealing with an outside adversary will not always coincide with the interests of the countries in which the leaders are domiciled. The two sets of interests may easily be at loggerheads, as when the governments want lower prices and the leaders higher prices. In social welfare terms, therefore, the eclipsing of the power of industry's leaders may be no bad thing – provided, of course, that the countries themselves have a capacity for finding a mechanism to define and to serve their common interests, whenever those interests seem egregiously threatened from outside.

The creation of the International Energy Agency in the full flood of the oil crisis suggests that such collective responses are not an utterly remote possibility. But the IEA case is an ambiguous precedent. It has never been tested; and if it were, the policies that emerged might be so weak as to represent an uncertain advance over no action at all. Accordingly, countries of North America and Europe can no longer turn to their respective companies to defend their separate national interests in the markets for basic materials, assuming they ever could; and it is not at all clear that the countries yet have either the capacity or the will to define and defend their collective interests by any other means.

The Capacity for National Planning

The elaboration of the concept of social welfare in the countries of North America and Europe has obliged governments to concern themselves with much more than the behavior of the prices of their basic commodities. Governments have found themselves charged with avoiding inflation, ensuring full employment, seeing to the equitable distribution of income between classes and regions, protecting the environment from degradation, and delivering the usual package of services in health, education, and recreation.

Different countries have tried to grapple with these responsibilities in different ways. Governments in small countries, such as the Netherlands and Sweden, for instance, have been in a position to deal with their big enterprises almost on a case-by-case and problem-by-problem basis. The opening or closing of individual plants and the fixing of prices in individual commodities, therefore, have been matters for negotiation with individual firms. Governments with dirigiste traditions, such as France and Italy, also have been in a position to address their leading enterprises with requests and commands tailored to the individual enterprise. In countries such as these, projects such as the development of backward regions or the nipping of an inflation surge, therefore, have depended partly on the capacity of the government to address individual firms in individual cases.

After World War II, at the very time when their ability to command individual enterprises took on greatly increased importance, the governments of North America and Europe committed themselves to a policy that would greatly limit their command role. With the liberalization of international trade and payments which began in the late "40's", enterprises could only respond up to a point, the point at which their competitive position in the national market or in export markets would be badly compromised. That ineluctable fact, of course, explains why governments with aspirations to command their own economies have characteristically been reluctant to open up their borders to unrestricted international trade and investment.

The multinationalization of big business has added a very complex element to the ability of governments to influence individual firms. Practically all the leading firms of North America and Europe now see themselves as quite capable of choosing among the national environments in which to expand their business; none is quite as fully committed to operating in a given national environment as it was, say, ten or twenty years ago. That means, of course, that the hold which Sweden has on SKF, or Holland on Philips, or France on Pechiney, or Italy on Snia Viscosa is not quite as strong as it had been. Already weakened by the liberalization of international trade, that hold has been weakened even more by the fact that the options of the target firm are painfully visible to any commanding government.

At the same time, however, governments are occasionally discovering that what their home enterprises are unwilling or unable to do in the national interest, foreign firms may be eager to do in their stead. That fact has been brought home in connection with the various programs of governments in North America and Europe to encourage increased business investments in backward areas: Italy in the Messagiorno, Holland in the Frisian region, Britain in Scotland and Wales, Canada in the maritime provinces, and so on. In a perfectly competitive, frictionless, and rational world, there would be no reason to anticipate that national firms and foreign-owned firms would respond differently to the incentives offered by governments for settling in such areas. But in a world of oligopolistic industries composed of a limited number of large firms, such a reaction is easily explained. For one thing, the constant efforts of the leaders to imitate the behavior of their rivals in a search for balance and stability have meant that many firms have placed a higher priority on expanding outside the home market than on expanding within. Firms based in the United States that had not yet followed the leaders in their industry into foreign markets were often eager to take the plunge. And firms in Europe that were concerned over the increasing multinational reach of their foreign rivals commonly responded to a similar set of priorities.

Besides, the national firms that did have an interest in expanding at home had to take into account the location of their existing nucleus of production facilities. When these facilities were already clustered in one of the richer industrial sections of the country, as Fiat in Turin or Philips in Eindhoven or Pechiney in Grenoble, their location sometimes provided strong reasons for placing the new facilities of the firm in the same general area. Foreign firms, on the other hand, could make their locational decisions as on a *tabula rasa*; and if the national government was prepared to offer enough inducements, the foreign firms were freer to consider a location in a backward area.

The eagerness of foreign firms to acquire a foothold in new areas has made them responsive to government inducements and commands in other respects as well. For example, foreign firms have been in a much better position than national firms to keep their prices low, at least at the time of their entry into new territories. Unlike the national firms, the foreigners were not relying on these new markets for their principal sources of income. Besides, in order to capture a share of these markets, foreign newcomers in any case would be obliged to shade their prices; if that policy happened to coincide with government objectives, as it sometimes did, so much the better.

All told, therefore, the swift acceleration in the spread of big enterprises has been a mixed blessing for national planners. It has increased the number of foreigners ready and willing to respond to the planners' invitations and demands, while making some of their own firms somewhat more impervious to those demands.

Once in place and operating, however, the subsidiaries of multinational enterprises have represented a difficult type of business structure for national planners to guide and control, more difficult perhaps than national enterprises of analogous size and function. That at least has been the assumption of national officials in Canada and Europe. The reasons for the assumption are easy enough to identify. Operating simultaneously in several jurisdictions, such enterprises are in a better position than national enterprises to withdraw their funds from an area whose currency is growing weak, and to reduce their production in areas whose costs are mounting or whose regulations are growing onerous.

It is exceedingly difficult to test whether, in actual practice, multinational enterprises exercise this seeming capability. Individual cases are not hard to find in which multinational enterprises have abruptly shut up shop because of declining demand, increasing costs, or onerous regulations. And in the mid-1970's the cases seemed to be multiplying. But the occasional efforts that have been made to compare their behavior with that of national enterprises similarly situated provide no support for the view that the capability is exercised more frequently than a national enterprise would exercise them.[9] On the other hand, managers of multinational enterprises have sometimes gone to some pains to remind national policymakers and national planners that the possibility was there, a reminder that has not helped to put these national officials at their ease.[10]

All told, therefore, the capacity for national planning has weakened in several important respects but strengthened in at least one. It has been weakened by the geographical diffusion of the interests of leading national firms and by the increased international traffic in goods and money conducted through the multinational networks. It has been strengthened by the increase in the number of firms in any economy that might be called upon to perform some specified national task. The weakening forces on the whole seem more potent than the strengthening ones; but not for every country nor for every objective that national planners seek.

Technological Capabilities

Many of the states of Europe and North America place great store on being able to produce, inside their national boundaries, the large complex chunks of hardware that represent the most challenging of industrial achievements – nuclear reactors, widebellied aircraft, powerful computers, extraterrestrial rocketry, and so on. The reasons for that driving need are not altogether obvious. In dollar-and-cents terms, it is not clear that the economy which absorbs the development costs of such gargantuan gadgetry is able to generate benefits for the economy that exceed its costs. In some cases, as in widebellied aircraft, nations have managed to develop a thriving export business on the basis of their industrial achievements. But in other cases, as in nuclear reactors, they have been obliged to exploit their advances largely through production in subsidiaries abroad and even through the licensing of independent firms. In general, as Japan has repeatedly demonstrated, imitators and licensees often seem able to secure the needed technology from the pioneer source at a relatively low cost, a fact that raises real questions as to the choice of policy for any country.

Yet the urge to be self-sufficient on the commanding heights of industrial technology is powerful and widespread. For one thing, capabilities of this sort help to create a pecking order among modern states, identifying the position of their industry and of their scientific community in relation to the others. Besides, as France has long recognized, the state that has the capability to produce its own hard-to-get items is less vulnerable to the political coercion of supplying states.

The link between the question of technological capability and the multinational enterprise is created by the fact that many of the industrial products that are technologically challenging demand very large enterprises for their production. In the average firm producing widebellied aircraft, employees are numbered by the tens of thousands, and annual sales in billions of dollars. The same is true for firms producing nuclear reactors. Neither the sales dollars nor the employees are necessarily linked directly to the technologically demanding products. But huge size and the development of demanding products are intimately associated.

The basic hurdle that firms confront in taking on these products is not usually created by the occult and exotic quality of the technology itself. It is rather the scope and uncertainty of the project as a whole. The heterogeneity of the inputs demanded for large industrial innovations requires a large organizational network capable of mobilizing and monitoring a diverse set of engineering and experimental activities. The unavoidable uncertainties of the process require an organization capable of mounting crash efforts to break bottlenecks and of financing long retreats from blind alleys. Sheer scale, therefore, has proved an important factor in bringing off successful industrial innovations of the gargantuan variety – scale in size of organization, in supply of financial resources, and in volume of sales for the completed project.

In this respect, firms with their principal markets in the United States have generally enjoyed an advantage over firms headquartered elsewhere. With the notable exception of the chemicals industry, firms in the United States have tended to be larger in size, to have more ample financial resources, and to face greater opportunities in the marketing of successful industrial innovations than those in Europe. A big internal civilian market has sometimes been the critical factor supporting the effort of US firms, as in the case of nuclear reactors. And a big government market has often provided an added boost, as in the case of communications satellites and supersonic aircraft engines. Operating from that initial advantage, US firms have often been able to take and have sometimes been able to hold a commanding lead in many of the technologically demanding product lines.

European states have chafed under the limitations imposed by their size. Partly to escape from those limitations, France originally pressed for the creation of a European Economic Community. A recognition of these limitations no doubt led de Gaulle to hold back from destroying the Community, contenting himself instead with suppressing its supranational tendencies and with scuttling Euratom. Although the Community has performed remarkably in many respects, it has been unable to do much about creating a large common market for the development and sale of technologically advanced products. Neither the British nor the French government could quite bring itself to merge national resources and national markets in a unitary effort. Instead, pairs and triads of governments have pooled their efforts for some limited objective, such as the development of the Concorde or the production of an earth-orbiting rocket. But in projects such as these, each participating country has retained its separate entitlement to a share of the production task and each has retained its hold on its own national market. The limited nature of the commitment has had the result of drastically limiting the benefits as well.[11]

In that sort of setting, a multinational enterprise that was based in one or another of the European states might conceivably have acted as an instrumentality for overcoming the European handicap. But European states have been unwilling to assign such a role to a multinational enterprise headquartered in another country. As a result, US firms often have drawn more support out of Europe's common market for their technologically-oriented business than the European firms themselves. Having taken their original technological gambles on the basis of the US market, many US firms have been able to increase the pay-off through exports, licenses, and subsidiary production in Europe. In the case of widebellied aircraft, exports have served that purpose. In the case of nuclear reactors, license fees and component sales have provided the principal route. And in the case of computers, the production of US-owned subsidiaries in Europe has generated most of the added profits. As a result, in default of an effective European response to the American challenge, US firms have commonly been able to parlay the initial advantages of a large home market into even greater rewards.

The Enterprise in Foreign Relations

Two economic facts dominate and condition the relationships among the states of Europe and North America. One is that any country which closed its borders to the goods and capital of the others would have to pay a high price in terms of productivity and income. That fact helps to explain many of the main developments in the economic relations of the region since the end of World War II, especially the persistence of the concept of European economic integration and the disposition of the states in Europe and North America to keep border restrictions in check. The other salient fact is that, of all the nations in the region, the United States stands to lose least from a closing of its national borders and to gain least from a further opening of those borders.

The spread of North American-based multinational enterprises into Europe and the spread of European-based multinational enterprises throughout Europe and North America add another major economic factor to the mix, one that is extraordinarily confusing in its implications. Until recently, an enterprise headquartered in a given national jurisdiction could reasonably hope for protection and support from "its" government whenever the interests of its overseas subsidiaries were being threatened. That expectation is less solidly based today than it was, say, five or ten years ago.

In the United States, a barrage of hostile comments from congressional committees, the press, and academics has raised questions whether what's good for General Motors in Barcelona is also good for Detroit. In Holland, Philips, Royal Dutch, and AKZO are constantly being challenged to justify their right to the protection and support of the Dutch government. Rumblings of a similar sort can be detected in Sweden, France, Britain, and Canada.

Behind those symptoms lies a widespread conviction that the management and stockholders of multinational enterprises are benefited more surely and more directly than labor and the home government. Although this is a conviction difficult to test, it is not one that altogether escapes rational analysis. First of all, labor must resign itself to finding its opportunities on the home turf, whereas managers and stockholders stand a chance of benefiting from their widened opportunities in other countries. On top of that, labor sees its welfare as more heavily tied to a strong state with strong national welfare programs, and sees the multinational enterprise as a factor that tends to weaken the executory powers of the state.

The attenuation in the identity of interests between parent enterprises and their governments reduces the risk that enterprises and their home governments might work hand-in-hand in foreign countries, each acting as an instrument, in support of the other. That risk in any case was never very widespread. For various persuasive reasons, most enterprises most of the time have tended to hold their own governments at some distance – American, Canadian, or German enterprises more so than French and Japanese, perhaps, but practically all enterprises in some degree. Besides, when enterprises have solicited the support of their governments, they often receive support that was perfunctory in nature or have been denied support altogether. Here again, the reasons have been straightforward enough. When the United States had been involved in situations of this sort, for instance, its response has been complicated by two critical questions. Were bigger fish in the process of being fried, whose culinary progress might be hurt by supporting the cause of the multinational enterprise? And were there other US firms whose interests might be imperilled by such support? With its tangled and complex set of external interests, the US government generally has found itself supporting individual cases in restrained, equivocal, and ineffectual terms.[12]

Nevertheless, even though circumstances have usually stayed the hands of most governments in support of "their" multinational enterprises, cases have occurred from time to time in which governments have seen their interests as altogether in conformity with those of a home-based multinational enterprise and thus have given the enterprise their unambiguous and energetic support.

Those occasional cases have given flesh and blood to the picture drawn by popular writers in North America and Europe of the multinational enterprise as the world's leading bogey man. Inevitably, when multinational enterprises have been in a position to call on the somewhat awesome resources of the United States for their support, the impact has been rather more impressive than when the support has come from Switzerland, Sweden, or Italy. It has been the seeming potential for such support, however, rather than the daily actuality of such support that has constituted a problem for harmonious international relations.

The potential partnership between enterprises and governments has also been seen as expressing itself in another form. Rather than enterprises using their governments, the possibility has been recognized that governments might use their enterprises to press official policies in foreign jurisdictions. The best advertised cases, of course, are those in which the United States has sought to pursue its antitrust, trading-with-the-enemy and corporate disclosure objectives by issuing commands through its parent enterprises to overseas subsidiaries, or by issuing commands to foreign-owned subsidiaries in the United States that could only be fulfilled by their foreign parents.

As long as the United States was the only country with active policies in those fields, other countries were up in arms over the unwarranted invasion of their jurisdiction. Little by little, however, other nations have also found themselves issuing commands to "their" enterprises on how they should comport themselves abroad. The Netherlands, for example, apparently would have no hesitation in chastising a Dutch multinational enterprise because the foreign subsidiaries of that enterprise were engaged in activities judged harmful by the Dutch government, even if the host government approved; the same no doubt would be true of the Swedish government's approach. In another variant of the problem of jurisdictional reach, the French government routinely expresses its support for the creation of foreign subsidiaries by French enterprises, whenever the effect of this investment will be to expose French firms to foreign technologies or to capture secure sources of raw materials abroad for the French economy.

In the abstract, one might have supposed that the disposition of countries to stretch their influence into the jurisdiction of other countries would provide all the necessary ingredients for a major political row. In practice, however, most countries in the Atlantic area have not wished to elevate issues of this sort to the level of high politics. When the intrusion of one country upon the turf of another has produced irritation or protest, the disposition of the offending country has been to reverse its field.

The disposition of governments in the Atlantic area to avoid major confrontations over their right to pursue the affiliates of the multinational enterprise into other jurisdictions has created a curious outcome in transatlantic relations. As enterprises of all nations have spread out into other parts of the area, national governments have taken an increasingly truncated view of the consequences upon the national interest of their firms' operations. Of course, if they had not done so – if each government had pursued the subsidiaries of its multinational enterprises vigorously wherever those enterprises settled – the consequences could easily have been disastrous. National restraint in these cases no doubt served a useful purpose.

But that same self-restraint also created a lacuna. Since each government was prepared to restrain its oversight of the foreign subsidiaries of its multinational enterprises, no public authority existed that was viewing the effects of any given multinational enterprise as a whole. Two kinds of problems therefore, eluded public authority. As a result of the growing interpenetration of economies, national governments no longer could be quite as much in control of the variables that affected their national well-being. At the same time, no effective supranational or multinational public authorities existed, capable of addressing the operations of multinational enterprises on a multinational basis. Issues such as the behavior of world markets or the pollution of outer space, therefore, eluded social control.

The gap in the capacity of nations in the Atlantic area to oversee the activities of multinational enterprises, however, has not necessarily increased the power of such enterprises. The interpenetration of the various economies of the area by multinational enterprises seems on the whole to have weakened the capacity of industries to reach agreements of a quasi-regulatory nature in individual product markets. For brief periods, such as the period of the oil crisis, enterprises have performed quasi-governmental functions, almost without being aware of the role into which they had been thrust. But more often than not, situations that might have been thought amenable to multinational or supranational treatment have simply had to play themselves out as best they could. From all the current signs, this incipient state of anarchy will have to progress much further before institutions are put in place that are capable of dealing constructively with it.

Notes

[1] This article is based on research financed by the Ford Foundation in a grant to the Harvard Business School and by the Rockefeller Foundation in a grant to Harvard's

Center for International Affairs. A more detailed account of many of the points summarized here appears in *Storm over the Multinationals: The Real Issues*, Cambridge, Mass.: Harvard University Press 1977.

² See for instance, Edward R. Fried and Charles L. Schultze, (eds.), *Higher Oil Prices and the World Economy*, Washington: The Brookings Institution 1975; and Raymond Vernon, (ed.), *The Oil Crisis*, New York: Norton 1976.

³ M. Z. Brooke and H. L. Remmers, *The Strategy of Multinational Enterprise*, New York: American Elsevier 1970, pp. 224–242; L. G. Franko, *The European Multinationals*, Stanford, Conn.: Greylock 1976, pp. 75–104; C. A. Michalet and Michel Delapierre, *La multinationalisation des entreprises françaises*, Paris: Gauthier-Villars 1973, pp. 17–61; M. Y. Yoshino, *The Japanese Multinationals*, Cambridge, Mass.: Harvard University Press 1976, pp. 127–159; H. F. Samuelsson, *National Scientific and Technological Potential and the Activities of Multinational Corporations – The Case of Sweden, Report of the OECD Committee for Scientific and Technological Policy*, Paris: OECD 1974, mimeo; J. M. Stopford, *Changing Perspectives on Investment of British Manufacturing Multinationals*, London Business School 1975, unpublished.

⁴ F. T. Knickerbocker, *Oligopolistic Reaction and Multinational Enterprise*, Boston: Division of Research, Harvard Business School 1973, pp. 193–196.

⁵ L. G. Franko, *The European Multinationals*, pp. 167–172; M. Y. Yoshino, *The Japanese Multinationals*, pp. 77–87.

⁶ For statistics on the number of firms operating in specified product lines in Germany, France, and Britain in 1950, 1960, and 1970, see my *Storm Over the Multinationals*, Chapter 4.

⁷ Concerning tractors see, R. T. Kurdle, *Agricultural Tractors: A World Industry Survey*, Cambridge, Mass.: Ballinger 1975, pp. 4, 113–140.

⁸ I have developed this point more fully in *An Interpretation* in: Raymond Vernon, *The Oil Crisis*, pp. 3–7.

⁹ John Gennard and M. D. Steuer, *The Industrial Relations of Foreign Owned Subsidiaries in the United Kingdom*, British Journal of Industrial Relations, No. 2, 1971, Vol. 9, pp. 143–159.

¹⁰ E. M. Kassalow, *Multinational Corporations and their Impact on Industrial Relations*, presented at the International Conference on Trends in Industrial and Labor Relations, Montreal, May 1976, pp. 13–15.

¹¹ For a more detailed analysis of these joint projects, see M. S. Hochmuth, *Organizing the Transnational*, Leyden: Sijthoff 1974; Roger Williams, *European Technology and the Politics of Collaboration*, New York: Wiley 1973.

¹² For an elaboration of this point see J. P. Einhorn, *Expropriation Politics*, Lexington, Mass.: Heath 1974; R. O. Keohane and J. S. Nye, Jr., *Power and Interdependence: World Politics in Transition*, Boston: Little Brown & Co. 1976; Raymond Vernon, *The Influence of the U.S. Government upon Multinational Enterprises: The Case of Oil*, delivered at the Second International Colloquium on Petroleum Economy, University of Laval, Quebec 1975.

Trade Unions in Search of a Role: European and American Experience

by Benjamin C. Roberts

Formative Influences

All trade unions exist to protect and promote the interests of their members, but the methods they use are to a great extent determined by the political ideology of the nation-state in which they have their existence. The differences in the powers and functions of trade unions in totalitarian states and democracies are considerable. There is no such fundamental difference in the role of the unions in the democratic countries of Europe and North America, nevertheless the unions in each country differ in many respects.[1] These differences arise from differences in national cultures, in ideology, membership, structures and patterns of activity. It is necessary to stress the significance of these differences in the character of trade unions and the industrial relations systems in which they play a critical role; but it is also important to recognize that there have been important similarities in trade union responses to common economic, technological and industrial trends, and that events in one country influence developments in another.

The focus of this paper is on the contemporary period and the years immediately ahead; in that context one of the most important questions to be raised is how far are the unions of Europe and America moving on parallel tracks.

However, before looking at crucial influences and developments, it is necessary to examine some fundamental differences. In the United Kingdom and the USA trade unions were, and to an important extent still are, based upon the occupations of their members. The classic union in both countries was a craft union of highly skilled workers. Today, however, few unions confine their membership to narrow organizational limits. Increasingly, the unions in Britain and America have widened their boundaries to take in the lesser skilled, but a significant group cling most tenaciously to the traditions of craft unionism. Unions in the USA were for many years acutely divided on this question and split into two national organizations; one, the AF of L emphasizing the "craft" basis of its membership; the other, the CIO, supporting the growth of industrial unionism. Eventually agreement to merge was reached, but the conflict over structure, which was also one of philosophy, was not easily healed and new divisions have recurred.

Two of the largest unions in the US, the Teamsters, and the UAW are not affiliated to the AFL–CIO. Though each is a broadly based organization, they differ greatly in structure and philosophy. The Teamsters, which was expelled from the AFL–CIO for violating its ethical codes, has a strong craft union tradition; the UAW which disaffiliated over issues of political policy, is a product of industrial unionism. Nevertheless in spite of those differences they both reflect significant features of the trade union tradition in that country.

In Britain the pattern of trade unionism, though based primarily upon occupational interests, is extremely diverse. There are craft, industrial, white collar, and general unions all competing for membership and it is not uncommon for each type of union to have members in a single enterprise. Commitment to a particular political creed is not a condition of union membership, but many unions are affiliated to the Labour Party. In spite of these divergences the trade union movement is united for the most part under a single trades union Congress.

In the Continental countries of Europe the unions are divided in a different way. Except in Scandinavia the unions in Europe were founded by political parties and religious denominations. In Belgium, France, Germany, Italy and the Netherlands, the pattern of union organization has owed more to ideological allegiance than to any other factor. However, in all of these countries there was a tendency for white collar workers to form separate unions. Although ideological divisions are still important, and acutely so in Belgium and France, there has been a tendency, especially during the last decade, for these divisions to become less significant. In Germany ideological unification was achieved with the assistance of the Western allies in the aftermath of National Socialism and the Second World War. No such renaissance was achieved in the other Western European countries, but economic, social and political trends during the past decade have led unions in Italy and Holland to take active steps to create a more unified trade union movement. In Italy agreement has been reached between the Socialists and the Communists to create a unified metal workers' union. At the level of the national association, there is common action on specific issues and discussions about the establishment of a common headquarters have taken place. In Holland fusion between the Catholic and Socialist trade union centers is in progress; although the Protestant unions refuse to participate the achievement of a united trade union movement is now not beyond the bounds of possibility.

Perhaps even more significant was the creation in 1974 of a European Trade Union Confederation which brought together trade union centers from the countries of the European Economic Community and the European Free Trade Area which were affiliated to the International Confederation of Free Trade Unions and in addition the trade union centers in the same countries which were affiliated to the World Council of Labor – formerly the International Confederation of Christian Trade Unions. The ETUC, also invited the Communist trade union center in Italy – the Confederation Industriale Generale Lavora and the French Communist controlled Confédération Générale du Travail to become members. The ETUC has accepted the affiliation of the Communist Trade Union Center in Italy, the Confederazione Generale Italiana del Lavoro, following its withdrawal from the WFTU. It has also had discussions concerning affiliation with the French communist controlled Confédération Générale du Travail. A difficulty in this case has risen from the reluctance on the part of the CGT to break its links with the WFTU.[2]

Not every trade union center affiliated to the ICFTU was particularly happy at this development. There are many trade union leaders who look with misgiving and distrust at the policy of unification between the Communists and Socialist trade union organizations which has been pushed extremely hard by the British trade union movement. The German trade unions and the French Force Ouvriers have in particular had reservations about unity with the Communist led trade unions. This reluctance has led to the slowing down of the proposed affiliation of the French CGT to the European Trade Union Confederation.

The movement towards ideological unification has been significantly encouraged and facilitated by the policy of *détente*. Although the International Confederation of Free Trade Unions remains resolutely opposed to the Communist concept of the trade unionism, its affiliates in Western Europe have increasingly accepted invitations to send delegations to the Eastern European countries and the Soviet Union. They have in turn received delegations from the Communist countries. These meetings have inevitably encouraged closer relations with Communist led unions in the Western European countries. Working class unity has been a prime goal of the Communists for many years and their continuous efforts to organize joint actions at many levels of political action have born fruit in the climate of détente.[3]

These developments have alienated the AFL–CIO, which disaffiliated from the ICFTU in 1969 because it was insufficiently anti-Communist. The AFL–CIO believes that détente will lead to the undermining of the principles of free and democratic trade unionism and a weakening of the will of the Western world to resist the relentless propaganda and pressure from the

Soviet Union in support of its world-wide goals, which are to turn free countries into Communist controlled subordinate satellites. Unfortunately, the disaffiliation of the AFL–CIO encouraged the trend towards ideological unification since it weakened the opposition to it. Although the US unions have links with the European trade unions through the International Trade Secretariats and directly with the British TUC and the German DGB their influence on European trade union developments is extremely weak. The influence of the AFL–CIO on international trade union movements will be further diminished if the United States withdraws from the International Labour Organization, as under Mr. Meany's pressure they threaten to do.

The Role of Collective Bargaining

Political ideology is not the only factor that separates the trade unions of one country from the trade unions in another. Collective bargaining which is regarded in Britain, the USA and in Scandinavia, as the classic activity of trade unions, has not had the same significance in France and Italy. In the countries in which trade unionism was established on a political and denominational basis, collective bargaining was less important than pressure brought against the state to secure protective legislation. This difference in trade union behavior was due not only to differences in trade union ideology, but also to the fact that the state played a much larger role in the determination of levels of pay and conditions of employment than in Britain, the USA and Scandinavia.[4]

There was also another reason, namely, that employers in the European countries were not prepared to negotiate with unions at the level of the enterprise. Rates of pay were established for each industry by collective bargaining between employers' federations and trade union federations. Issues that arose at the place of work in relation to the application of wage settlements or conditions of employment were settled in the main through works councils that were by law established in most enterprises above a certain size.

This characteristic pattern of industry-wide wage agreements and works councils through which day to day problems at the place of work could be resolved is still a predominant feature of European industrial relations systems, but it has been changing in a number of important respects over the past twenty years under the influence of social, economic and industrial developments.

The most important change across Europe has been a greater emphasis on collective bargaining and the settlement of issues in conflict at the shop floor level. In every country there has been a trend towards company and plant trade union activity.[5]

Although the system of industry-wide negotiation and settlement at the Länder-level remains strong, in Germany there has been a notable increase in the activity of trade union representatives at the place of work. This development has led to the unions playing a more prominent role in the enterprise and greatly influencing the membership and activities of works councils.[6]

In France there has been a similar trend towards increased trade union bargaining activity at the level of the enterprise. This development was encouraged by a change in the law after the events of 1968 which gave the 'section syndical' in the enterprise statutory protection. The relation of plant and company bargaining to nationwide bargaining is complex. The unions and employers' associations are frequently in conflict over what questions should be settled at one level and what at another. Nevertheless there has been a considerable development in collective bargaining which has become a more significant feature of industrial relations than was traditionally the case in France.[7]

In Belgium, Holland, Italy and the Scandinavian countries there have also been radical changes in the patterns of collective bargaining. New laws and new agreements have greatly extended the bargaining power of the unions and in all of these countries there have been significant developments in the role of the unions within the enterprise.

The shift from industry-wide bargaining to company and plant bargaining has been most dramatic in the United Kingdom, where it has been closely associated with the growth in power and influence of the shop stewards which has taken place since the Second World War. Under general inflationary conditions, with in particular shortages of labor, shop stewards were in a position to negotiate substantial improvements on the terms agreed at industry-level by employers federations and trade unions. The assertion by shop stewards of their bargaining power in the "50's" and "60's" was a significant factor in the persistent tendency for wages to outrun productivity and in the upsurge of unofficial strikes and restrictive practices which had become a dominant feature of British industrial relations. In no other country in Europe did the unions on the shop floor exercise such a degree of influence and control over productive performances. The widespread belief that it was the chronic character of this situation which was primarily responsible for the abysmally poor performance of important sectors of British industry led, in 1965, to the appointment of a Royal Commission into the role of trade

unions and employers' organizations. This inquiry generally referred to after
the name of its chairman as the Donovan Commission concluded that there
were in effect two systems of industrial relations in Britain: one at the level
of the enterprise, which was informal and disorderly, the other at the level of
industry which was formal and orderly, but which had little relevance to the
bargaining process in the enterprise. The two systems of industrial relations
were in conflict with each other. What had happened was that the unions had
lost control of their own representatives at the place of work.[8]

The main recommendation of the Donovan Commission to remedy this
situation was the establishment of a Commission for Industrial Relations
which, by inquiry and report, would help strengthen the unions and promote
more orderly collective bargaining at the level of the enterprise. The Donovan
Commission rejected proposals to make collective agreements legally binding
contracts and to limit the freedom of shop stewards to call strikes. The
Labour Government then in power was disappointed with the recommendations of the Commission which it believed did not go far enough and it
decided to take powers to impose a "cooling-off" period in strikes of national
importance and to fine unions and union leaders if they called strikes which
were in defiance of such an order.

This attempt by the Labour Government in 1969 to bring about an
improvement in industrial relations by regulating the right to strike in breach
of a government order was defeated by the unions threatening to withdraw
their political support from the Labour Party at the forthcoming general
election. Faced by this revolt the Labour Government withdrew its proposals.

The unions had made their point and demonstrated their political, as well
as economic power. They were to show even more dramatically when the
Conservatives came to office in 1970 that no government could make
fundamental changes in the law relating to industrial relations without the
cooperation and agreement of the trade unions. It is not only in Britain where
unions have the power to make government impossible unless substantial
concessions are made to satisfy their interests. This situation exists potentially
in many countries in Europe.

By contrast with Britain, collective bargaining in the USA has exhibited
"a combination of stability and innovation that by most standards has
effectively served both labor and management."[9] Nevertheless, when
compared with most countries in Europe, a much smaller proportion of the
labor force is unionized and protected by collective bargaining. While
unionization has spread rapidly in the public sector and collective bargaining
become increasingly accepted as a means of determining terms of
employment, there is little unionization of white collar workers in private

industry and the service sector. American unions have been particularly weak in organizing and protecting the interests of minority groups and of young workers and women employees by collective bargaining.

Although the unions in the USA are immensely powerful in certain industries and among certain groups of skilled workers, they have not been able to exercise the same degree of influence and control over management or governments, as is often the case in Europe. The fact that in the US a larger number of strikes occur and a larger number of Mondays are lost compared with most European countries in part reflects the weakness of the unions, as indeed does the ability of management to innovate and to avoid making massively inflationary pay increases.[10] If the American unions are to become stronger and to continue to use their aggressive bargaining tactics they might find as they did in wartime that collective bargaining would become subject to far reaching legal regulations and administered controls. Whether they could win in a serious conflict with the US government is doubtful, but it seems less likely than in Europe that such a conflict would occur.

The Problem of Inflation

The growth in trade union bargaining power was seen by many observers as a prime cause of the rising levels of inflation throughout the Western world in the "60's" and "70's". For those who drew this conclusion income restraint imposed through some form of national incomes policy was an essential element in the achievement of a more stable economic situation. All the countries of Northern Europe and the USA and Canada have tried for shorter or longer periods to control inflation with the help of voluntary or legally imposed incomes policy and not infrequently prices policies.

The countries most successful in containing inflation have been Germany and Switzerland which have had the least formal systems of pay control. Germany has relied since 1966 on a policy of 'concerted action' between the government and the employers and unions reached through meetings at which the parties have exchanged information and discussed their response to the economic situation. Although this policy has been limited to exchanging information it has been extremely successful if measured by the low rate of increase in money wages, the low level of industrial conflict and the high level of economic growth. Switzerland, which has followed a similar type of informal incomes policy has been equally successful. Although this success cannot be seen simply in terms of the style of incomes policy which has been followed, Germany and Switzerland have been able to pursue monetary and fiscal policies which have been rather less expansive than many other countries. They have nevertheless enjoyed high levels of industrial growth and maintained high levels of employment. At bottom the economic success of Germany and Switzerland has had much to do with social attitudes and behavior patterns which have been generated by factors peculiar to these countries and which have affected not only the trade unions but all sections of society.

In most other countries more precisely formulated incomes policies have for a time effectively curbed the collective bargaining process, but they have then usually come under intense strain and have had to be greatly modified or abandoned. In spite of this recurring experience countries have come back to national incomes and price control policies as indispensable weapons in the fight against inflation. It is clear, however, from the continuous and escalating rise in wages and prices over the postwar period that centrally imposed incomes policies have not prevented, and of themselves probably cannot prevent, inflation. Nevertheless it may also be true, as the supporters of incomes policies would argue, that without these systems of pay and price restriction the rate of inflation would have been substantially greater.[11]

Although centralized incomes policies have a doubtful record as devices for preventing inflation, they have long been established in Norway, Sweden, Austria and the Netherlands as virtually permanent features of the industrial relations systems of these countries. In these countries incomes policies have had other goals as well as to control inflation. They have also been linked to the social objectives of raising the relative level of the lowest paid and the narrowing of differentials. At their most sophisticated they have been linked to fiscal policies and price controls. The Swedish and Norwegian trade unions have perhaps had the most clearly defined social aims. Scandinavian incomes policies have been designed by the unions to foster their solidaristic goals. It is not easy to say, however, how far the trends towards a more egalitarian pattern of income distribution in Scandinavia has been materially advanced by the incomes policies pursued. There has been a significant redistribution of income in the Scandinavian countries, but this has been achieved largely through fiscal and social transfer policies. There is evidence that 'solidaristic' pay policies and the redistributive tax and social income policies are now giving rise to serious difficulties. The limits of these policies are felt by many Scandinavians to have been reached and that some retreat from income egalitarianism achieved by compressing pay structures and high personal taxation is necessary.[12]

Although the British Labour Government abolished the incomes policy established by the Conservatives when it came in power in 1974 because it had become intolerable to the trade unions, the rate of pay and price increases soared to over 30 percent. Faced by runaway inflation a voluntary incomes policy was jointly agreed as one element in a "social contract" arrived at between the Labour Government and the trade unions in Britain in 1975. The "social contract" played a major part in the reduction of the rate of inflation from over 30 percent to below 15 percent by the end of 1977. Whether it will be possible for the Government and the unions to agree to continue this policy until the rate of inflation is lowered to a point even remotely near that of elimination is a question that few would answer with confidence.

The USA is another country which after a number of experiments with legally regulated wage policies and official guide lines, has returned to uncontrolled collective bargaining. However, this is not to say that the Government does not seek to persuade the unions that it is in their own interest to keep their pay demands to levels which do not force up labor costs excessively. Canada on the other hand has recently followed the European pattern of a formal wages and price policy. This policy has had some success, but it is widely disliked by employers and unions, and evasions and anomalies have stimulated considerable criticism of its real value.[13]

The difficulty with any centralized incomes policy is that it prevents managers from adjusting wage and salary structures so as to meet the particular needs of a company at a particular time. This inevitably distorts the pattern of pay and creates tensions and conflicts. Unions are also adversely affected since they cannot respond to the felt needs of their members in different employment situations without running into conflict with the requirements of the policy to which they have given their support. This situation places union leaders in an extremely difficult situation, since no matter how powerful the case for general wage restraint may be and how much trade union members may in general benefit from the curtailment of inflation, any individual or group of members may be adversely affected by restrictions which prevent an adjustment in their personal income level. The problem is particularly acute for unions, as in the USA and Great Britain, which are primarily concerned in their activities with negotiating and servicing collective agreements at the plant and company levels, since there are often likely to be clear cut differences of interest between local and national leaders. The shift to plant and company negotiations has been a significant factor in the difficulties which have arisen in the continuance of such long established centrally determined pay policies as those in Holland and Sweden. There are many who believe that the conflicts and distortions which are an inevitable feature of national incomes policies are a needless sacrifice, since the basic problem of inflation at bottom has little to do with the unions. In the opinion of those who hold a monetarist view of inflation, the fundamental cause of excessive increases in pay and prices lies in the failure of governments to effectively regulate monetary and fiscal policies. If money supply is held to a low rate of increase, unions could only price their members out of jobs by insisting on excessively high wage increases. This doctrine contains a good deal of truth, but it has too austere consequences for most governments for it to be carried to its ultimate end. Higher levels of unemployment may be an inescapable alternative, if unions refuse to exercise restraint in their pay demands, but this political cost may be higher than the imposition of wage and price controls. Restrictions in the freedom of unions and companies to fix freely pay and prices, though uncomfortable and in the last resort intolerable, becomes a political necessity if pay and prices, even though for only a short period, are to be held in check without forcing up the level of unemployment and curtailing the rate of growth through raising the costs of borrowing.

What has become evident is that without incomes policies severe monetary and fiscal policies may be necessary to check inflation and it may be impossible to avoid far higher levels of unemployment. There is no mystery about the causes of inflation, nor is there any mystery about the causes of unemployment, though there are immense difficulties in preventing either from happening. The overexpenditures of governments and the inevitable cutbacks which have had to be made to curb the inflationary consequences of these policies have inevitably led to upsurges in inflation followed by upsurges in unemployment.

Unions and Unemployment

The attempts by governments to curtail expenditure and to cope with the problems created by the decision of the OPEC countries to increase the price of oil exports by 400 percent and the loss of confidence these developments entailed, produced a worldwide recession in 1974–1975. Unemployment rose in every advanced country to higher levels than had been experienced at any other time since the end of the Second World War. The recession slowed down the rate of price increase, but in many countries only to rates of increase well above those which were normal in the "50's" and "60's". This left most countries in a situation in which there was both inflation and unemployment.

There had been a feeling in probably every country in Europe that if unemployment rose much above three percent this would lead to a violent political response from the trade unions. This level has been far exceeded in most countries during the past few years and on present indications there would seem to be little likelihood of a return to the very low levels of unemployment which were a feature of the immediate postwar decades. The reaction from the unions has been far less radical than was generally expected. There have been protests, but these have been relatively muted in most countries.

One of the reasons for this perhaps rather surprising behavior has been the fact that much of the higher unemployment has come in sections of the labor force which tend to be less well organized and less able to make effective protests. In particular, those leaving school, women workers, migrants and the elderly have been relatively more badly affected than adult male workers generally. Certain industries such as construction, which have a high proportion of highly mobile workers who therefore drift out of the industry in a recession, have suffered rather more than other industries. Thus structural factors which have been of considerable importance in the higher totals of unemployment have tended to inhibit mass reaction.

Other factors which have cushioned the impact of unemployment have been the high levels of unemployment benefit, the substantial payments made to workers laid off and the improvement in retraining facilities. These provisions have enabled workers who have lost their work to take much longer in finding a new job. In both Europe and North America the costs of layoffs have become much more expensive than used to be the case. In the United States unemployment in the automobile industry completely emptied the supplementary Unemployment Benefit funds of General Motors and Chrysler, but the Ford fund was not depleted to this extent. Nevertheless these funds served their purpose well if not with total adequacy. The recovery of demand came in time to prevent the social disaster which was feared in Detroit and other major car production centers. The strengthening of these benefit funds will be a major objective of the unions during the recovery period, thus it is likely that companies will have to set aside large sums to provide for the income maintenance of their employees in recessions. In Europe it is becoming difficult to discharge any group of workers without giving advance notice and providing substantial compensation to those who lose their jobs. One effect of this development has been to make employers more cautious about hiring workers. High security of employment is likely to lead to employers seeking a greater degree of occupational flexibility as is the case in Japan where employees of the larger companies expect to enjoy security of employment for their working lives. Developments in this direction in Europe have important implications for trade unions which are based upon occupational principles.

The higher levels of unemployment during the mid "70's" have had a significant effect of the bargaining power of unions in Europe and in North America, but they have not brought down the rates of increase in negotiated pay levels which had been forecast in the "50's" and "60's". The Phillips curve which had a considerable impact on the thinking of many economists on the relation of wage increases to unemployment, has proved to be a less precise indicator of the effect of rising unemployment on wage increases than expected. Experience during the past decade has demonstrated that there is a relationship between unemployment and inflation, but this relation is not as simple and clear cut as suggested by many conclusions drawn from the Phillips curves. Certainly the notion that a modest increase in unemployment would be sufficient to bring an economic system into a stable situation has proved wanting. Changes in the structure of the labor force, in market organization, in industrial technology, in political and social factors have altered economic relationships and undermined the statistical correlations which Phillips demonstrated had existed in the past.

This does not mean that unemployment does not have an important influence on the level of pay settlements; it does, but any given level of unemployment may leave a scope for pay increases that could be highly inflationary. Although there is in all countries a tolerance of higher levels of unemployment and this is likely to continue in the future, it does not follow that rigorous steps should not be taken to deal with some of these structural problems which if successful would make it possible to have lower average levels of unemployment without incurring other adverse effects. It is possible that unless these structural problems are successfully tackled it will be impossible to return to lower average levels of unemployment without running the risk of stimulating high levels of inflation again.

A serious problem facing the unions and society as a whole is the fact that much of the new investment that is being made is investment in high technology is by its nature labor-saving and not job-creating. Given the high cost of labor in the US and the advanced industrial countries it is inevitable that goods requiring a great deal of labor to manufacture will be imported and labor intensive services will be expensive, thus limiting their growth. Overcoming this problem will not be easy and it is likely that unemployment will be far higher in the future than it has been in the recent past. The unions will seek to prevent lay-offs and reduction in the labor force when technological innovation takes place. Unfortunately this policy can only succeed by slowing down the pace of economic development and by loading the costs of labor displacement on the successful innovators. Although a strong case can be made for making firms with seasonal fluctuations in labor demand bear the cost of making a part of its labor force idle at regular intervals, a tax on innovation and efficiency in labor utilization could be seriously damaging to general economic welfare. Equally dangerous in this respect is the demand made by the unions in the advanced industrial countries, especially in the United States, that multinational enterprises should be prevented or discouraged from exporting capital to start new ventures overseas by penal taxation or downright prohibition, or that goods from less developed countries should be denied entry.

Unfortunately unions are often reluctant to cooperate in the adjustment of pay structures, in opening entry into occupations and to transfers within occupational hierarchies, out of fear that such flexibility will weaken their organizational strength and bargaining power. The resulting overmanning and excessive labor costs may be factors of decisive importance and have a potent influence on economic growth. This type of problem is of far greater significance in some countries than in others. It has had particular relevance in the United Kingdom. Although the problems of structural unemployment and the achievement of high levels of economic growth are by no means entirely problems of union attitudes and behavior, the co-operation of the unions in overcoming them is of considerable importance. It is only likely to be effectively achieved if the degree of union participation at both national and enterprise level in the making of key decisions is greatly extended.

Collective Bargaining and Co-Determination

The political and economic role of the unions at the national level has been closely related to their role in the enterprise. In Europe one of the most significant developments has been the establishment in Germany of a system of co-determination in the boards of directors of private and public enterprises. The achievement of co-determination in which the unions were assisted by the allied occupying powers after the Second World War had a profound political significance. It followed logically from the abandonment of any support for a revolutionary Marxist philosophy, and the adoption of pragmatic social democratic principles which entailed the acceptance of a pluralist society based essentially upon the private ownership of capital. The desire for co-determination also reflected the fact that German trade unions were relatively weak at the level of the enterprise and that at the national level they were unlikely to be able to achieve more than a moderate influence on governments.[14]

The establishment of works councils by statute also reflected the weakness of German trade unions. However, over the past twenty-five years German trade unions have grown much stronger and they have been able to exercise a considerable and growing influence over the election of employee directors and works' councilors. The unions have found support from the great majority of German workers for what has been an essentially consensus role in participation in the work of supervisory boards and works councils and also in their role as collective bargaining agents. This acceptance of responsibility for solving problems in a way which would bring most benefit to their members through the maintenance of industrial peace has been remarkably successful if measured by the level of wages and working conditions enjoyed by their members. Although it is impossible to measure the specific contribution made by the trade unions to the remarkable performance of German industry and the German economy, there is a large body of opinion inside and outside of Germany that believes it to have been very considerable. This view would not necessarily be fully accepted by a number of managers who believe that the trade unions have tended to become more radical and there is a very deep apprehension that the recent decision to extend the parity principle, though on a different basis from the system which prevails in the iron, steel and coal industries to the private enterprise sector will have an adverse effect on the management of German enterprises.[15] There is perhaps an even larger group of younger members of the trade unions who after twenty-five years are beginning to doubt the consensus basis of German industrial relations. This emergence of a Marxist oriented group of young radicals, who look towards a greater degree of conflict leading on to a challenge to the existing structure of industry, its ownership and management and the ultimate socializing of the state is a new and potentially significant development, although it harks back to an older tradition.

The fundamental issues of consensus and conflict, of pluralism and socialism are central to this debate on co-determination and collective bargaining which is taking place in every European country. This debate and the changes in the systems of industrial relations which are occurring have been produced by economic, social and political forces which are world-wide in their signficance. Full employment, rising standards of life, greater educational opportunity, technological advance, the information explosion and the breakdown of traditional class structures and social systems and their replacement by more open societies have brought a challenge to established patterns of authority.

Throughout Europe and North America trade unions have called into question the legitimacy of managerial prerogatives. This challenge is of course, not new, it was implicit in the establishment of trade unions, and it has always been explicit in the Marxist view of capitalist industry. What is new, however, is the widespread adoption of some variant of the German model of co-determination as an answer to the problem. It is now evident that managerial legitimacy can no longer be founded on a right to make and execute decisions which is derived largely from the ownership of capital, whether this be private or public. Ownership of capital is a necessary, but not sufficient basis for the making of managerial decisions. The source of managerial authority must reside inherently in the managerial function, which can only be effectively carried out in modern circumstances if decisions are based as far as possible upon the consent of labor as well as capital. It has, therefore, become necessary to make this explicit in the structure of corporate organization, through representation on board of directors or some other machinery of decision making.

Most countries in Europe with the exception of those with a strong Marxist tradition in their trade union movements have introduced, or are in the process of introducing employee participation on boards of directors, or by other means, at the shop floor level in the enterprise. In France and Italy the two largest trade unions, the CGT and the CGIL, which are under the domination of the Communists, refuse to have anything to do with the idea of co-determination which they see as class collaboration. The CFDT in France, the former Catholic oriented trade union movememt, and FGTB in Belgium are also against co-determination, not only because it smacks of class collaboration, but because they are in favor of workers self-government. This syndicalist aim is, however, anathema to Communist controlled organizations as well as to those who believe that a significant degree of managerial authority is still required for the efficient conduct of most enterprises.

The British TUC, after showing a guarded interest in employee participation for some years, decided to adopt as an immediate policy aim the achievement of parity representation of employees on boards of directors. This demand is now the subject of a Commission of Inquiry, which was due to report by the end of 1976. It was confidently expected that the Commission would endorse the establishment of employee directors on a similar basis to that suggested by the European Commission in its draft statute for the European Company. This would provide for one third shareholder representatives, one third employees representatives and the remaining third jointly chosen.[16]

Not all British trade unions are in favor of the TUC's proposal; those influenced by the left and the right would prefer for different reasons to see their collective bargaining power strengthened, rather than be represented on the boards of directors of companies. In the light of the strength of this opposition it is likely that the report of the Commission of Inquiry will recommend that any reform of company law that the Government is pledged to make will be permissive rather than mandatory. It would give the unions the right to have employee directors if they so wished, but companies would not be compelled to make provision for employee directors if the unions were not in favor of such a development. Opposition to co-determination is also strongly voiced by most of the trade unions in the USA and Canada for the same reasons as the right wing trade unions in the United Kingdom. The unions in the United States are against co-determination, since they fear that it would undermine their bargaining power by confusing their role with that of management. The US unions see no advantage in participating in the decisions of management. They believe that by negotiating with management on an independent basis they can force management to modify policies for the benefit of their members more effectively than they could by being represented on a Board of Directors. If they were on such a board they would be jointly responsible for the decisions of management and, therefore, they would lose their freedom to continue to oppose decisions they did not like. This would lead to enfeebled unions and to weak management. American unions and managers both strongly support the adversary concept of industrial relations. The adversary process has deep roots in American society; it is entrenched in its political and legal systems and it is sustained in industrial relations by a persuasive body of theory as well as a long established institutional framework. There are, however, straws in the wind which suggest that changes may occur which could bring the American system of industrial relations closer to the European models.

An important factor influencing unions and managers in the USA is the rising cost of industrial conflict. The cost of the last major strike in the steel industry so scared managers and unions that they decided to negotiate an agreement lasting for six years, from 1974 to 1980, in which the union agreed not to call a strike on certain conditions. Among these conditions was the establishment of a joint planning committee, through which union leaders would have access to all the information available to the directors of the steel companies and be able to participate in discussions with management in advance of major investment and other decisions that might have a significant affect on union members.

More recently Mr Leonard Woodcock, President of the Union of

Automobile Workers, has been reported as saying in the course of negotiations for a new wages agreement in the motor car industry that the union could see some advantages in having a representative on the board of directors of the General Motors Corporation. Trade union leaders have in fact been appointed to the boards of some enterprises taken over in the public interest by state agencies. There are moreover a number of private enterprises which have appointed employee directors to their boards.

There is a deep concern in the US about the role of the large modern corporation; its political and economic power and the legitimacy of its management is under attack from public interest groups concerned with environmental protection, as well as from unions. One response of American management to this criticism has been a considerable expansion of employee stockholding schemes. Many American managers see this development as an alternative to co-determination, and as an answer to the issue of managerial legitimacy and arbitrary power.

There is virtually no questioning by the trade unions in the USA of the virtues of private capitalism; though there is plenty of criticism of its vices. American unions do not wish to see any form of socialism introduced into the United States. They would, however, like to see a larger proportion of the labor force unionized and they constantly attack state laws which make union shop provisions illegal. They also expect the Government to create economic conditions under which the unions can make full use of their bargaining power. They would like to see the government expanding the economy at a pace which would reduce the unemployment level to not more than a few percent, but they would bitterly oppose any resultant wage controls.The desire to see collective bargaining strengthened is not just an American concern. The trade unions in Sweden, having obtained the legal right for employees to be represented on boards of directors on all companies employing more than one hundred, have preferred to seek to achieve co-determination by collective bargaining rather than to adopt the German model of parity representation on supervisory boards.[17]

The aim of the Swedish trade unions is effectively the same as the German trade unions, but the method is significantly different. The new law relating to collective bargaining which comes into effect on 1 January 1977 compels an employer to bargain on any issue relating to the management of the company. There is no longer any area of sole managerial responsibility on which the union has no right to bargain. The law requires the employer to provide employees with full information on the company's plans relating to production, future developments, and changes in personnel policy and the employment situation. The union must be given access to any documents arising from the activities of the employer in connection with his business. Where conflict over a decision arises which is not covered by an agreement on participation, the union will be free to strike.

Notwithstanding the constructive and responsible role played in the past by Swedish trade unions, employers fear that this far-reaching extension of union bargaining rights will lead to increased conflict between union representatives and management at the workplace. Others, however, believe that union representatives will behave responsibly and the these new rights will be used with discretion.

The LO, the largest central federation of trade unions in Sweden, at its conference in 1976 adopted a plan, named after its author, Rudolf Meidner, which if realized will give the unions an even greater control over the policies and future of Swedish industry than is implicit in the new collective bargaining law. The aim of the new proposal is to create "wage-earner investment funds" which will be managed by the unions. The funds will be created from compulsory issues of stock which will be based upon a percentage of profits set aside by each company for this purpose. These funds will not be distributed as a cash bonus to individual employees, since the prime purpose will be to ensure that capital gains accrue to wage earners who will benefit from dividends declared on the shares held in their name. The collectivizing of the capital ownership of private companies will also give the unions an influence over and ultimately control of corporate finance and thus on the making of industrial policy.[18]

The Meidner plan is highly controversial, as is a similar plan put forward in Denmark, since the plan is essentially a radical syndicalist alternative to either classic capitalism or state socialism. It could be developed in a number of different ways, it need not necessarily involve a central fund which would give the trade union organizations an immense economic power. An alternative would be to establish separate funds in each enterprise; in this model the employees eventually own and control the company, which would have far-reaching implications for the unions and the traditional processes of industrial relations.

These issues are far from decided but it is likely that the unions in other countries will be influenced by the Swedish and Danish proposals and will press for similar schemes. If they do and they are politically successful the fundamental basis of private capitalism will be substantially changed. A development of this kind would have significant implications for both management and trade unions. It would remove the fundamental conflict between employees and managers that arises from the ownership of capital, but it would still leave a need for effective management and a need to continue the role of collective bargaining, which might give rise to serious problems.

From the earliest times trade unions have been concerned to protect the immediate economic and social interests of their members. Throughout their history unions have used their bargaining power to extract better terms of employment, in the context of democratic capitalist societies, and they have sought to influence governments through the exercise of political pressure to create economic, social and legal conditions that would make this task easier to achieve. At the same time most trade union movements have sought more radical goals, including the creation of democracy in the workplace as well as in the state, and often the elimination of private capitalism and its substitution by state socialism. The issues which dominate the activities of trade unions in every country reflect to greater or lesser extent the divisions of interest and ideology which afflict their members and the societies in which they exist. The roles of the unions in Europe and America have been changing, but they have clearly not evolved to a situation in which it could be said that they have now become much the same everywhere. The unions in contemporary democratic societies have become more powerful and in so becoming have revealed the contradictions and uncertainties of their role. The crucial problem which faces unions which desire to see pluralist democracy maintained is how they might achieve their goals without destroying their independence and with it the system which has made their development possible.

If under modern circumstances unions use their bargaining power to the full extent they may well destroy the efficiency of private enterprise and undermine the ability of democratic governments to maintain a stable economy and a pluralist political system. It is thus essential that unions co-operate with management and governments to the extent of ensuring that enterprises are profitable and a multi-party political system is maintained. There is a danger, however, that unions may fail to satisfy their members if they limit their conflictual role; they may lose their credibility and become rent by internal dissensions. On the other hand, if they threaten to undermine economic and political stability governments will be compelled to impose constraints upon them. It is in these circumstance that the role of unions as instruments of participation in managerial and governmental processes would seem to have something more to offer than reliance solely on the classic role of collective bargaining.

Unions in democracies which have a revolutionary ideology are concerned with the question of the exercise of trade union power and responsibility only to the extent that the maintenance of a democratic political system facilitates their activities which are aimed at destroying the pluralist structure of capitalism. Although few of the unions which are wedded to the aim of destroying pluralist capitalist societies would admit to it – especially those whose ideological goal is a form of democratic socialism – in all probability the creation of a socialist society, that is to say a society in which all the means of production were owned by the state, would mean an end to their independence. This is certainly what has happened to the unions in all the socialist societies that have so far been established.

Since they have the power to make management and government weak and ineffective the search by unions for a constructive role in which they can satisfy the legitimate concerns of their members and survive as independent institutions is a matter of fundamental concern for all democratic societies. If it is not found pluralist societies will shift to the left or the right; in either case restrictions will be imposed on unions which will limit their role. Trade union freedom is an essential element in a democratic society, but as with all other freedoms, it must be exercised in such a way as not to destroy the freedoms on which trade union freedom itself depends.

Notes

[1] Everett M. Kassalow, *Trade Unions and Industrial Relations: An International Comparison*, New York: Random House 1969.

[2] B. C. Roberts and Bruno Liebhaberg, *The European Trade Union Confederation: Influence of Regionalism, Détente and Multinationals*, in: *British Journal of Industrial Relations*, Vol. 14, 1976, No. 3.

[3] John P. Windmuller, *Realignment in the I.C.F.T.U.: The Impact of Détente*, in: *British Journal of Industrial Relations*, Vol. 14, 1976, No.3.

[4] Kassalow, op. cit.

[5] *Collective Bargaining in Industrialised Market Economies*, Geneva: ILO 1973.

[6] O. Blume, *Erfahrungen und Möglichkeiten der Mitbestimmung im Unternehmen*, Tübingen: Mohr 1956, and Ivor L. Roberts, *The Works Constitution Acts and Industrial Relations in West Germany: Implications for the United Kingdom*, in: *British Journal of Industrial Relations*, Vol. 11, 1973, No. 3.

[7] J. D. Reynaud, *Les syndicats en France*, Paris: Seuil 1975. G. Adam et al., *La négociation collective en France; Evolution et perspectives*, Paris: Editions Ouvrières 1972.

[8] *Royal Commission on Trade Unions and Employers' Associations, 1957–1968*, London: HMSO Cmnd 2623.

[9] Donald E. Cullen, *United States*, in: *Collective Bargaining in Industrialised Market Economies*, Geneva: ILO 1973.

[10] Sumner Rosen, *The United States: A Time for Reassessment*, in: S. Barkin, Ed., *Bargaining System Challenged: Worker Militancy and its Consequences 1965–1975*, New York: Praeger 1975.

[11] F. Blackaby, (ed.), *An Incomes Policy for Britain, London:* Heinemann Educational Books 1972, and L. Ulman and R. J. Flanagan, *Wage Restraint: A Study of Incomes Policies in Western Europe*, Berkeley: University of California Press 1971.

[12] K. O. Faxen, *Wage Policy and Attitudes of Industrial Relations Parties in Sweden*, Paper submitted to 4th World Congress of the International Industrial Relations Association, 1976, and J. Fulcher, *Joint Regulation and its Decline*, in: R. Scase, (ed.), *Readings in Swedish Class Structure*, New York: Pergamon 1976.

[13] *The Inflation Dilemma*, Economic Council of Canada 13th Annual Review, November 1976.

[14] Joachim Bergmann and Walther Muller-Jentsh, *The Federal Republic of Germany: Co-operative Unionism and Dual Bargaining System Challenged*, in: S. Barkin, (ed.), *Worker Militancy and the Consequences 1965–1975*, New York: Praeger 1975.

[15] Thomas Kirkwood and Horst Mewes, *The Limits of Trade Union Power in the Capitalist Order; The Case of West German Labour's Quest for Co-determination*, in: *British Journal of Industrial Relations*, Vol. 14, 1976, No. 3.

[16] *Employee Participation and Company Structure in the European Community*, Communication of the Commission of the European Communities, November 1975.

[17] Lennart Forsebäck, *Industrial Relations and Employment in Sweden*, Stockholm: Swedish Institute 1976.

[18] op. cit.

PART THREE

DIMENSIONS OF SECURITY

Atlantic Security Policy in an Era without Great Alternatives

by HANS-PETER SCHWARZ

In the American-European security dialogue of the past 25 years the demands for a comprehensive conceptual reshaping of the existing system and the corresponding concrete initiatives have often played a disproportionately great role. The last impulses of this sort could be observed in the late "60's" and early "70's" when détente policy appeared to improve fundamentally the relationship with the Soviet Union and again during the negotiations in the "Year of Europe." However, all these grandiosely staged endeavors towards new departures which were in many cases carried with keen far-sightedness brought, in reality, little or no results. The changes which did occur were not so much the result of great plans and dramatic reversals as of partial shifts. Mostly they were the indirect repercussions of large changes which took place outside the security system in its narrow sense. The security system itself has remained relatively constant in an era of profound transformation in world politics. Today one can observe not only a disillusionment with "grand designs" and great alternatives but also a new reflection upon the original goals and functions of the Atlantic alliance.

Thus it seems realistic to proceed from the assumption that the present security system has a future well into the "80's" – not to mention the desirability of its continuance.

Provided that the international climate does not take an alarming turn for the worse in the coming years, one can assume that the system will only change slowly in the near future as well. Those who optimistically hope to realize their "grand designs" and those others who with a deep-seated pessimism fear fundamental set-backs in the Western security situation will probably both be equally disappointed or equally relieved.

Nor should one expect too much of the great alternatives and fundamental changes. It is much more sensible to consider the positive possibilities and the dangers which – to use Nietzsche's words – proceed in a pigeon-toed gait and which only bring about gradual shifts, shifts which taken as a whole can indeed bring about far-reaching restructuring.

But before we discuss a number of constellations in which gradual changes occur and which will, indeed, probably have even greater repercussions in the future, we must furnish evidence for the thesis that the great alternatives have failed in the past. At the same time we can sketch those basic "givens" of American-European security relations upon which all reflections on the future must be based.

The present European security system of the postwar period required ten years to develop its basic structure: from 1947 to 1957. Although its basic elements are the result of *one* basic decision, numerous important partial modifications, which eventually shaped the present system, followed later. The basic decision consisted in basing the security system of the United States and European democracies on an anti-Soviet alliance. The alternative would have been a flexible, polycentric balance of power system with the great powers acting more or less autonomously. Such a system has been characteristic for Europe with the exception of all but a few periods since the seventeenth century. Even the allied statesmen of the war years were thinking along such lines: Roosevelt, who took the "grand design" of a security system of the "four policemen" as his point of departure, General de Gaulle, whose Central Europe concept represented a combination of Richelieu's testament with Poincaré's practices, Winston Churchill who despite the evocation of Anglo-Saxon blood ties thought little of permanent alliances.

The bipolar system which later was to become reality was at best feared by the leaders of the war coalition but not actually expected and certainly not planned. And in the formation of its basic structures one can by no means observe a logical conceptual consistency as, for example, the Truman Doctrine would possibly suggest.

Only the retrospective view of the historian and the advocate of a leftist Hegelian school of thought recognizes the historically inevitable. When the Marshall Plan was initiated the Atlantic pact was by no means a closed matter. When the United States and Great Britain resolved to create the Federal Republic of Germany, hardly anyone wanted to admit that a lasting central element of the European security system had thus been established and that a stable basis – now almost thirty years old – for US military presence in Central Europe had been created which, in practice, made the United States a European power. It is questionable whether we would have arrived at a German defense contribution as early or at all had there been no Korean War, although this contribution has in the meanwhile proven to be one of the decisive preconditions for the present system. Uncertainty prevailed for some time as to the form this contribution should take (in the framework of the EDC or of NATO). Not even the presence of strong American armed forces in Germany was programmed from the very beginning, although it has for some time now been considered the be-all and end-all of American-European security policy. This first came about as a result of the "great debate" of 1951. And one of the elements so decisive today – the equipment of the American troops with tactical nuclear weapons – was resolved only in 1957. The three elements of the triad on which today's deterrence system in Europe is based were brought into play one at a time: 1948/49 the strategic nuclear components, since 1951–1954 the conventional and 1957 the tactical nuclear components.

Since that time, however, the security system has remained constant in its basic characteristics, even though partial elements and surrounding conditions have changed more or less greatly. The significant alternatives – which never lacked advocates – remained mere programs or led at best to marginal modifications.

Even if one realizes that these alternatives were to a great extent the expression of self-delusions as to the stability of the existing system, a glance at these alternative concepts is, nonetheless, informative, in particular in so far as it makes clear which forces *hindered* the realization of these alternatives.

Since 1947 when the Western powers after some hesitation abandoned their endeavors to regulate European security matters within a system of consensual cooperation with the Soviet Union, demands were voiced again and again to return to this concept and to create a fundamentally new security system which must be based on the principles of *polycentric balance of power politics* and *collective security*. However, all these impulses have bogged down in the inertia of the bloc system established since 1948. They were not put into action, above all, because no government, if not under extreme pressure, can agree to fundamental changes in the system of European states the repercussions of which by the very nature of the problem are incalculable. It was the role of the respective opposition parties or individual critical dissenters (the British Labour Party, the German SPD, journalists and scholars like George Kennan or Walter Lippman or Senators in the US Congress who opposed Eisenhower and Dulles) to make such demands. Governments are by nature more cautious and incomparably more inhibited; thus it was natural that neither the conference on Germany of the "50's" nor the campaigns for disengagement could change the basic structure.

For the threatened Western democracies – above all the German Federal Republic – the fear was and is exceedingly strong that, given the return to a system of non-allied European nation states, sooner or later the potential European hegemonial power would force the weaker European nations to the wall and cut off the influence of the United States.

Nor did the so-called *policy of liberation* which found many protagonists in the early "50's" (in particular in America and the Federal Republic) succeed in bringing about a fundamental change in the system. Already at that time one viewed this policy principally as an instrument of domestic policy which in 1952 was above all predestined to "roll back" the Democrats out of the White House; present research on John Foster Dulles shares this interpretation. Nonetheless, we must not forget that this policy of the Eisenhower administration vis-à-vis Germany was more than mere rhetoric. In the Paris Agreements (*Deutschlandvertrag*) the three big Western powers committed themselves vis-à-vis Germany to no more and no less than a policy which refuted the right to existence of the communist German state created by the Soviet Union and which would have meant – had the goal been realizable – liberating Eastern Germany and rolling back the Soviet Union through a combination of diplomatic pressure and request.

But this alternative also proved to be unrealizable, primarily for three reasons: with good reason, the West rejected any actions which would have threatened peace and also rejected liberation through use of direct force; the Soviet Union was so strong that a strategy of applying diplomatic pressure would have been absurd; Moscow succeeded in resolutely holding together the East European bloc.

Not only these approaches which we have just sketched bogged down. The so-called *détente policy* has not succeeded in creating fundamentally new conditions for a changed European security system either.

Western détente policy was and is heterogeneous. As a conservative program it aims at a modus vivendi which is meant to avoid or master collision, make possible pragmatic and carefully limited partial agreements and so salve the conscience of those Socialists and Liberals who regarded military alliances and systems of deterrence as immoral and atavistic. Many also hoped that in the long run one could bring about changes in the Eastern bloc, but the basic approach of conservative détente policy is defensive.

As a progressive program, détente policy includes those various concepts of Liberals or Socialists which all aim at changing the bipolar security system – to be sure, not overnight but nonetheless fundamentally. Viewed in the short run, even the progressive schools of thought take the status quo as their starting point. Still the system of alliances are to be overcome in the end through a comprehensive policy of smaller and larger steps, whereby internal changes on both sides must go hand in hand. Those concepts proposed and experimented with above all in the late "60's", which could be captioned the "framework of East-West reconciliation" (Brzezinski), a "European peace order" (Brandt), and the restoration of a Europe seen as one single entity, were as a rule oriented towards the progressive view of détente.

The motives, final goals and rhetoric of the conservative and the progressive schools of détente policy thus differ in many ways; with regard to short run policy, however, there were common views which made a compromise between the détente concept of politicians like Kissinger or Pompidou and those of progressives like Brandt or Nenni possible.

The fact is, however, that détente policy as it has been implemented in many variations since Stalin's death has only confirmed the basic assumptions of the conservative schools of détente. The minimum goals set by these schools have been reached for the most part: a certain normalization of the status quo of the political and economic division of Europe; a certain degree of institutionalization of the coexistence and conflict between the systems; improvement in the general climate; decreased threat of war.

However, the basic elements of the security system could not be changed and in view of the policy of the Eastern bloc will not be alterable in the future. The Conference on Security and Cooperation in Europe (CSCE) welcomed by the progressive schools of détente policy as an instrument of continuous change has, for good reason, become an instrument for stabilizing the status quo, an instrument which to a great extent and for good reasons excluded questions of security policy. MBFR has proved to be a "non-starter". If the CSCE and MBFR have any effect at all, it is the paradoxical effect of stabilizing the blocs – i.e., the exact opposite of that to which the politicians advocating dynamic détente aspire. Almost nothing has so consolidated the unstable Western system of the late "60's" as effectively as the multilateralization of détente policy as exhibited in the CSCE and MBFR. They have succeeded in channelling the destabilizing détente-bilateralism of the Western governments – the Americans, British, Germans, to a certain extent the French, and likewise the smaller NATO Partners – in domesticating and fusing these developments into integrated approaches.

It is to a great degree a matter of common agreement among politically responsible elites in the West today that a change in the bloc without risks and based on a consensus which does justice to the respective security interests is not feasible. In this sense progressive détente policy loses a long-term perspective in security policy. It has today reached a bottleneck similar to that which confronted the policy of comprehensive solutions or the policy of liberation of the "50's".

Yet another fundamental approach has proven unrealizable: *the Gaullist concept of partially autonomous security policy* of the European big powers. France could only afford the posture which it has taken since the early "60's" because the military shield of American and British presence in Germany and the German army provided "cover" for such a course. And since the big powers did not have to reckon with corresponding psychological burdens, the French nuclear armament was likewise tolerable in the international political scene. To be sure, the developments in armaments technology in the past years show that the French nuclear weapons would only open minimal additional options for the French government in the case of crisis.

The French approach has remained an isolated case for a number of reasons. Great Britain opted from the very beginning for the NATO concept which since 1962 conceded the British government – thanks to the corresponding clauses in the Nassau Agreement – sovereign powers to dispose over its nuclear weapons in case of crisis. For the Federal Republic, on the other hand, the French approach would have been suicidal; and it would certainly have transcended the possibilities of the smaller Western and Northern European NATO states.

It is by no means unjust if one describes the French concept as parasitic. It depends to a great extent on the security structures which are only maintainable through the output and the sacrifice of sovereignty of other states, in particular the Federal Republic.

It is theoretically conceivable that other Nato states could also choose to rely on such a calculation (such tendencies are visible in the Netherlands and in Denmark). This would not, however, represent a Gaullism of strength but a Gaullism of weakness. In the last analysis France remained isolated with its approach and was unable to change the system as a whole. And whether France actually expected or aspired to such change is questionable in any case. General de Gaulle's rhetoric alone does not provide sufficiently clear insight in the matter.

Another alternative concept – the establishment of a *West European security community* has always remained chimerical. This concept would only then have a practical chance if the United States tolerated the build-up of an eventually autonomous European defense community and were willing to shield this undertaking against Soviet pressure during the long and dangerous period of development. Such a defense community presupposes the establishment of a European Federation – a goal almost as remote as that of the classless society in the countries of the Eastern bloc. It cannot be realized without France and without the Federal republic; but both countries, for different motives, do not wish to involve themselves. Great Britain, which under Heath's government took a relatively positive attitude to this idea, has once again taken a reserved stance. And even if it were fully integrated in the alliance with the United States, and if all institutional prerequisites were fulfilled, a European defense community would imply such immense increases in Western European defense budgets that it would be unattainable even as a long-term security alternative. The idea of a European defense community is like a beautiful woman whom all find attractive but whom no one can possess merely on the strength of this attraction.

Thus in the mid "70's" every one of the "grand designs" has been more or less exhausted. Despite all the striving toward significant alternatives, the existing system remains for the most part intact. In the following pages it remains to be asked whether the concepts sketched here could not – given certain conditions in the future – once again stand in the foreground of interest. Yet any predictions will nonetheless have to be based on the expectation that attempts at pre-planned, coordinated fundamental changes of the previous system have no great chance – a prediction which previous experience would corroborate. An analysis of the future problems of European-American security relations can today with much greater assuredness than would have been possible ten or even five years ago assume that in the medium term no fundamentally new, comprehensive alternatives will be realizable, though they will certainly continue to find advocates in one camp or the other.

This does not, of course, imply that no change can and must ensue in these areas. On the contrary. But they will in all probability be partial changes, as in the past, changes which must respond, with modifications, to the present policy. If, however, these modifications fail to occur, then one cannot exclude the possibility that the supporting foundation of the system will begin to erode.

Gradual changes and the necessary responses: an endless topic! We shall limit ourselves here to those questions which will presumably occupy the center of planning and also of controversy. They are, in part, the old familiar problems which pose themselves again under new conditions, but, in part, also new challenges to which answers must be found. They all are related to one basic state of affairs, which could be described as follows: the European democracies depend upon the stability of the NATO system as a guarantee of their freedom and independence, and this system would not be viable without the full American commitment. This is, to be sure, conventional wisdom. But sometimes there is a grain of truth in it.

From the multitude of constellations let us here extract only five important problem areas:

1. The Permanence and the Credibility of the American Presence in Europe

Can one count on this presence for the next ten or twenty years? Will the American presence in conjunction with the allies be sufficient in terms of strength and quality of equipment to maintain the military balance of power?

Is the US determination to venture extreme risks in defense of Europe sufficiently credible? Or, posed differently, under what conditions would the lastingness and the credibility of this presence be called in question? And finally, what can be undertaken to counteract such tendencies toward erosion?

2. The Goals and Possibilities of the Soviet Union and Their Consequences for the Atlantic Alliance

What does the Soviet Union plan in the medium term and what options does it have? How and where will it employ the instrument of military power in the coming years? What repercussions does its global expansion have on the security situation in Europe? Or, to put it more precisely, will the Soviet Union only further develop its military potential, will it employ this potential only at the diplomatic level outside its hegemonial realm, or must one even fear that it will make concrete use of this potential in respect to Europe? The answers to these questions raise many others. Can NATO continue to live off the myth of deterrence policy or must it prepare itself for defense? If so, in what regions, under which conditions, with which risks and at what costs? As we shall point out in the following, each of these questions is very closely connected with the American willingness to take great risks in Europe in order to avoid even greater security risks. America's willingness is in turn dependent upon the willingness and ability of the West European states to allocate adequate budgetary means and to demonstrate the necessary flexibility for cooperation in armaments and between the armed forces. Can this be expected?

3. The Organizational Concept of the Atlantic Alliance

Is a concept which limits NATO to primarily military questions realistic? Or should and can, rather, all security questions be dealt with collectively in a wider sense? (i.e., détente diplomacy and security policy in tension areas outside the NATO sphere, the direct and indirect security policy aspects of foreign economic policy and the indirectly relevant overlying conditions of American-European economic relations). Is a security policy which operates in various, though mutually coordinated, functional areas (NATO, EC, Summit of 7) appropriate? Or must new institutions be developed which make possible a comprehensive approach? And directly connected: against which threats is Atlantic security policy directed? Is it only directed against the external threat by the Eastern bloc? Is it also meant to prevent communist take-overs within the Western sphere, which are supported only very cautiously from outside, if at all? Or must the circle of possible enemies be extended in the future even farther to include radical developing nations and perhaps also Middle Eastern states which in more or less open cooperation with the Eastern bloc could endanger the future of Western Europe in a great number of different ways? A further conceptual topic area is dependent on the solution of these organizational problems.

4. The Range of the Alliance

Is the traditional delineation as set down in the NATO Treaty still tenable? Tenable in a double sense: on the one hand, when one considers that a new shrinking process has been taking place amongst the NATO members since the mid "70's" which could in the future make it questionable whether certain member states still want to be and can be defended in case of crisis. To put it more concretely, can Central, Western and Northern Europe still be defended in the long run if NATO's southeastern flank deteriorates? What can be done to channel or eliminate tension in the Eastern Mediterranean?

On the other hand, we must consider whether NATO's membership and sphere of influence should not, in fact, be extended. The question of NATO's ties with Spain is raised in this connection, for example. Above all, NATO must decide whether its crisis planning as well as its maritime presence should not finally be extended to those overseas tension zones which could vitally affect the Atlantic world, in particular Western Europe. In what forms could cooperation with friendly states in the Middle East, in South Africa or Latin America be organized, i.e. with those states, which for various reasons neither at the present nor in the future can belong to the alliance? In short: how narrow or how broad must the framework for multilaterally organized Atlantic security policy be set?

5. The Inner Erosion of NATO in Western Europe

Within the NATO sphere three problem complexes in particular could in the future lead to irritation between alliance partners, especially to undesirable repercussions for the United States' willingness to remain in the alliance:

(a) inter-state conflicts involving the danger of war between alliance partners (for example Turkey and Greece or in certain respects the Iceland fishing rights conflict);

(b) deep-seated political differences and domestic crises within individual

European states in the alliance which have repercussions for the security situation and organization of the alliance as a whole (for example Portugal; further developments in Italy; and possibly France's development from 1978 onwards);

(c) the erosion of defense capability due to insufficient financial and organizational efforts to maintain strong armed forces.

Each of these strains on the alliance is in itself hard to predict and will in one way or another have repercussions for all other problem complexes. Needless to say they are all interrelated. Crises, changes and innovations in the individual area influence each other reciprocally.

The Europeans' Nightmare: Is US Commitment to Europe Lasting and Credible?

From the very beginning the shadow of doubt as to the lastingness and credibility of American presence has hung over the Atlantic alliance.

When the United States together with its war allies defeated the Third Reich, it was not geared to remain in Europe after the victory for a longer period of time. Even an internationalist like President Roosevelt pleased Marshal Stalin when he stated on 5 February 1945 in the Lividia Palace in Yalta: "I can get the people and Congress to cooperate fully for peace, but not to keep an army in Europe for a long time. Two years would be the limit."[1] To be sure, in the latter half of the "40's" and in the "great debate" of 1951 the force of postwar neo-isolationism was broken; but the return to a modified concept of "fortress America" could never be excluded as a conceivable option.

European statesmen with broad historical perspective have always skeptically assumed that the self-sufficiency of the great continental power was, as it were, the natural basic attitude of the USA and that its presence in Europe would sooner or later come to an end. Chancellor Adenauer, for example, was constantly plagued by this worry. His bold European policy in the "50's" as well as the German-French bilateralism under de Gaulle can be understood as alternative concepts in case of American withdrawal.[2]

It is not really the isolationist tendencies in the United States which are astonishing;[3] on the contrary, it is amazing that, despite much criticism, the willingness to station strong armed forces in Central Europe since the "great debate" in 1951 has so far been able to assert itself so clearly.

After the great controversy over the Mansfield Resolution, the situation appears to have stabilized for the foreseeable future, but certainly not indefinitely. In any case Americans have today for the most part recognized that the presence of the 7th Army equipped with nuclear weapons in Germany and of the 6th Fleet in the Mediterranean fulfils to a high degree political-psychological functions. It simply cannot be overlooked that the Soviet Union is the potential European hegemonial power. Without the presence of American military units the tendency to arrange oneself in good time with one's future lord and master would be irresistible in many corners of Western Europe. One cannot, for example, overlook the fact that the relatively "soft" policy of the Federal Republic vis-à-vis the Soviet Union in 1970/71 was conceived against the backdrop of the Mansfield Resolution.[4]

The psychological-political effect of US military presence does not limit itself to those regions in which US armed forces are stationed or could operate. It radiates into the peripheries as well (Norway, Finland, and Denmark in the North; Austria in Central Europe; Yugoslavia in the Mediterranean region).

Whereas in the past the US military presence tended to be seen primarily in the light of its political-psychological stabilizing function, the aspect of its actual fighting power has come again into the field of attention in recent years. As long as the myth of deterrence strategy was accepted without reflection the consideration whether considerably fewer armed forces would not possibly have the same effect was logical. The psychological-political problem of reduction would then essentially consist in presenting this process as deftly as possible (for example, as part of an East-West agreement on balanced troop reduction), so as to avoid a panic reaction on the part of the European democracies affected. One may well doubt whether even the most tactful presentation could completely avoid the shock and the policy of adaption to the Soviet line which would ensue. But in recent years planning has had to accustom itself – much more directly than in the optimistic early "70's" – to the idea that a convincing fighting strength is not only irreplaceable in the medium term but is, indeed, a central component of this presence.

In this connection the question as to equipment and strategy is raised: in particular the question as to the US nuclear strategy in Europe – a problem almost as old as the hills. We do not intend to recapitulate here the endless arguments for and against the *rationale of escalation*, about *threshold* and *pause*. At any rate, experts agree that in the case of extensive military action the time span between the first great battles between conventional armed forces and the threat or the deployment of nuclear weapons will be very brief.[5] If the use of nuclear weapons were not credibly threatened as actually demonstrated, then scenarios could unroll, such as those sketched by Drew Middleton in his study "Can America Win the Next War?":

Soviet armored and mechanized infantry divisions, moving in a week or ten days to the Channel ports and overrunning the Ruhr, most of Northern Germany, Belgium and the Netherlands would find themselves in a predicament similar to that of the German armies in 1940. . . . The fighting is likely to end . . . with the Russians ruling most of Western Europe and with the Americans, perhaps with Britain as an outpost, perhaps not, concentrating on a Fortress America on which the next phase in the duel will be based . . .[6]

Whether the USA would employ nuclear weapons in the case of conflict is not completely predictable. It is important, first of all, that a certain probability of this cannot be ruled out. But the fundamental prerequisite for the maintenance of this probability is the 7th Army being equipped with tactical nuclear weapons. In this sense, substantial troop reductions, East-West agreement over a "no-first-use" clause, nuclear-free zones and the like would be counterproductive given the present state of defense technology and would not enhance but rather endanger security.

Within the limitations of such a brief sketch we cannot discuss in detail those cases in which the implementation of American military power would likewise be necessary, for example, in the case of military action in Norway or in the Mediterranean region. It is essential to realize in this context that a *lasting American presence* alone is not sufficient if in case of crises the willingness and capacity for *effective action* is lacking. The strategy of flexible response so convincingly advocated by the United States stands or falls with the capacity to actually vigorously carry through limited military action.

Under what conditions could the desire for reduced engagements,[7] latently or openly present in America today, or the tendency to question the reliability of effective American defense readiness be enhanced? Observed theoretically, a number of conceivable constellations which could lead to such a negative development can be recognized.

1. Discontent with the European alliance partners

The future most certainly holds just as many causes for transatlantic discontent in store as the past, perhaps more. Differences amongst the alliance partners (e.g., Greece-Turkey), economic tensions with the European Community or a combination of differences over economic and security policy with individual allies (paradigm: the sale of reactors by France or the Federal Republic involving proliferation risks), supply of weapons by European states to certain countries against the will of the USA, systemic crises in individual allied countries with irritating repercussions (paradigm:

Portugal 1974–1976; in the more distant future perhaps Italy or after 1978 in France); differences over Middle East policy and cooperation during Middle East crises (for example, the crisis in the alliance in the fall and winter of 1973/74); an indolent attitude of European states concerning military burden sharing; differences of opinion over the most effective détente policy.

Much speaks for the probability that these and similar problems which are by no means new will be handled through cooperation in the future as well, without grave damage to the alliance. But this is by no means certain. It is thoroughly conceivable that irritation with individual European states and their policy in the most various areas could accumulate and lead to an agonizing reappraisal of American presence with far-reaching repercussions for the security system as a whole.

The alternative to the present system would with relative certainty not involve an imminent subjection of Western Europe or at least Central Europe to Soviet power. Various forms of "Finlandization" would be imaginable, for example, a precarious, armed neutrality similar to the Swedish model. The increasing alienation of the USA with a parallel increase in Eastern predominance could ensue gradually, so that face-saving institutional arrangements for such a change in orientation could be found. And there would certainly be no lack of short-sighted politicians and journalists on both sides who would defend such measures as being not only not dangerous but, indeed, constructive. One need not even point to the armistice agreements in Vietnam or to the appeasement policy of the late 30's to be reminded that unstable systems only finally collapse in crisis situations – and such situations are bound to occur sooner or later.

2. The costs of American commitment

In the past, the inner-American controversy over reduction of armed forces in Europe has always been seen primarily under the aspect of the cost of stationing troops. The changed monetary constellation has eliminated this permanent bone of contention in American-German relations. Today the realization that a withdrawal of troops stationed in Europe would not lead to any substantial savings appears to have taken hold in the United States.

A new discussion over decisive reductions in Europe would hence probably involve the demand not only to bring the units back to the United States but to dissolve them entirely. American critics of costly military expenditures already recognized some time ago that the share of general purpose forces in military expenditures by far exceeds the share of strategic components. If radical savings seem desirable, a quantitative reduction of the 7th Army and the 6th Fleet would be unavoidable, since both lay claims to a lion's share of such expenditures. That under the present conditions this would be a unilateral measure with destabilizing effects on the entire system is obvious. It is, therefore, questionable whether the cost argument alone can lead to a fundamental change of course in the future.

On the whole it was astonishing that US political leadership succeeded in fully maintaining, in fact, in increasing military presence in Europe even under the most unfavorable conditions of the past recession as well as the aftermath of the Vietnam trauma. Why should it then not continue to be possible under psychologically more favorable conditions?

At the present and in the foreseeable future the American determination to maintain a strong military presence in Europe is quite convincing. Yet no one can guarantee that this attitude will remain unchanged in the middle or long run. Nor will one be able to overlook the fact that any attempt at drastic savings measures in this area would meet with weighty economic counter arguments (securing jobs in armaments industry and in the armed forces) and, on top of this, would have to overcome the perseverance and longevity of the military bureaucracy.

A future reduction would probably make itself particularly noticeable in a negative sense if key European states were to engage themselves in a demonstrative military policy of calculated "under-insurance" in security matters in order to save costs, whereby the Federal Republic would occupy a key position.

3. American-Soviet bilateralism

The fear that, with an eye to its global interests or primarily for domestic motives, the United States would be willing to accept bilateral American-Soviet arrangements is a well-known nightmare of European statesmen. Cases where American admistrations have succumbed to the temptation are as easy to find[8] as counter-examples which demonstrate that good and well-presented arguments from the allies were not without effect.

The sensitive points which might become controversial in the future are well-known:
- quantitative and qualitative concessions in the MBFR negotiations;
- the direct or indirect inclusion of land-based FBS and comparable carrier systems of the *Bundeswehr* in American-Soviet agreements;
- the decision to give in to Soviet pressure to include the cruise missiles in the SALT agreement, although the significance of this weapons system could be great for the self-defense of the European states;[9]

– agreements over a substantial thinning-out of tactical nuclear weapons in Central Europe.

Although the influence of the arms control bureaucracy and its associated scientists has always represented an important component in American security policy, there are signs that, due to technological developments, the arms control approach is moving increasingly into a dead-end street. To this extent, this realm of American-Soviet bilateralism – today still so vital – will at a future time possibly become less important. This would, in turn, make one chronic irritation in the American-European relationship more bearable.

On the whole the weight and importance of the European states for American global policy is so great that future administrations will most likely withstand the temptation to practice American-Soviet bilateralism at the cost of its European allies.

In all probability such tendencies would only gain footing if the European governments were at odds amongst themselves or were weakened and were themselves under the spell of an appeasement policy which traded short-term advantages for middle and long-term risks.

It is unnecessary to say that a troop reduction arising as a direct consequence of Soviet pressure or military action would most dramatically shake the equilibrium in Europe. That reactions such as those observable in the end phase of the Vietnam war are also imaginable in relation to Europe and the Middle East is obvious; but all reflection over such constellations is extremely speculative.

How these and other conceivable possibilities for development can be counteracted can likewise only be described in most general terms – based on observations stemming from 30 years of East-West tension and European-American security endeavors.

There is no universal recipe for mastering the manifold differences between the allies. Decisive is, however, the realization that American presence represents a *conditio sine qua non* for the long-term chances of survival for the European democracies. Priorities must be set accordingly on both sides of the Atlantic, not only in relation to the USA but between the European states as well. Patience, a feeling for the interdependence of the problems and a permanently intermeshed dialogue at the most various levels will continue to be indispensable. The "costs" argument which will probably play a considerable role in the future as well can only be neutralized through a willingness of the European allies to play their part in fair burden-sharing.

In the last analysis there is no sure prophylactic cure for the temptation of American-Soviet bilateralism at the cost of the allies. In a multipolar system the temptation for a power of the stature of America to engage in neo-

Bismarckian balance of power policies is great, as the example of Nixon and Kissinger shows. One should, however, not forget that European states have also played with the concept of traditional balance of power policy at the cost of the other allies; de Gaulle is a classic example. It is unnecessary to point out that a multilateral alliance in which the leading power or one of the other big powers takes up the classical game of multipolar balance of power politics will be undermined. In this respect the post-Kissinger era provides a chance for a new start. Not even a world power like the USA can dance at two weddings simultaneously; it cannot see itself as the leading power in an anti-Soviet alliance on the one hand and on the other as a great power who plays the game of balance of power politics if necessary against its own allies.

The institutionalization of multilateral Western détente policy, permanent consultations at all levels, and Europe's foregoing the possibility of itself practicing provocative bilateralism can all work to counteract such tendencies.

If one considers one of the greatest long-term dangers for the US presence in Europe to be an armed conflict in the European area or in the Middle East in which the USA would become or would have to become involved, then it is only rational to undertake all possible endeavors not to let such situations arise in the first place. In the last 20 years most European statesmen have distinguished themselves in their preference for pussyfooted cautiousness rather than vigorous action; in this respect they hardly need tutoring.

The Permanent Worry of the Alliance: What are the Plans of the Soviet Union?

If appearances do not deceive, Western public opinion's evaluation of Soviet policy is undergoing profound changes at the moment, through a process of reassessment. The interpretation which prevailed in the last ten years that East and West were moving out of the epoch of the Cold War into an era characterized by better understanding and closer cooperation, meets with increasing skepticism. Instead one must accept the fact that Western democracies are only at the beginning of an era of successful global Soviet expansion. Even if one does not fail to recognize that the formation of a new system of independent post-colonial states and the problems of development still represent central determinants of the international system, one can no longer ignore the fact that the neo-imperialism of the Soviet world power will in the future be one of the decisive determinants of international politics.

If one analyzes the present goals and military options of the Soviet Union against the background of this process, the second half of the "70's" offers a fairly clear picture.[10]

The new realities in the constellation can be sketched as follows:

1. The improvement of the offensive capacity of the Warsaw Pact, in particular of the Soviet Union, exceeds all defense needs. This applies not only to the well-known quantitative reinforcement of the Soviet armed forces in Central Europe but also, and above all, to their qualitative improvement: the introduction of a third generation of combat airplanes which could in case of war pose a serious threat to the Western sovereignty of the air over NATO territory; shift in armaments from medium range missiles aimed at Western Europe over to mirved missiles; the impressive increase in air transport capacity and in general the increased capacity for spontaneous *Blitzkrieg*.

Pessimists, such as the Belgian General Robert Close,[11] Drew Middleton, or politicians with a sober but not necessarily catastrophic view, like Senators Nunn and Bartlett, fear that the superiority in the conventional field makes the option of a comprehensive conventional attack more attractive. In this event they could not exclude the possibility of an occupation of large portions of Northwestern and Western Europe in a short span of time given exclusively conventional defense by the West.[12] Moderately skeptical German ex-NATO Commanders like General Ulrich de Maizière or General Steinhoff avoid going into detail as to time and geography in designing their scenarios, but they agree that without resorting to nuclear weapons the front cannot be defended for long against a comprehensive attack.

Of course the precarious situation is not quite new. But the rapid qualitative improvements on the side to the Warsaw Pact, on the one hand, and the fact that this concentration of armed forces capable of *Blitzkrieg* action occurs in an era of détente, on the other, is unsettling. Optimists in the West, such as George Kennan, still interpret this as an expression of the Soviet tendency to over-insure themselves in military strategy, and point by way of explanation to the trauma of 1941.[13] But this argument becomes increasingly unconvincing. It is more and more difficult to contradict with conviction those voices which point out that the time for a dogmatization of the strategy of nuclear deterrence has passed. Conventional military action in Europe can no longer be excluded as totally impossible; the heyday of the old, respected theory of the decreasing importance of military violence seems to be passé in Europe as well.

Moreover, one is continually astonished to discover that in general public debate the capacity of the East to employ nuclear weapons demonstratively or in surprise attack is very much commonly repressed. The classic scenarios of Russian military strategy in the First and Second World Wars still dominate the public imagination to a large extent.

Still not even today's unsettling developments can wipe away the memory of the previous maxims of Soviet behavior which has as yet always been characterized by a certain cautiousness and the attempt to avoid direct confrontations with USA. However, this argument is only valid in a qualified sense, since the American-Soviet power balance is shifting in favor of the Soviet Union at many levels.

2. The Soviet Union's conventional options have increased, above all, because nuclear strategic parity is by now a reality. The debate today centers around the question whether parity still exists or whether the Soviet Union does not already enjoy a superiority in certain areas of strategic forces.

As far as the chances of conventional defense in Europe are concerned, this would imply that in the case of a catastrophe one would have to posit scenarios involving limited warfare, regardless of whether it is carried out with conventional forces or with nuclear weapons.

To be sure, it is still true that nuclear escalation cannot be calculated. Yet this incalculability is not only a problem for the opponent but also for the Western European states which depend upon the American atomic umbrella. A certain "fear of escalation" (Schlesinger) in the USA is understandable; but it also allows for a certain inner decay in deterrence strategy. Skeptical observers regard the so-called "security guarantee" as little more than the preparedness of the USA to conduct a limited conventional war or a war with tactical nuclear weapons on the continent, if necessary, whereby the territory of the Soviet Union would be avoided in the counter-attack.

3. This negative trend in Central Europe which also predominates in Northern Europe, is taking shape against the background of a considerably altered geo-strategic constellation. To be sure, the Soviet Union has been trying to carry out overseas expansion with a variety of instruments since the beginning of the Khrushchev era (since 1955 in the Middle East, since 1960 in Africa and in the areas bordering on the Indian Ocean, and since the early 60's even in the Caribbean area). But not until recently did it have the necessary military capacity at its disposal to make possible a policy of global expansion (overseas fleet, air transport capacity and geo-strategic positions).[14] In many respects, the Soviet Union has copied the United States' successful policy of expansion which since World War II has moved into many positions vacated by the European colonial powers.

So far the Soviet Union has operated quite cautiously and made use of the classic tools of military aid, the diplomatic exploitation of regional opposites, military base policy, indirect influencing via other dependent states such as

Cuba, the GDR or through nationalist organizations in Africa. The recent infiltration in the decaying substance of the former Portuguese overseas empire also follows the familiar basic pattern, although the intervention of Cuban armed forces shows that the Soviet overseas instrumentarium in the meanwhile allows for the implementation of military force without risk. In any case, Moscow already has at its disposal strategic positions and possibilities for influence which neither Wilhelmenian Germany nor Hitler's Germany even dared to dream of in their bid for world power. And the fear is not unfounded that we have reached a state in which the Politburo could see itself increasingly tempted to view the occasional direct use of armed forces as productive and relatively free of risk.

These realities also create a new security situation for Europe. Above all, the vulnerability of Western European oil imports, but also in the long run of sea transport in general, no longer exclude the possibility that in a crisis the Soviet Union would directly or indirectly put pressure on the Western democracies from overseas. Given the acts of military aggression in Europe and today's situation one still cannot exclude the possibility that a nuclear escalation spiral might be set in motion; whereas a direct or indirect implementation of Soviet military potential overseas might not cross the nuclear threshold but nonetheless paralyze Western Europe.

These insights find expression to an increasing degree even in the augmentation of the Federal Republic's official security policy which originally had been related almost exclusively to Europe.[15] France and Great Britain, on the other hand, have always been more aware of these interconnections.[16]

4. And finally, after a good decade of Sino-Soviet tensions we recognize that the effect of the military-strategic diversion was considerably less than had been assumed at the outset.[17] Since China's efforts in the military field are on the whole not very impressive, not much should change in this respect in the near future. The calculation that Soviet predominance in Central Europe can be balanced through a multipolar balance of power diplomacy has not brought any impressive results, at least not in the narrowly defined military-strategic sense. One reason was America's hesitation to give its support of China at least equal status to that of American-Soviet détente.

This new situation has far-reaching consequences for the European-American relationship. In this light, all optimistic notions that the Western European states will one day be able to defend themselves without the USA appear illusory. The military presence of the American forces and the strategic backing from the United States are more indispensable than ever. Even given the immediate creation of a European Federation which would then drastically raise the defense expenditures of its member states (both points are completely Utopian), full American presence would continue to be unavoidable for a long transitional period in view of the rapid increase in Soviet armament. This is particularly valid if one realistically assumes that the present confederate system of the Atlantic alliance will still represent the basic structure of the European security system in the "80's".

The option of a partial autonomy of the European nuclear powers, France and Great Britain, is also becoming increasingly less credible. Soviet progress in the nuclear strategic field puts the deterrence systems of these states in a relative context.[18]

Even if one assumes that the Soviet Union will continue its course of moderation in the future as well and one rejects a foreign policy which orients itself in theory to the worst of all possible cases, the military presence of the USA in its present strength is indispensable if a psychological erosion in Western Europe is to be avoided, erosion which could lead in the direction of "Finlandization" or to collapse during a crisis.[19] Any reduction of the American commitment would necessitate efforts in Western Europe which cannot realistically be expected, or which could only increase the factors of insecurity – as, for example, a quantitative and qualitative strengthening of the *Bundeswehr*. We must, in fact, consider whether the US forces in the European region should not be increased.

The dependency on the United States is not only increasing in Europe with regard to the power balance. The above mentioned possible direct or indirect threats to Western Europe's energy supply or its maritime traffic likewise would indicate America as the only potential protective power. Only the USA has naval forces and maritime positions at its disposal which could match those of the Soviet Union. If one envisions certain crisis scenarios in the Persian Gulf area, one can at first have a certain degree of confidence in Iran as a force of order; but within the NATO alliance in this area in the last analysis only the USA has sufficient mobile armed forces to intervene if necessary and to successfully carry out limited military action.

This not only brings up the question of crisis planning for regions outside the present NATO sphere, which shall be discussed later. At the same time it shows that the pillars of the so-called American security guarantee for Europe are not merely its military presence on the continent and the capacity for nuclear strategic deterrence. Taken as a whole, Western Europe is still just as dependent on the United States in questions of security as it was in the early "50's".

This often discussed asymmetry of interdependence in the security field will probably persist in the coming years. Nor is it out of the question that we will in the future experience paradoxical situations similar to those which arose during the oil crisis in 1973/74. At that time it was the United States which, much less affected by the embargo, tended towards a more energetic policy of confrontation, while the European states, more vulnerable to blackmail, tried to operate with more reserve and moderation, although they in particular had good reason to defend themselves. States with the means for military action are, indeed, more apt to consider violent options in crisis situations or at least to threaten with such possibilities. States which are more dependent in matters of security policy must restrict themselves to negotiation.

On the other hand, the successful Soviet breakthrough overseas has given the key alliances with Europe and Japan new value from the American perspective. After all, vast areas are controlled by the USA with the help of these states. The industrial potential of the Western democracies still far exceeds that of the Soviet Union (about 65 percent of the world production capacity and 70 percent of trade). This tool can be implemented at the diplomatic level to balance growing Soviet military power and its improved geo-strategic possibilities. Without close European cooperation in the framework of the alliance an anti-Soviet balance of power policy, which is still feasible today, would not be very promising under worsened conditions in the future. Thus, American self-interest also speaks for a common policy in overseas crisis areas, after the original Kissinger concept of American-Soviet entente has largely failed as a means for stabilizing the system.

So far NATO's military policy has only brought forth pragmatic answers to the changes we have sketched here. On the whole, the basic elements of the Atlantic security community are characterized by a considerable degree of stability. They changed just a little in the past détente era as they are now changing at the beginning of the new era which is taking shape at present. The tendency toward unilateral reduction of the 7th Army disappeared and likewise the hopes for risk-free reductions of the European armed forces as they had been articulated in the détente climate of the early "70's". In their stead, efforts are being intensified to shift from a no longer completely credible deterrence concept to a military strategy which would if necessary open up broader options for conventional defense. Considerations as to how well the alliance would stand the test of a *Blitzkrieg* in terms of organization and weapons technology are the focus of attention.[20]

It is striking how little today is still expected from the proposed solutions of the détente period. The normalization approach which was typical of the détente policy of the late "60's" and early "70's" has not paid good dividends in the realm of military security. In reality the Soviet Union used the era of détente to achieve military superiority and to improve systematically its positions overseas. The MBFR approach has also led to a dead end and could at best bring about a short-term improvement of climate – should any agreements be reached at all in the next few years.

Those impulses with which the European states, and the USA as well, responded to doubts as to the American nuclear guarantee at the beginning of the 60's cannot be observed at present. The non-nuclear states in the alliance no longer plan to change fundamentally their situation of vulnerability to nuclear blackmail and their total dependence upon the strategic and tactical nuclear deterrence of the USA by building up their own nuclear capacity in a newly-conceived MLF framework. Not even the European nuclear powers are undertaking greater efforts to counteract the relative weakness of their potential through bold decisions for a cost-saving common nuclear deterrence and to close the modernization gap within the Western European framework or – as in the case of France – through association with the USA. Resignation has apparently set in for all those involved; the financial and political costs of a convincing independent nuclear deterrent appear too high. A shift in orientation in this realm could only be expected in the wake of dramatic developments in the East-West relationship or if the employment of nuclear weapons by one or more of the present nuclear powers were to create a completely new psychological situation for the non-nuclear powers.

All this allows for the assumption that the gradual changes in the Eastern camp in the coming years will not move either the United States or the Western Europeans to make fundamental changes in their security policy.

The Organizational Concept for New Dimensions of Atlantic Security Policy:
Integration or Pragmatic Flexibility?

The statement that "the political, military, and economic problems in Atlantic relations . . . are coupled together by reality"[21] hints at the interdependence of security issues and other areas, but offers no practicable solution. Kissinger, who mentioned these interconnections with welcome clarity, himself quickly became aware of this when his initiative for a comprehensive review of American-European relations in Europe met with cold reserve. In reality the European cabinets shied away from this comprehensive approach above all out of fear that the USA would exploit Europe's dependency in security questions in order to obtain concessions in those areas which are not directly related to military security. Nothing has changed in this reserved stance since the tedious negotiations leading to the Declaration of Ottawa – not without good reasons, whereby we do not only mean reasons of negotiation tactics:

(a) Foreign economic policy, military strategy, foreign policy vis-à-vis the countries of the Middle East and the Third World are each such complex phenomena in themselves that they can hardly be forced into the framework of an integrated dialogue. It is impossible to imagine at present what kind of institution could make such a total alliance policy on the part of the Western democracies possible.

(b) The fact that any attempt at a concerted economic policy would have to include participants from outside the Atlantic region (in particular, Japan) likewise makes an institutionally flexible approach necessary.

(c) The existence of the institutions of the European Community also proves to be an obstacle; for they can, on the one hand, no longer be excluded from the transatlantic economic dialogue and, on the other hand, are for good reason still unable to play a pronounced role in security policy.

(d) And finally, France still hesitates to engage herself in an integrated military policy; France also shies away from Atlantic coordination of economic diplomacy because in France's opinion this would involve advantages primarily for American hegemonial power (and for Germany).

In reality the period since 1973/74 has demonstrated that it is not the institutional link which is decisive, but the basic conceptual attitude of the governments. If the governments recognize the interdependence of the problems and behave accordingly, then it is perfectly possible to treat the individual problem complexes in various institutional frameworks (within NATO, in summit meetings of the European-Atlantic big powers including Japan, within the OECD, between the EC and the USA, bilaterally, etc.). It is certainly not easy, but it is possible and in any event more promising than any attempt to build up a complex apparatus for coordinated multilateral consultation and coordination, or to rely upon summit diplomacy, the PR value of which usually stands in an inverted ratio to its actual output.

When it finally becomes clear that the European-American relationship cannot be shaped in the spirit of multipolar balance of power politics but rather in the spirit of partnership, then progress can be made even with numerous heterogenous mechanisms.

Even if the conscious avoidance of an institutional linking of the problem areas brings certain tactical advantages for those European states organized in the EC in their relationship with the USA, a concept of *separate functional areas* is, in the last analysis, also in the American interest. For the United

States can hardly desire that institutions which functioned successfully in the coordination of the respective policies in the last half decade be overburdened by the inclusion of new problems. This would apply to the European Community which is not yet mature enough to deal with military questions. This would also apply to NATO which functioned quite satisfactorily in the military field in the "70's" but whose institutions would be hopelessly overburdened if the attempt were made to transfer to these institutions coordination of policy vis-à-vis the OPEC cartel, for example, or consultations and decisions in other questions of foreign economic policy with relevance to security policy.

Nor could complicated new institutions offer any solutions to those questions of security policy which are of a more narrow military nature. In this context, the experience of the last 28 years testifies in favor of maintaining the tried and tested organizational framework of NATO and to make modifications only where new tasks are likewise of a primarily military nature.

To be sure, the Preamble and Article 2 of the NATO Treaty describe a field of competency of the alliance which by far transcends the military constellation in the narrow sense; but so far NATO as an institution has only been useful in coordinating such matters of "high policy" which were at the same time primarily military questions: for example, in passing the resolution to establish and further develop an integrated military organization and miltary strategy, in deciding to introduce tactical nuclear weapons and in attempting to realize the MLF concept in the first half of the "60's". According to the assumption of the Harmel Report, NATO has, indeed, been used as a vehicle for developing multilateral détente diplomacy, but seen in the light of day this image has only taken hold where either genuine questions of military security were involved (i.e., the MBFR complex), where, given a specific constellation, a multilateralization of détente diplomacy appeared opportune (in coupling MBFR, getting CSCE rolling and the decisions in the field of *Deutschlandpolitik* in the early "70's") or where other coordinating bodies had done considerable preliminary work, as in the case of European Political Cooperation (EPC) during the CSCE negotiations.

Those who would like to burden NATO with the tasks of "high policies" should realize that even in its days of glory countless basic questions of great import in security policy were negotiated primarily in bodies outside the alliance. This applies to *Deutschlandpolitik* and the Berlin question, to the détente bilateralism of the "60's" and early "70's", and to many crisis decisions of the United States. As a center of planning, opinion formation, and decision-making for primarily non-military matters, the NATO institutions are not at all suitable.

This will continue to apply in the future to the questions of European Atlantic economic diplomacy. The necessary apparatus is for the most part lacking. It would be impossible to restrict the circle of participants artificially to the NATO states. Nor are the NATO organs suited to confer or indeed decide upon the strategy of the allies in response to those economic crises of individual partners in the alliance which have far-reaching effects on security issues.

A harmonization of policy (including foreign economic policy) in overseas tension zones (Middle East, South Africa, Persian Gulf) could in principle be realized within the organs of the alliance, but the interests of the USA and the individual Western European states are so difficult to synchronize in this field that the inclusion of these questions in the NATO framework would probably have a more destructive than integrating effect. A primarily functional military alliance simply does not stand up well when overburdened with disfunctional tasks.

The question then, of course, poses itself: Where should the coordination of planning in those problem areas be located which have obvious importance for security policy but which cannot be handled from a primarily military perspective? A glance at present practice shows the direction which such considerations must take.

Questions of basic principle can and must indeed be cleared at summit meetings of the major Atlantic powers. This may well evoke resentment on the part of the smaller partners in the alliance but that is to a certain degree unavoidable given the present situation. Certain individual problems could be dealt with in *ad hoc* working groups. The Group of Four, for example, which is concerned with the German problem, has done efficient work. The allies were informed through NATO channels.

On the whole it will be of secondary importance which institution is associated with such ad hoc working groups (for example OECD, coordinating committees of the UN ambassadors, coordinating committees of the CSCE ambassadors, etc.). More essential would be the organizational feedback loops to the NATO security apparatus on the one hand and the national decision-making bodies on the other.

However, in recent years there has also been a whole series of military questions where planning and decision by consensus have not as yet been feasible within the alliance. The problem of a regional extension of emergency planning for the case of war is an example, like crisis planning which primarily affects only a few of the partners in the alliance. Wherever

individual governments for domestic reasons or because of greatly diverging
foreign policy strategies fail to fulfil functions in the planning or the
realization of tasks important to a majority of the allied partners, or in cases
where practical considerations speak against the participation of all NATO
states (as, for example, in the case of NPG) the establishment of flexible
working groups could be an appropriate solution. Suggestions such as those
made recently by Johan Jørgen Holst[22] for establishing such study groups
should be taken into consideration here alongside the long accepted practice
of bilateral and trilateral regulations of certain questions with the tacit
toleration of the alliance partners (as, for example, in the American-German,
or in the American-Turkish-German relationship). As a rule this kind of
flexibility favors the strongest partner, the USA, which is logically involved
in almost all constellations involving crisis planning outside the sphere of
competence set down by a treaty. But this still is to be preferred to a situation
in which in a crisis the United States, as the only power capable of action,
makes the decisions and then confronts the entire alliance with accomplished
facts. Precisely these new tasks and the new threats which grow out of the
Soviet Union's intensified overseas expansion must be met to a large extent
with such a flexible apparatus.

This flexible approach is particularly important for cooperation with
friendly states outside the NATO region. In such cases only direct ties with
an alliance through bilateral treaties and agreements has helped: a classic
example is the American-Spanish security treaty. A complex network of
bilateral agreements on military assistance can also serve as a substitute for
a full membership which would be objectionable for practical or ideological
considerations. The bilateral bridges have in the past primarily been built by
the United States and Great Britain. In part France also assures a certain
security presence of the West even today in West Africa.

But since all West European governments have realized that their security
stands or falls with "Europe's Oil Tanks" on the Persian Gulf, the question
of intensified cooperation with friendly powers in the problem zones poses
itself more forcefully than before. Even outside Great Britain there is more
understanding today for the British "East of Suez" strategy of the past.

At any rate we can no longer expect the United States in the long run to
secure Europe's vital interests in these areas in the case of crises and to
concern themselves with crisis planning singlehandedly. And we will have to
recognize that despite all partnerly cooperation, interests and evaluations of
the situation can differ drastically. This all speaks in favor of a more intense
involvement of the Western European NATO partners in planning and
coordination with respect to these areas.[23]

Due to the ideological sensitivity of some Western European NATO states commitments of the alliance *in toto* are not conceivable, whereas bilateral agreements or the activity of flexible working groups of alliance partners would be. This would apply to relations with Spain or Iran as well as the particularly controversial question of a certain degree of security policy cooperation with South Africa[24] (and in the not too distant future perhaps with Brazil and Argentina) in matters of security policy.

It is a matter of common knowledge that the West European states depend primarily on the instruments of foreign economic policy and diplomacy in maintaining their security interests overseas. This should not change in the future. But the instruments of diplomacy and foreign economic policy which are normally quite useful in stabilizing and exerting influence often prove to be dull weapons in acute crisis situations. New forms of crisis planning are thus absolutely indispensable.

In any case, cooperation within the alliance must gear itself to an increasing degree to the fact that domestic variables within the individual partner states and the pressure on each partner to practice diplomacy with individual nuances make coordinated action of the alliance vis-à-vis the outside world more difficult. Under these circumstances Western Europe cannot afford either solitary American activity (with destructive repercussions for the alliance) or the renunciation of all concrete crisis planning.

In this context only an approach which combines an indispensable optimum of information and opportunities for consultation between *all* alliance members with an indispensable minimum of group formation and concrete preparation amongst a limited group of the alliance partners can be effective. Since, given the variety of questions to be dealt with, the groups will vary in their respective composition, the negative repercussions of such a procedure for cooperation in the alliance should be nipped in the bud. It is unnecessary to say that preference should always be given to integrated planning procedures and that in many cases they are absolutely indispensable. But whenever they do not appear feasible, and wherever the risks of inactivity are great, a more flexible procedure must be chosen. In any event, for the future of US cooperation with Western Europe much depends on the solution which will be found with regard to these constellations.

Systemic crises within NATO states involving the danger of extension of influence or, indeed, a coming to power of Communist parties, represents a particularly sensitive problem. Those governments which observe with trepidation the advances of strong but legally operating Communist parties in their own countries will make sure that the alliance does not discuss or plan any sanctions or other measures. Even in the case of a civil war intervention by the alliance would be a double-edged sword, not lastly because of the consequences for the mood of public opinion in the states involved. Since NATO – in the interest of its own functional capacity of an uncomplicated American-European relationship – is working primarily as a military alliance, emergency planning by NATO with regard to one of its members could be interpreted as intervention which can obviously not be allowed – except in the case of war between East and West. Nonetheless, certain situations are conceivable in which consultation and coordination of common measures vis-à-vis a member state are necessary. But such consultations cannot take place within the framework of the alliance. The agreements in the framework of the EPC vis-à-vis Portugal or the discussions at the summit meeting in Bermuda with regard to Italy were good examples for the usefulness of such an approach which indirectly also stabilized the security situation.

With respect to the domestic policies of the individual states as well as to the ideological orientation of the member governments, NATO is a heterogeneous alliance. Thus it should avoid endangering the functioning of its integrated military organization in case of a crisis by exerting political influence on one of its members.

However, this certainly does not imply that the alliance partners should remain idle. For if the European states place any value in linking the USA as an active world power with their interests, then those of them which are capable of action and wish to act must not leave the leading power to its own devices in crises management. They will have to develop methods and ism had burned itself out once and for all in the fires of World War II. Such phenomena continue to threaten with shake-ups.

The New Task of the Atlantic Security Community: Crisis Management Overseas

From the very beginning NATO has understood itself as an alliance whose major task was to protect Western Europe from the Soviet Union. The threat posed by the ground forces of the Warsaw Pact occupied the foreground in this context. The importance of securing the flanks and the peripheries of the alliance (the North Sea, Norway, access to the Baltic, and the Eastern Mediterranean) has, to be sure, always been recognized,[25] but the alliance partners considered this to be primarily a task of those partner states in the respective regions, or of the USA, and (until the late "60's") of Great Britain.

It is well known that beyond the Mediterranean peripheries, further sea and land areas must also be included in security planning. Above all SACLANT pointed this out on various occasions, without any consequences, however, for strategic planning and for the sphere of competency of the alliance.

The continental European states take quite a comfortable stance in this respect. They take the US presence for granted and are not prepared to involve themselves in a coordinated approach to the peripheries. Great Britain, which still held combat troops and bases in the Eastern Mediterranean and East of Suez in the "50's" and "60's", was in this respect an exception. Today, Great Britain only plays a very modest role in Cyprus.

As we have already mentioned, the exertion of influence is primarily the task of diplomacy and to a great extent of foreign economic policy. The European Community has geared itself accordingly with regard to the Mediterranean. This insight explains the Mediterranean policy of the European Community,[26] the Euro-Arab dialogue and the increasing attention given to Iran's importance.[27] Participation in defusing the explosive Middle East conflict, cautious contributions to stabilizing the conservative Arab governments and rolling back Soviet influence are the high priority goals of this foreign policy strategy. Here the EC is guided by the consideration that those Arab governments in this region, which, economically strong and politically independent, are the most resistent to Soviet attempts at penetration. Attempts at economic cooperation without trying to force these states into dependency or to draw the governments into a Western alliance system are the fruits of this insight.

It is a well-known fact that considerable differences in operative approach appear in this context and will in all likelihood continue to arise. But in the European-American rivalry the line is drawn at the very latest where the danger exists that key states for oil supply might slip into the Soviet sphere of influence. Crisis planning intensified, based on a consensus between the USA and Western Europe, should and could focus on such possibilities.

Theoretically speaking crises in the regions mentioned could grow out of various factors:

1. Successful activity of subversive movements manipulated from the outside (until recently a major problem in the emirates on the Persian Gulf).

2. Power take-over by pro-Soviet forces in key states as regards Western energy supply.

3. An alarming expansion of the system of Soviet military bases.

4. Embargo measures against the West under conditions similar to those of fall/winter 1973/74.

5. Blockade measures or other impediments to sea traffic through states

acting as proxies for the Soviet Union or, indeed, directly through the Soviet navy – in case of world crisis.

6. Military occupation of centers of oil production or other geo-strategically crucial areas by the Soviet armed forces.

"Remote-control" subversion can be counter-acted – in so far as it is still necessary today – through bilateral military aid. Now that the conservative dynasties and Egypt have attained a considerable financial margin of maneuver, not lastly as a result of the oil price increase, Western states need no longer be so active in this point. Supplies of military equipment on a particularly commercial basis seem to be sufficient to stabilize the situation. In the future we will be able to depend to a great extent on the influence of leading pro-Western regional powers (Iran, Saudi Arabia).

Within certain limits, the maritime presence of Western powers can contribute to avoid a situation in which pro-Western governments get the impression that the Soviet Union is not the dominating future world power in the strategic region from the Eastern Atlantic to the Indian Ocean. If the contrary impression were to persist it could once again encourage pro-Soviet forces within the Arab states to take new action.

Should power take-overs actually occur, one must first wait to see whether the new rulers are in fact willing and – from the point of view of the interest constellations of their states – able to impede the supply of the West. Only in the latter case would measures of a military nature have to be considered, in particular in reaction to possible embargo or blockade measures or, indeed, in the case of direct Soviet military activity.[28]

Crisis management in the regions of the Middle and Near East, the Indian Ocean, and the South Atlantic would have to be supported by naval forces, military bases of harbour rights, as well as on sea or land-based, highly mobile combat units. The preparatory planning must include cooperation with friendly governments in the region which, in turn, raises the question as to the extent to which bilateral or multilateral agreements are necessary in this context. In such cases one cannot rely on improvisation. Building up and maintaining military bases with all the detailed work involved in logistics and treaty negotiations is, as the United States and Great Britain have learned, a difficult, expensive and time-consuming task. The same is true of building up and maintaining combat troops which would be at immediate disposal should a crisis occur.

Obviously, such crisis preparations run the risk of being misinterpreted by the countries of the region as offensive neo-colonialist measures of the Western states. One would have to reckon with corresponding criticism within the West from leftist oriented groups. Yet, despite all intention to proceed cautiously and without provocation, such planning must not be so faint-hearted that it would be ineffective should intervention to prevent a breakdown of the Western European energy supply actually become necessary.

The continental European NATO states whose crisis planning to this day is focused on the security situation in Central Europe (to be sure, with consideration given to the NATO flanks in the North and Southeast) will soon have to ask themselves whether they should not in the future also train and maintain combat troops for such purposes. Although this would have to be prepared without dramatics in order to avoid negative diplomatic reactions it could prove decisive to have such an instrument at hand in case of crisis. It would, furthermore, be wise to examine whether the Western European naval forces can afford to limit themselves indefinitely to protecting only the North Atlantic sea area.

In any case, the states of Western Europe cannot in the long run expect the United States to maintain combat troops and the necessary transport capacities, or carry the necessary financial and political costs of military bases singlehandedly only in order to secure the West Europeans against threats to their flanks. To be sure, in the Middle East tremendous investments of American companies are also at stake; and the United States' increasing dependence on crude oil imports would put the American administration under considerable pressure in a crisis regardless of any consideration of Western Europe. Nevertheless, the United States could come to terms with a short-term, partial lapse in Middle and Near East oil supply. Western Europe would not be in the position to do so until at least the mid "80's". Hence the governments have good reason to concern themselves with corresponding crisis scenarios more than they have in the past.

Any failure to do so would in a crisis necessarily put American-European relations to the test as it did in the Middle East war of 1973 with the oil embargo and its repercussions. In this context as well one must remember that the society of states has for a long time been moving into an era where the use of military force is understood as a legitimate political tool. The Western democracies must, of course, continue to strive for a world in which inter-state conflicts are acted out with other instruments, but it would be highly dangerous to trust the behavioral patterns and concepts of a deterrent policy which guaranteed freedom and stability in Europe for thirty years also to be sufficient to provide defense against overseas threats in all events and for an unlimited period.

Erosion Tendencies and Tensions in the European NATO Area

In the past, when one spoke of erosion tendencies in NATO, this was directed primarily at erosion in the defense budgets and at the reluctance of the alliance partners to integrate armaments and armed forces planning. Such tendencies have frequently seriously strained the European-American relationship.

The difficulties are well-known and are the permanent concern of NATO. In the following we shall only select two major points for discussion.

1. Arms Procurement as a Bone of Contention between Europe and the United States

The first problem category arises as a result of the sky-rocketing costs of armaments production and of maintaining armed forces. Both would in themselves call for a continuous expansion of the military budgets, as it is in fact the case in the USA and the Federal Republic. But various factors work to counteract this development. In most of the NATO states tax income has decreased as a result of the recession. Expenditures for social policy and for structural reform compete with armaments expenditures (in the Mediterranean this is particularly true of Turkey, Italy, and Portugal and is becoming a great problem for Great Britain). Leftist parties tend by nature to regard the defense budget as a kind of piggy bank which can be cracked open should one come to power. But the parties of the center and the right which compete with the leftist parties do not wish to neglect the non-military tasks either. Those NATO partners which lie somewhat farther out of the line of fire, like the Netherlands or Great Britain, tend at the moment to trust the bulwark of Central Europe and to neglect their defense efforts. Small countries, such as Denmark, which would not be able to defend themselves on their own are tempted to contribute not even the small segment which they could indeed manage.

The development unrolls against the backdrop of a frightening inability to standardize[29] or coordinate common armaments planning and production. The financial costs and the negative repercussions on the combat potential of the military units are both equally great. General Goodpaster asserted that up to 50 percent could be saved in expenditures for the acquisition of armaments through standardization. General Steinhoff is somewhat more skeptical but at the same time points out that in the deployment of multinational NATO troops of the AMF type up to 50 percent of their effectiveness is lost because these related weapons systems do not meet the standards of interchangeability, interoperability and compatibility.[30] This would have devastating consequences in the case of war.

We have already mentioned that the erosion tendencies only sketched here could in the long run impair the US willingness to defend Europe. But the difficulties mentioned above represent a burden to European-American relations from another point of view as well.

An increasing disparity can be observed today between strong and willing contributors amongst the NATO members on the one hand and a large group of partners which are no longer able to fulfill their functions either completely or in part on the other hand. NATO cannot function in the long run – certainly not without many tensions – if within the alliance a leading duo consisting of the United States and the Federal Republic is established, which to an increasing degree carries the burden of integrated programs and takes responsibly for stability in Central Europe. The primarily American-German bulwark in Central Europe cannot be sustained under unlimited political or economic strains. It is most irresponsible of the European partners to allow an erosion of their own defense expenditures and to rely on the USA and the Federal Republic. This attitude is sooner or later bound to weaken the willingness of the US and Germany to carry the burden alone. They not only have the major burden to carry in Central Europe, but they also make considerable contributions to integrated infrastructure programs and to military aid to weaker partners (the United States more, but the Federal Republic also to a certain extent). One need not be a prophet to foresee that for the weaker partners these circumstances will sooner or later lead to resentment over American-German "bi-gemony" in the alliance. Certain West European states are not sufficiently aware that the entire continental European security system would begin to totter should a majority be found either in America or the Federal Republic in favor of a decisive reduction in their respective contributions.

Another related aspect of the European-American relationship is the well-known rivalry in the field of armaments acquisition. NATO commanders, groups of experts and the NATO institutions have pointed out the problems involved often enough and have suggested solutions. The United States is also aware that no road can lead back into the golden "50's" when the near exclusive outfitting with American equipment led, without great effort, to a considerable degree of standardization in the armaments of the NATO forces.

Today no one would contest the fact that a European arms industry is an essential prerequisite for a certain degree of independence in European security policy, which should also be in the interest of the United States. That

European-American armament cooperation cannot be a one-way street is in principle recognized by all sides. And the insight that coordination alone, as it has been attempted for the last quarter century in various bodies, cannot solve the problem, finds steady approval.

The suggestion of creating a common arms market is still being discussed. In this market, decisions on acquisitions would be made by an alliance organ which would have its own budget – as does the EC Commission in the area of agriculture – which could be used to buy arms in Europe or in America. It is clear that such a body could only be established in gradual steps. Even in the most favorable case, the states would probably be willing to let only a small portion of their acquisitions be determined centrally, but this would, nonetheless, be a start.

One should not delude oneself in this respect. National armaments interest would not disappear as a result but would simply be articulated at the level of an integrated armaments office instead. The capacity of the particular groups to realize their interests is only in part a function of the activities of companies and lobbyists. Their most important representatives are the individual state governments which expect a certain yield from the state investments in the armaments field, which grant high priority to job security and which would not like to do without the tax revenue. Fortunately, the goal of armaments autonomy is not stressed as strongly by all states as by the United States and France; but this motive naturally plays a role, and its legitimacy within certain limits cannot be denied.

To make matters more complicated, the idea of an armaments pool is at present seen by certain governments as an inducement to draw France closer to the NATO organization again. For Paris, participation in such a NATO armaments pool is out of the question for reasons of both foreign and domestic policy. If France's participation is nonetheless desired, then the not too attractive alternative is posed between a European armaments pool which would make the matter acceptable for France, or a NATO-pool (with a naturally strong European component) without France. When faced with this alternative a state like the Federal Republic tends to hesitate.

Various political groupings which would like to extend European unity to include the military realm as well are also in favor of a European armaments office. The report of the Belgian Minister President Tindemans on the European Union[31] includes suggestions along these lines, for example. Such considerations are usually based on the hope that functional cooperation in the realm of weapons systems acquisition could lead to a synchronization of strategy. As a tacit long term goal one can recognize the idea of a new European defense community.[32]

However, even with a positive attitude to initiatives towards greater European unity this idea is not convincing either from the aspect of defense policy or of European policy. The military utility as well as the savings which a Europe-centered approach offers are out-weighed by the disadvantage that such an approach could sooner or later lead to tensions with the United States. To be sure, the American representative in the NATO Council has given his blessing to the establishment of a European study group in which France also participates, and the advocates of the European pool are, of course, contemplating orders in the United States. But those who are judging by previous experience with the egotism of the states which would be involved in such a pool have their doubts as to whether the good intentions will actually be put into action. In such a case, this most welcome measure towards cutting costs could prove to be the new bone of contention in the European-American dialogue.

After all, many different cooperative projects have been launched in the past (bi-national projects such as the Bréguet "Atlantique", multinational-European projects such as MRCA or "sidewinder", multinational Euro-American projects such as "Starfighter"). Why should a functional European organization not also be given a chance? One thing is certain: the road from European armaments cooperation to a European defense community is just as long and stony as the road from the Common Market to a European Economic and Monetary Union. Moreover, it hardly seems imaginable that the European states would entrust a European body with a considerable portion of their acquisitions; the egotism of national armaments interests is simply much too strong. Such considerations are, to be sure, well suited to dampening the enthusiasm of those who regard armaments functionalism as a new vehicle to get stagnating European integration rolling again. But they can also dissipate the worries of those who see the European armaments pool as a future burden to European-American cooperation.

On the whole one can hardly dispute the fact that an armaments pool in the NATO framework would be the more constructive solution, if one agrees that France will not be willing to give up its sovereignty in the realm of security policy in the foreseeable future anyway.

Thus, all will proceed more or less in the same manner in this field as well. If it were only possible at least in part to reduce higher costs through more standardization and co-production, much would be gained.

Two points appear of equal importance in regard to the European-American relationship. On the one hand the European NATO states must not become completely dependent on the USA in the field of conventional armament. Washington might otherwise be tempted to exploit this

dependency at a diplomatic level if necessary. The situation in Israel is a
warning. The West European NATO partners need a modern arms industry
not only to meet their own demands but also in order to employ the
instrument of military aid to enhance their own interests overseas. On the
other hand, the legitimate wish to maintain a certain degree of independence
in the field of conventional armament must not be allowed to lead to incurable
American-European conflicts of interest.

2. Tensions between European Members of NATO and Systemic Crises

Along with these already classic irritants to European-American cooperation
we must also draw attention to other threats of erosion which have their roots
in the European NATO realm. In the past years there have been more than
enough occasions to question whether the European-American alliance will
not be threatened by the inner erosion resulting from tensions between the
alliance partners or from systemic crises in the individual states in the future
as well.

We have become accustomed to staring spellbound at such possible
developments. The Greek-Turkish conflict over Cyprus and over offshore
drilling rights in the Aegean which is still not settled, the advances of the
Communists in Portugal and Italy and the prospect of a victory of the
popular front in 1978 in France did, indeed, in recent years give the
impression that the alliance was dissolving with increasing rapidity from
within.

Here one is reminded of the melancholic comment of Jacob Burckhardt:
Ever since politics have been based on the inner fermentation of nations we
have been experiencing the end of all security.[33] Tension-laden modern
societies do, in fact, demonstrate a considerable degree of instability;
surprises can never be excluded. The unexpected renaissance of Marxism in
the late "60's" which today has already come to a close, or the systemic crises
of the supposedly stable 5th Republic in May 1968 are, for example,
reminders in the recent past. And it would certainly be unrealistic to believe
that in Europe of all places the flame of nationalism and interstate antagonism had burned itself out once and for all in the fires of World
War II. Such phenomena continue to threaten with shake-ups.

One can, for example, hardly exclude the possibility that the south-east
flank of NATO would break down if a Greek-Turkish war should occur (or
if Turkey should turn its back on the West in frustration). NATO is already
seriously, even if not incurably, crippled in this region.

It is likewise easy to imagine groupings in which Western Europe is polarized between socialist-communist popular front governments on the one hand and on the other hand a bloc of states in which European governments of the center and the right together with the United States try hard to stabilize the situation by means of balance of power politics in the West European framework. It is, moreover, conceivable that such ideological conflicts could influence the orientation of security policy and that new fears of the possible reciprocal use of force could grow out of the inevitable ideological tensions between West European states, above all if the political polarization were to lead to civil war like controversies in the domestic area of one of the alliance partners. These are, nonetheless, all rather vague future possibilities which are not at all certain to occur and which can by no means be included in any calculations or planning.

In fact, NATO has had to live with Greek-Turkish tension since 1964.[34] The situation, however, has improved in that region since the overthrow of the military dictatorship in Greece.

For the first time in its history, NATO includes exclusively states with democratic political systems. Nor should we forget that it has often been necessary with respect to these countries to reinforce the integrated military organization through bilateral measures on the southern flank where above all the United States, and to a limited extent Great Britain in Cyprus, have made considerable contributions. The Federal Republic has for some time exerted its influence in this area bilaterally (though always in agreement with NATO) through armaments aid.

This bilateral involvement would probably continue in one form or another even under conditions of intense Greek-Turkish rivalry, whereby the American element would have to be supplemented by a greater involvement of Western European states. More differentiation from region to region and a more complicated organizational structure will probably be inevitable in the entire NATO sphere. If they are more prominent in certain regions, this need not result in fundamental changes of the European-American alliance. It seems quite clear that the USA would in principle welcome a compensation of receding American influence, above all in Turkey, through stronger West European presence. The more clearly a policy of "burden sharing" is established in this context the less it must be feared that American frustration in the Eastern Mediterranean will affect its attitude toward the alliance as a whole.

The situation in Portugal and in Italy has stabilized for the moment. From the point of view of the security dimension, the situation in Italy will probably worsen gradually. But even if one considers the worst possible development, that of Communist participation in the government, the negative repercussions for security policy could possibly be averted.[35] The Portuguese model has, to be sure, demonstrated that Communist participation in government makes the problem of secrecy acute in the integrated NATO staffs and in other NATO bodies. Experts differ in their opinions as to whether the procedure developed for the Portuguese case could be repeated in the Italian case; it would depend on the exact circumstances. The Italian bases would most probably still be placed at NATO's disposal, though perhaps under more complicated conditions and at higher cost. Italy's willingness to uphold an alliance in case of a crisis or of war would – judging by various experiences collected in the twentieth century – have to be taken with a certain skepticism in any case; although Italy would hardly become more reliable through Communist participation in government.

Nor would the assumption be wrong that such a government would belong to the particularly outspoken advocates of détente in the alliance. Italy's already minimal inclination to make sufficient investments in modernization of its armed forces would probably be reinforced (Italian military expenditure has already sunk to 2.8 percent of the GNP); particularly unsettling are the insufficient investments in aviation equipment.[36]

All these dimensions would be troublesome and not unobjectionable in the long run, but we would have to live with them and probably could. Seen from the point of view of the European-American relationship it would probably be wise to develop an elastic and undramatic attitude toward undesired domestic developments (in so far as they remain halfway controllable). If we assume that American presence in Europe is most apt to be called into question if the conviction should take hold in US public opinion that its continued presence on the Continent and in the Mediterranean will lead to constantly recurring diplomatic or military crises, then a watchful but not dramatizing attitude would be advisable. In times of crises or indeed of war almost everything depends on the circumstances, the various groupings at the time, and not least on the strength and determination of the West as a whole.

This does not only apply to Italy. The alliance, especially the Central European alliance partners, will have to use the instrument of military aid vis-à-vis the weaker allies in the future as well. This is also an area in which the capacity of those economically stronger European NATO states can and must supplement the American contribution.

It has often been pointed out that the NATO states on the southeastern flank in particular, but Portugal as well, demand special attention and solidarity from the alliance as a result of unsolved structural problems in their societies and their economic weakness. The stabilizing effect must ensue primarily through economic instruments in this context as well. In this sense, security in the Mediterranean is just as much the task of the EC as of NATO.

Alongside the factor of economic stabilization the instrument of supra-state cooperation between the political parties has recently played a role – a possible channel which once again can only be exploited by Western European alliance partners and which brought visible positive results for security policy above all in Portugal.[37] The consolidation of the European Community which leads again and again to the familiar European-American frictions in the field of foreign economic policy, could represent an element of cohesion in the field of security.

In future internal crises of alliance partners it will not, for the most part, be possible to avert or channel the repercussions of such shake-ups for security policy through military measures. Only the political network of multilateral and bilateral reciprocal influence which has taken shape in the EC would be of any use here – in so far as the situation can be influenced from the outside at all. In this respect much speaks for limiting the alliance largely to its military function and not to overburden it politically. Any attempt to bring the military alliance into play in controversies within NATO states is almost bound to be counterproductive.

A period of inner instability in France, as could have occurred after the national elections in 1978 would by nature have had considerable psycholog-ical repercussions for Western Europe as a whole and for the EC in particular. The direct short-term and probably also medium-term effect on NATO would, on the other hand, probably not have been too substantial. After all, France has not belonged to the NATO military organization since 1966 so that a fundamentally new security policy would not be expected, regardless of how the domestic battle for power was decided.

All in all, a glance at possible internal crises of alliance partners need not lead to the catastrophic predictions for the security situation as have been made in recent years. To be sure, the situation will become more difficult. It will demand conceptional, and, above all, political-psychological adaptation in the future as well. But since the changes will ensue gradually for the most part, a pragmatic adaptation to the new realities should be possible.

Most dangerous would probably be the psychological-political repercus-sions of systemic crises. They would, for the time, make clear that the prerequisites for a continuation of political unification of Western Europe are for the foreseeable future no longer at hand. And the internal tensions in the Western security alliance could coincide with previously mentioned threats from overseas and could be manipulated diplomatically by the militarily superior Soviet Union. Even in the still stable NATO states a tendency to compliance and adaptation to the seemingly irresistible trend could prevail in the long run. But this would not necessarily happen, quite apart from the chance that it might be possible to keep the Communists in Italy out of the vital power centers of government through patient temporizing, and to find a majority for a reform course without Communists in France.

Moreover, the free peoples of Western Europe and the USA will have to accustom themselves to the fact that the security situation at the end of the "70's" and in the early "80's" will be more dangerous. We have entered an era of greater instability and heightened external threat to security. This is new. A pleasant feeling of security has developed in Western Europe since the Berlin and Cuba crises which is painful to lose. But in broad historical perspective and in the light of recent Western European history such an experiment is neither new, nor does it confront Europeans with insoluble tasks. The illusions of progress which experienced a revival in Europe after World War II evaporate in the realm of security policy as well. But one should not mourn lost illusions. Their fading at the same time sharpens the eye for the harder realities upon which the survival of Western democracies depends.

One of these realities is the unconditional security presence of the USA in Europe and in the Mediterranean. Only if the United States in fact sees itself as a European power and acts accordingly, will the present and probably future period of weakness of certain West European democracies avoid a collapse. And only if the democratic élites in Western Europe orient their foreign and domestic activity towards the reality that there is no substitute for US presence will they be able to find productive answers to the manifold burdens facing the alliance in the future.

Notes

[1] Foreign Relations of the United States. Diplomatic Papers. *The Conferences of Malta and Yalta* 1945, Washington: US Government Printing Office 1955, p. 628.

[2] Cf., for example, the basic speech of August 28, 1948 in: Konrad Adenauer, *Reden 1917–1967*, Hans-Peter Schwarz, (ed.) Stuttgart: Deutsche Verlags-Anstalt 1975, p. 129. A richly documented analysis of Adenauer's policy vis-à-vis the United States is found in: Kurt Birrenbach, *Adenauer und die Vereinigten Staaten in der Periode seiner Kanzlerschaft*, in: *Konrad Adenauer und seine Zeit*, Vol. 1, Stuttgart: Deutsche Verlags-

Anstalt 1976, pp. 475–509, see also pp. 481 f. and Klaus Dohrn, *Das Amerikabild Adenauers*, ibid., p. 513.

[3] Cf. J. Robert Schaetzel's essay in this volume.

[4] Chancellor Brandt's expectations in 1971 in this regard have now been described quite convincingly by him in retrospect: "My considerations . . . were based on the expectation of the day, that by the end of the 70's only a part of the American armed forces will still be in Europe": Willy Brandt, *Begegnungen und Einsichten. Die Jahre 1960–1975*, Hamburg: Hoffmann & Campe 1976, p. 348. For the moment, however, we must point out that the presence of American armed forces in Europe has ceased to be controversial in Congress. Yet it is not certain whether the group of critical Senators and Representatives will tolerate the situation for long (cf. Phil Williams, *Whatever happened to the Mansfield Amendment?*, in: Survival XVIII, No. 4, 1976, pp. 146–153).

[5] The official German formulation of the triad upon which the military doctrine of NATO in Central Europe is based can be found in the federal government's most recent White Paper on security matters. *White Paper 1975–76: The Security of the Federal Republic of Germany and the Development of the Federal Armed Forces*, Bonn: Press and Information Office of the Government of the Federal Republic of Germany 1976, pp. 20–23. In a study made for WEU on April 2, 1975 General de Maizière formulated quite clearly with regard to Central Europe: "only a limited aggression, as far as the goals and the region are concerned, can be maintained with purely conventional means with any chance of success." (In: *Verteidigung in Europa-Mitte. Studie im Auftrag der Versammlung der Westeuropäischen Union*, Munich: Lehmanns 1975, p. 22, § 103a.) Similarly General Steinhoff: "If the present trend in Central European land forces continues, in cases of limited or large-scale attack, there will be no combat action lasting weeks or months but at best days" (*Wohin treibt die NATO? Probleme der Verteidigung West-Europas*, Hamburg: Hoffmann & Campe 1976, p. 133). Likewise skeptical is ex-General Johann Adolf Graf Kielmansegg in his comprehensive new study, *Probleme eines kriegerischen Konflikts, insbesondere in Mitteleuropa*, in: Karl Kaiser, Karl Markus Kreis, eds., *Sicherheitspolitik vor neuen Aufgaben*, Frankfurt: Metzner 1977, p. 325: "The chances for success of a conventional attack in Central Europe are greater than many are willing to admit."

[6] Drew Middleton, *Can America Win the Next War?* New York: Scribner 1975, pp. 256 ff.

[7] Corresponding programs of reduction are still being propagated, for example by Earl C. Ravenal *After Schlesinger: Something Has to Give*, in: Foreign Policy, No. 22, Spring 1976, pp. 71–96. As further examples of neo-isolationist budget suggestions oriented around the concept of Fortress America, we could mention the suggestion of the MCPL Task Force on Defense Policy of May 1976 (*Defending America: An Alternative US Foreign Policy and Defense Posture Statement*. Congressional Record, May 19, 1976, pp. 7507–7533). According to Ravenal the costs of a "non-interventionist force structure" would amount to 60 billion dollars given Fiscal Year prices for 1976. (By way of comparison ca. 177 billion dollars have been estimated for FY 1977.) Cuts of this proportion would necessitate the withdrawal of all land and air

forces from Europe and the Asian continent as well as the naval forces in the Mediterranean.

[8] Robert Schaetzel points to the brusque decision of the Johnson administration to give up the MLF project which the allies had previously been encouraged to begin for years as a classic example of American willingness to give preference to bilateral agreements over planning in association with the allies. (*The Unhinged Alliance: America and the European Community*, New York: Harper & Row 1975, pp.162 f.)

[9] Cf. Richard Burt, *Das Dilemma mit den "Cruise Missiles"*, in: Europa-Archiv, No. 14, 1976, pp. 457–468. The author sees cruise missiles (for which he thinks Western Europe has the necessary technology and strategic conception) as a chance for increasing both its own chances for survival and the destructive power of French and British deterrence forces (p. 465). Besides the difficulties which arose in the SALT negotiations as a result of the multitude of development configurations (tactical/strategic), the variable range of this weapon system can also lead to disturbances in the MBFR negotiations (ibid., p. 466); cf. also Richard Burt, *New Weapons Technologies: Debate and Directions*, Adelphi Papers 126, London; International Institute for Strategic Studies 1976 and Alexander R. Vershbow, *The Cruise Missile: The End of Arms Control?* in: Foreign Affairs, No. 55, October 1976, pp.141 f. For the German point of view, see Hubert Feig., *Marschflugkörper mit strategischer Einsatzmöglichkeit*, in: Wehrkunde, No. 5, 1976, pp 240 ff.

[10] See also Stefan T. Possony, *Die NATO und das Aufkommen neuer Technologie*, in: Europäische Wehrkunde, No. 9, 1976, pp. 433–440. Possony sketches among other things the various possibilities of Soviet strategy in Europe.

[11] The Belgian General R. Close calculates that in the case of a successful surprise attack the Rhine would be reached in two days (*L'Europe sans Défense?*, Brussels: ed. Arts et Voyages 1977, pp. 263–288).

[12] Drew Middleton, *Can America Win the Next War?*, loc. cit. (footnote 6), pp. 213, 256–259. Most striking, since it avoids dramatic effects and is nonetheless based on the latest expert information, is the report of Senators Nunn and Bartlett (*NATO and the New Soviet Threat. Report of Senator Sam Nunn and Senator Dewey F. Bartlett to the Committee on Armed Services, US Senate, January 24, 1977, 95th Congress, 1st Session*, Washington: US Government Printing Office 1977).

[13] George F. Kennan, *Europe's Problems, Europe's Choices*, in: Foreign Policy, No. 14, Spring 1974, pp. 3–16.

[14] Cf. Michael MccGwire, Ken Booth and John McDonnell, (eds.), *Soviet Naval Policy: Objectives and Constraints*, New York: Praeger 1975; and Michael MccGwire, *Naval Power and Soviet Oceans Policy*, Halifax, Nova Scotia: Center for Foreign Policy Studies, Dalhousie University, Feb. 1976; and Dieter Mahncke: "Stützpunkte als Faktor maritimer Macht", in: Dieter Mahncke and Hans-Peter Schwarz, (eds.), *Seemacht und Außenpolitik*, Frankfurt: Metzner 1974, pp. 414–444. The best descriptive survey of Soviet overseas expansion can be found in: *Osteuropa-Handbuch, Sowjetunion, Außenpolitik 1955–1973*, Cologne: Böhlau 1976.

[15] Cf. White Paper 1975/76, loc. cit., footnote 5, pp. 40–44. The CDU/CSU

opposition has a similar view. Cf. Manfred Wörner, *Neue Dimensionen der Sicherheit*, in: Wehrkunde, No. 2, 1975, pp. 61–65.

[16] Worries over Great Britain's energy supply played a major role in the British strategy, "East of Suez"; see Phillip Darby: *British Defence Policy East of Suez 1947–1968*, London: Oxford UP 1973. Geostrategic views were advocated by French military journalists above all during and after the Algerian War, for example by André Beaufre and Ferdinand O. Miksche.

[17] The following data are cited in the latest estimate of IISS, Soviet armed forces in Central and Eastern Europe – 31 divisions of category I; the European Soviet Union – 64 divisions (ca. 1/3 of them category I); Chinese-Soviet border area – 43 divisions (only 1/3 of category I) (*The Military Balance 1976/77*, London: International Institute for Strategic Studies 1976, p. 9).

[18] The need for an effective European deterrence component was analyzed in detail by Geoffrey Kemp in 1974 (*Nuclear Forces for Medium Powers*, Adelphi Papers 106/107, London: International Institute for Strategic Studies 1974). This study makes it quite clear that the deterrence value of the present French and British systems is constantly decreasing, while the costs of maintaining sufficiently effective deterrence armed forces is sky-rocketing and already today exceeds the limited means of France or Great Britain. The former NATO General, Johannes Steinhoff, is similarly skeptical (*Wohin treibt die NATO?*, loc. cit. (footnote 5), pp. 227–232. Particularly critical of the Force de Frappe from the German point of view is Hans Rühle, *Der "Neo-Gaullismus" in der Bundesrepublik Deutschland*, in: Wehrkunde, No. 8, 1975, pp. 385–389. That this argument is well-known to critical French analysts is demonstrated in a new essay by Raymond Aron, *La force française de dissuasion et l'Alliance Atlantique*, in: Défense Nationale, January 1977, pp. 31–46.

[19] R. J. Vincent who recently developed a scenario of possible dangers and who would like to hang on to a rather forcedly optimistic interpretation of Soviet intentions also admits to this (*Military Power and Political Influence. The Soviet Union and Western Europe*, in: Adelphi Papers 119, London: International Institute for Strategic Studies 1975, pp. 28 f.).

[20] The Nunn/Bartlett Report (footnote 12) lists the following short-term measures: 1. revision of the political and military-technical planning which were based on a preliminary warning time of several weeks; 2. deployment of units in order to make the concept of forward defense plausible again (reinforcement of defense in the northern German lowlands; forward displacement of units at present stationed on the Rhine and/or west of the Rhine); 3. considerable strengthening of the firepower of the NATO units; 4. heightening instant preparedness for action; 5. improvement of air defense, above all of military bases; 6. introduction of an Airborne Warning and Control System (AWACS) to improve the leadership and information functions; 7. increased airlift capacity for American and British reinforcements in case of crisis; 8. constant improvement of standardization and interoperability.

Mid-term reforms for stabilizing the situation commonly mentioned are: introduction of newer more advanced weapons systems (PGM, etc.) for combating tanks; greater centralized planning and decision making in the acquisition of armaments goods. Robert Lucas Fischer comes in part to the same conclusions:

Defending the Central Front. The Balance of Forces, Adelphi Papers 127, London: International Institute for Strategic Studies 1976. As the conference of NATO Defense Ministers in May, 1977 showed, the evaluations formulated in the Nunn/Bartlett Report are well on their way to becoming the common platform of the alliance.

However, purely military-technical answers to the new situation would be meaningless without changes in the basic political attitude of Western public opinion and its élites. Here we must realize that war in Europe can best be prevented if the Western democracies would quickly and decisively accept the fact that the case of defense could actually arise in the coming years. – For the official position of the NATO commander-in-chief, see General Alexander Haig, *The Challenge for the West in a Changing Strategic Environment*, in: NATO Review, No. 3, 1976, pp. 10–13.

[21] So Kissinger in his New York speech of April 23, 1973 which set off the frustrating dialogue over the Year of Europe (as quoted from Europa-Archiv, No. 7, 1973, p. D 221).

[22] Johan Jörgen Holst, *Lehren der Nahost-Krise von 1973 für das Atlantische Bündnis*, in: Europa-Archiv, No. 7, 1976, pp. 205–214.

[23] See William Wallace, *Atlantic Relations: Policy-Coordination and Conflict. Issue Linkage Among Atlantic Governments*, in: International Affairs, No. 2, 1976, pp. 163–179. – For information on present crisis management in NATO see Admiral Sir Peter Hill-Norton, *Crisis Management*, in: NATO Review, No. 5, 1976, pp. 6–10.

[24] We cannot go into the many faceted topic of policy vis-à-vis Southern Africa which has occupied not only Western cabinets but to an increasing extent experts on security from science and administration since the power take-over by pro-Soviet forces in Angola and Mozambique. From the strategic aspect, the sea routes in the Indian Ocean and the South Atlantic as well as the significance of South Africa play a major role in Western raw material supply (gold, chromium, uranium, manganese, platinum, vanadium). Cf. the sketches of the problem from various points of view by Walter F. Hahn/Alvin J. Cottrell, *Soviet Shadow over Africa*, Miami: Center for Advanced International Studies, University of Miami 1977 and from the German perspective Hans-Christian Pilster, *Südafrika und die Verteidigung des freien Westens*, in: Wehrkunde, No. 3, 1976, pp. 127–133 as well as William E. Griffith, *Die sowjetisch-amerikanische Konfrontation im südlichen Afrika*, in: Europa-Archiv, No. 2, 1977, pp. 31–40.

[25] For the present situation in the Eastern Mediterranean see Lothar Ruehl, *Die Allianz in Südeuropa*, in: Karl Kaiser und Karl Markus Kreis, eds., *Sicherheitspolitik vor neuen Aufgaben* (footnote 5), pp. 27–49. On the situation on NATO's northern flank see Jochen Löser, *Militärische und politische Balanceakte an der Nordflanke der NATO*, in: Europäische Wehrkunde, No. 8, 1976, p. 392 f. See also the corresponding analyses of Edward Wegener and Gerd Linde, in: Dieter Mahncke und Hans-Peter Schwarz, (ed.), *Seemacht und Außenpolitik*, loc. cit. (footnote 14), pp. 299–338.

[26] Compare Avi Shlaim, *The Community and the Mediterranean Basin*, in: Kenneth J. Twitchett, ed., *Europe and the World. The External Relations of the Common Market*. London: Europa Publ. 1976; Heinz Andresen, *Über die Verwirklichung einer gemeinschaftlichen Mittelmeerpolitik*, in: Wolfgang Wessels, (ed.), *Europa und die*

arabische Welt. Probleme und Perspektiven europäischer Arabienpolitik, Bonn: Europa Union Verlag 1975.

[27] Karl Kaiser, above all, addresses himself to the economic possibilities of far-sighted security relations with Iran: *Iran and the Europe of the Nine: A Relationship of Growing Interdependence*, in: the World Today, No. 7, 1976, pp. 251–259. On the problem of security in the Gulf region in general, see W. A. C. Adie, *Oil, Politics and Sea Power. The Indian Ocean Vortex*. New York: Crane, Russak 1975; Patrick Wall, ed., *The Indian Ocean and the Threat to the West. Four Studies in Global Strategy*, London: Stacey International 1975; Wolfgang Höpker, *Wetterzone der Weltpolitik. Der Indische Ozean im Kräftespiel der Mächte*, Stuttgart: Seewald 1975. For an understanding of the historical background of Iranian policy, see Rouholla K. Ramazani, *Iran's Foreign Policy, 1941–1973. A Study of Foreign Policy in Modernizing Nations*, Charlottesville: UP of Virginia 1975.

[28] Such arguments are more frequently voiced by American defense politicians and admirals than by Western Europeans. See Worth H. Bagley, *Die sowjetische Seemacht und ihre Konsequenzen für die Strategie der NATO*, in: Europa-Archiv, No. 20, 1975, pp. 633–641 and Robert Ellsworth, *Folgen des Energieproblems für das strategische Gleichgewicht*, ibid., No. 21, 1975, pp. 653–662.

[29] General Goodpaster listed several examples for 1974:
– 23 different kinds of combat airplanes;
– 7 different groups of combat vehicles;
– 8 different groups of transport tanks and troop transport vehicles;
– 22 different anti-tank systems.
Marine:
– 36 different models of radar guidance and targeting systems;
– 8 different ground-to-air missiles;
– 6 different torpedo classes;
– more than 20 different calibers in weapons up to 30 mm;
from: Jean Laurens Delpech, *La standardisation des armements*, in: Défense Nationale, May 1976, pp. 19–35.

[30] Johannes Steinhoff, *Wohin treibt die NATO?*, loc. cit. (footnote 5), p. 248; and similarly Ulrich de Maizière, *Verteidigung in Europa-Mitte*, loc. cit. (footnote 5), pp. 75 f. The relatively minimal success of earlier attempts is made clear in the study by Roger Facer, *The Alliance and Europe: III, Weapons Procurement in Europe. Capabilities and Choices*, Adelphi Papers 108, London: International Institute for Strategic Studies 1975; John Simpson and Frank Gregory, *West European Collaboration in Weapons Procurement*, in: Orbis, No. 2, 1972, pp. 436–439. The official German position has been sketched by the present General Inspector of the Bundeswehr, Harald Wust, *Militärische Aspekte der Rüstungsstandardisierung*, in: Wehrkunde, No. 5, 1976, pp. 224 ff.

[31] Tindemans suggested: "to work together in armaments production in order to lower defense costs and to enlarge Europe's autonomy as well as the capacity for competition of its industries. The present endeavors to create an organization for the European NATO countries which would bring about the standardization in weapons on the basis of a common program would have significant consequences for industrial

production. This would make it all the more important to pursue a common industrial policy in the area of armament production in the framework of the European Union. The foundation of a European armaments agency could be considered here (*Der Tindemans-Bericht über die Europäische Union vom 29. 12. 1975*, in: Europa-Archiv, No. 3, 1976, p. D 64).

³² P. H. Scott, *Beyond the Eurogroup: New Developments in European Defense*, in: The World Today, No. 1, 1976, pp. 31–38.

³³ Jacob Burckhardt, *Briefe. Vollständige und kritische Ausgabe in 8 Bänden*, Basel, Stuttgart: Schwabe 1966. Vol. 6, p. 230.

³⁴ On the development and the problems of Greek-Turkish relations, see Jacques Menoncourt, *Dangereuse rivalité greco-turque en Méditerranée orientale*, in: Défense Nationale, May 1976, pp. 75–91 and the essay by Lothar Ruehl (footnote 25). See also Johannes Steinhoff, *Wohin treibt die NATO?*, loc. cit. (footnote 5), pp. 97–113.

³⁵ Which problems would, however, arise are disclosed by Alberto Jacoviello, *The Italian Situation and NATO*, in: Survival, No. 4, 1976, pp. 166 f.

³⁶ Johannes Steinhoff, *Wohin treibt die NATO?*, loc. cit. (footnote 5), p. 98.

³⁷ That the Federal Republic has for some years been quite effective, through its political parties as well, in influencing individual countries below the diplomatic level first became clear to many foreign observers during the Iberian crisis of 1974–1976; see Robert Gerald Livingston, *Germany Steps Up*, in: Foreign Policy, No. 22, Spring 1976, p. 122.

The Evolution of East-West Relations: The European Context

by KLAUS RITTER

A Narrowing Margin of Maneuver

Détente has become more difficult in recent times, and it is hard to see how the momentum of the early "70's" can be recaptured. Helsinki represented the zenith of this upswing; no doubt, the success of this past phase of détente was largely conditioned by the complementarity if not convergence of American and German *Ostpolitik*. To be sure, nobody wants to shelve détente – also known as the "policy of normalization" or "co-existence". Yet the policies of the various countries do obey different sets of imperatives and national interests. Moreover, the unplanned – sometimes rather unpleasant – side-effects of détente have in the meantime become ever more apparent on either side of the East-West divide. As result, the earlier euphoria has subsided, and the margin for future maneuver has narrowed. Future Helsinki-type conferences will resemble – rather like SALT II – arduous mountain climbs where it is more important to keep one's balance and to conserve energies than to scale distant peaks at maximum speed. Still, détente and stability remain the foremost task of East-West diplomacy, all the more so because conflict remains an ever-present possibility in a world composed of different and competing societal systems. There are bound to be ups and downs as the East-West relationship continues to unfold, but a return to the rigid confrontation of yesteryear appears unlikely – and certainly not desirable. In short, the issue is not whether, but how we are going to continue the détente process.

Leaving aside the fundamental incongruence between "peaceful coexistence" and "détente", East and West are faced with two different sets of problems. The Soviet Union is caught between the demands of the "class struggle" – its very raison d'être as a revolutionary power – and those of détente and related criteria of political performance. It has sought to escape from this conflict by falling back to enforcing uniformity at home and a remarkable drive to acquire more and more military power. As a result, its "coexistence policy" is bound to lose credibility abroad.

The pluralist West has to cope with different structural weaknesses. Its political style is shaped by pragmatism and the superior moral claim of the individual. Both make it difficult to forge a conceptual and political consensus which lives up to the complex needs of deterrence and détente. The rights of the individual and power politics are felt, to some extent, to be mutually exclusive; hence, the recurrent and ultimately inconclusive debates between moralism and realism in foreign policy. The mixed results of détente have, until now, only served to exacerbate these conceptual conundrums.

The current state of affairs affords few hopes for significant progress. Certainly, we cannot expect some kind of "system convergence" – a highly unrealistic and misleading concept to begin with. Yet it should be possible to maintain a process which will lead to diffusion with the effect of a *rapprochement*, not of systems but of responsibilities on ideas, and expectations across the lines of ideological demarcation. To some extent, this has already happened in the wake of Helsinki. Success in these terms, would be measured by the growth of "vested interests" in détente (as Henry Kissinger once put it) and not by the realization of "grand designs" or fundamental structural change. At best, détente will be a kind of holding operation which stabilizes the existing collective defense structures while widening the scope for cooperation and communication between the blocs. In short, the basic task of Western policy is to preserve the strategic balance, to strengthen the vital link between global and regional (i.e., European) deterrence and, last but not least, to fashion an alliance consensus on the limits of political risk-taking. Put differently, there are two fundamental questions: Given the challenge of Eurocommunism, how much political diversity can the West safely absorb? Given the challenge of détente, which kind of flexibility should or could promote its objectives?

Détente: The Divergence of Goals and Methods

There is yet another challenge to Western cohesion – the increasing diversity of conceptual and political approaches to détente. From the very beginning in the late "60's", the main Western protagonists – the United States, France and the Federal Republic – have pursued different détente objectives. The Federal Republic had to cover the greatest distance. Bonn's traditional insistence on progress to reunification as a precondition for détente had lent it a certain veto power over the general course of East-West relations, as long as this injunction was honored by the entire Alliance. When, from the early "60's" onward, the West (first John F. Kennedy, then de Gaulle) embarked on their own *Ostpolitik* – regardless of German claims and complaints – the FRG's veto rapidly degenerated into an irritation that threatened diplomatic isolation. The essence of Willy Brandt's policy of reconciliation was a diplomatic salvage operation. First, he "decoupled" West Germany's "special conflict" with the East (i.e., the issue of reunification) from the overall East-West agenda (i.e., détente) by recognizing the territorial postwar status quo. Then he inverted the traditional link between German and European détente: Reunification was no longer a precondition of détente, but détente based on the status quo was to prepare the road for the "reassociation" of the two Germanies in terms of "organized coexistence". In other words, the issue was no longer reunification but the *quality* of German-German coexistence as measured by the increase in contacts and cooperation between the two German states.

The United States, on the other hand, was primarily interested in stabilizing the *global* balance through arms control and conflict muting rules of superpower politics; Washington was thus less interested in *structural* change à la CSCE or *regional* arms-control measures à la MBFR. In fact, MBFR became almost a tool of domestic politics – grasped by the Administration to hold at bay those who, like Mansfield, kept insisting on unilateral US troop withdrawals from Europe. France, finally, regarded both processes with mixed feelings. On the one hand, Paris greeted West Germany's new realism with some satisfaction. On the other hand, France was less happy with the sudden multiplication of West German policy options toward the East and the new dangers of "Big Twoism" built into the Soviet-American rapprochement. Yet, at least in the early phase of détente, this heterogeneity of objectives and muted rivalry between the protagonists remained manageable even without an explicit Alliance decision-making process which might have defined purposes and allocated tasks.

In the meantime, the process has become more complicated. The stumbling stones and costs of détente have begun to loom more prominently. The rapid advances of arms technology (e.g., cruise missiles and "neutron bombs") have confused the "count-and-compare" mechanisms of traditional arms control. The old compromise formulae which were devised to obscure the underlying conflicts of objectives have become increasingly precarious. Finally, the muting of bipolarity and the emergence of new conflicts and stakes have tended to shift Western attention away from the problems of the East-West balance. To be sure, the growing arms potential of the East does preoccupy Western chancelleries. Yet there are other problems which are more urgent and immediate – long-term unemployment, the increasing costs of energy and raw materials, deteriorating balances of payments, inflation, the "North-South" conflict, and so forth. In short, the classic issues of East-West diplomacy, troop reductions à la MBFR or security systems à la CSCE, no longer seem to occupy the top of the East-West "normalization" agenda.

Surely, MBFR is a good illustration of this shift in priorities; MBFR has stagnated for years without really affecting the détente process for better or for worse.

Additional uncertainties have grown out of the new mix between globalism and moralism in American policy under President Carter. The old fixtures in American diplomacy are weakening. There seems to be a plethora of new questions and answers on the entire gamut of American policy concerns – non-proliferation, energy, the North-South dialogue, arms control, the Middle East and Latin America. The Carter Administration's reappraisals have not made the search for a Western consensus any easier. Indeed, on the Atlantic plane, new disagreements have arisen which are far from conceptual – let alone consensual – clarification. The newly discovered (or reemphasized) link between civilian nuclear energy and nuclear proliferation, for instance, added a new element of dissension to trans-Atlantic relations which threatened to surpass the squabbles over non-proliferation a decade ago. The Carter Administration and the major West-European powers do not see eye to eye on matters nuclear – whether on nuclear exports, reprocessing, or "Fast Breeders". In East-West and West-West relations, there is a growing tendency toward bilateralism which threatens to erode the prospects for joint action even further. To sum up: A unified Western approach to East-West and North-South relations does not seem in evidence – or very likely.

The Lack of Conceptual Consensus

Today's divergencies in Western détente policy are rooted in the past. Hence it is necessary to go back a bit in order to elucidate the various national concepts operating today. In retrospect, the intensity of the East-West confrontation in the "50's" and early "60's" appears more directly determined by the imperatives of bloc-consolidation than by the real or imagined imminence of aggression from the other side. Diplomacy, therefore, was primarily alliance management and hence directed against anything which might have unhinged the rigid separation between East and West. The relationship between the West and the Federal Republic, as contractually defined in the so-called "Bonn Convention" of 1952 (and as amended in 1954), is a perfect illustration of this tendency. The Western alliance system has always had two functions; to contain the Soviets and to control the West Germans. Similarly, Adenauer's "linkage policy" ("no détente without reunification") was not so much designed to achieve reunification, as to block any Western approaches to the East which might have prejudiced and diminished the military and political status of the Federal Republic in the evolving European context.

The result of this link – as long as it was honored by each and all – was of course, political stalemate in Europe. Yet, and this was the essence of Adenauer's linkage policy, stalemate was better than any movement which might have ended up in a kind of security system (very much *en vogue* in Soviet thinking of the time) thrown up *around* and *against* Germany – reunited or confederated. Toward the end of the "60's", West Germany's veto power eroded. Having realized that the general trend towards East-West détente could no longer be resisted – except at the peril of increasing diplomatic isolation, the Federal Republic under Willy Brandt embarked on an *Ostpolitik* of its own. Its results were the recognition of the territorial status quo and the quasi-recognition of the German Democratic Republic, without the formal renunciation of the claim to eventual reunification. Instead, the *idea* of reunification was subtly transformed. The issue is no longer a matter of territorial but of *political* change; not the nature of the border but the nature of the relationship between the two German states is at stake. The very affirmation of the border was – and is – supposed to make it more permeable – for people, goods and ideas. Thus the German approach essentially parallels that of Helsinki where the ratification of the territorial status quo ("Basket One") was to unfreeze the social and political status quo in terms of humanitarian improvements ("Basket Three").

In addition to changing the *content* of reunification, Bonn has also reversed its old priorities. Traditionally, only evolution in Germany (i.e., progress towards reunification) was thought to permit and justify evolution in Europe (i.e., détente, arms control and regional security measures). Now détente in Europe is supposed to pave the way for an as yet undefined measure of reassociation between the two Germanies.

The new German *Ostpolitik* has created its own ambiguities and tensions which have not made the overall Western approach to détente any easier. In the old days, the West was contractually committed to reunification (as laid down in the famous Article 7 of the Bonn Convention). The article and the commitment is still on the books, yet it is clear that it is no longer operative – not even in the negative sense of precluding any Western overture or concession to the East which would add solidity to the status quo based on the division of Germany. On the other hand, how far can the Germans go themselves without colliding with another part of the 1954 compact which reserves all rights "pertaining to Germany as a whole" to the former occupying powers? How far can Bonn go in its attempt to improve relations with GDR without forfeiting completely the idea of one nation indivisible?

Berlin is a good example for dilemmas that have withstood the soothing impact of détente. Berlin is still a continuous source of tensions because it remains a symbol of national identity for the West Germans – and of fractured sovereignty for the East Germans.

And then there is the tension between stability and evolution which besets all of détente policy. The former is supposed to lead to the latter, but beyond certain limits (which we do not fully know) evolution undermines stability. We want less confrontation and more evolution – and end up with phenomena like Eurocommunism and the dissident movements which might, ultimately, return to haunt the very stability that spawned them in the first place. To some extent, West Germany's policy of small but steady steps toward inter-German "normalization" and the new American human rights policy are parallels and complement each other. Yet there is a danger that both policies will fall out of step, that a human rights policy pursued too stridently and too insistently will achieve the opposite of what it intended. The pursuit of lofty principles, proclaimed without due regard for the sensitivity thresholds of the other side, might ultimately rekindle the very repression it was designed to mute.

The issue is not either-or but complementarity and prudence. Both require a hitherto unrealized degree of intra-Western coordination and consensus-building. The task is all the more urgent in view of a permanent build-up of Soviet and Warsaw Pact forces, which might threaten the military stability which is the *conditio sine qua non* of all détente efforts.

The Dilemmas of Soviet Coexistence Policy

"Peaceful coexistence" is a form of the international class struggle which purports to exclude war as means towards its consummation. Up to a point, the Soviet Union's renunciation of force is credible not only because of the horrendous destructiveness of nuclear weapons and danger of escalation but also because of the deep-seated trauma the ravages of World War II have etched into Soviet conciousness. Yet for the Soviets "peaceful coexistence" does not necessarily imply the permanence of international arrangements, mutual self-limitation or even respect for spheres of influence. For "peaceful coexistence" proceeds on the iron premise of "historical necessity" inexorably paving the way for the ultimate victory of the forces of Socialism. As such, the concept contains a built-in element of inevitable growth and expansion which does not exactly dovetail with Western détente notions of "parity", balance and coexistence with socio-political systems inimical to one's own value system. To be sure, the Soviet view of the world does not exclude arms control or intensified economic exchange. Indeed, Moscow is eager to strengthen its lagging economy with infusions of Western credits and know-how. But economic cooperation *à la russe* should not be confused with Western visions of ever-increasing "interdependence" turning the Soviet Union into a status quo power willy-nilly. In the final analysis, the COMECON system is based on self-sufficiency and not on a global division of labor. Trade and exchange is a vehicle for badly needed economic modernization, not for long-run systemic transformation. And détente notwithstanding, the Soviet Union does remain a revolutionary power – at least as far as its intentions are concerned.

Its raison d'être is the revolutionary class struggle; hence the inherent limits to Soviet détente policy. The Soviet system is badly in need of modernization and flexibility, but the ideological imperatives of the system impose rigidity, repression and stagnation. Faced with the choice between permeability and reform, on the one hand, and retrenchment and recentralization, on the other, the Kremlin leadership – captured by certain fixations – will necessarily tend to opt for the latter. At best, the Kremlin will balance and maneuvre, but it cannot really ditch its dogma or system of rule – no matter how pressing the need for movement and modernization. Moreover, Russia's key historical experience is that of revolution, not evolution. Hence, whosoever talks reform is automatically suspected of subversion.

The resort to ever more arms must partly be seen as reaction to internal (dissidents) and external (Eurocommunism) troubles: the Soviet Union has no other way of countering. Armaments are thus a form of compensation and not necessarily preparation for military aggression. Military power is a symbol of strength and a factor of domestic discipline in a system which has few other ways of compensating for its loss of influence. Yet no matter what the real function of the Kremlin's armament policy may be, it does tend to limit the scope and credibility of its normalization policy. The clash between system efficiency and system stability remains a crucial and cruel dilemma. The Soviet leadership seems to be rather intrigued by it.

The Global Dimension of the East-West Conflict

The West cannot solve this dilemma for the Soviet Union, nor should it. Yet neither should the West sharpen the dilemma's horns through a policy of moralizing pathos which hits home where it hurts most. Such a policy may sharpen repression within the Soviet orbit. The attempt to "sell" economic benefits for political concessions or a straightforward conflict strategy appear equally unpromising. The "internal crisis of Socialism", stoked by Western pressure, will not give way to liberal-democratic confrontation.

Basically, only small steps are possible. What should their purpose be? They should help or encourage the East to make qualitative progress in the evolution of its system, yet deny them any offensively conceived objectives. We should encourage the Soviet Union to assume more responsibility for world order and less for world revolution. The Soviet Union should be inspired to participate actively in the shaping and ordering of global interdependence, and less actively in military support for so-called wars of national liberation. Ideally, the West would seek to present the Soviet Union with the right mix of incentives and constraints which would lead Moscow to revise and modify its antiquated dogma and objectives.

Yet the West has to make a qualitative "leap forward" in its own conceptions of world order, too – most urgently on the North-South axis. The old approach toward the Southern Hemisphere was really an extension of the East-West conflict: The Third World was regarded primarily as a stake and pawn. A creative approach to the Third World, one that would mute and defuse conflict, might also end up changing the nature of the East-West conflict for the better. This would be a truly *trilateral* task, one that would offer a new and constructive role to Europe. The two parts of Europe would not act at being a "third force" but rather as a double-jointed link between the two superpowers. This would in no way relieve the West of the necessity to keep a watchful eye on the overall military balance. Everything is crucial – the improvement of security as well as progress in economic and human relations.

European Ostpolitik: The Next Phase

In the wake of Helsinki and Belgrade, the East seems to be moving away from all-European gatherings and toward MBFR and SALT-type operations. The reason is twofold. Firstly, the Soviet Union and its cohorts are sensing that they are losing the ideological struggle, at least in Central Europe. Helsinki has brought them dissidents without bringing Moscow-leaning Communists to power in Western Europe. As result, they are now more interested in defending a kind of ideological Maginot Line than in competing freely for the hearts and minds of men. Secondly, they have been forced to learn that arms races are counterproductive; the West has tended to match and sometimes even to surpass their technological pace of armaments. Arms have not brought influence but instead have activated the resistance and suspicions of the West.

This is not to say that the West should set aside, for the time being, any efforts for the qualitative improvement of East-West relations and instead concentrate all of its efforts in the arms control arena. The real issue is to preserve the (humanitarian) gains of Helsinki *and* to advance on the SALT and MBFR level. Even if the Soviet Union has so far sought to compensate domestic insecurity with arms, a creative Western policy should not exhaust itself in pure arms-matching. The first MBFR agreements might not result in more than simple stabilization measures. Yet as MBFR goes on, the West should make it increasingly difficult for the Soviets to use guns as a vehicle for influence while driving home the ultimate incompatibility between arms competition and coexistence.

SALT and MBFR require two different approaches. In the MBFR context, the task is to duplicate on the regional level the principles of stability, balance, and parity already accepted – if not always realized – on the SALT level. One criterion of parity is the progressive equalization of manpower figures within an agreed area of reduction. Right now, the problem is one of quantitative as well of qualitative and geographical disparity, even though arms and equipment imbalances loom more prominently than the Warsaw Pact edge on men. Yet the Soviet Union has always denied these disparities or shrugged them off by pointing to their purportedly legitimate function as a compensating factor in the global balance. In the meantime, Soviet superiority has become ever more apparent. Yet precisely because of stable nuclear deterrence on the global level, which contributes significantly to Western "self-deterrence", conventional forces have become more important on the regional level. If the East puts its faith in numbers, the West has to compensate in terms of quality and modernization – at least until arms control begins to work. Senator Nunn's recent report for the ASC has issued a clear warning that the East is gaining a nuclear edge in Europe, too. Hence it will become even more critical than it is now for the West to count on its nuclear weapons to balance the long-standing conventional superiority of the Warsaw Pact.

To be sure, the portents do not point to Soviet military aggression but to the use of arms superiority as a vehicle for political influence. This makes it all the more important to aim for numerical equality and collateral measures, such as stringent limits on deployment and movement. The principle of "no unilateral advantage" enshrined in the Moscow Summit of 1972 should be extended to the regional, European level as well, all the more so because "parity" remains an ambiguous measure of equivalance. In MBFR we are dealing with very complex and disparate weapons systems. How does one balance an advanced tank against a third-generation anti-tank missile? Parity, however defined, does not necessarily make for stability; hence MBFR should go beyond the mere numbers game and evolve codes of conduct which will inhibit and constrain the use of weapons disparities for unilateral political gains. Arms control as constraints policy is a kind of demonstrative "cost-benefit analysis" for the other side. Its purpose would be to put not only military but also political and perhaps economic "price tags" on the other side's decisions so as to minimize temptations and encourage the best possible behavior.

Codes of conduct, however important, should not be overestimated. They cannot really constrain a deliberate Soviet decision to break previously accepted commitments. Hence, the ultimate guarantee of good behavior is still the qualitative balance of force potentials. Such balance is threatened more closely by the rapid, almost revolutionary development of weapons systems (which make geographical limitations almost irrelevant) than by mere numbers of troops (which have, at any rate, remained relatively stable in the past). The Soviet formula of "the materialization of military détente" makes sense if there is an equilibrium between weapons systems. Certainly, the rash and somewhat transparent Warsaw Pact proposal for the "no first use of nuclear weapons" in Europe can be comtemplated only after regional parity has gained sufficient substance. Equal feelings for man-power as a possible achievement in a first round of MBFR agreements could – limited as it is – certainly not meet both objectives, but meaningfully manifest regional parity as the agreed term of reference for further decision-making on both sides in this context.

The Course of American Foreign Policy: Problems and Prospects

We started out by emphasizing the complementarity between (military) deterrence and (political) détente. Both are equally important, and both require a good deal of coordination between the various Western policies. On the European side, institutionalized consensus-building with regard to détente has worked fairly well in the past. Yet the consensus is fragile and there is no guarantee that it will persist in the face of, say, pressures from the East or one-sided undertakings on the part of the United States. Serious peril might arise from the uncertainties enveloping the stability of governments in various European capitals. Regime or governmental instability effectively inhibits even small progress toward talking with "one European voice". Moreover, matters will be further complicated by the admission of new members to the European Community. However, unless there is a powerful shift to the Left in Paris or Rome, the basic convergence of détente interests will probably suffice to lend continuity to the established practice of "conceptual syncretism" – the unity of the weaker nations against the threat from a single strong power.

Future American policy toward the East and toward Europe poses additional uncertainties and question marks. Clearly, Jimmy Carter's hand in foreign policy matters, as that of most American presidents, is stronger than that of most European executives. Yet for all his moral and political strength and regardless of his many pronouncements, his directions are still shrouded. Almost anything seems possible – ranging from Brzezinski's old "peaceful engagement" to a new moralist globalism and rather idealistic visions of arms control. The gamut is wide, and the distinctions between these options are vague and fluid.

Three potential changes of direction might have a decisive impact on European-American relations. First, what priority will the Carter Administration assign to Europe? For instance, if the scales are tipped in favor of North-South "world order" politics, then the Atlantic relationship will probably be scaled down to a mere holding operation *cum* new demands for European (financial and economic) contribution. The strains will grow because Europe and America have different views of a new world economic order. The importance hitherto attached to the superpower relationship as key factor in world order could decline. Perhaps the American commitment to the defense and stability of Western Europe might even weaken in the process. Hence, in order to avoid conflict, it is paramount to reach an understanding on a harmonious distribution of roles and to define more closely the tasks and responsibilities of the European Community than was either possible or necessary in the more narrow East-West context.

Secondly, which priorities will shape American security policy? Presumably, the Carter Administration will opt for continuity and thus use force cautiously, aiming to assure stability through diplomatic and consensual means. Yet as far as Europe is concerned, the danger is that a persistent imbalance of military potentials might be further consolidated by arms control measures oriented primarily towards feasibility and speedy agreement rather than true stability. Those risks would increase if the reduction of tactical nuclear weapons in Europe were to proceed more rapidly than the pace of conventional force modernization.

Last but not least, it will be crucial to evolve means which will eliminate the dangers of alienation or even a "decoupling" process between Europe and America – especially in the face of leftward swings in various European capitals. The resort to bilateral links between the United States and the politically most reliable partners in Europe seems hardly to be a promising way out – interdependence in Europe has gone too far for such tactic to work. Falling back to traditional inter-state alliance politics would give the Soviet Union the political chance it has always sought, i.e., to draw Europe piece by piece into a kind of all-European neutralism under Soviet predominance. The vitality of the Atlantic Alliance, enabling it to envelop diversity within unity, is the cornerstone of a policy which can profit from the forces of pluralism, creativity and movement far more than the rigid and inflexible systems of the East. But if there is such a thing as the "cunning of reason", and if it operates in favor of innovation and against stagnant dogma, it needs the helping hand of creative coordination – and the strong arm of deterrence and defense.

The Communist and Socialist Parties in Italy, Spain, and France
"Eurocommunism," "Eurosocialism," and Soviet Policy

by WILLIAM E. GRIFFITH

This essay considers the usefulness of the terms "Eurocommunism" and "Eurosocialism" and analyzes the most recent developments in West "European socialist and communist parties[1] and in Soviet relations with them, especially the communist-socialist split in France and the controversies surrounding the publication of Santiago Carrillo's "*Eurocomunismo*" *y Estado* and the November 1977 Moscow sixtieth anniversary of the Bolshevik Revolution.[2]

To begin, let us dispose of a few of the "terrible simplifications" which, as the great nineteenth century Swiss historian Jacob Burkhardt so presciently predicted, have become the curse of our times.

...."Eurocommunism" and "Eurosocialism" are labels which by now more conceal reality than they illuminate it. As Secretary of State Vance has said:

... It is misleading and incorrect to lump together the various Communist movements in Europe that are striking out along different roads from Moscow. They are different and separate parties, as in Yugoslavia, Italy, Spain and France. We must move away from the habit of simply calling them "Eurocommunists.". . .

... We Americans often trap ourselves by grabbing on easy code words that in fact misdescribe what we are talking about. . . .[3]

Carrillo's reformism and Marchais' rigidity have little in common. The French socialist party is both to the right and to the left of the French communist party. Socialism (or, rather, social democracy) in West Germany is much to the right of socialism in France and Spain. I therefore deliberately do not use these two labels in this essay.

... The left is not, as is so often claimed, rising in all of Western Europe, but only in three Latin countries: Italy, France, and Spain. Even there, the French communist party has not increased its power, for the communist-socialist split has hurt the left and helped the center and the right; and in northern Europe conservatism, not the left, is gaining.

... The Latin communists have not become social democrats. They declare that they are not and will not, and they have not abandoned Leninist democratic centralism, i.e., they still forbid opposition within the party. Yet the Italian and Spanish communists, but not the French, seem to be steadily moving in that direction, and some experts maintain that they are almost there.

... It is not clear whether at present and in the near future the rise of communism in Western Europe will be favorable or unfavorable to either the United States or the Soviet Union. Indeed, it may be unfavorable to both.

The Causes of the Rise of the Latin Left

Rightist parties, ranging from the moderate Christian Democrats in Italy through Gaullism in France to Franco's authoritarianism in Spain, have been in power in Latin Europe for a quarter-century or more, and voters increasingly want a change. The Italian Christian Democrats are laced with corruption; the Gaullists have done little to bridge the high French rich-poor income gap; and Francoism has been discredited in Spain. The post-1973 economic crisis, caused by the end of the dollar standard, the quadrupling of oil prices, and the resultant recession and stagflation, has also favored the left.

Scenting power, the left has improved its electoral image. Realizing how completely the Soviet model has lost its attractiveness in Western Europe, the left has established a nationalist image by distancing itself from Moscow's invasion of Czechoslovakia and its repression at home and in Eastern Europe. The left has also profited from the tarnished image of the United States, because of the Vietnam War and Watergate, and from the détente-induced decline in West Europeans' fear of the Soviet Union.

The Latin Socialists

The Latin socialist parties, unlike the north European social democrats, support large scale nationalization and workers' self-administration (*autogestion*) and oppose much of US foreign policy. In France and Spain they, not the communists, are the strongest leftist parties. In Italy, where the socialists are split, the communists and the left-wing Christian Democrats fulfill the function of the French (PS)[4] and Spanish (PSOE) socialists. By its simultaneous support of civil liberties, European unity, and *autogestion*, the PS threatens the communists from the left as well as the right.

Historically, the French, Italian, and Spanish socialist parties have been stronger than the communists. Indeed, we may well see the temporary weakness of the French socialists in the "'70's" as only an interruption in this situation. The Italian socialist party (PSI) allied with the Italian communists during the fascist period. During the Cold War period a small social democratic party (PSDI), led by Giuseppe Saragat, split off from Pietro Nenni's PSI. Only after the 1956 Hungarian Revolution did the PSI break with the communists. However, Italy's worsening tensions, the slow decline of the DC, the PCI's superior skill and increasing moderation, and the continuing socialist split gradually brought the PCI to its present position of greater electoral superiority to the socialists and close to the DC.

One other point must be made, about which little published material is available. Within the context of the Socialist International, and aided by the Swedish and Austrian socialist parties, the West German Social Democratic Party (SPD) has been very active in recent years in supporting and financing the Spanish and Portuguese socialist parties. Indeed, the SPD was in part responsible for their re-creation and success. The SPD has primarily worked through the Friedrich Ebert Stiftung, a SPD-controlled organization with a world-wide program of support for socialist parties, whose funds come primarily from West German governmental appropriations. (So do those of the Konrad Adenauer Stiftung, a CDU-controlled organization with similar global functions for Christian Democrats.)

The SPD's operations in the Iberian peninsula, its position to the right of and of frequent rivalry with the PS, and its opposition to the PS/PCF alliance[5] increased PS-SPD rivalry, notably for influence in Portugal, Spain, and Italy and within the Socialist International. This rivalry has lessened in the last year or two and the PS-PCF break will probably lessen it still more.

Latin socialists are much more heterogenous and less disciplined than Latin communists. Although the Italian socialists are split and weak, the French and Spanish socialists are united, albeit heterogenous, and strong. Indeed, the PS today somewhat resembles the inter-war French radical socialists, and the programmatic distance between its right (e.g., Defferre) and its left wings (CERES) is far greater than the minor differences within the PCF. Finally, the socialists have two leaders, Mitterand in France and González in Spain, with great charisma and organizing ability.

Latin Communists[6]

The French, Italian, and Spanish communist parties now have varying mixtures of independence (from Soviet control), domestic reformism (parliamentary pluralism and civil liberties), and regionalism (West European unity and independence from the US and the USSR). Each of these three differs in all three parties in intensity, duration, and degree of doctrinal expression. The Italian communist party has exhibited these trends the longest, the Spanish the most extensively, and the French the most briefly and least. Moreover, none of the three characteristics is confined to West Europe alone. Independence also characterizes the Yugoslav and Romanian parties in East Europe and the Japanese and Australian parties in Asia. Indeed, independence (and reformism) first appeared in East Europe: in Yugoslavia when Stalin broke with Tito in 1948, and later in the Polish and Hungarian parties in 1956 and in the Romanian party in the early "60's". It only began thereafter to rise in the Italian and Spanish parties and was first decisively expressed by them in public by their criticism of the 1968 Soviet invasion of Czechoslovakia, because of the third East European wave of independence (and reformism) there. The Japanese and Australian CP's, i.e., all major communist parties in the industrialized world, are reformist, except those in North America. Only regionalism is a West European phenomenon, and even there only in part: the French communists oppose it.

Independence from Soviet control represents a revival in these communist parties of the national traditions submerged by Stalinism and the Cold War. Reformism (as it did among pre-1914 West European social democrats) reflects these parties' increasing awareness that in an age of affluence revolution is increasingly unlikely but participation in political power through parliamentary means is increasingly possible. Regionalism reflects popular support for West European unity in Italy and Spain. The fear of failure and the scent of success, not ideological conversion, are moderating southern European communist parties. And, let us remember, in politics pragmatic changes are more genuine and long-lasting than is intellectual conversion, for their causes are broadly based and reflect permanent trends. The ideology to justify them comes, as usual, later.

Independence. All three major West European communist parties, the French (PCF), Italian (PCI), and Spanish (PCE), have gained autonomy from Soviet control or predominant influence. They have done so by following essentially nationalistic policies. They have furthered their independence by maneuvering so successfully in their relations with the Soviet Union (notably in the context of the Soviet-sponsored preparations for and holding of two multi-party communist conferences, an international one in Moscow in 1969 and an all-European one in East Berlin in 1976), that Moscow's attempts to contain or reverse the erosion of its influence have only eroded it further and have contributed to the consolidation of the independence of the Italian, Spanish, French, Yugoslav, and Romanian communist parties.

The PCE needs nationalist legitimacy to erase Spaniards' memories of its servility to Moscow during and after the Spanish Civil War. Spain is now fervently democratic and pro-European. The PCE is a small minority and badly needs electoral support. It therefore stresses independence from Moscow more than the PCF and even the PCI. For example, in his recent book[7] its leader, Santiago Carrillo, insists not only on independence from Moscow but also on West European communism's superiority to Soviet communism. Moreover, he declares that it is not only the right but the duty of all communist parties to criticize repression in the Soviet Union (which is not an "authentic workers' democracy") and the 1968 Soviet invasion of Czechoslovakia, *inter alia* in order to establish their own electoral credibility.

In contrast, the PCF, fearful of alienating its pro-Soviet supporters, has occasionally criticized specific Soviet repressive acts but has never generalized, as Carrillo has done, on the ideological level. The PCI has until now been somewhere between the PCE and the PCF on systemic criticism of the Soviet Union. While by far the greater part of its criticism of Moscow has been specific, more recently some examples of PCI systemic criticism have appeared, but to date they have had nowhere near the completeness and authority of Carrillo's book.

Finally, all three major West European parties are determined not to break with the Soviet and East European parties, a step from which they would gain little, lose influence in Eastern Europe, and face some dissension within their own ranks. The question, therefore, is whether Moscow will break with them and thus precipitate the third great communist schism, after those with Yugoslavia in 1948 and with China in 1959.

The independent Yugoslavs and autonomous Romanians strongly support the Latin communist parties in their opposition to Soviet control and their determination not to break with Moscow. Since both are in Eastern Europe and in power, they are more important to Moscow than the West European parties. Yugoslavia is also valuable to the Soviets in the non-aligned world.[8] Both have good relations with Washington, and since Tito's August-September 1977 visit[9] there Yugoslavia has quite good relations, as Romania has always had, with Peking. Belgrade and Bucharest thus help to deter Soviet pressure on the West European communist parties. Since Romania must be circumspect toward the Soviet Union and the PCF differs with the PCI and the PCE on regionalism and reformism, the center of the independent tendencies in European communism is a Belgrade-Rome-Madrid alliance.

Beginning in 1974 Yugoslavia took the lead in resisting Soviet pressure during the long preparations for the June 1976 East Berlin European communist meeting.[10] (Of the other ruling communist parties, only the Hungarian has shown some sympathy for "Eurocommunist" tenets, but Moscow has always brought Kádár back into line.)[11] Moreover, although Tito's visit to China did not result in resumption of Chinese-Yugoslav inter-party relations, it did further heighten his prestige, including vis-à-vis Moscow. It also made improvement in Chinese-West European inter-party relations seem possible. In December 1977 Chinese Vice Foreign Minister Yu Chüan remarked that West European communist revisionism was bad but their opposition to the Soviet Union was good.[12] (Meanwhile, Albania virtually broke with China because of Peking's rapprochements with Washington and Belgrade, a move which further weakened the declining "Maoist" splinter groups in Western Europe.)[13]

Reformism. Reformism may be defined as the acceptance of a permanent multiparty parliamentary system, civil liberties, and willingness to gain and to leave power by parliamentary victory or defeat. It therefore means the abandonment of the Leninist doctrines of the vanguard role of the communist party and the dictatorship of the proletariat but not of democratic centralism or of socialist economic transformation, i.e., it remains different from social democracy.

The PCI has been increasingly reformist since 1944. For that reason, because of its anti-fascist record, and because Italian nationalism has always been weaker than French and Spanish, the PCI's electoral appeal has steadily grown. In the June 1976 elections for the first time it gained enough seats in parliament so that the Christian Democrats could not rule without its acquiescence.

Thereupon, the DC, the PCI, and the other "constitutional" parties (i.e., all except the neo-fascist MSI) agreed on a program of economic austerity and reforms which deprived parliament of any real power, now exercised by a *de facto* DC-PCI coalition, with the PCI abstaining on all important parliamentary votes. This led to differences within the PCI leadership, PCI losses on its left and among its youth, trade union opposition to PCI support of economic austerity, and to a feeling among left intellectuals that the PCI, like the DC, is primarily interested in power and its perquisites rather than in reform – to say nothing of revolution.[14] In December 1977, while the DC still opposed PCI entry into the government, the PCI (and the PSI and Republicans) urged it, because of the economic strains caused by deflation.

In March 1978 a prolonged governmental crisis, caused by the other "constitutional parties" withdrawing their support or abstention from the minority DC government, was "solved" by a new minority DC government which all the constitutional parties except the Liberals (i.e., including the

PCI) agreed to support in Parliament. It is too early as of this writing (March 1978) to venture an opinion as to whether the communists will win or lose as a result. They won insofar as this was the first time since 1947 that the communists will be in the governmental majority and will therefore be consulted on all issues. Thus, the PCI won in status and in reinforcing its image of progress toward participation in the cabinet. It lost insofar as it dropped its initial demands to have ministers in the cabinet.

The question now is whether or not Andreotti can continue to maneuver so that the PCI will lose worker support because of a deflationary economic program which it will now have more clearly to support. In any case, the most recent crisis was not decisive. All parties are waiting for the December 1978 presidential elections. Thereafter, new parliamentary elections seem likely.[15]

The PCE's reformism, as Carrillo's book has most recently shown, is the most extensive and the most generalized and absolutized at the doctrinal level. Indeed, it has so departed from the Leninist model that it is not surprising that it proposes to call itself only Marxist, not Marxist-Leninist.[16] It includes peaceful parliamentary transition to socialism, by "hegemony" of a "historic bloc" (Gramscian phrases) of workers and cultural forces, indefinite continuation of a permanent multi-party system and full civil liberties, alternation of parties in power (i.e., it rejects the dictatorship of the proletariat), denial that the communist party is the leading or only party of the working class, the aim of merger of communists and socialists (i.e., it rejects the Leninist vanguard concept of the communist party), full toleration of religion, and no objections for the present to the Spanish constitutional monarchy. Carrillo differentiates the PCE from social democracy in that he proposes to institute socialism, not to reform capitalism but even so he favors continued small peasant proprietorship and privately-owned businesses. He also supports the Marxist concepts of dialectical and historical materialism and of revolution in underdeveloped countries or in developed countries if the bourgeoisie undemocratically prevents the left from coming to power peacefully. The Catalan communist party (PSUC) is if anything even more reformist.[17]

The PCF, however, because of its tradition of Jacobin nationalism and its hard-line base, has tended to give priority to nationalism over reformism. Although it continues to preach the latter, its September 1977 split with the PS weakened what little credibility its reformism had achieved.[18] Indeed, the major reason for the PCF's attack on the PS was its (justified) fear that if the left were to win the March 1978 parliamentary elections, it would be weaker than the socialists, thus damaging its image as the "vanguard of the working class". (The PCF also insisted on more nationalization of more industrial firms in order to get more positions in them.)[19]

Throughout the election campaign the communists continued to denounce the socialists. That plus fear of economic crisis and of communist participation in the government produced, contrary to all the public opinion polls, a solid victory for the incumbent center-right coalition in the parliamentary elections on the 12th and 19th of March 1978. The communist vote remained steady at 20.5 percent. The center gained vis-à-vis the Gaullists. The socialists were the main losers. Whether they will move toward the right or the communists toward reformism remains to be seen.

Regionalism has three aspects: attitudes toward West European unity, East-West relations, and NATO. Not surprisingly, in the two strongly pro-European unity and quite pro-American countries, Italy and Spain, their communist parties have been influenced by these views. The PCF, in contrast, is, like most Frenchmen, against NATO, European unity, and West Germany. The PCE urges a united, independent Western Europe equidistant between East and West. So, less strongly, does the PCI. The PCF, however, advocates a French nuclear force *à tous azimuths*, aimed against the West as well as the East, i.e., it proposes General de Gaulle's policy of armed neutrality. Finally, the PCI and PCE have recently taken a fairly positive attitude toward NATO. Both advocate that their countries remain in it until all blocs are dissolved, that is, indefinitely. However, both want NATO modified, in some unspecified fashion. The PCF, on the other hand, remains as anti-NATO as it is anti-EEC.

Most of the minor West European communist parties, especially the British, Swedish, and the "interior" Greeks, are also independent, reformist, and regionalist. The Portuguese communist party remains adamantly anti-"Eurocommunist" and pro-Soviet.

The Soviet Attitude toward the West European Left

The Soviet leaders have become increasingly hostile to the West European left, and most of all to the communists. This is not surprising, for Moscow has always opposed social democrats and even more reformist communists, in Western Europe and elsewhere. After all, the orthodox have always found heretics much more pernicious than heathen.

It is even less surprising now, for the West European socialists threaten Soviet orthodoxy from the right, because of their social democratic tendencies and their relation with the North European Social Democrats, notably the

SPD, and, for Moscow even worse, also from the left, because of their support of *autogestion*. The West European communists are even more threatening to Moscow because they not only reject Soviet primacy but even criticize the Soviets for deviations from Marxism-Leninism. Indeed, Carrillo has written that Eurocommunism is rightly different from and certainly more advanced than Soviet socialism, that communism can only be the vanguard of the working class by earning political and cultural "hegemony" (Gramsci's famous concept), and that the communist party is in any case not the only representative of the working class.

Moscow rightly fears the impact of West European communism in Eastern Europe, where dissidents feel encouraged and legitimatized by it, as they do by the Helsinki CSCE Final Act. The Soviets probably also fear that the rise of the left in Latin Europe will push West Germany to the right and toward the United States. And since Soviet policy in Western Europe gives first priority to the Federal Republic, such a development would weigh heavily in Soviet calculations.

Moscow has several reasons to view the West European communists positively. The West European left, most of all the communists, generally oppose the US and hold views parallel to Soviet foreign policy. Were they to dominate their governments – which is unlikely – US influence and presence in Western Europe would probably decline. With Sino-Soviet relations frozen, Moscow needs the West European communists, despite their deviations, to try to assert its primacy in the "international communist and workers movement." (Ironically, the more it has tried to do so, the more West European communist parties have successfully maneuvered to increase their independence from Moscow.) One of these communist parties, the Italian, already *de facto* shares power in Rome, so the Soviet Union must take into account its state relations with Italy in dealing with it.

For several years past the Soviet Union has been intermittently and increasingly unsuccessfully campaigning against West European communists' "deviationist" theories and practice. After its 1968 invasion of Czechoslovakia, Moscow hoped to bring West European communist criticism of it under control. However, the 1969 Soviet-sponsored international communist conference in Moscow further diminished Soviet power and influence in the international communist and radical world. Soviet losses were even greater at the 1976 East Berlin European communist conference, where Carrillo, whom in the early "70's" the Soviets unsuccessfully tried to overthrow, declared that the international communist movement no longer has either a Vatican or a Pope and Berlinguer and Marchais said that they would refuse to attend such a conference again.[20]

Soon after the 1969 conference, Moscow began to reiterate its basic objections to the line of the major West European communist parties: that it has developed particularly during a period of East-West détente, when the imperialists become increasingly active and more flexible in their attempts to subvert communism, that it increases the dangers arising from electoral collaboration with non-communists, and that these dangers can only be overcome by strict adherence to proletarian internationalism (to which the East Berlin statement had not referred, on the insistence of the West European communists) and to the "general laws" of socialist construction.[21]

For some time evidence has been accumulating of differences of view within the Soviet leadership about the best tactics to use in dealing with West European communism. Suslov, Ponomarov, and Zarodov seem to favor a frontal attack, while the more moderate, such as Zagladin, perhaps (until he was replaced) Katushev, and (less clearly) Brezhnev, have preferred a combination of carrots and sticks. These differences, which first became apparent in Soviet theoretical articles dealing with Cunhal's 1975 bid for communist power in Portugal and in references to "proletarian" or "socialist" internationalism,[22] became clearer in 1977. In early March at the Madrid Eurocommunist summit meeting Soviet pressure reportedly prevented Berlinguer and Marchais from joining Carrillo in open criticism of Moscow.[23] Moscow then cut key passages out of its version of the Madrid communiqué.[24] In March and April Soviet-sponsored multiparty meetings at Sofia[25] and Prague,[26] the Czechoslovak and Bulgarian delegations led the attack on Eurocommunism, Ponomarev took a less extreme position, and the Poles and Hungarians even more moderate ones. Carrillo's book [27] was published in April. In June the Soviet *New Times* (*Novoe Vremya*) published a slashing attack on it. It charged that Carrillo "counterposed" West and East European communist parties on an "anti-Soviet platform," discredited socialism, especially the Soviet Union, and renounced a joint multi-party line in favor of division of Europe and a stronger NATO. "Eurocommunism," the *New Times* went on, weakens and splits communism "for the interests of imperialism," leads to a "split in the international communist movement," and interferes in internal Soviet party affairs because of its "conscious anti-Sovietism" and "renunciation of Marxism-Leninism." Communists must struggle, the Soviet article concluded, against "those who would insert divisive ideas into the communist movement."[28]

The PCE replied to Moscow in at least as violent a tone.[29] The Yugoslavs supported Carrillo the most strongly of the other communist parties.[30] The Romanians reiterated their autonomist position.[31] The PCI downplayed the dispute[32] but sent a delegation to Moscow which reportedly got the Soviets to agree to suspend polemics against the PCE,[33] and Moscow did for a time execute a partial tactical retreat.[34] The PCF downplayed the issue almost completely. Among Moscow's allies, the Czechoslovaks, Bulgarians, and East Germans joined in the Soviet attack. The Poles[35] and Hungarians[36] were more moderate until Moscow brought them back into line. Even the East Germans took a less hard line than the Soviets, Czechoslovaks, and Bulgarians.[37] Later, Kádár reportedly sponsored another attempt at mediation between Moscow and the Eurocommunists.[38] The Soviets then invited Carrillo to attend the November 1977 Moscow ceremonies for the sixtieth anniversary of the Bolshevik Revolution,[39] but when he arrived he was not called on to address the gathering and was seated in a back row.[40] Thereupon he left Moscow before schedule for Belgrade,[41] Rome,[42] Madrid – and the United States, where he lectured at Yale, Johns Hopkins and Harvard.[43] As he said to western correspondents in Moscow:

... There must be some kind of debate. Otherwise, they simply would have told me right from the beginning they weren't going to allow me to speak. But as to who is on what side – I do not know the secrets of the Kremlin. . . .[44]

And in Belgrade:

... Eurocommunism is going well: when Kissinger agrees with some of the Soviet comrades in affirming that Eurocommunism does not exist and Lister associates himself with this judgment, this confirms that Eurocommunism exists and is in good health. . . .[45]

Shortly thereafter Suslov and Ponomarov, while disclaiming Soviet hegemonic intentions, reiterated the importance of "proletarian internationalism" and the "common objective laws" of the construction of "real socialism" and communism, i.e., that while the West European parties may for tactical reasons come to socialism differently than Moscow did, once they do their socialism must follow the Soviet model, which they must not criticize. In January 1978 Moscow violently attacked the PCE leader Manuel Azcárate. He, the PCE, the PCI, the PCF, and the LCY criticized the attack.[46] In February 1978 Moscow was thus continuing to polemicize with the West European communists and attempting to assert its primacy *de facto* while denying it in theory.

The question is not whether the "Eurocommunists" will break with Moscow but whether Moscow will break with the "Eurocommunists." Arguments in Moscow against a break probably include the blow it would strike at Soviet prestige; the danger of driving these parties farther toward Washington, and perhaps even Peking; the shock to Eastern Europe; and the absence of any authoritative Soviet-dominated international mechanism to pronounce an excommunication. The main arguments for a break would be "Eurocommunism's" infectious impact on Eastern Europe and eventually on the Soviet Union itself, as well as on other extra-European pro-Soviet communist parties. Moreover, Moscow has always excommunicated deviationists and it goes against the grain not to do so now.

Finally, Moscow has aided party splits in the past. It has unsuccessfully tried to split the PCE and Japanese communist party. It has aided in splitting the Israeli, Australian, and Swedish communist parties.[47] True, none of these Soviet moves would have as great an impact as a Soviet attempt, successful or not, to split the Italian or French communist parties. But one should assume that Moscow would in principle be prepared to try.

The Soviet decisions, therefore, will be ones not of principle but of tactics. But when, why, and if they will occur we cannot know.

To sum up: "Eurocommunism" is at present not a useful label for increasingly complex and diverging mixtures of independence, reformism, and regionalism which now characterize the major West European communist parties. (It was until recently; it may be again; but it is not now.) The major West European socialist parties are perhaps even more in flux; "Eurosocialism" is therefore also not useful. Soviet policy toward the West European parties, although cyclical and disputed in Moscow, remains more hostile than conciliatory. The results – whether or not the Latin left will come to power, and when and where, and whether or not Moscow will break with one or more West European communist parties – remain in doubt. As the *Guide Michelin* so wisely remarks in another connection, *nos recherches continuent.*

Problems for Western Policy

The Political Background. The problems created by the Latin left for Western policy are not susceptible to easy solutions nor in all likelihood to direct public Western pressure. They arise primarily for the United States and for the strongest economic power in Western Europe, the Federal Republic of Germany. They are generally of two kinds, economic and military.

Let us first, however, be clear what the nature and limits of these problems are. The PCF and the PCE are very unlikely in the near future to become majority parties in governing coalitions, for both are much weaker than their actual or potential socialist allies. The left will hardly come to power in Spain for several years; and in any case the PSOE rejects a coalition with the PCE. In France, a left victory in the March 1978 parliamentary elections, which already seemed unlikely before the recent communist-socialist split, did not occur. In Italy the issue is not a left coalition, which the PCI does not want, but Berlinguer's *compromesso storico*: a coalition between the Christian Democrats (DC) and the PCI, with the former at least initially the majority member. The PCI is neither in nor out of the government, but somewhere in between, and thus the future is in doubt.

Economic Crisis? The immediate result of a left coalition in a southern European country would be an economic crisis in that country and in the European Economic Community. Rightly fearing rapid wage increases and resultant spiralling inflation, capital investors would fulfill their own prophecies: massive disinvestment and capital flight would follow. Washington and Bonn, the only states with money and the political motives to prevent this, would therefore have to decide whether or not to undertake a massive aid and stabilization program, presumably through the IMF, and what conditions they would demand for their aid.

Military Crisis? Of the three, only the PCF wants to leave NATO, but France is barely in it anyway. US defense policy calls for continued use of Spanish and particularly of Italian bases. The PCI and PCE have declared that they will agree to this, but the PCI has also said that it is opposed to continued Italian participation in NATO "in its present form." Long and difficult negotiations would threaten if the PCI entered the Italian government. Yet as a minority party in a governing coalition with the DC it would unlikely to be able to create insuperable obstacles to NATO.

The West German SPD-FDP government is opposed to the PCI entering the Italian government and far more so to the PCF entering the French. (PCE entry is most unlikely and therefore not an issue.) However, it has preferred publicly not to express its opposition but rather to keep communications open with the PCI through the SPD and to aid Italy to overcome its economic problems. In Spain the SPD strongly supports the PSOE, as it does the Portuguese socialists. Former Secretary of State Kissinger publicly and uncompromisingly opposed (and still opposes) the entry of West European communist parties into goverments. He has declared that this would not only subvert democracy but also endanger continued congressional support for American troop deployment in Europe. This overt attempt to tell West Europeans how to vote runs contrary to rising West European nationalism.

The Carter Administration seemed at first to modify Kissinger's position. It declared that the decision was one for the West European electorates and that the US did not intend to interfere in it. However, it went on, the US reserved its right to express its views on the subject and favored governments formed by parties with democratic traditions and convictions. Secretary Vance even said that it was conceivable that this present policy would have to be revised if relations between the West European communist parties and the Soviet Union worsen sharply. In sum, therefore, Washington (like Bonn) continued to oppose communist entry into West European governments, but initially and for tactical reasons expressed this position indirectly so as not to antagonize West European nationalist sensitivities.

But in January 1978 the PCI withdrew its support from the Andreotti government, which fell soon thereafter. Washington was thus faced with the possibility of the PCI entering the government, concerned with offending conservatives in Congress (whose votes it needed for ratification of the Panama Canal treaties and SALT II), and under pressure from the US Embassy in Rome and at least some elements in the DC. On 12 January the State Department issued a statement which reflected a considerable hardening in US policy, in particular by its declaration that the PCI did not share with the United States and Italy "profound democratic values and interests."[48] True, the statement repeated the Administration's view that the peoples of Western Europe alone could decide how they were governed, but the change in emphasis was unmistakable. Bonn made no similar statement.

By March 1978 the left had been defeated in France, the communists had won little if anything in Italy, and US relations with the Soviet Union were again deteriorating, in large part because of differences concerning the Middle East and the Horn of Africa. It seemed unlikely, therefore, despite its initial qualifications of its position, that the Carter Administration would become any less hostile to the West European communist parties.

Notes

[1] This is a revised and updated version of my "*Eurocommunism*": *The Third Great Communist Schism?* Cambridge: MIT Center for International Studies, C/76–19, mimeo., November 1976, published as "L'Eurocomunismo: Sara il terzo grande schisma comunista?", in Sergio Segre, (ed.), *A chi fa paura l'eurocomunismo*. Florence: Guaraldi 1977 and in revised form as "Das Problem des 'Eurokommunismus'", in Karl Kaiser and Hans-Peter Schwarz, (eds.), *Amerika und Westeuropa*. Stuttgart: Belser 1977, pp. 218–246. See also my "The Diplomacy of Eurocommunism", in Rudolf Tökés, (ed.), *Eurocommunism and Détente*. New York: New York University Press for the Council on Foreign Relations 1978.

[2] This study is primarily based upon discussions in Western and Eastern Europe in June, July, and September 1977. I am grateful to *The Reader's Digest*, of which I am

a roving editor, and to its editor-in-chief, Edward T. Thompson, for sponsoring my trip, and to the Earhart and Carthage Foundations for research support. I have profited from discussions with Kevin Devlin of Radio Free Europe, Munich; François Fejtö, Annie Kriegel and Neil MacInnes, in Paris, and Wolfgang Berner and Heinz Timmermann of the Bundesinstitut für ostwissenschaftliche und internationale Studien in Cologne, and with various West European socialist and communist leaders. For backgound on West European communism, see Neil MacInnes, *The Communist Parties of Western Europe*. New York: Oxford UP 1975 and *Euro-Communism*, The Washington Papers, No. 37. Beverly Hills and London: Sage 1976 and Donald L. M. Blackmer and Sidney Tarrow, (eds.), *Communism in France and Italy*. Princeton, N.J.: Princeton University Press 1975. There is unfortunately little analysis available on recent developments in the PS and the PSOE; the best sources, apart from their own publications, are *Le Monde* and *El Pais*. Italian socialism, on which considerable data is available, especially in Italian, is, however, much less important.

3 In an interview with C. L. Sulzberger, *The New York Times*, 6 November 1977. See also an interview with Frane Barbieri, who coined the word "Eurocommunism," in *Deutschland Archiv*, April 1977.

4 Norman Birnbaum, *Squabbling Toward the Election*, in: *The Nation*, 29 October 1977; Jean-Pierre Worms, *The Rise of the French Party*, in: *Dissent*, Summer 1977; Patrick McCarthy, *The French Socialist Party: Its Place in the Politics and Society of the Fifth Republic* (unpub. MS., Bologna, SAIS, 1977).

5 The SPD's opposition to socialist-communist alliances is above all due to its opposition to one within the Federal Republic, where the minuscule DKP is essentially an extension of the SED.

6 In addition to my own papers, cited in ftn. 1, supra, I have relied heavily on the analyses by Frane Barbieri in *Il Giornale*, Kevin Devlin in *Radio Free Europe Research*, and Heinz Timmermann in the *Berichte des Bundesinstituts für ostwissen-schaftliche und internationale Studien* and the running coverage in *Le Monde*. See also, *Eurocommunism*, in: *The Economist*, 5 November 1977; Annie Kriegel, *Un autre communisme?* Paris: Hachette, 1977; Heinz Timmermann, *Moskau und der europäische Kommunismus nach der Gipfelkonferenz von Ost-Berlin*, in: *Osteuropa*, April 1977 (plus documentation in ibid., pp. A180–A208) and *Der "Eurokommunismus" in Mehrzahl*, in: *Schweizer Monatsheft*, July 1977; James O. Goldsborough, *Eurocommunism after Madrid*, in: *Foreign Affairs*, January 1977; Charles Gati, *The "Europeanization" of Communism?*, ibid., April 1977; Joan Barth Urban, *Moscow and the PCI: Kto Kovo?*, paper prepared for a meeting of the Conference Group on Italian Politics, APSA Annual Meeting, Washington, D.C., 2 September 1977 (the best analysis of recent PCI policies, particularly vis-à-vis the CPSU), her previous *West European Communist Parties and the Soviet Union*, paper prepared for a conference on Foreign Policy of Eurocommunism, Airlie House, Warrenton, Va., May 1977, and *The Impact of Eurocommunism on the Socialist Community*, (MS), to be published in Andrew Gyorgy, (ed.), *Innovation in Communist Systems*. Boulder, Colo.: Westview, forthcoming. For foreign policy, see Heinz Timmermann, *Die Entspannungskonzepte der "Eurokom-munisten"*, in: *Berichte des Bundesinstituts fur ostwissenschaftliche und internationale*

Studien, No. 48, August 1977. For the PCF, in addition to the new Kriegel book, cited above, see the articles by Ronald Tiersky, notably his chapter in the forthcoming collective volume edited by Tökés (cited in ftn. 1, supra). For the PCE, see the articles by Eusebio Mujal-León, notably his chapter in the forthcoming Tökés volume and his *Spanish Communism and the Transition to the Post-Franco Era* in: David E. Albright, ed., *Communism and Political Systems in Western Europe*. Boulder, Colo.: Westview 1978. I also profited from a conference on "Eurocommunism and Regional Institutions" sponsored by the US Department of State and held at Airlie House, Warrenton, Va., on 12–14 May 1977.

⁷ Santiago Carrillo, *"Eurocomunismo" y Estado*. Barcelona: Critica 1977 (tr. as *"Eurocommunism" and the State*. London: Lawrence and Wishart, 1977), esp. p. 199. Analysis: Kevin Devlin, *"Eurocommunism and the State": Carrillo's Challenge to "Real Socialism"*, in: *Radio Free Europe Research*, 30 June 1977.

⁸ Aleksandar Grličkov (LCY secretary in charge of international affairs), *The National and the International*, in: *Borba*, 22–28 February 1977 (FBIS/EEU/18 March 1977/I6–21) (analyzed in Slobodan Stankovic, *Party Official Defends Primacy of "National Interests"*, in: *Radio Free Europe Research*, 8 March 1977) and his interview in *Politika*, 31 December 1977 and 1 and 2 January 1978 (FBIS/EEU/19 January 1978/I6–15); Viktor Meier from Ljubljana, *Der Eurokommunismus vor Jugoslawiens Tür. Die Entwicklung der Partei Berlinguers verunsichert Slowenien*, in: *Frankfurter Allgemeine Zeitung*, 2 March 1977; Paul Lendvai and Irena Reuter-Hendrichs, *Die sowjetische Jugoslawienpolitik 1972–1976*, in: *Berichte des Bundesinstituts für ostwissenschaftliche und internationale Studien*, No. 38, 1977; and F. Stephen Larrabee, *Balkan Security*, Adelphi Paper No. 135. London: International Institute for Strategic Studies 1977.

⁹ Slobodan Stankovic, *The "Heretic" Tito Rehabilitated at Peking's "Gate of Heavenly Peace"*, in: *Radio Free Europe Research*, 7 September 1977 and *"After Tito's Visit to Moscow"*, ibid., 22 August 1977.

¹⁰ For details, see my *The Diplomacy of Eurocommunism*, cited in ftn. 1, supra, and a Brussels lecture on 11 October 1977 by Grličkov, in TANJUG in Serbo-Croat, 11 October 1977, 1900 GMT (FBIS/EEU/13 October 1977/I2–8), analyzed in Slobodan Stankovic, *Grličkov Anticipates New Conflicts within Communist Movement*, in: *Radio Free Europe Research*, 14 October 1977.

¹¹ William F. Robinson, *The Wind and the Willow Tree*, in: *Radio Free Europe Research*, 7 October 1977; Kevin Devlin, *Eurocommunists on the Budapest-Belgrade Circuit*, ibid., 6 October 1977.

¹² Browne from Belgrade, *Chinese Diplomats Making Overtures to Eurocommunists*, in: *The New York Times*, 15 September 1977; interview with Vice Foreign Minister Yu Chüan in *El País* (Madrid), 30 December 1977 (FBIS/CHI/12 January 1978/A 1–2.)

¹³ The Sino-Albanian rift first became publicly clear in *The Theory and Practice of the Revolution*, in: *Zëri i Popullit*, 7 July 1977 (FBIS/EEU/8 July 1977/B1–14) and *The Theory and Practice of the Revolution*. Tirana: 8 Nëntori 1977, written in the form of a polemic against the (unidentified, but actually Chinese) theory of the "three worlds."

(The Albanians distributed the English version of this article to foreign embassies and correspondents in Peking – an overtly anti-Chinese move.) By far the best analyses of the Sino-Albanian rift and its consequences are by Louis Zanga; see his *Albania and China in the View of the "Marxist-Leninist" Splinter Parties*, in: *Radio Free Europe Research*, 1 March 1977; *Albania, China and the "Marxist-Leninist" Parties*, ibid., 12 July 1977; *The Sino-Albanian Rift and the "Zëri i Popullit" Attack: An Assessment*, ibid., 25 July 1977; *Western "Marxist-Leninists" Support Albania's Criticism of China*, ibid., 10 August 1977; *Peking and Tirana on Collision Course*, ibid., 29 September 1977 (re Sino-Albanian struggles in West European "Marxist-Leninist" parties); *Albania Braces Itself for Tensions with China*, ibid., 20 October 1977; *More Evidence of Tension within the Albanian Party*, ibid., 4 November 1977; and *The Sino-Albanian Ideological Dispute Enters a New Phase*, ibid., 15 November 1977. The last paper also analyzes the first major Chinese (implicit) reponse to the Albanian attacks, *Chairman Mao's Theory of the Differentiation of the Three Worlds is a Major Contribution to Marxism-Leninism*, by the Editorial Department, in: *Jenmin Jihpao*, 1 November 1977 and *Peking Review*, 4 November 1977. (This Chinese article also represented a further escalation of Chinese attacks against the "fascist" Soviet leadership and a further theoretical justification of Peking's attempts to ally with Western Europe against the Soviet Union and, secondarily, the United States.)

[14] Robert Solé from Bologna, *Une nouvelle "nouvelle gauche" est née à Bologne*, in: *Le Monde*, 27 September 1977. See also Massimo Teodori, *On the Italian Reds*, in: *The New York Times*, 24 November 1977.

[15] Ulrich Nitzschke, *Wohin geht Italien? Zur Frage einer Regierungsbeteiligung der Kommunisten*, in: *Berichte des Bundesinstituts für ostwissenschaftliche und internationale Studien*, No. 49, September 1977; Fabio Basagni and Gregory A. Flynn, *Italy, Europe and Western Security*, in: *Survival*, May–June 1977; A. Ross Johnson, *Italy and Yugoslav Security*, RAND P–5898. Santa Monica: RAND Corporation, June 1977. For two stimulating views on the PCI, see the interview with Altiero Spinelli by George Urban and the article by Enzo Bettiza in *Encounter*, January 1978. For the latest developments, see Robert Solé in *Le Monde*, 22 December 1977 et seq.

[16] *The New York Times*, 27 November 1977.

[17] See, e.g., Joaquim Semperè, *Sobre les relacions entre Democràcia i Socialisme dins de la tradició de la Tercera Internacional ahir i avui*, in: *Taula de Canvi* (Barcelona), October 1976 and *Sobre la tradició comunista i la seva vigencia*, in: *New Horizons* (Barcelona), October 1977; Jordi Borja, *Socialistes i comunistes davant la democràcia*, in: *Taula de Canvi* (Barcelona), November–December 1976. For analysis, see Mujal-León, *Spanish Communism and the Transition to the Post-Franco Era*, cited in ftn. 6, supra.

[18] The leading PCF intellectual Jean Elleinstein continues to intensify his reformism: see his *Lettre ouverte aux Français sur la Republique du programme commun*. Paris: Albin Michel 1977 and the review of it by Alain Duhamel in *Le Monde*, 19 November 1977.

[19] Very few good analyses of the PCF-PS split have yet appeared. See Fernando Claudin (an ex-PCE leader), *La dimension pathologique du P.C.F.*, in; *Le Monde*, 5

October 1977 and Thierry Pfister, *La Gauche sans union*, ibid., 22, 24 December 1977.

[20] See my *The Diplomacy of Eurocommunism*, cited in ftn. 1, *supra*.

[21] See the detailed analysis of the development of this Soviet line, with full bibliographical citations, in Borys Lewytzkyj, *Zur Auseinandersetzung mit dem Eurokommunismus in der UdSSR*, in: *Berichte des Bundesinstituts für ostwissenschaftliche und internationale Studien*, No. 16, February 1977.

[22] Joan Barth Urban, *Contemporary Soviet Perspectives on Revolution in the West*, in: *Orbis*, Winter 1976. In 1976–1977 Suslov and his associates stressed "proletarian internationalism" and omitted any reference to "socialist internationalism." Brezhnev and his associates did the contrary. See Christian Duevel, *Entwicklungen in der sowjetischen Führing seit dem XXV. Parteitag*, in: *Berichte des Bundesinstituts für ostwissenschaftliche und internationale Studien*, No. 58, 1977, pp. 18–31. In my view this reflected differing Soviet views on what concessions to make to the Yugoslavs, Romanians, French, Italian, and Spanish communist parties, who before the June 1976 East Berlin multi-party conference successfully obtained the omission of "proletarian internationalism," the code phrase for Soviet hegemony, from the conference declaration.

[23] Communiqué: *L'Humanité* and *L'Unità*, 4 March 1977; various accounts in FBIS/WEU/4 March 1977/N1–5.

[24] CD [Christian Duevel], *Moscow Uses Censorship to Dissociate Itself from the Madrid Communiqué*, in: *Radio Liberty Research*, 4 March 1977.

[25] Frane Barbieri from Budapest, *L'antivertice di Sofia*, in: *Il Giornale*, 12 April 1977; Manuel Lucbert, *La virulence des attaques contre le P.C.E. embarrasse les Polonais et les Hongrois*, in: *Le Monde*, 26–27 June 1977.

[26] Ponomarev speech, *Pravda*, 28 April 1977 (FBIS/SOV/2 May 1977/D1–4); *An Important Political Meeting of Communists*, in: *Pravda*, 9 May 1977; Kevin Devlin, *Soviet Hopes Dashed at Prague Meeting*, in: *Radio Free Europe Research*, 3 May 1977; *Soviet Interpretation of Prague Meeting Stirs Controversy*, in: *Radio Liberty Research*, 14 May 1977; Frane Barbieri, *Ponomariov al contrattacco*, in: *Il Giornale*, 30 April 1977.

[27] See ftn. 7, supra.

[28] *Contrary to the Interests of Peace and Socialism in Europe*, in: *New Times*, No. 24, June 1977.

[29] PCE-CC communiqué, 25 June 1977 and Carrillo conference, 27 June 1977, and interview in *Le Monde*, 28 June 1977 (FBID/WEU/29 June 1977/N1–6; wha. [Walther Haubricht] from Madrid, *Die Führung der spanischen Kommunisten wehrt sich gegen Moskauer Pressionen*, in: *Frankfurter Allgemeine Zeitung*, 27 June 1977 (with text of PCE-CC communiqué); Kevin Devlin, *Spanish CP Counterattacks: Moscow Rebuked*, in: *RFE Research*, 28 June 1977 and *Carrillo: "Others Split Communism"*, ibid., 2 September 1977. For a general analysis, see Kevin Devlin, *Interparty Echoes of the Carrillo Case*, in: *Radio Free Europe Research*, 6 July 1977; C.A., *Eurocommunist Stocktaking*, ibid., 4 August 1977; Leo Mates, *Why Moscow*

Must Live with Eurocommunism, in: *The Observer*, 4 August 1977; Frane Barbieri, *Mosca: pluralismo formula famigerata*, in: *Il Giornale*, 25 June 1977.

[30] Milika Sundić, Radio Belgrade, 24 June 1977, 1400 GMT and Radio Zagreb, 26 June 1977 and *Vjesnik*, 25 June 1977, cited from Slobodan Stanković, *Belgrade Defends Carrillo Against Moscow Attacks*, in: *RFE Research*, 28 June 1977.

[31] *Scinteia*, 5 July 1977 (FBIS/EEU/7 July 1977/H2–7); V.M. [Viktor Meier] in *Frankfurter Allgemeine Zeitung*, 2 August 1977 (re Carrillo visit to Bucharest).

[32] *Eurocommunism, "Novoye Vremya", and Us*, in: *L'Unità*, 28 June 1977 (FBIS/WEU/30 June 1977/L1–3.)

[33] *Eurocommunism, "Novoye Vremya" and Us*, in: *L'Unità*, 28 June 1977 (FBIS/WEU/30 June 1977/L1–3); CPSU/PCI communiqué: 3 July 1977 (FBIS/WEU/7 July 1977/E1); *Le Monde*, 5 July 1977; Romano Ledda (PCI-CC), *Diversity and Internationalism*, in: *Rinascita*, 1 July 1977 (FBIS/WEU/20 July 1977/L1–3); *L'Unità*, 7 July 1977 (FBIS/WEU/14 July 1977/L9–11); Urban, *Moscow and the PCI: Kto Kovo*, cited in ftn. 6, supra, and especially Frane Barbieri from Belgrade, *"Tu quoque, Santiago"*, in: *Il Giornale*, 1 July 1977, from Budapest, *Il Pci ha deluso Carrillo rimasto solo contra Mosca*, ibid., 7 July 1977, and from Madrid, *Avallato da Pajetta l'attaco a Carrillo?*, ibid., 8 July 1977.

[34] *Putting the Record Straight*, in: *New Times*, No. 28, July 1977. For PCE reaction, see the interview with Azcárate (PCE Politburo and Secretariat member responsible for international affairs), *"Non esiste eurocomunismo che non parte da un guidizio negativo sull'Unione Sovietica"*, in: *Il Giornale*, 9 July 1977.

[35] Bogumił Sujka (Deputy Head, International Department, KC PZPR), *Wkwestii solidarności internacjionalistycznej*, in: *Nowe rogi*, August 1977; Kazimierz Zamorski, *Polish Criticism of Carrillo: Support for "Red Socialism"*, in: *RFE Research*, 27 September 1977; Jerzy Kraszewski in *Trybuna ludu*, 3 August 1977 (FBIS/EEU/7 August 1977/G1–7).

[36] See Kádár's favorable references to Eurocommunism in press conferences in Austria in December 1976 and in West Germany and Italy in June 1977 (*The New York Times*, 6 December 1976; *L'Unità*, 10 June, 1 July 1977). For retreat, see Janos Berecz (head, international dept., CC MSzMP), *Our Debates and Our Unity*, in: *Népszabadság*, 24 July 1977 (FBIS/EEU/26 July 1977/F1–4).

[37] Heinz Timmermann, *Die Beziehungen Ost-Berlins zu den jugoslawischen und zu den "Eurokommunisten"*, in: *Berichte des Bundesinstituts für ost-wissenschaftliche und internationale Studien*, No. 41, July 1977 and *Carrillo, Moskau und die SED*, in: *Deutschland Archiv*, No. 8, 1977.

[38] Yankovitch from Belgrade in *Le Monde*, 6 October 1977.

[39] See the interview with the CPSU emissary Viktor Afanasyev (editor-in-chief of *Pravda*), in *El País*, 18 October 1977 (FBIS/SOV/26 October 1977/E1–4), e.g., *"Novoye Vremya's* criticisms of Santiago Carrillo ... were not the opinion of an official party organ. ..."* See also Acoca from Madrid in the *Washington Post*, 24 October 1977.

[40] *Pravda*, 11 November 1977 (TASS, English, 10 November 1977, 1545 GMT, in FBIS/SOV/11 November 1977/A1–8). See also Suslov in *Pravda*, 3 November 1977 (FBIS/SOV/2 November 1977/P1–18) and K. Zarodov in ibid., 26 August 1977 (FBIS/SOV/30 August 1977/A6–11); Flora Lewis, *Tug-of-War Reported in Moscow on Approach to Eurocommunism*, in: *The New York Times*, 17 October 1977. For background on the incident, see *Le P.C.E. conteste la version soviétique*, in: *Le Monde*, 9 November 1977; Afanasyev in TASS, quoted in the *The New York Times*, 7 November 1977; and especially Kevin Devlin, *Soviets Block Carrillo's Speech*, in: *Radio Free Europe Research*, 7 November 1977.

[41] LCY-PCE communiqué, TANJUG in Serbo-Croat, 10 November 1977, 1049 GMT (FBIS/EEU/11 November 1977/I1–3) (very cordial).

[42] See the Italian press coverage in FBIS/WEU/14 November 1977/L1–8, and *M. Berlinguer marque ses distances à l'égard de M. Carrillo*, in: *Le Monde*, 12 November 1977.

[43] Kevin Devlin, *Eurocommunism and the States: Carrillo's Historic Visit*, in: *Radio Free Europe Research*, 15 November 1977.

[44] Whitney from Moscow in the *The New York Times*, 4 November 1977.

[45] Quoted in Barbieri from Belgrade in *Il Giornale*, 10 November 1977. Lister, who recently returned to Spain, headed a Soviet-supported effort in the early and mid-"70's" to depose Carrillo. See *La dernière bataille du général Lister contre l'"euro-opportunisme" de M. Carrillo*, in *Le Monde*, 10 November 1977. See also Zdenko Antic, *Yugoslavs, the October Revolution and Carrillo*, in: *Radio Free Europe Research*, 14 November 1977 and Kevin Devlin, *Lister "Against Form and Timing" of Soviet Intervention in CSSR*, and *The Return of the Native: Carrillo's pro-Soviet Rule*, ibid., both 10 November 1977.

[46] In speeches at an international scientific-theoretical conference on "The Great October Revolution and the Contemporary Epoch," *Pravda*, 11 November 1977 (TASS summaries: FBIS/SOV/11 November 1977/A1–4). See also L. I. Brezhnev, *A Historic Stage on the Road to Communism*, in: *World Marxist Review*, December 1977; Alexander Sobolev, *Common Heritage of the Revolutionary Forces*, in: *New Times*, No. 44, October 1977; and, for analysis, Frane Barbieri, *Stato guida cercasi*, in *Il Giornale*, 11 November 1977. Suslov's position was perhaps most authoritatively set forth in his *Marksizm-Leninizm i revolutsionnoe obnovlenie mira*, in: *Kommunist*, No. 14, September 1977, pp. 13–28. Significantly, this article was reprinted in *Einheit*, No. 12, 1977, pp. 1369–1383 but not, through the January 1978 issues, in: *Nowe Drogi, Nová Mysl*, or *Társàdalmi Szemle*.

For the attack on Azcárate, see B. Andreyev, *Playing Up to Imperialist Anti-Soviet Propaganda*, in: *New Times*, No. 3, January 1978; for criticism of it, Azcárate in *El País*, 15 January 1978 (FBIS/WEU/19 January 1978/N2); Veyrier in *L'Humanité*, 13 January 1978 (FBIS/WEU/19 January 1978/K9); *L'Unità*, 12 January 1978 (FBIS/WEU/18 January 1978/L6); Teslić in *Borba*, 23 January 1978 (FBIS/EEU/25 January 1978/I1–3); analyzed in Slobodan Stankovic, *Belgrade Daily Sharply Attacks "Novoe Vremya"*, in: *Radio Free Europe Research*, 26 January 1978; for a renewed Soviet attack, *Why This Distortion of the Truth?*, in: *New Times*, No. 6, February 1978;

Un anti-euro primitivo, in: *Mundo Obrero*, 19–25 January 1978, analyzed in Kevin Devlin, *Spanish-Soviet Polemics Intensify*, in: *Radio Free Europe Research*, 6 February 1978. See also Devlin, *Eurocommunists Hail Prague Spring: Anniversary Articles* by Kriegel and Huebl, ibid., 27 January 1978.

The PCE's position was made more difficult by the publication of Jorge Semprun's *Autobiografía de Federico Sanchez*. Barcelona: Planeta, 1977, a strong attack on Carrillo's and the PCE's Stalinism before 1968 by an ex-leader of the PCE, expelled with Claudin in 1964. See the reply by Azcárate in *El País*, 4 January 1978 (FBIS/WEU/18 January 1978/N1–5) and a rejoinder by Semprun in ibid., 8 January 1978 (FBIS/WEU/18 January 1978/N5–10).

[47] See Kevin Devlin, *Rival Swedish Communist Delegations in Moscow: "Official" CP Protest*, in: *Radio Free Europe Research*, 10 November 1977.

[48] Text: *The New York Times*, 13 January 1978.

PART FOUR

STRUCTURAL PROBLEMS IN THE WEST

Western Europe, the United States and Japan – Structural Problems of an International Triangle

by WILHELM G. GREWE

I

Nothing pulls the rapidly changing scenery of the international political arena into sharper focus than a glance at developments in the global triangle USA-Western Europe-Japan, whereby I am using this term for the time being in its most general sense, leaving it open as to whether it has any substance, and if so, what that substance consists of.

In 1973, on American initiative, the first concrete diplomatic attempt was made to structure and organize this global triangular relationship. The attempt was made in connection with Kissinger's plan, following years of American overengagement in South East Asia, to inaugurate a "Year of Europe" and to reorganize American-European relations within the framework of a new "Atlantic Charter."

In his programmatic speech on 23 April 1973, the Secretary of State sketched the "new realities" which necessitated "new approaches"; he included – aside from the revival of Western Europe and its successful movement toward economic unification, the "near equality" in the East-West strategic military balance, the conditions in a period of relaxation of tensions, the new demands for cooperative action by, for example, industrialized nations to ensure the supply of energy – the growing significance of other world regions: "Japan has emerged as a major power center. In many fields, 'Atlantic' solutions to be viable must include Japan." The new Atlantic Charter, he proclaimed, should create a new relationship for the Atlantic nations in which Japan has a share in the general progress.

This invitation to participate in a trilateral declaration of the democratic industrial nations was often repeated later and elucidated in more concrete form. The Japanese government showed active interest, beginning with a statement by Prime Minister Tanaka in Washington on 31 August 1973, and was reinforced several times in the following months.

However, the "Year of Europe" turned into a crisis year for European-American relations. The Yom-Kippur War in October, 1973, and the oil crisis which it triggered, fundamentally changed the overall picture of global relations by moving entirely new problems into the foreground. After a year of difficult, often delicate negotiations, an "Atlantic Declaration" could finally be signed in June, 1974, which in the end no one wanted to call a "Charter" any more.

The concept of Japanese participation in an all-encompassing trilateral declaration had been lost by the wayside, and along with it the idea, which had been discussed on occasion, of a parallel declaration of principles by Japan and the European Community.

The failure of the initiative launched by Kissinger in the spring of 1973 raises a number of questions:

1. Were the methods used inappropriate?
2. Did the events of 1973 destroy the prerequisites for an otherwise promising undertaking?
3. Or was the trilateral concept doomed to failure from the outset due to insufficient substance?

The replies to these three questions must be combined to answer the basic question which is not only of historical relevance but of great significance for the future: Is the concept of a "global triangle" in international politics (USA-Western Europe-Japan) more than a mere scheme, more than an artificial diplomatic construction without sufficient substance, i.e., without a solid basis of common interests amongst those involved? Does the concept show any promise and deserve to be taken up again under new conditions and perhaps with other methods and made the subject of a new *relance*?

II

From my point of view the three questions should be answered as follows:

1. The methods used by Kissinger in carrying out his spring initiative in 1973 were in many respects injurious to the ends pursued. The preliminary consultations with those involved, which should have preceded the public proclamation of the program, were by no means sufficient. Such consultations could have assured the project a better start. On the other hand, it appeared questionable from the outset and even more so in retrospect, as to whether the vehicle of a general statement of principles was necessary or appropriate as the basis for trilateral cooperation. It proved to be most difficult to find a common denominator for the interests and goals of the three regional partners within the framework of general principles, or indeed to formulate the particular nuances of Europe's relations to America on the one hand and Japan's relations to the United States on the other. More flexibility and pragmatism in the selection of instruments of cooperation would probably have led more easily to success.

2. The developments which arose in 1973 proved to be extremely unfavorable for the realization of the Kissinger project for integrating Japan, in connection with the reorganization of American-European relations, into a world-wide trilateral relationship. Two complexes which influenced each other reciprocally played a major role: The reorganization of American-European relations proved to be much more difficult than predicted; the "Year of Europe" unexpectedly developed into a crisis year in these relations. In view of these difficulties the willingness on the part of Americans as well as Europeans to increase the already existent complications by including Japan in the framework of a triangle relationship flagged rapidly. This dilemma was mirrored in the suggestion of the Nine in November, 1973, to discuss a bilateral declaration of cooperation with Japan. The "Declaration on European Identity," passed in Copenhagen on 14 December 1973, includes only a relatively pallid formulation on cooperation with Japan: "The Nine also remain determined to engage in close cooperation and to pursue a constructive dialogue with the other industrialized countries, such as Japan and Canada, which have an essential role in maintaining an open and balanced world economic system. They appreciate the existing fruitful cooperation with these countries, particularly in the OECD." Concrete negotiations over the suggestion to formulate a Japan-EC declaration concerning Japanese-European community relations never came about.

All developments were overshadowed by the outbreak of the Jom-Kippur War in October, 1973, and the ensuing proclamation of the Arab oil boycott. The new Middle East War began on 6th October – the Japanese Prime Minister Tanaka, accompanied on his European tour by his Foreign Minister Ohira, left Bonn on the same day enroute to Moscow, in order to complete the last stage in his journey after prior conversations in London and Paris. The decision by the oil-exporting Arab states to use oil as a weapon was announced on 17 October, that is, one week after Tanaka had left Moscow.

Despite the lip service paid to the necessity for increased cooperation between industrial countries in coming to terms with the escalating energy crisis, retrogressive and diverging tendencies made themselves apparent. The Japanese and the Europeans became aware of their dependence on Arab oil exporters and were not willing to take up the strategy of a tough defensive stand proposed by Washington – which could rely on its better secured oil supply. On the contrary, the Japanese and the Europeans tried to adapt their Middle East policy to the demands of their supply situation. The concrete expression of this endeavor was the Middle East declaration of the EC Foreign Ministers on 6 November 1973, which in turn was outdone in a statement by the Japanese government on 22 November 1973; the Japanese pronouncement went several steps further and, in contrast to the European declaration, sharply and clearly demanded Israel's withdrawal from "all regions occupied during the 1967 War," while ending with the ominous sentence, the Japanese government would "have to reexamine her policy vis-à-vis Israel depending upon further developments."

Both statements, which were in clear contrast to the American Middle East position, took on further, in part even more pointed accents in the course of tactical maneuvering by the governments involved; this was especially true of the European offer of a "dialogue" with the Arab states which came close to offering a conference of Foreign Ministers and thus considerably irritated the US with respect to their peace initiatives in the Middle East.

Japan sent its Deputy Prime Minister Miki on a good-will tour to the Middle East. Other high-ranking politicians followed; development aid promises, some of which involved considerable expense, were made, but these activities did not pay off in the further course of the oil crisis.

New controversies broke out amongst the industrial nations at the energy conference in Washington (11–13 February 1974), in particular between France and the United States. Kissinger sought in vain to convince the Foreign Ministers of the twelve other participating states (the Nine, Norway, Canada, and Japan) that there could be no isolated solution, that without the cooperation of all countries the world would be caught up in a vicious circle which would inevitably lead to a break-down of the world economic order similar to the depression in the 1930s. The French Foreign Minister, Michel Jobert, sharply countered all attempts to create a grouping of the industrial states and defended the French practice of bilateral negotiations with the oil producers and the suggestion of a general energy conference of all countries under the auspices of the United Nations – without previous consultation between the consumer groups. The French delegation did not approve the program of action passed by the conference, in particular the implementation of a coordinating group. It was only without the French that the "International Energy Agency," after extensive preparations, could finally be formed within the framework of the OECD on 15 November 1974. The harshness of the controversy is made clear by statements such as President Nixon's comment made during the Washington conference at a dinner for the participants: A policy in which each country tries to secure the greatest possible advantage for itself was "bad statesmanship"; or Jobert's statement after his return to Paris on 25 February: The United States has pursued a conference goal which had little to do with the energy crisis, namely to bind Europe even closer to the US and impose its leadership upon them.

In such a controversial climate an ambitious project for organizing trilateral cooperation between Japan, the United States and Western Europe had no real chance.

3. Was the concept of such cooperation itself thus refuted? This could only be maintained if the unfavorable constellation of 1973/74 had proved to be permanent. Such an assertion could only be justified if all those factors which speak for trilateral cooperation had been carefully analyzed and a negative – or at least insufficient – balance had been determined. Studies with such results have not as yet been presented. Nor could one assert that the constellation of 1973/74 still persists.

The question as to the possibilities and prospects of "relaunching" the trilateral concept against the backdrop of a more favorable international political constellation and with improved methods thus remains open; at any rate a new attempt would not be prejudiced in the negative sense. Thus it would seem admissible and sensible to pursue the search for an answer.

III

The failure of the American Secretary of State's "trilateral" initiative in the spring of 1973 does not alter the fact that real trilateral cooperation has existed since long before 1973 and has a good chance of being practiced successfully in the future, indeed of becoming more intensive. This cooperation is rooted in a fundamental identity or at least parallelism of interests of the three regional partners: as the world's leading trade nations they are all equally interested in a world order which guarantees free trade, free shipping lines, competition within a market economy, monetary stability, the secured supply of raw materials and energy, and access to markets.

Japan's membership in the OECD since 1964 had already given Japan an institutional basis in its cooperation with the leading industrial nations of North America and Western Europe in questions of economic policy. Towards the end of the sixties a close – even if not institutionalized – cooperation developed in the field of world monetary policy had found its expression in frequent informal meetings of the Ministers of Finance from Japan, the USA, France, Great Britain, and Germany. Many of the important decisions made at international monetary conferences, the World Bank, and the World Monetary Fund were prepared in this framework.

The development of the energy crisis since 1973/74 posed the question as to the possibilities for trilateral cooperation in the field of energy policy as well. Despite all the peculiarities of Japan's interests and all her initial endeavors to withdraw from an action of solidarity of the large consumer nations through a bilateral policy vis-à-vis the Arab oil producers, Japan was one of the participating nations in the Washington Energy Conference of February, 1975, and finally also became a member of the International Energy Agency. When the Conference on International Economic Cooperation (CIEC) convened in December, 1975, and the extensive dialogue between developing and industrialized countries began, Japan took her natural place in the group of industrialized countries; ever since the committee consultations of this conference began on 11 February 1976, Japan has belonged to that group of countries, along with the USA, the EC and Canada, which hold a co-chairman in the four committees.

The more clearly the front of developing nations is formed (for example, in the Group of "77") and the more radically the demand for a new world economic order is articulated (for example, during the special General Assembly of the UN in April, 1974), the more inevitable Japan's association with the industrial nations of North America and Western Europe will become.

Japan thus did not hesitate a moment in accepting the invitation to the economic summit in Rambouillet in December, 1975. It is of no decisive significance if at such meetings on one occasion North America is represented solely by the USA and at another time (in Puerto Rico) by Canada as well; whether the nine Europeans present themselves as the "EC" with the presidents of the European Council and Commission thus participating or whether, as in Rambouillet, they are represented by the four larger powers in the Nine – Germany, France, Great Britain, and Italy; or whether a non-EC member like Norway is also included as in the Washington Energy Conference. In substance, all these meetings fall within the framework of the concept of trilateral cooperation.

Rambouillet was as yet the most spectacular symbolic peak in this trend: for the first time since World War II a Japanese Prime Minister met in a conference with the American President and two European heads of government – in a conference which did not, indeed, aim at resolving a conflict or at bridging over controversy but rather served solely to promote cooperation, a conference which was based on the insight that a common endeavor and solidarity are necessary in coming to terms with the problems of recession, inflation, stagnation, and unemployment. The renewed consultations of the same circle of government leaders in Puerto Rico in July, 1976, even if the domestic situation more strongly motivated several participants, was nonetheless the expression of the desire to continue on this course. The disinclination to present themselves to the Third World as members in a rich men's club still expressed by the Japanese in 1973 was more than outweighed by the feeling of satisfaction in finding recognition as a fully-fledged and respected member of this group of economically leading nations.

On these foundations a pragmatically oriented trilateral cooperation will continue to develop in the future: wherever policies on economics, energy, raw materials or development are at stake, whether in the framework of UNCTAD, GATT, the World Monetary Fund, regardless of the organization the partners in the "cooperative triangle" will come together even if position differences become visible in divergent voting behavior; they will consult, synchronize policy, and cooperate. No treaty or Charter is needed in this context. The compelling objective necessities (which will presumably increase) deriving from common interests and an identity in a number of basic principles concerning their state and economic order, will suffice.

IV

Independently of initiatives and activities at the diplomatic level and one step ahead of them in terms of time, a significant initiative towards activating trilateral cooperation between the USA, Western Europe and Japan was undertaken at the unofficial level: in the so-called *Trilateral Commission*, inspired by David Rockefeller and Zbigniew Brzezinski, outstanding scholars, politicians, business and union leaders convened to thoroughly examine the problems involved in such cooperation and announced their willingness to place their findings and advice at the disposal of interested governments. After a series of preliminary contacts to sound out the problem in the summer and fall of 1972, the former director of the US Arms Control and Disarmament Agency and chief delegate for SALT, Gerald Smith, and Professor Zbigniew Brzezinski of Columbia University in New York, began preparatory discussions in Tokyo in January 1973. Here, as in Washington and several European capitals, the project met with interest and sympathy and the promise of support. The former President of the Asian Development Bank, Takeshi Watanabe, put himself at the Commission's disposal as coordinator of the Japanese contingency. Following a preparatory European-American conference in Amsterdam in March 1973 the first trilateral conference of the executive committee of the Commission was convened in Tokyo. The goals, tasks and organizational structure of the Commission were defined more precisely at the conference.

Three goals were mentioned:

1. Close cooperation of leading personalities from the three regions in order to avoid breakdowns in communication as they had previously occurred, and to reach a common understanding of the problems which affect them mutually;

2. The proposal of policies which could be pursued by Japan, the nations of the European Community and North America in their economic, political and military relations, and in their relationships to the developing nations and Communist states;

3. The promotion of interest and support for the recommendations of the Commission at governmental as well as at private levels within the three regions.

The following topics were mentioned as possible objects for study by specific "task forces":

– Economic relations, including monetary problems, problems of trade and investments;

– security, arms control, nuclear proliferation;

– relations with the developing nations;

– the political implications of the energy crisis;

– international institutions and political consultation;

– relations with communist states.

In the first four years of its existence the Trilateral Commission has demonstrated a remarkable productivity. A dozen reports have been published, each of which was written by three outstanding experts – one from each region. The topics of the reports were as follows:

1. Ways to a New World Monetary System.

2. The Crisis of International Cooperation.

3. A Turning Point in North-South Economic Relations.

4. Guidelines for World Trade in the "70's".

5. Energy: the Necessity for a Trilateral Approach.

6. Energy: A New Strategy for International Action.

7. OPEC, the Trilateral World and the Developing Nations: New Forms of Cooperation, 1976–1980.

8. The Crisis of Democracy.

9. A New Order for the World's Oceans.

10. In Search of a New Order for the World Raw Materials Market.

11. The Reform of International Institutions.

12. The Problems of International Consultations.

Further reports are now in preparation on constructive worldwide cooperation between the Trilateral and the Communist states in mastering global problems and on a new international system. A new three year program beginning in 1976 will concentrate on three topic groups: trilateral problems, North-South problems, internal problems of highly developed, democratic industrial nations.

To be sure, it is difficult to formulate a brief, general evaluation of the quality of these reports. And it is even more difficult to determine whether the Commission has succeeded in attracting attention in decisive places and in influencing the policy of the governments; such judgments and evaluations, however, are in any case not decisive in and by themselves. The significance of the Trilateral Commission is not a function of its publications, nor is it dependent on the recognition of the governments involved. Its significance lies rather in the initiation of lively intellectual cooperation and understanding, and in the exchange of ideas between the scholarly and the political elites of the three regions. The bulletin of the Commission bears the terse title "Trialogue." It is, indeed, the decisive contribution of the Commission that this "trialogue" has been set in motion.

The existence of the Commission and its work are living proof that a basic stock of common spiritual and political qualities exists which has in turn stimulated the political, economic and intellectual elites of the three regional partners to systematically search for ways and means for practical cooperation.

This still does not necessarily prove that trilateral cooperation is or could be a promising goal for diplomatic endeavors. However, the work of the Trilateral Commission remains, nonetheless, significant and useful whether or not this is the case. In the long run the Commission could take over a role similar to that played by the "European Movement" in the process of European unification – regardless of whether one evaluates the consequences which this development has brought for Europe as positive or negligible.

V

How stable is the agreement reflected in the pragmatic work of the governments and in the "trialogue" of the regional elites? Will it ever extend beyond the previous fields of cooperation to include the realm of general politics and defense matters, which, in the last analysis, was the goal of the Kissinger initiative? The areas of study selected by the Trilateral Commission leave no doubt as to the Commission's intention to examine these more far-reaching perspectives as well.

When such dimensions are brought into the discussion the question arises as to other competing groupings into which Japan could be integrated. In recent years, in every discussion of Japan's future role in world politics, the various "triangle-relations" in which Japan considers herself involved have always been mentioned: beyond the triangle Japan-North America-Western Europe (central to this essay) which Brzezinski has termed the "cooperative" triangle, there is the "competitive" triangle USA-Soviet Union-China. It forms the decisive system of coordinates for Japan in her foreign relations within which she must orient, engage and delimit herself.

Another school of thought centers around the triangle USA-China-Japan and involves the possible formation of an alliance-like group which could be promoted by the danger of further Soviet advances in the Asian Pacific region. Many consider such a grouping to be the only possible solution for filling the power vacuum left in this region after the reduction of American military presence and alliance engagement in Asia.

The first steps towards such a development and its perspective chances have been described in a series of articles by Robert Guillain, the experienced and long-standing Far East correspondent of "Le Monde" ("La bataille diplomatique du Pacifique", 11–13 February 1976).

His thesis can be summarized as follows:

1. A "triple entente" to counter Soviet hegemonial expansion in Asia was the goal pursued systematically in Chinese foreign policy by Chou En-lai from 1969 on. The new rapprochement with the United States, which was more his work than Nixon's, served this goal. Fear of encirclement by the Soviet Union motivated such efforts. A consequence of this policy was the changed (namely positive) evaluation of the American-Japanese Security Treaty and the inclusion of Japan in the American-Chinese entente which after initial complications in the years between 1971 and 1974 (between Peking and Tokyo as well as between Washington and Tokyo) gradually led to a growing convergence. From the very beginning the core of this policy was the "anti-hegemony clause" which not only figured in the Nixon and Tanaka communiqués of Shanghai and Peking in 1972 but can be traced back as far as the Chinese statements and documents at the time of the Soviet invasion in Czechoslovakia (1968). The clause also appeared later in the Program of the Ninth Congress of the Chinese Communist Party and was presented at every suitable occasion to visitors from all parts of Asia (and in certain cases from other parts of the world) who were asked to sign statements of concurrence.

2. The "Pacific Doctrine" proclaimed in Honolulu by President Ford immediately after his return from Peking on 4 December 1975, was the expression of the United States' definitive shift towards this concept of "triple entente." It put an end to the United States' "disengagement" which

had been introduced towards the end of the Vietnam War. In contrast to Nixon's "Guam Doctrine" it reinforced America's determination to remain "present" in Asia, to honor the commitments remaining after Vietnam and henceforth to build up a new position of strength in cooperation with China and Japan which could stabilize the balance of power in Asia. Although the Soviet Union is not mentioned explicitly in the formulations of the Pacific Doctrine it is nonetheless focused upon implicitly as the potential enemy.

3. Moscow understood the Pacific Doctrine in this sense. Gromyko's visit to Tokyo in January 1976 was a warning addressed equally to Tokyo and Washington – the cut at Peking was obvious. Behind this warning stood the threat of weighty reprisals which could hardly be taken lightly by Japan: cessation of all talks and negotiations over the return of the "Northern Territories" (the four Southern Kuril Islands which the Soviet Union occupied in 1945) and over the conclusion of a peace treaty; interference with the Japanese fishing fleet and demonstration of military strength by the Soviet marine and air force in the immediate vicinity of the Japanese islands.

4. The United States encouraged the Japanese with increasing clarity to join in building the concept of "triple entente" and to forget her reservations over signing a peace treaty with China on the basis of the "anti-hegemony clause." It is in this sense that one must interpret Kissinger's speech on 19 June 1975, in New York in which he already declared the thesis of "equidistance" (in relation to all points of the "competitive" triangle Washington-Moscow-Peking) which had been posited not by the Japanese government but by the news media in Japan, to be a myth.

5. At the beginning of 1976 the way was finally paved for a consensus within the Japanese government and the leadership of the governing party in favor of signing the treaty with Peking, if possible largely on the basis of the interpretation of the anti-hegemony clause advocated by Foreign Minister Miyazawa. Immediately after Gromyko's departure Prime Minister Miki expressed the determination of the Japanese government when he stated that the Soviet Foreign Minister's visit would have no influence whatever on the conclusion of the China Treaty; he expressly agreed with Kissinger's view that "equidistance" is a myth. However, all this did not imply that Japan was thus willing to join an anti-Soviet bloc. In awareness of its own military weakness and in harmony with the pacifist mood of its population, Japan continues to try to avoid confrontation and the build-up of new tensions with the Soviet Union.

Guillain closed his presentation with the open-ended question as to whether such a foreign policy does not represent an impossible feat of acrobatic agility. In any case, the controversies involved, in their confusion

as well as in the range of their repercussions, in his opinion do remind one of
the difficult decisions of 1939–40.

Two questions can be derived from this deduction:

1. Is the thesis that Japan is in the process of integrating itself in such a
"triple entente" against the Soviet hegemonial drive in Asia really
compelling?

2. How would such a constellation relate to trilateral cooperation in the
triangle Japan-North America-Western Europe? Do two such groupings
exclude one another or is a complementary relationship conceivable in the
sense that the one serves the balance of power vis-à-vis the Soviet Union
while the other promotes Japan's economic and financial integration into the
world of the Western industrial nations?

VI

As interesting and stimulating as Guillain's theses are, they call for a number
of reservations and questions. The first reservation stems from the events and
developments which have taken place since the publication of his series of
articles. At the moment of publication *Chou En-lai*, the initiator of the
concept of "triple entente," was no longer alive. Later in the year, Mao died.
Contrary to the original expectations Teng Hsiao-peng, the designated heir
to power, could not hold his own; a furious "life or death" (as the Chinese
newspapers put it) battle for power ensued. It increased after Mao's death
and is still continuing. To be sure, the new leadership under Hua Kuo-feng
is trying to emphasize the continuity of Chinese foreign policy; and there are
no signs which would point to a change in the anti-Soviet fixation of Chinese
foreign policy in the foreseeable future (on the contrary, even the radical left
wing of the Shanghai group, the "gang of four," tended to be rather
more outspokenly anti-Soviet than were the pragmaticians amongst the
followers of Chou and Teng). Nor are there any signs of a change in relations
to the United States. But once again everything is uncertain. Even without
a fundamental alteration of the course vis-à-vis Moscow or Washington
profound changes could ensue in the event of a renewed battle for power. A
new period of immobility and self-isolation in foreign policy – similar to that
seen in the cultural revolution – cannot be excluded. Beyond this, in the
course of such a power battle one must reckon with surprises of all kinds,
including changes in the foreign policy course. In other words, the course of
the most important factor in the concept of a "triple entente" cannot be
calculated or predicted for some time.

A second reservation must be made with regard to the United States. The value and emphasis which Guillain puts on the Pacific Doctrine are already subject to certain doubts. Can it really be taken as the starting point of a well thought out US Asian policy which is once again taking shape? The evaluation of the doctrine's importance given by semi- and unofficial American spokesmen would suggest the contrary: no new policy, but rather the recapitulation of principles already in practice; a domestically motivated and domestically oriented attempt to justify the China trip (which had met with mixed feelings within the United States) by integrating it into a general conception of American Asian policy, a policy which was, however, never carefully examined or made concrete with regard to Japan's role; hence, a policy which covers no more far-reaching goals than those actually stated. Nor did the Japanese side perceive either direct or indirect American signals inviting them to join in such a "triple entente." This policy did not fit into the general conception of the Ford-Kissinger foreign policy, for despite all the soberness which had set in in America as to the results and the chances of détente, thus making détente a campaign issue, and despite President Ford's verbal disassociation from "détente," the fact remains that nothing has changed in the basic guidelines of this policy and that there are no certain indications for President Carter's willingness to change them. The United States will, in all probability, remain interested in a special relationship between the superpowers which enables them to continue their dialogue, the SALT negotiations and possible new bilateral agreements on single issues. Only under such preconditions could Kissinger's concept be realized that under conditions of a strategic balance of power between the superpowers the task of American foreign policy must be to encourage the Soviet Union to "moderate" its claims and actions. A policy of encirclement and alliance clearly directed against the Soviet Union in the Pacific region would throw this special relationship into question. As a presidential candidate, Carter (perhaps under Brzezinski's influence) has occasionally spoken in favor of the development of trilateral relations between North America, Western Europe and Japan. Whether or not as President he will urge Vance, his Secretary of State, to pursue this line, whether he might even be inclined towards the more far-reaching concept of a "triple entente" remains an open question. As long as the basic conception of future US foreign policy is unknown, the American component of a "triple entente" remains an uncertain factor.

As far as the third partner, Japan, is concerned, Guillain himself formulated his thesis of a "triple entente" in conjunction with cautiously limiting qualifications: by no means did Japan intend to let the projected treaty with China be interpreted as the third pillar in an anti-Soviet bloc. Even if Japan gives preference to its relationship with China over its relationship with the Soviet Union, it still does not mean that Japan wishes to make the Soviet Union its enemy. In addition to this subjective element, which makes Japan unsuited as a partner in a "policy of encirclement," is the objective element, Japan's military weakness and its incapability for action, which has the same effect. The "capacity for self-defense" is at most sufficient to ward off a limited conventional attack in the short run. Offensive operations or any kind of operative deployment outside Japan's own territory are out of the question: Japan's constitution forbids such deployment and, as a result, the corresponding weapons and equipment are nonexistent. A distrustful opposition and no less distrustful news media zealously guard against violation of this constitutional stipulation. Another element of uncertainty is the long range effect of the December elections (1976) and the weakening of the ruling conservative party. For the time being, speculations on this subject are premature.

What then is left of the concept of "triple entente"? Basically only its potential for development in the future, the realization of which will depend on further changes in the world political constellation: a consolidation of the Chinese ruling elite after Mao's death together with the maintenance of a pronounced anti-Soviet foreign policy, an increasingly sober attitude of the United States as to the prospects and possibilities for its bilateral "special relationship" with the Soviet Union; the possibilities for SALT and other similar partial agreements on détente; the new President and the new Secretary of State who do not tend to take Moscow's reaction into consideration to the same degree Ford and Kissinger did; a change of climate in Japan in favor of greater defense efforts and a greater willingness to take diplomatic risks in relation to the Soviet Union which presupposes a stronger awareness of Japan's endangered situation. Only given such a change of climate would Japan ever conceivably overcome its characteristic dodging in foreign policy, its fear of binding commitments and its strategy of keeping all options open. Only then could parallelism of interests, which doubtless exists between the United States and the People's Republic of China with regard to containing the expanding Soviet superpower, fully develop. For the moment none of these preconditions exist.

VII

If the "triple entente," USA-China-Japan, is not an actual but at best an uncertain, potential constellation in the Asian-Pacific region, then the question as to its possible relationship to the "cooperative triangle" USA-Western Europe-Japan, likewise loses its pressing topical interest, especially since it cannot be answered abstractly but only against the background of a concrete situation.

It would seem much more fruitful to explore the question of whether the already existing pragmatic and barely institutionalized forms of trilateral cooperation in the realms of economic, monetary and development policy within the cooperative triangle could possibly take on a political dimension in the course of the near future.

In order to guard against premature projections it will be useful to examine the considerations of the governments which were involved in 1973 in one or more of the declarations of basic principles of the trilateral project – their motives, expectations, fears and reservations.

There can be no doubt that, after some initial hesitation, the Japanese government showed active and positive interest, that it would have preferred to have seen such a project realized in the form of one common declaration of basic principles. To this end the Japanese government circulated its own confidential draft of a statement while suggesting it merely as a basis for discussion. This draft confirmed, what other statements of Japanese spokesmen had intimated, that is, that Japan placed decisive value on the political dimension of trilateral cooperation (and was, therefore, prejudiced against a – by necessity – economically accentuated declaration in the framework of the OECD). The preamble and a good third of the declaration contained political statements in programmatic form. The only procedural suggestion for the realization of trilateral cooperation addressed itself to the entirety of the common interests and did not limit itself to the traditional field of economic and monetary policy.

One can, of course, only speculate as to the motives for the Japanese interest in the political dimension of trilateral cooperation. I would interpret these motives as being based upon a strong Japanese interest in the past, present and future in overcoming its geographically and historically rooted isolation and in associating itself with a larger international grouping. This interest grew proportionally as the exclusive ties and association with the United States (as a result of the "Nixon-shock," the post-Vietnam situation and the Lockheed scandal) loosened and necessitated a more independent foreign policy. Given this situation, the trilateral concept offers a favorable constellation in that it makes it possible to preserve the Japanese-American Security Treaty and the American nuclear umbrella while allowing for Japan's integration in a larger group. Apparently this positive motivation was stronger than the reservation which caused the initial hesitation of the Japanese government after Kissinger's speech in April, 1973: the fear that Japan could compromise itself in Asia, and vis-à-vis the Third World as a whole, by joining the "rich man's club" and could possibly maneuver itself into an unwanted confrontation with the developing countries.

Meanwhile it has become clear (in the course of the UN Special General Assembly in April, 1974, the Conference for Industrial and Economic Cooperation (CIEC) and the Fourth UNCTAD in Nairobi in the spring of 1976) that Japan cannot possibly escape its image as member in the group of highly developed industrial states and that it is more auspicious to work together with them towards a relaxed, fruitful relationship with the developing countries which is oriented towards dialogue and balance of interests. The quick and unconditional willingness of Miki's government to take part in the summit at Rambouillet appears to prove that Japan is no longer hestitant to expose itself in the circle of leading industrial nations. Moreover, the style of Rambouillet and Puerto Rico seems to have reinforced the Japanese governmental elites in their willingness to integrate themselves in this circle. Nor did the desire to intensify relations with the ASEAN group and to closen their relationship with Australia and New Zealand seem to stand in the way in the final analysis.

How strong is Europe's interest in a trilateral cooperation which may even include the political dimension? The course of the discussion in 1973 basically promoted more doubt and reservation than active interest. The Europeans also expressed their misgivings over a "rich man's club." Whether their doubts were substantive or rather more a pretext to void off a momentarily unwelcome American initiative, is a moot point. From the very beginning, Kissinger's concept for the trilateral declaration of basic principles met with a cool reception. The inclusion of Japan in such a declaration was rejected for several reasons: The "Declaration on European Identity" of 14 December 1973, had been developed in lengthy and laborious negotiations. The synchronization and gearing of this statement to the "Statement on Atlantic Relations" which was being developed simultaneously and was finally passed in June, 1974, proved to be no less difficult. The task of tying both these Declaration projects to the problem of the integration of Japan seemed to be too much for European diplomacy. It was feared that a further trilateral declaration would devaluate or water down the other two declarations which were specifically tailored to European-American relations.

Two aspects played a role in this context: In the "Year of Europe" and following the easing of the US military burden through withdrawal from Vietnam, the emphasis of European interest lay in reconfirming and strengthening America's defense commitment for Europe. It was believed that this interest could hardly be expressed in a declaration in which Japan also took part. The Japanese did not wish to become involved in European defense matters nor did the Europeans want to involve themselves in Pacific defense problems. The second aspect was related to the role of the United States in the political triangle: Kissinger's construction seemed to many Europeans to be an instrument for "mediating" relations between Japan and Western Europe. They saw it as an incomplete triangle with the United States at the top and only two lines connecting Washington with Tokyo and Brussels, but without a connection between these poles at its basis. No one wanted to forgo the direct connection between Europe and Japan, i.e., the links not directed by Washington. The practical consequence was drawn and in November, 1973, the suggestion was made to Japan to formulate an independent declaration on the relations between Japan and the EC, which could possibly be merged with the European-American document and with a third American-Japanese declaration into a triangular relationship.

Many of the European reservations were more directly related to the concrete form of Kissinger's initiative, as presented at the time, than to the general concept of trilateral cooperation. Nonetheless, it cannot be denied that a binding declaration committing the Europeans to a politically accentuated triad is still lacking to this day. The 15th paragraph of the Declaration on European Identity which acknowledges the concept of cooperation with Japan and Canada points to an "essential role of this cooperation for maintaining an open and balanced world economic system."

Consequently, it refers to the "productive cooperation with these countries above all in the OECD." There is no mention of political cooperation. A certain interest in this dimension could at best be read into the idea considered occasionally at the end of 1973 to suggest to the Japanese ad-hoc consultations at the directorial level with the respective chairmen of the political committee of the European Political Cooperation of the Nine. Considerations of this nature, along with the project of a common declaration between Japan and the EC, were submerged in the turbulence of the oil and energy crisis.

In the future, the strongest impulses toward trilateral cooperation with a political dimension are to be expected, as usual, from the United States. There is no doubt as to its interest in a political coordination of the European and Pacific allies. Whether such a political trilateral cooperation can be activated will depend on the American role in world politics in the next years and on the diplomatic ability of its leaders. They will have to respect the interest of the Europeans in not having their relations to Japan be mediated. Flexible, pragmatic forms of cooperation will stand a greater chance than attempts to institutionalize or to formulate dogmatic basic statements of principle. From the Europeans one would have to expect a broadening of their global horizons.

Tasks of Trilateral Cooperation

by HENRY OWEN

Introduction

The relationship between Western Europe, and the United States, and Japan reflects several factors:

- the growing economic interdependence among these three industrial regions;
- a common interest in certain political issues, notably some aspects of North-South and East-West relations, even though security ties continue to run bilaterally between the United states, on the one hand, and Western Europe and Japan on the other;
- increasing contact via travel and media among peoples of the three regions;
- the growing interest that each region takes in the way that other industrial regions are tackling problems of the advanced societies;
- a widening awareness of certain values, held in common, which distinguish these three regions from other developing countries and communist countries.

These factors have increasingly brought governments of the three regions together, in ways that are discussed in some detail below. It is worth noting that these inter-governmental relations are shadowed by the fact that Western Europe cannot speak with one voice, as Japan and the United States can. Inter-governmental relations are thus trilateral in only a conceptual sense; until European governments delegate power to the European Commission, or otherwise achieve greater unity, more than three political entities will continue to be involved in relations among the industrial nations.

The above factors have also spurred a growing network of non-governmental links among the peoples involved. Tripartite meetings sponsored by the Trilateral Commission, and by the Kiel Institute of World Economics, Brookings, and the Japan Economic Research Center are among the resulting ventures. One result of this widening private and governmental trilateral dialogue has been increasing contact between Western Europe and Japan. Not since Lafcadio Hearn have so many Europeans been interested in exploring Japanese culture, while Japanese tourists are becoming common-place in most large European cities. The main links of Europe and Japan will continue to run to the United States, which is their largest market and strongest ally, but the postwar US monopoly on their attention is gone. Indeed, both these regions find it easier, in some situations, to deal with the United States in a trilateral context than in bilateral forums, where each is decisively overshadowed by superior US power. This is the more true since on some issues (e.g., agricultural trade policy) they tend to agree more with each other than either of them does with the United States. Thus, the third bar of the triangle – the tie between Europe and Japan – is growing stronger.

Despite the closer links described above, suspicion and hostility remain. Some Europeans view the United States as a relic of old fashioned capitalism and somewhat imperialistic at that; some Americans view Europe as unduly dependent and demanding, weakened by social structures that are either archaic or overly socialistic; some Japanese wonder if the seeming reluctance of the other two regions to treat Japan as a full and equal partner is not a product of persisting and lingering racist attitudes. In each region, there are pressures for policies that look to greater autonomy, rather than greater interdependence: Some Japanese want agricultural self-sufficiency, so as not to have to rely on unpredictable US export policy; some Americans want to bring the troops home from Europe, so as not to be unduly involved in other people's defense; and some Europeans want to reorder their economies to make them less dependent on trade with Europe and Japan, so as to insulate their efforts to achieve social justice in greater degree from external pressures. It is all too easy to conceive how these nostalgic and parochial impulses could be enhanced by inter-regional disputes on specific issues that divide the United States, Japan, and Europe from each other. This trend could lead to shifting adversary coalitions within the trilateral relationship or, more likely, to a general weakening and fragmentation of that relationship.

On the other hand, growing concern on specific issues among the three regions could help to strengthen the concept of an emerging community of developed nations. It would not be a matter of building a super-government but rather of creating a wide variety of ad hoc instruments for more effective joint action. The OECD, along with recurring economic summits of major OECD governments, would surely remain the main focus of such action, but other instruments might be created to enable the industrial countries to concert their approaches toward a wider range of problems.

Which of these two directions – widening fissures or growing concert – is taken will depend, in good part, on how specific issues are addressed. To these we now turn.

The Economic Agenda

1. Trade

The most important item on the economic agenda of the three industrial regions is the Tokyo Round trade negotiations among them and others. At the moment, each of the industrial regions is approaching the negotiations with somewhat different views and priorities. It is not yet clear whether they will reach an agreement that will substantially reduce trade barriers.

On the one hand, there is a consensus in all three industrial regions that none of their interests would be served by returning to the trade wars of the 1930's. There is also some belief that protectionism is more likely to be avoided by reducing trade barriers than by trying to stand pat. Many in each region also perceive that widening trade can give a powerful impetus to the most innovative sectors of modern economies and thus to rates of growth. In addition, specific groups – e.g., US grain farmers, European dairy farmers, and Japanese electronic producers – want to see their export markets enlarged. And, at least among government officials, there is an awareness that reducing trade barriers would do more than anything else the industrial nations could do to help some of the developing countries. All this creates substantial support in all three areas for pushing ahead with the Tokyo Round of trade negotiations.

Nonetheless, powerful obstacles remain. For one thing, there are different perceptions as to how trade barriers should be reduced among the three areas. The European Community wants a tariff reduction formula that would help to harmonize its variable tariff structure, while the United States wants to cut tariffs equally across the board. Japan has so far favored more modest tariff cuts than the United States. The United States wants to link agricultural and industrial tariff negotiations more closely than either of the other two regions do. Specific groups within each region are also anxious to protect domestic markets for their products. Resulting problems are enhanced by the fact that some countries, notably the UK and Italy, face severe economic problems, which create domestic pressures for policies that can only be pursued behind high tariff barriers.

The favorable factors seem sufficiently powerful to create a fair chance of success in the Tokyo Round. The obstacles are formidable enough, however, to ensure that if the negotiations fail protectionist pressures will revive and governments that find themselves unable to advance will be hard pressed to avoid retreat. In this event, trade disputes will once more be at the center of relations among the industrial countries.

In short, the status quo is unlikely to be maintained: The developed nations will either go forward or retrogress in the trade field.

2. Food

The Tokyo Round should result in an agricultural agreement which has three elements: opening the US dairy market wider to European exporters, opening European and Japanese grain markets wider to US exporters, and creating an international system of national grain reserves which gives Europe and Japan reasonable assurance that US exports will continue to be available in time of global shortage. The last of these three elements may be the most difficult to achieve.

Negotiations on grain reserves have been underway in the World Wheat Council since the Rome World Food Conference. They have proceeded slowly, partly because of European and Japanese reluctance and partly because the Ford administration shared (or was reluctant to confront) the opposition of some US farm groups to an international system of national reserves. The Carter administration is reported to take a more favorable view of the matter.

If these negotiations fail, the results are predictable: The next time there is a conjunction of bad harvests in major exporting countries, as in 1973, lack of adequate reserves will cause enhanced inflation in the industrial world and real hardship in the poorer developing countries. In this circumstance, the United States might well impose export controls, with resultant damage to US relations with Europe and Japan – a damage that would probably be compounded by protectionist responses to these controls in Europe and Japan.

In food, as in trade, the industrial regions will either go forward to greater interdependence or retreat into heightened parochialism.

3. Energy

When the energy crisis was most acute, the developed countries pledged to take cooperative remedial action. In some respects they have succeeded; agreements between Europe, Japan, and the United States about sharing and stockpiling have been reached which should enable these regions to meet a future oil shortage more effectively than in the past.

But in other respects they have failed. Insufficient progress has been made in reducing energy consumption – especially in the United States. And not enough has been done to try to diversify sources of energy supplies. Such longer term actions are needed if the industrial countries are not to be exposed to the periodic external shock of large oil price increases, since only with these measures can the bargaining position of the major oil importers vis-à-vis exporters be improved.

The Carter administration's task in trying to persuade the American public and Congress of the need for action may be eased if a cooperative program can be negotiated among the industrial regions, so that the US executive branch's proposals to the Congress can be made within the framework of an agreed multilateral program.

If this is not done, the industrial regions my find themselves bidding against each other for scarce oil and trying to make special deals with oil exporting countries, as in 1973, and the European countries and Japan may come increasingly to resent the seemingly profligate American use of energy. Here, too, opportunities for dispute will multiply, if greater interdependence is not attained.

4. Coordination of Domestic Economic Policy

The Rambouillet and Puerto Rico meeting were, among other things, the first attempts by heads of government of the major OECD nations to concert their domestic economic policies. Prior experience had shown how disastrous the effects of a simultaneous excess of inflationary or deflationary zeal in the main industrial countries could be. The move to flexible exchange rates, which was supposed to insulate national economies against external influences, did not have the expected effect; inflation and deflation are evidently still contagious.

The political obstacles to progress in coordinating domestic economic policies are formidable, quite aside from the technical difficulties involved. Each government responds to a domestic constituency that is influenced by different history and circumstance. If needs for international cooperation and domestic approval thus come in conflict with each other, the latter are likely to prevail.

Still, most governmental leaders perceive that the economic trends on which their political fortunes depend hinge, in part, on actions beyond national frontiers. So a halting search for improved cooperation will likely continue to be made. To the degree that it succeeds, the governments of developed countries will find themselves brought more closely together in a matter of great import. To the degree that it fails, periodic inflation or recession will heighten the economic nationalism that is still the most serious threat to the US-European-Japanese relationship.

5. North-South Relations

Trilateral economic concert is also important to progress in North-South relations.

The developing countries that are already achieving respectable rates of growth (Brazil, Korea, Taiwan, etc.) need access to widening import markets, particularly for manufactures, in the developed world. This hinges less on trade preferences, whose economic advantages have been exaggerated, than on a general reduction in tariff and non-tariff barriers in the Tokyo Round.

The poorer developing countries – in South Asia and Africa – cannot achieve growth without a larger infusion of resources than they are likely to achieve through trade and private investment. They require substantial amounts of concessional aid – bilaterally, and from such multilateral instruments as the World Bank, its soft loan affiliate (the International Development Association), and the regional development banks in Asia, Africa, and Latin America. Whether these institutions can secure the requisite resources depends largely on whether the United States, Europe, and Japan agree to provide them. Recently, these regions have been divided on this issue among themselves: The United States has lagged behind Europe and Japan in its willingness to increase the callable resources of the World Bank and in its willingness to authorize a generous replenishment for IDA.

Resolution of other economic issues listed earlier will also affect North-South prospects. Higher oil and grain prices contributed notably to distress in developing countries in recent years. If the industrial nations can agree to create an international system of national grain reserves and to reduce energy consumption and diversify energy supplies, this will alleviate future price pressures on developing countries. If the industrial nations can also concert their domestic economic policies so as to maintain stable rates in growth in the developed world, this would help to create an economic environment congenial to the developing countries' growth.

The industrial countries will have to deal with two other issues in North-South relations – debt rescheduling and commodities. These issues' economic importance has been exaggerated, but they are politically sensitive.

The majority of developing nations do not need or want debt rescheduling; it would only threaten their ability to secure new loans. The few countries that do need rescheduling are generally getting it now – quietly and informally. Dramatizing this action would only frighten creditors and impair the credit worthiness of other developing countries.

Some developing countries have proposed that agreements be negotiated that would stabilize the prices of commodities at higher price ranges than could be sustained by market forces. They have also proposed that financing for these agreements be provided through a common fund. This course would be damaging to many developing countries, which import more raw materials than they export, and it would stimulate pressures for import substitution in the developed world. The industrial countries will not agree to these proposals, but they might be willing to negotiate agreements which would stabilize prices of a few commodities – at prices consistent with those dictated by the market. This would be of some help to developing countries.

Political-Military Agenda

1. Nuclear

Strong pressures exist in the United States for restricting exports of nuclear fuel and of processing facilities to countries that might conceivably use these exports to create national nuclear weapons programs. European countries, notably Germany and France, take a more relaxed view of the issue – doubting that technical restraints and safeguards will be decisive in shaping prospects for proliferation. Japanese sentiment on this issue is not clear. Evidently, the makings of dispute are present. Whatever may be the short term prospect, this issue will come to the fore increasingly over the longer term: Countries that want to develop a capability for producing nuclear weapons will continue their efforts to do so, and the question of what policy the industrial nations should follow toward these countries will force itself on governments.

2. Middle East

Europe and Japan's attitudes toward the Middle East will probably continue to diverge from those of the United States. Neither of these areas has as large a commitment to Israel as the United States, and both consider themselves – energy sharing agreements notwithstanding – more vulnerable than the United States to Arab oil pressures. In the event of renewed Arab-Israeli conflict, serious differences among the trilateral countries would thus be likely to recur, with the United States being more willing than either Japan or Europe to risk both Arab hostility and confrontation with the USSR in order to support Israel. If this US policy leads to an increasing danger of renewed Arab oil embargo or US-Soviet conflict, European and Japanese objections to it will be very strong indeed – the more so since these regions see little opportunity to insulate themselves from either the oil embargo or US-Soviet clashes that might result.

The best way to avoid all this will be to secure a Middle Eastern settlement. But even this effort may trigger US-European-Japanese arguments along the way, since the United States is likely to be more sympathetic to Israeli concerns in the unfolding negotiations than either Western Europe or Japan.

3. East-West Relations

Both Europe and Japan adjoin large aggregations of Communist power, and both rely on defense ties with the United States to assure their security. This reliance makes Europe and Japan sensitive to any indication of US indifference to allied concerns. That sensitivity, in turn, could have a large effect on East-West relations.

If the withdrawal of substantial US forces from Northeast Asia or a more nationalistic US economic policy caused Japan to doubt the reliability of US security guarantees, Japan might move toward a policy of neutralism or greater accommodation with its Communist neighbors. But the obstacles to such an accommodation would be powerful; the past history of Sino-Japanese and Russian-Japanese relations underlines the difficulty of reconciling neighboring great powers, which are surrounded by weaker areas (Korea and Southeast Asia) in which they compete. An alternative outcome, i.e., greater reliance by Japan on its own power to assure its own security, could lead to large scale Japanese rearmament which, even if it did not produce a national nuclear weapons program, could have profoundly destabilizing effects in Asia. Korea might well become the focus of resulting tensions, and peace in East Asia would be at greater risk.

European confidence in the United States, similarly, could be shaken if US troops were withdrawn from Europe or if US policy toward negotiations with the USSR did not take adequate account of Western European concerns. Bitter recriminations might be exchanged across the Atlantic as each side blamed the other for the resulting fraying of security relations. This would be all the more likely if, at the same time, the two regions were trying to devise a common reaction, against the background of widely differing perceptions, to the imminent and unnerving prospect of Communists sharing in political power in France and Italy. How all this would affect European attitudes toward East-West relations is hard to foresee. On the basis of present evidence, a weakening of Western European resolve seems more likely than a greatly increased European defense effort. Soviet influence would likely grow.

US relations with Japan and Western Europe have been treated separately in the above discussion, but they would probably interact, for two reasons:
– Japanese attitudes would be influenced by what was happening to US-European ties, and vice versa. Doubts in each region about America's alliance could reinforce doubts in the other region. Alternatively, growing confidence in the United States by one region might mitigate the other's concerns.
– US forces' deployments between these two regions are justifiable, to some extent. The United States now has six carrier groups in the Pacific and six in the Atlantic. The number in the Pacific may be in excess of post-Vietnam Asian needs; there have been proposals to increase the number in Europe to meet the growing Soviet naval threat. The United States has six infantry divisions (Army and Marine) in the Pacific and on the US West Coast that are too lightly armed to fight in Europe; it is not clear that all six are needed in Asia, but more ground strength may be required in Europe, or in the United States earmarked for Europe, to offset increasing Soviet capabilities in Central Europe. Decisions as to whether to redeploy US carriers, and to redeploy and re-equip US infantry divisions from Asia to meet European needs cannot be made without assessing both European and Japanese concerns. Any US decision to shift forces between these two regions is bound to affect the interests of both.

For these reasons, US security policies toward Europe and Japan will probably interact. As this becomes increasingly evident, European and Japanese reluctance to treat security questions trilaterally may wane somewhat.

Whether conflict or cooperation shapes the US-European-Japanese relationship will depend most immediately on how economic issues are handled. These issues have a decisive claim on domestic politics in each of these regions.

On the main issues involved – trade, food, energy, and concerting domestic policy – the choice is clear: Either the industrial regions will move toward greater interdependence or they will drift apart. The status quo is unlikely to be maintained.

The outcome will depend largely on US policy. This is true not only because of large US economic power, but also because of special problems that limit Europe's and Japan's capacity for leadership: So long as Western Europe remains divided, it will have difficulty making large proposals for economic initiatives; and Japan still lacks confidence in its newly acquired economic power. If the United States does not lead the way, no one will.

The advent to power of a new US administration creates an occasion for new US initiatives. Whether these initiatives prosper will depend heavily on how the wider public – in Europe, Japan, and North America – reacts to them. The public's reaction, in turn, will depend in part on whether people come to perceive that what is at stake are not merely the specific issues under discussion but also the stability of their countries' alliances and of relations with potential adversaries, which shape prospects for wider peace. Needed economic compromises are more likely to be made in this larger perspective than if they are addressed only on their merits.

The periodic economic summits that began with Rambouillet and Puerto Rico may provide a framework in which the heads of government can move in this direction – making clear that they are addressing economic issues in a context that takes account not only of their own countries' economic welfare but of the need to maintain and strengthen the fabric of international relations – among industrial countries, between developed and developing countries, and with the Communist nations. Over the long term, these trilateral conferences might even address some of the non-economic issues defined under II, above. In any event, efforts should increasingly be made in private forums to link discussion of economic and non-economic issues confronting the industrial nations. In widening both the agenda of trilateral discourse and the context in which that discourse takes place will be found the best means of strengthening the European-Japanese-American connection in the period ahead.

The European Community and its Global Responsibilities

by François Duchêne

From 1971 to 1974, American relations with Europe and Japan were suspicious and bad-tempered. Indeed, they were so bad-tempered that David Rockefeller launched his Trilateral Commission, now made famous by President Carter's cabinet appointments, precisely in order to salvage, through a private framework, some of the threatened shipwreck of cooperation at the official level. However, since 1974 the storm clouds have dispersed even more suddenly than they appeared. From both sides of the Atlantic one hears echoes of official and mutual self-congratulation on the serene climate of relations. How can the weather have changed so abruptly? How did the storm gather in the first place? If it broke once might it not break again? What might cause it to break? What does the present serenity consist of, anyway? The questions teem, but they have been muffled in comfortable silence, what may in itself say something about the relationship that now exists. For there is no doubt that the very fact of the bad patch of 1971–74 has, however, tacitly, changed the scenery. The cracks beneath the surface have been revealed, measured and tested. That is not necessarily to be deplored. One of the most beautiful passages in modern English poetry even suggests it is a form of maturity, of waking up.

> Now, Ariel, I am that I am, your late
> and lonely master, Who knows now what
> magic is; – the power to enchant that
> comes from disillusion.

Nevertheless something has changed. What? Why? and with which implications?

One of the underlying tendencies of the "60's" was that although the debate over Gaullism in Europe was full of sound and fury, – and definitely less significant than its volume would appear to indicate – the gradual dissociation of the United States from its former concentration on priorities defined in common with Europeans was far more important. When the tide turned in 1971–74, it was this underlying development that really mattered. During those years, Nixon and Kissinger seem to have tried to achieve two aims in relation to their allies. The first was to gain a free hand in great power

relations with the Soviet Union and China, in order to profit from the rift
between the two Communist giants; this did not mean abandoning America's
cold war allies but it did mean taking them for granted, and is the real reason
why the "Nixon shock" knocked the stuffing out of the Japanese. The second
aim was to free America of the economic shackles imposed on it by the
successful cold war policy of reviving the weakened allies, which had meant
endless credits and open home markets for potential competitors. The
competition had begun to hurt. By 1971, the Japanese were prevailing over
whole industrial sectors on the American market itself and Germany
overtook the United States as the world's greatest exporter of manufactures.
Nixon-Kissinger policy was a total success in the attainment of both goals.
This led to a third discovery – that the allies of the United States needed her
more than she needed them and that she could afford to manipulate them to
a considerable degree. Though some of the less aware Americans made it a
cliché to explain America's post-Vietnam policies by her weakened position
in the world, this was not at all true in relation to her allies. By shaking free
of the burdens of looking after them and by beginning to mobilize her
immense resources in the tactical as well as strategic pursuit of the "national
interest," or whatever appeared to be so at the time, the USA was easily able
to demonstrate that weakness is relative and that when it came down to it,
she had far more muscle than her allies. As the two regional economic
leaders, Germany in Europe and Japan in East Asia, are peculiarly vulnerable
to such pressure (and the US, Germany, and Japan produce 75 percent of
"trilateral" GNP) the United States has in effect been able to retain economic
leadership through these two countries. The International Energy Agency
has grouped her allies behind her in what Kissinger, its creator, himself
called an "economic Nato," and deservedly so. Despite demonstrations of
independence by France, the heart of the matter remains, although America's
allies are far more vulnerable than the US in the energy area; energy priorities
of the industrial world continue to be defined by the Americans. The 1973
dispute over whether the United States should be consulted about European
Community policies before or after the Nine themselves had made their own
decisions was absurd in one way, but deeply significant in another, because
it showed the determination of the United States, under Kissinger at any
rate, to remain the sole center of policy formation in the West. The final
compromise, that the President of the Community's Council of Ministers
should regularly inform the United States, at least partially confirmed that
primacy, real as it was before being spelt out in such a clumsy way. All this
was sufficient to substantiate if not justify Kissinger's imperial distinction
between the "global responsibilities" of the United States and the "regional"

ones of Europe. Thus, the period of supposed retreat after Vietnam has, as regards allies and particularly the Europeans, been in many ways a period of greater American hegemonial assertion than the cold war period when the apparent disparity of power was much greater. During the cold war common purpose was a basic assumption. Now, common purpose can be assumed only up to a point. Where there are differences, the United States, though amenable to discussion, has become far more used to exercising its leverage to see that its view prevails against potential dissent.

In a sense this change in American attitudes has been paralleled by an evolution in Europe, where the years 1968 to 1974/75 have also been a period of pivotal importance. European wage inflation began to become critical in 1968, the year of revolutions, and led to the cumulative divergences in performance of the member states of the Community that have made a nonsense of the dreams of a European Monetary Union by 1980 on which Pompidou and Brandt build their *relance* of integration after de Gaulle's abdication in 1969. These divergences have been rather more the cause than the consequence of the recession which has in turn, magnified the differences, but whatever the ultimate chain of cause and effect, the result has been a weakening of the European Community worse than had ever been feared in the heyday of the Gaullist assault upon that organization. Some progress has been made in diplomatic cooperation between the Nine, but the substance of the Community itself has become dangerously thin and the agricultural policy, the one area of partial European, as distinct from national, government is under such strain that the last European farm Commissioner, Pierre Lardinois, justified his resignation in 1975 by its threatened collapse. In Europe, as in America, there has been a domestication of political purpose and priorities, but with different effects. Because the United States is a great power, domestication tends to stress unilateral great power purposes in the world. In Europe it simply tends to divide, weaken and encourage provincial tendencies. Germany, the exporter to the world and to some extent the mistress of her inflation has tended to emerge from the pack, though she may well depend upon it more than is immediately apparent. But the total effect has been to underline the gap between America as the leader and the disorderly camp followers carrying, aside from Germany, little weight.

Thus, today, the power of the United States over Europe is far more heavily felt than ever before. This would not automatically, of course, ensure the serenity of transatlantic relations which has been such a marked feature of the Ford administration. On the contrary, it could have led, especially in a period of recession, to more difficult and angry relations. Anyone hearing an accurate Cassandra of the mid-1960's predicting the present situation might indeed have assumed that this would be the case. That it has not occurred is due to a number of specific factors.

An important element is the predicament of the European Communists. They can only emerge from their political ghetto and attain their goal of merging into the mainstream of West European politics, by throwing off the electoral albatross of the Soviet Union which is beginning to look more and more like a modernized version of the old czarism. They must steer clear of all the familiar cold war themes that alienate the new strata of society to whom they hope to appeal. They cannot attack the United States, since this would lose them significant margins of votes. Instead they must ignore the US as far as possible, as did the Italian Communists even when Kissinger let it be known in April 1975 that the Ford administration would not countenance their participation in the government. The dynamo of anti-Americanism has been turned off and a strange silence has ensued. There is still widespread potential anti-Americanism, mostly in southern and latin Europe, but there is currently no political force to turn it on.

The second important factor is that since East-West affairs have faded into the background of political fashion, as they have since Willy Brandt steered through the *Ostpolitik*, foreground has been occupied by economic issues which point primarily West and South, not towards the East. This has placed the emphasis on aspects of European-American relations which generate quite different reactions than those evident during the cold war. The problems here are not who protects whom, who might unleash a preventive war or who predominates – which all produce the traditional power responses – but rather how does one overcome recession or reach a *modus vivendi* with the OPEC as the marching wing of the Third World? The pattern of interests is quite different. To countries faced with the problems of recession, unemployment and inflation, the United States, like all the stronger economies, is in an ambiguous relationship to the weaker systems. On the one hand it is widely recognized that only America, Germany and Japan can take the lead as they are the sole countries capable of leadership. To be sure, America stands alone in her equivalent NATO function. In the economic sector, however, the US is not the only ant telling the grasshoppers that a price has to be paid in the winter for dancing through the summer. Germany and Japan use the same language. Moreover, unlike the ant in the fable, America, Germany and Japan do lend money to the weak. The weak might still close their frontiers as the Italians have done in part and as the British have threatened to do. But they also are aware that this would impoverish them even more. As a result the predominant Western relationship has, so far at any rate, been the feeling that everyone is in the same boat.

When the excesses and limits of American power were displayed by Watergate and the Lockheed scandal, both of which had been exposed by a triumphant Democratic Congress, or when, to the irritation of most men of government, the Congress queers American relations with Turkey because of Cyprus, the message conveyed to other Westerners is that this is truly a democracy. In such ways, America's very weaknesses tend to identify it with the democratic process in other countries and to divest it of the cruder traditional associations of power with which it was saddled in many quarters of Europe during the cold war. Strangely enough this may be the positive legacy of the Vietnam crisis in American relations with Europe just as the New Deal underprimed its leadership after the war. Moreover, to the extent that developments in West European countries are felt to depend on indigenous trends in opinion, it is not felt that America, which betrays some of the same symptoms, is really the manipulator of events. From this point of view there is only a limited analogy between Latin America and Europe, despite the parallels drawn on the left in France and Italy between the fate of Allende and the possible difficulties of Berlinguer. Even the Portuguese crisis does not seem to have affected such analogies very much, because the European countries and socialist parties threw themselves more wholeheartedly and successfully into the revolutionary fray than the Americans, and prevailed by political means, not through the naked exercise of power. A revival of Communist interest in anti-American campaigns could change this. In practice it has not.

Another important factor is that in so far as Europeans and Americans can build a front against the OPEC or the poor, the assumption is made that Western interests are identical. Whatever their differences, Europe and America are felt essentially to sit on the same side of the fence. This has been equally true of East-West issues such as the respect of the human rights inscribed in the Helsinki agreement, or the reaction to the attempt of the Portuguese Communists to pull off the crude kind of coup that once worked in Stalinist eastern Europe. It is, perhaps, too early to speak of a Western patriotism, but in a world of "global bargaining" and instinctive tightening of the ranks of the rich, the preconditions for something of that sort can be discerned.

When one adds to these developments the failure of the European Community to cohere as a partner or adversary of the United States, it is not surprising that *ad hoc* relationships have been fairly serene. Once the Americans had readjusted the postwar system, most of the practical purposes pursued were almost bound to stress the identity of culture and interest of Europe and America. In a way, it is possible to think of the early "70s" in

Atlantic relations as the period in which Americans and Europeans have both really begun to adjust to the enormous shift in power produced by the Second World War. The Americans have grown used to leadership, the Europeans are reconciled to provincialism as never before. This is linked to the increasing preoccupation of all advanced industrial societies with domestic problems and their declining interest in the "high" politics so fascinating for the "elites" in hierarchical societies. This tends to defuse power issues and to gut notions like imperialism of much of their relevance. Perhaps this is an unconscious tribute to the political standards and compatibility of the industrialized societies. However, it would not occur to East Europeans looking East nor to Latin Americans looking North. In a way, the serenity of current transatlantic relations is a reflection of the domestication of international affairs amongst the advanced industrial societies all of whose governments in varying degrees have to answer to the same pressures and feel a similar weakening of their traditional authority.

Does that mean that the present calm will probably endure? In view of the recent turbulence a certain skepticism is bound to linger, even if it is clear that between 1971 and 1974 some adjustments in the system took place which will not need to be repeated in the immediate future. Nonetheless, there is no national harmony which dictates that domestic Lobbies seeking their own advantage in ignorance or indifference of their impact on foreigners will produce a spirit of benevolence and concord; rather the opposite will be more likely. Can this absence of conflicts last?

In many ways, Europe and America are likely to have common interests and environmental perceptions. The United States will remain vital to the security of the Western European nations as long as they are unable to integrate sufficiently to provide for their own protection and the Soviet Union remains highly armed; both conditions which show every sign of lasting. There is clearly a need for cooperation between the industrial powers to handle the problems of their own threatened prosperity, a prosperity which had long been taken for granted. There is also the innate conservatism of the rich and traditionally powerful in the face of the clamorous second and third worlds making demands which must, at the very least, place a constant psychological strain on the "satisfied" powers. Even deeper than that conservatism is the cultural compatibility of the advanced industrial democracies and a *fortiori* of the Europeans and their American descendants. Affinity breeds rapport, all the more so because the advanced industrial democracies are now surrounded by a sea of dictatorships. As politics become more and more "global" and international negotiation begins to take on the air of bargaining between huge regional groups of countries, this factor is likely to become increasingly important. In this context it must be seen that the European tends to place a very high priority on the relationship to the United States.

Nonetheless, this simple and very general picture is likely to be modified and possibly even undermined by changes taking place in the world. The problem is essentially one of cumulative divergence in the behavior and outlook of the industrial powers themselves, the unity of which was the very fulcrum of the common postwar *Weltanschauung*. This has a number of aspects and all of them are of great potential significance.

One of them is the growing importance of the structural gap between the United States, Canada and Australia on the one hand and Japan and Western Europe on the other. Canada and Australia are net exporters of raw materials, and the United States is a limited importer which could attain self-sufficiency in most cases if it were necessary. Europe and Japan are uniquely dependent on their capacity as competitive transformers of imported raw materials to maintain their standards of living. For them, the energy crisis of 1974 marked the end of empire in a more significant way than a political retreat from former colonies. It showed that a combination of economic and political factors could, in the future, raise the price of, and even potentially cut them off from, the basic resources of their industrial prosperity. True, oil is a special case in several ways. Firstly, even before 1973 it represented about half the (non-food) raw material import bill of all the major industrial countries. Secondly, its sources are concentrated in the hands of a single cartel leader, that is, Saudi Arabia; the United States position on the grains market offers the only parallel. And thirdly, oil conditions the whole range of production as no other material does. For all these reasons the energy crisis should not be taken as the cloud no larger than a man's hand; it is the storm itself – and has been weathered better than most Westerners would have expected beforehand. Nevertheless, it is difficult to imagine that Saudi Arabia will indefinitely expand its output, and that in return for money which would be troublesome to spend. This factor could even raise the price of oil much further than it has in the past. Other raw material prices could also rise in the medium term if resource nationalism and conservation were to increase in major exporters such as Canada and Australia. The effect of these trends could be to favor the basic producers and the more flexible societies among the industrial countries against those that are not in such a position. Nor will there necessarily be much solidarity between the two factions; the history of the IEA offers a case in point.

Of course, the demand for oil of the whole industrial world has been rising extremely rapidly since the early "60's" due to the low prices fixed by the

Seven Sisters. Yet, after 1970 it was the shift in the United States from continental self-sufficiency to imports from the Middle East which gave the OPEC the bargaining power to point the gun not primarily at the United States, but rather towards the more vulnerable Europe and Japan. Even though American imports have continued to rise vertiginously, it still remains far less dependent, actually and above all potentially, on imported energy than its smaller associates. The reason why Project Independence, with its goal of attaining energy self-sufficiency, has failed in the United States has been that the various domestic lobbies have resisted price increases or major saving in energy consumption, a consumption which is more than twice as high per capita than in any of the other advanced industrial countries. In short, the United States, by concentrating on the domestic rather than international politics of energy, has weakened the global bargaining power of its own allies. But these allies have done very little to influence American policy. The International Energy Authority, their common organization, does, to be sure, provide an insurance system against catastrophe in that North American domestic production would be shared in a Western rationing scheme if OPEC were to launch another embargo. But to rely on this rationing scheme as if it solved the problem is to throw away the time it has bought for more lasting alleviations of the underlying problem, and which were implicit in the IEA's two other priorities, conservation (where little has been achieved) and research and development (which boils down to bilateral contracts between the United States and any other country that may have interesting technologies to offer). As long as the United States pursues its present policies, the basic problems for its allies, – as well as for itself – will be made worse, not better. IEA may be an economic Nato, but Japan and Germany, which have done so well on the basis of the "low posture" so far, may be making a major mistake if the IEA continues to function as it has in the past when the needs of Japan and Europe on the one hand, and the US on the other, at least partly diverge as they have in the energy sector. They may be in for a rude awakening. But until they show a more resolute attitude towards the United States and make it plain that American *domestic* politics must take their own situations into account, they will be aiding and abetting their own subordination in an area where the United States is potentially one of the main architects of their troubles. In this sense, the later years of Kissinger's regime were really the beginning of an imperial situation, that is where the weak begin to acquiesce to the flouting of their interests by the "protecting" power. This should be taken into account in inter-allied politics. The common interest is not served by leaders who out of habit, lack of imagination or "low posture" fail to point out and try to overcome conflicts of interest where they arise. To ignore them is to court far worse trouble later. Thus, there is a very real crack in the Western system in a manner never present during the cold war, at that time allied interest were similar, now they diverge in some crucial respects.

In themselves, mechanical differences of this kind can be important, although they are not likely to be decisive. Life is too various and the ability of the vigorous and flexible to overcome apparent obstacles (i.e., Sweden, Switzerland or West Germany since 1949) too great. Probably more decisive in the present situation are the signs of increasing divergence between the industrial powers which are deeply rooted in their socio-cultural differences. Western Europe in particular is in danger of radical division as a result of the diverse paths being taken by those demanding a redistribution of income and power within different countries. The countries of the Deutschmark zone, West Germany itself and the rich minor states whose economies gravitate around it, are more or less satisfied with, or well adapted to the postwar mixed economy. This is true of the apparently radical Sweden as well as conservative Switzerland. Most of the rest of the region, essentially all of the big countries except Germany – Britain, France, Italy, Spain – face considerable difficulties in handling inflation, which is, in turn, the symptom of their domestic social tensions. This is the root of the recent monetary troubles of Western Europe and their extension in the failures of the European Community. Until these tensions are resolved or have worked themselves out – and how long will that take? – a number of dangers will face Europe. One that is very seldom talked about is the effect on security. What would happen to the politics and doctrines of deterrence if Germany were by 1980 surrounded to the west and south by neo-gaullist regimes in Britain, France and Italy? This is not at all impossible. The social contract in Britain will face a crisis when strict controls are lifted, as they almost certainly must be, in 1977 or 1978. The frivolity of the Italian politicians could still create the kind of crisis in which the Communists who are creeping into social democratic shoes could be discredited and replaced by their more totalitarian party colleagues. The weaknesses of the French constitution, with its division of authority between the President and Prime Minister, seem calculated to make a possible shift to the Left after the legislative elections of 1978 as damaging and difficult as possible. Which direction would Germany move under such circumstances? Would it shift to the right or to the east? Probably, all things considered, further towards America. But there is no denying that with two potential neutrals athwart the main lines of communication between Germany and America, it would soon be much more difficult than in the past to produce that rational and coherent strategy of deterrence which Henry

Kissinger, reasonably enough, called for in 1973. And even if matters do not go that far, the reinforcement of the American-German link, deepening the lines of demarcation between the two Western Europes, would be full of dangers, as indeed it already is today both for the economy and the political processes of the region.

In the final analysis, the biggest problems will probably lie in the general politico-economic stance of the West in the face of the great changes that seem now to be looming up. It is difficult from our present perspective to gauge the significance of the changes that have taken place in the "70's". But two seem to be particularly important. On the one hand, due to political and social reasons it seems that the concurrent growth and politics of the industrial world will be far more difficult to maintain than in the generation during the cold war. The "West" is potentially divided, and will only remain united by conscious effort to that end. On the other hand, the Third World is beginning to become an active participant on the political stage, and not only in OPEC. The offshore countries of East Asia and some of the largest Latin American countries, as well as the Moslem world, are emerging as forces to be reckoned with in some if not all sectors of international affairs. The upshot of this situation is that there are many signs that industrial competition throughout the world is going to become more intense, although by the same token there will also be an expansion of potential markets. The Europeans and Japanese, who have monopolized the export markets along with the Americans, may find they have to struggle for the control of such commerce more than they have in the past. Thus, the automobile industry may go the way of cotton as more and more countries enter the field, first preempting import markets and ultimately themselves competing in the countries that used to monopolize the exports. In such a situation everything will depend on the natural strength of particular economies and, where that is lacking, the toughness and flexibility of the society that has to face the challenge. Many European societies having become, since the war, essentially more demanding as consumers and less so as producers, show signs of becoming a great deal less flexible and able to adapt. Britain is an extreme example but even Germany shows some indications of the same phenomena, and in between these two countries lie a whole range of responses. Under these circumstances, the sheep are likely to be sorted out from the goats. For instance, the Japanese, and to a lesser extent the Germans, already seem to be talking about long-term strategies to maintain their export supremacy. The Franco-German rebellion against American-sponsored restraints on the sales of plants to reprocess nuclear fuels seems to have had at least something to do with the desire to be first in a field which is thought to be a potentially key future market. Such efforts will not always be either successful or wise, and where they fail are likely to lead to a climate of increased competition and reduced growth, and a revival of economic nationalism. This will be essentially protectionist in nature, as was the case in the "30's". The major problem, therefore, in a period of reduced growth or recession and of gradual transfer of power from the few to the not so few, will be to maintain the effectiveness of an international system that has worked well so far. It cannot be done simply by carrying on with the old mechanisms and prescriptions.

All this is not to say that European-American relations are necessarily going into a period of turbulence or degradation. Too many factors can affect developments from month to month and year to year. But it does mean that there has almost certainly been a fundamental change from the period of cold war and economic miracles. The whole network of domestic and world relationships is different, and so are the dangers and the directions in which remedies need to be explored. The years from 1968 to 1974 really do seem to have been a kind of watershed. The structures of the cold war period have been handed down to the contemporary scene but the old purposes have disappeared. They have been replaced by a radicalization of politics both in the domestic and international spheres. There is a growing demand for the redistribution of incomes and power within many societies in the rich part of the world. Similarly, there is a demand for the redistribution of incomes and power internationally between the rich societies and the poor, on a global scale. The central problem that has now emerged is the competition between these two processes. It supersedes at least one of the central problems of the preceding period, that is the competition for power between the Soviet Union, and the other major participants led by the United States. The Soviet leadership, placing this in a traditional Marxist context, doubtlessly now hope that they may be able to profit by divisions in the capitalist world and further their own predominance. All these complexities have to be faced as flexibly and as effectively as they were after the war, and it must be admitted that in some ways it is more difficult to do so. The main reason is that no power now has the capacity to shape the total environment that the United States once had, and which it used, on the whole (certainly from Western Europe's point of view) in a remarkably effective and beneficent way. The effort now has to be collective. The whole problem posed by the divergence of Western societies is whether they, or at least the Americans, Germans and Japanese, will be able to cooperate, and at what cost.

There seem no easy, ready-made solutions in face of the new situation posed by the cumulative divergences in the political and economic comportment of the rich countries, the proliferation of states, the means of action towards the Third World, and sluggish instead of easy growth possibly throughout the world. Two main approaches seem necessary; firstly, the strategy to be adopted to attain international control over the difficult and turbulent process of socio-economic change in the present period of diminished growth, and secondly, the strategy to be taken towards the Third World.

As regards the international economic system as it has been built up under the aegis of America since the war, it is becoming more and more evident that free trade rules, on the one hand, and unilateral economic nationalism, on the other, will both fail in the new and more competitive phase. The disputes between the European Community and Japan over trade in 1976 point clearly to the dangers. They could produce chain reactions of protectionism. Even if the problem were to be handled largely on a basis of free trade it is evident that issues are likely to be exaggerated out of all proportion to their real importance because of inadequate instruments and insufficient political will to treat the different elements, such as Britain's political problems and Japan's deflationary policies, as connected parts of the total picture. In addition, it is evident that such a problem cannot be handled simply as a free trade question, partly because of the political salience of unemployment issues in Europe, and partly because of the centralized control of the Japanese import market, which require special methods. But if trade policies become politicized in such a manner, there will be disaster unless there are more international rules and procedures to make countries more responsible to their peers for their domestic policies, both in general and in specific sectors. Disputes, however, are the political equivalent of fevers. The real problem is preventive medicine. This is really a question of how best to deal with the issues of industrial strategy that are becoming increasingly important as countries realize that basic changes may be taking place. It is one thing for Japan to adopt an "industrial strategy" and through its vigor achieve a well deserved advantage over its competitors. It is quite another for everyone else to charge down the same road at the same time. There must then be some sense of direction in the world economy as well as of the scope and limits of particular approaches. The answer possibly lies in some kind of international indicative planning that would not be capable of directing national policies, but might cast some light upon them. Such a move is no more than a step and would clearly be insufficient in itself. The needs of the new situation will unfold with the problems. Without more cooperative action, sharing of responsibilities and accountability to each other, the countries of the world will have great difficulty avoiding the pitfalls of a period of gradual, but probably deep change.

A second and related problem is the attitude to be taken towards the Third World. The tradition of providing "aid" to the poor tends to divert attention from the real issues as well as the real achievements of the postwar boom, which has been to create the beginnings of new industrial states in the Third World. If this industrialization takes root and spreads the problems of the Third World may at last begin to seem more manageable. The difficulty, of course, is that this is precisely where the shoe could pinch the industrial powers of the First World. It will at least give them potential incentives for shifting the emphasis of their industry, possibly as MITI has suggested for Japan, that is, into sectors requiring less raw materials and more value added by human skills – perhaps in other directions as well. But change is apt to be difficult even in a period of rapid growth, and especially in societies where the labor force has become increasingly immobile. Yet, allowing the more successful of the present-day poor to industrialize and thus to be coopted into the company of the present-day rich may ultimately be the only long-term solution to the problems of poverty in the world. The attitudes of the OPEC countries, contrary to all the atavistic fears the West certainly entertained about them before the energy crisis, has shown that many if not most or all of them, once they begin to industrialize, will in effect wish to be integrated in the system. This will not be an easy process, because the psychological difficulties of integration, the domestic upheavals in countries undergoing accelerated development, and the constant tendency of *ci-devants* to concede too little and too late will all make crises a virtual certainty. But crises here and there are different from the systematic confrontation between North and South which has often been predicted. One of the great changes that has taken place through the miniaturization, cheapening and potential spread and vulgarization of weapons of high accuracy and power is that it has now become conceivable that the gap between governmental and non-governmental violence, and between the destructive power of rich and poor may be sufficiently narrow as to make international terrorism a technically conceivable strategy. In the long run, cooptation of the relatively successful defuses the black and white of wealth and poverty, and is the only solution which avoids greater dangers, even if it undoubtedly contains risks of its own. But such a strategy will demand more of the industrial powers than "aid" because it involves responding encouragingly to potential competitors and not the mere distribution of hand outs scooped from the accumulated treasure of superior economic performance. One costs money, the other is a threat. Control remains in the first case in the hands of the donor, in the other case he may lose it entirely. To pursue such a strategy, when its costs become more obvious from day to day, will call for clear-sightedness about priorities.

This is only possible if the international system is seen to be strong enough to define and maintain those priorities and cushion the costs of the process of change. In a controlled climate it may turn out that many of these changes take place spontaneously and remain almost unnoticed. That will certainly not be the case if the industrial nations are seriously at odds with each other and thus protectionism and divisions ensue.

To stress the potential problems and dangers of the European-American relationship and of the international system built around is not equivalent to drawing up a balance sheet of failure. On the contrary, in some ways the system has stood up well under the strains placed upon it. The energy crisis has not proved the catastrophe that was once feared; recession has not led to the protectionist excesses of the "30's", the potential confrontation with the OPEC has evolved into a tense and conditional cooperation (but cooperation all the same) typical of the latter part of the twentieth century; and economic leadership continues to be maintained by the trio of America, Germany and Japan even if the weaker brethren complain that they are too concerned about cutting inflation and not concerned enough about raising employment. Of course, the balance remains fragile. The control over inflation is patchy, unemployment is so stubborn that even in Germany there is talk of it being "structural," and a certain anxiety has arisen about the future of cooperation between government and labor unions. Recession is hard to shake off, growth looks like it will remain indefinitely constrained, mainly by social pressures, in a way that would have seemed disastrous to the postwar generation. Nevertheless, the leadership system, as such, cannot really be blamed for troubles that lie deep in the growth of a new society which places new demands on government and the productive machinery and shows less willingness to accept the discipline and hierarchy which achieved economic success in the past. Within limits, the leadership system, far from failing, has shown itself fairly solid and flexible in the face of these new issues. The United States remains the final repository of the security of the whole First World as it has been ever since the war; there is complete continuity in this field. In economics there has been more change, but the triangular leadership of the United States, Germany and Japan also seems solid, in part because of the special dependence of these two upon their wartime conqueror. This is not the leadership system that had been imagined in the postwar Grand Designs; but politics – because it is part of nature – abhors a vacuum, if the blueprints fail, real power will fill that vacuum. In itself, this is a natural development and must be accepted as such.

In spite of these factors, one cannot ignore the gradual accumulation of weaknesses in the system and the potential for reaching new thresholds of difficulty if these weaknesses are not corrected. The gap which has opened up between the United States and its allies in the area of defense lends itself to trouble. The United States, which demands – as is, indeed, essential to nuclear deterrence – that decisions be centralized in Washington, has acquired the habit of command to the point where the distinction between leadership and manipulation has become blurred. Of course, Nixon and Kissinger were conscious and enthusiastic manipulators and this was a serious charge against them in an alliance of democratic countries. But one has only to observe the frequent impatience in Washington with its allies to see that the temptation goes deeper and to some extent lies in the situation. It is a temptation, amongst other reasons, because it has serious costs in the resultant behavior of the followers. The mirror image of centralization and manipulation is irresponsibility and egression. This is the malady afflicting NATO. All of the allied governments, except Germany, which is on the frontier and takes part in the real decision-making, are having major difficulties maintaining defense expenditures even in the face of a major Soviet military build-up. It is true that peace has lasted so long that the public is less and less inclined to pay for it. There may be some realism in this. But no one in his right senses lowers his insurance premiums during a time of inflation – which, in military terms, this undoubtedly is. The failure to commit all the European countries to a genuinely common decision-making process means that more and more of them, including large countries like Britain, France and Italy, tacitly rely for their defense on Germany and America, while gradually shifting their expenditures to other priorities.

There is something somewhat similar, *mutatis mutandis*, in the economic field. Cumulative divergences between the performances of the industrial countries mean that, to some extent, the success of the few is a partial reflection of the failure of the many and vice versa. If the price of commitment to the system becomes too high a number of consequences can result. One is that if half of Western Europe (in economic terms) labors under great tensions and difficulties, there is no certainty that the German economy itself can remain healthy. The links between the member countries of the European Community have become very profound and while this is a binding force up to a point, beyond that point it could become a factor communicating not strength to the weak but weakness to the strong. The fact is that, collectively, the weaker European economies are large enough to infect the international system. The dispute between Japan and the European Community is, in part, a symptom of this danger (though it also shows the need for special methods in dealing with a country, like Japan, whose economy is centrally controlled). The kinds of reactions that may become routine in the weaker

European economies – increased state intervention in industry, the whole range of concealed as well as open instruments of economic nationalism, planning in a restrictive rather than embracing sense – can divide the First World at the very moment when problems of dealing with the Third and perhaps even Second Worlds are becoming greater than ever before. Failure to control the economy, in the sense of reducing unemployment and trade imbalances at the very least, increases the risk of the success on the left of a kind of nationalism heavily influenced by the Eurocommunists, or their British equivalent, the Tribune.

To cope with such problems is a collective responsibility. For instance, American manipulation of energy policy must be reduced, but that will only occur if the Europeans, and especially Germany and Japan, make up their minds that a "low posture" no longer pays automatic dividends and that it is therefore necessary to exert pressure on the United States in the IEA. If restrictive nationalist "planning" is to be avoided, there must be more expansive internationalist planning, of the kind implied in an industrial strategy which would reconcile the old industrial leaders with the new countries seeking integration into the system from below. If there is to be less minority leadership, the member states of the European Community must increase their domestic and collective efforts to act coherently. Of course, this is easier said than done. While the European electorates are consistently moderate, some of the strategic lobbies which tend to determine political outcomes are considerably more radical. But this is not the whole story. The "pragmatic" nationalism of various governments frequently makes matters worse and tends to obscure the fact that the European Community is not only a source of strength and hope but is also a principal method of control over member countries. The manner in which the borders are kept pervious is not merely dependent upon free trade because the Community is political as well. Maintaining open borders could well be the key to the ultimate outcome of the turmoil in Europe today and of its impact on the outside world. But they will not be kept open if states play fast and loose with the detail of their Community commitments to the point where people wake up one day and see the emperor has ceased to wear clothes. American policy, of course, is important. Attempts to bypass and quietly downgrade the Community, the way Kissinger did, are bad; the more traditional good resolutions of the incoming Carter administration are a cause for hope. The United States impinges on Europe at so many points, through its troops, its multinationals, its economic leadership and its many Trojan horses, that it can make cohesion in the region more difficult to achieve. The fact is, however, that where the Europeans have cohered the Americans have always been prepared to talk, to adapt and to cooperate. Moreover, the Germans have shown on a number of occasions that when they see their interests as differing from those of the Americans that they are as ready as the French are to act accordingly. They are not as theatrical, and are sometimes more stubborn. In 1976, the French showed more willingness to retract their policy of selling nuclear fuel reprocessing plants than did the Germans.

The fact is that if the weaker Europeans want to master their economic and social troubles, they will have to face the challenge of an open economy while seeking support from the framework of the European Community and the international system. If the Americans and Germans want to avoid the degeneration of their leadership into a losing struggle to plug holes in the system then they will have to encourage coherence in Europe, as the weakest of the "trilateral" regions. If the advanced industrial democracies are to deal with the difficult spread of industry to new countries at a time of constrained growth, they will have to act in concert in areas where such planning has been tabu. This may seem to go beyond Europe and America, but however close the two countries are today, even their mutual relations can now only make sense in a global framework.

The Future of the European Community as a Problem of American-European Relations

by MARTIN J. HILLENBRAND

A sensible American approach today towards the future of the European Community must necessarily involve both historical considerations and a realistic assessment of current possibilities. Reviewing the past record, one finds consistent, sometimes emotionally tinged, support for the concept of supranational integration in Europe as announced American policy, although the intensity and genuineness of such support and the nuances in its verbal formulation have varied over the years as concrete problems have arisen or administrations in Washington have, in the light of their own prejudices, adapted to changing prospects in Brussels.

Although schematic presentations sometimes distort reality to make a point, it is useful, I believe, to think of the past relationship of American policy to European unity as having gone through three phases. The first of these, which might be designated as the romantic-idealistic phase, grew out of the postwar necessities which inspired the Marshall Plan. It soon developed a momentum of its own, a coalescence of the creative European leadership provided by such personalities as Robert Schuman, Alcide de Gasperi, Konrad Adenauer, Jean Monnet and Paul Henri Spaak, and a group of enthusiastic American officials located either in Paris or in the State Department in Washington. To many it seemed then that a truly supranational Europe was in the making. The negotiation of treaties to create a European Coal-Steel Community and European Defense Community, to be capped by a European Political Community, moved along at a rapid pace given the complexity of subject matter and importance of national interests involved. The forward movement, however, came to an abrupt halt with the rejection by the French National Assembly in the summer of 1954 of the Treaty to Establish a European Defense Community, and with the realization that the *Ad Hoc* Assembly of Parliamentarians created to draft the Political Community Treaty had gone far beyond what at least some national governments were prepared to accept. The Mission headed by Ambassador David Bruce which had been set up in Paris in 1952 to provide the beginnings of American representation to the emerging Europe, and more specifically to do what it could to insure that the French Assembly ratified the European Defense Community Treaty, went about its task with deep dedication to the cause of Europe. When the EDC Treaty collapsed and Sir Anthony Eden then seized the initiative within the framework of the Western European Union and NATO to provide some sort of substitute which would permit a West German military contribution to the common defense, the Bruce Mission quickly dissolved.

The Treaty of Rome signed in March, 1957, seemed to recapture some of the lost momentum. It was quickly hailed by the US Government, and the institutionalization of European unity seemed once again on its way. However, the reappearance on the French political scene of Charles de Gaulle in the following year brought with it the second phase of American policy towards European unity – the era of President de Gaulle. French emphasis on the Common Agricultural Policy, while hampering the execution of other supranational features of the Rome Treaty, and on the exclusion from the Common Market of the United Kingdom, provided many points of conflict with the United States. It is true that the fine words of President Kennedy in his Philadelphia speech of 4 July 1962 expressed the continuing American support of European union as part of a "grand design." He stated that "the nations of Western Europe ... are joining together ... to find freedom in diversity and unity in strength. The United States looks on this vast new enterprise with hope and admiration. We do not regard a strong and united Europe as a rival but as a partner. To aid its progress has been the basic objective of our foreign policy for seventeen years."[1]

In practice the actual record of the decade was essentially one of frustration for American supporters of the Common Market and a source of fuel for those who attacked it for protectionist practices as essentially inimical to American economic interests. The argument so often made that the United States must be prepared to swallow certain economic disadvantages because of the greater political advantages expected to flow from European unification rang somewhat hollow given the practices and the actual progress towards an organized Europe.

When President Nixon visited a number of Western European countries in February, 1969, at the very beginning of his administration, he inaugurated the third phase of American policy towards European unity. The old endorsement was there, but he gave it a new twist and point of emphasis. His first Report on US Foreign Policy to the Congress, made on 18 February 1970 put it this way, after a traditional statement of support for the strengthening and broadening of the European Community:

"The structure of Western Europe – the organization of its unity – is fundamentally the concern of the Europeans. We cannot unify Europe and we do not believe that there is only one road to that goal. When the United States in previous administrations turned into an ardent advocate, it harmed rather than helped progress.

"We believe that we can render support to the process of European coalescence not only by our role in the North Atlantic Alliance and by our relationships with European institutions, but also by our bilateral relations with the several European countries. For many years to come, these relations will provide essential trans-Atlantic bonds; and we will therefore continue to broaden and deepen them."[2]

In other words, we would be there cheering on the sidelines but we were no longer part of the game. We would deal bilaterally with problems as we saw fit including those which might, in whole or in part, fall within the competency of the Community. Subsequent annual Reports to the Congress on Foreign Policy reiterated this basic stance.

Despite all the fine words about Europe, the preference and the practice of the first Nixon administration clearly favored bilateral dealings with the individual members of the Community. There was little evidence in the way we conducted our relations with the Community to indicate much understanding of its purposes or our fundamental interest in its success.[3]

Then came 1973 – the proclaimed Year of Europe, certainly not one of the notable diplomatic accomplishments of the Nixon years. In his address to the Associated Press in New York, Dr. Henry Kissinger, who was still Assistant to the President for National Security Affairs, announced in effect, that 1973 is the Year of Europe because, having dealt with other presumably more urgent problems, the US Government now had the time and the inclination to turn to our relations with Europe. It was proposed that, by the time President Nixon traveled to Europe toward the end of the year, a new Atlantic Charter be worked out setting goals for the future and creating for the Atlantic nations a new relationship in whose progress Japan could share. We would continue to support European unity, but the emphasis was on the economic frictions between the Community and the United States.[4]

The aftermath was a shambles. The Europeans resented the patronizing tone of the approach as well as the fact that it had been sprung on them without prior consultation or warning. The initial confusion was compounded both by the choice of spokesman and the assurance of Secretary of State Rogers, with whom the speech had not been cleared, that it need not be taken seriously. In the debate that followed, to the degree that an issue was discernible, it seemed to involve the process of consultation to be followed by the European Community and the United States.[5] The arguments on both sides, in prolonged meetings of the so-called Political Directors of the 10 countries concerned, were reminiscent of the decadent period of Scholasticism; they certainly made little contribution to better relations between the Community and the United States – and the scars remain. A compromise on consultative procedures was finally worked out and has been in effect up to the present. The passing from the scene of President Pompidou and Jobert made its own contribution to a mellowing of the atmosphere. The grand proposal for a new Atlantic Charter spluttered out in a Declaration on Atlantic Relations – full of fine words and platitudes but conveying no really new impulses to the American relationship with Europe or to NATO.[6]

Meanwhile, the primary attention of the Atlantic world had turned to more urgent problems, either in other geographical areas or primarily in the economic field, while it morbidly watched the drama of Watergate and its aftermath being played out in the United States. The European Community itself was going through a difficult period of attempted adjustment to energy crisis, economic recession and growing disparities between the economies of member states. At the same time useful consultative mechanisms for handling common economic problems came into being, particularly within the OECD context; but an impartial observer would hardly argue that the recent past has been a creative period for the US relationship with the European Community.

While in a reflective mood Secretary of State Kissinger was willing to admit, in his Alastair Buchan Memorial Lecture, given in London on 25 June 1976, that "It is academic to debate now whether the United States acted too theoretically in proposing to approach these challenges through the elaboration of a new Atlantic Declaration, or whether our European friends acted wisely in treating this proposal as a test case of European identity." He added, however, that "The doctrinal arguments of 1973 over the procedure for Atlantic consultations, or whether Europe was exercising its proper global role, or whether economic and security issues should be linked, have in fact been settled by the practice of consultations and cooperation unprecedented in intensity and scope. The reality and success of our common endeavours have provided the best definition and revitalization of our efforts."[7]

Allowing for the hyperbole in his description of the present situation, that is where we are today – the deed always falling somewhat behind the promise. If it falls too far behind, and the disparity between words, sentiments and practices becomes too great and too obvious, we engender a form of relational anemie. Even when the practice is compatible with the promise, the question inevitably arises whether this is enough, whether the interests of the United States and the European Community are sufficiently served by an exchange of information and views that does not go beyond the instrumentalities of conventional diplomacy. The time has come for a new appraisal of the American interest in the European Community, starting from the realities of the present. If the thrust toward the making of Europe has lost its momentum, that is a fact American policy cannot ignore. If, on the other hand, American attitudes and practices are themselves a potential source of difficulty, this is another important fact.

To an American observer, there is lacking in Europe today any clear and agreed conceptual framework for the kind of Europe which the US has traditionally said it would like to see. The report on European Unity submitted by Belgian Prime Minister Leo Tindemans,[8] early in 1976, attempted to provide such a framework, but it was limited both by his sense of what the traffic would bear, and by the generally restrained welcome which the member countries gave even to the relatively modest recommendations which his report put forward. It seems to be tacitly accepted by many that major Governments within the Community are mainly interested in burying the report rather than in seriously attempting to implement it. In any event, the need for an over-riding theory of European unity on which consensus can be obtained remains, and the prospect for achieving this in the foreseeable future is not good. A continuing lack of clarity about goals, purposes and institutions is likely to lead to amazing inconsistencies such as attacks by European leaders on the Commission bureaucracy in Brussels as somehow working counter to the Community's purposes when, in fact, it represents the major institutional embodiment so far of European integration.

If the Europeans have failed adequately to think through their vision of the future, the American side has likewise never been able to work out a consistent and agreed conceptual framework for its long-term association with Europe. In the early days of the "50's" the analogy of concentric circles was used to describe the relationship of an integrating Europe and the NATO area including the United States; another analogy which became popular, but also added little to understanding of the real problem, was that of the dumbbell symbolizing a relationship of two centers of power of comparatively similar weight. In his "grand design" speech, noted above, President Kennedy called upon the European Community to join the United States in an "Atlantic Partnership of Equals" and the dumbbell concept was revived unofficially as an appropriate metaphor. The problem was that American thinking did not advance much beyond figures of speech and phrase-making; a clear definition of the American role in relation to possibilities was lacking.

Another fact that has become clear in the recent past is that a basic assumption of the Treaty of Rome is no longer valid: namely, that there would be a coherent and more or less equivalent economic development of all member countries, allowing for some transfer of capital and wealth through the devices of the regional fund, the common agricultural policy, and other internal payments systems of the Community. What we see today instead is an ever-growing disparity between the economic situations of member states. This has not only doomed the objective of monetary union in our time, but has strained the common agricultural policy almost to the breaking point. The highest priority for the advanced industrial countries, both within and without the Community, must be to restore a measure of stability and predictability to the weaker industrial economies lest the more prosperous also be dragged down by those that are sinking. Without such return to general economic health, it is difficult to see how the Community can hope to regain its forward momentum.

It is regrettable that the European Community should be in the state in which it finds itself today. No one concerned about American ties with Europe can be happy about the situation. Despite all these problems, however, a sober reappraisal of the possibilities will, I believe, lead to the conclusion that there is still life, both potential and actual, in the European movement which it is in our interest to encourage. The broad endorsement which American official spokesmen have been giving for more than 25 years retains its basic validity; and the "practice of consultation and cooperation" of which Secretary Kissinger spoke, must remain our consistent objective.

Why is this the case? One must begin with certain elemental facts about the relationship of Europe and the United States. It has been a postwar truism that American security begins in Europe and is identified closely with the independence of the other free Western nations bound together in an alliance for self-defense. This security is not just a matter of maintaining the military balance, as important as that may be, but also of insuring a healthy and viable economic and political society in the West. It is difficult to see these conditions being fulfilled purely on the basis of individual national development. Most observers would argue that, not only can the clock not be turned back, but that the requisite forward movement of a Europe which is not to stagnate and disintegrate can only take place within the framework of increasing cooperation and unification.

One question worth asking is the possible effect on American attitudes towards the European Community of the revisionist approach to postwar history which, during the past decade, has had considerable influence in American academic and intellectual circles. While the main thrust of this approach has been to rewrite the history of the cold war and American economic penetration around the world, some of the revisionist conclusions, if valid, would have direct relevance to the American approach to the Community. If American policy towards Europe in the postwar period has essentially been guided by neo-imperialist motives, or by groundless fears of supposed Communist threats of aggression, then much of the thinking which has supported American relations with the European unity movement would have to be reconsidered in terms of a radically different world picture. This is not the place for a detailed discussion of American revisionism. Historical truth is not likely to emerge from the ideological constraints of a neo-Marxism which never gives the benefit of doubt to the leaders of yesterday, shows little insight into the actual motives of those leaders, and attributes only benignity or innocence to those who were once the object of fear for their possible aggressive intentions. Suffice it to say here that the more balanced appraisal of American motives and actions in the postwar period which is emerging out of the academic conflict of revisionists and anti-revisionists is not incompatible with a supportive American relationship to the European Community. Even if American motives were, in certain cases, less idealistic in their composite content than might have seemed to be the case at the time, the broad identity of our political, military and economic interests with those of a developing Europe would remain no less of a basic fact.

This is the point at which three other contemporary currents of thought in the United States which have a bearing on our relationship to the Community should also be discussed: the new isolationism, neo-protectionism and the "put all emphasis on NATO" approach. If the validity or inevitable triumph of any of these is accepted, fundamental changes in the traditional American attitude towards the Community would necessarily follow.

Many observers of trends in the United States have detected what they describe as a new "inwardness," a turning away from world responsibilities and the demands of a global foreign policy to a pre-eminent concern with local problems and their solution. In the aftermath of Vietnam, the generational upheaval of the late "60's", and the growing anxiety over environmental spoilage and the future quality of life, one can indeed detect a certain weariness of spirit, a declining sense of obligation to the outside world and a willingness to be satisfied with a much narrower area of interest. Whatever the psychological reasons for such a development, its existence in scattered form throughout the country, and even in the academies, is a fact. It is not true, however, that its eventual dominance of policy in Washington is inevitable. One could indeed argue, with some justice, that neo-isolationism in this form was clearly time-conditioned, has already passed its zenith, and is probably destined to take its historical place alongside the American First Movement of the immediate pre-World War II era. The mood of the current

US Congress does not seem to reflect any deep constituent pressures for withdrawal but rather a sober awareness that the defense of the West and its institutions remains a major American policy imperative in terms of our own interests. While popular confidence in the Federal Government has undoubtedly declined in recent years, this has not (in the light of recent public opinion polls) apparently dulled the appreciation of the role which we must continue to play.

More troublesome, perhaps, is the phenomenon of neo-protectionism. It was probably inevitable that a time of serious recession would bring with it the revival of old trade union support for restrictions on imports as a panacea, supported by the spokesmen of those industries suffering the most from foreign competition. As far as the AFL-CIO is concerned, a highly emotional new element is the conceived role of the American multinational corporation as an exporter of jobs from the United States as well as the source, from foreign productive facilities, of imports into the United States which further undermine the American manufacturing base. No one who has listened to labor spokesmen on this subject can doubt the intensity and sincerity of the emotions involved. Nor is it possible to view certain features of the Trade Act of 1973 without concern that they could be used to further essentially restrictive purposes.

But so far at least the basic thrust of US Government policy continues to favor general trade liberalization. The classical arguments based on comparative advantage, despite deviations in practice, remain persuasive, especially for a country like the United States which has so many natural advantages and which, since its currency is no longer over-valued, is beginning once again to attract foreign capital because of those advantages. Continued vigilance will be required to prevent erosion of liberal principles. Perhaps the single most helpful thing that could happen would be a clear movement of the United States economy into a new growth phase relieving some of the pressures created by an intolerably high unemployment total.

On the agricultural side, the United States' urge to export will, of course, remain, and continue to provide a major source of support for liberal trade policy. If the Common Agricultural Policy of the Community itself operates, as it has at times in the past, so as to severely limit US agricultural exports to the Common Market area, this can only have the effect of weakening in the United States the voice of the single most important pressure group still favoring liberal free trade principles.

Obviously, neither the individual interests within the Community nor within the United States can have all they want. The common interest in providing mutually acceptable compromise solutions remains so great, however, in terms of the general relationship of the two, that it is difficult to imagine that arrangements to avoid confrontation cannot be found, as they have generally, if not always, been found in the past.

From the very beginning of the European Movement, there were some Americans who feared that any progress towards integration in Europe was bound to be at the expense of the Atlantic Alliance. It was never clear precisely why this needed to be so, but it was assumed that no basic identity of interests existed between the European Community and the larger Atlantic Community, or at least that they represented potential rival poles of power. While this strain of thought never effectively determined official US policy, it has persisted as an undercurrent of uneasiness, heightened each time that the Community seemed to be moving forward into a new phase. Such an attitude reflects in part that lack of any satisfactory and developed theory of the American relationship to Europe, which we have noted, but it also involves the fear of inevitable economic strife between organized Europe and the United States which has from time to time been the inspiration for direct opposition to the Common Market. The author can recall participating, some years ago, in a symposium held in New York during which a reputable American economist defended the view that it would be far better for the United States if the Market ceased to exist. Apart from the political obtuseness of such a position, it overlooked completely the role which the Market has played in that general growth of economies and of trade which has been such an outstanding characteristic of the postwar period and from which the United States has certainly derived great national benefit.

What does all of this mean then in a practical sense? It means that the traditional American support of European unification remains valid policy in terms of national interest, and that the deviations in practice of the past decade, which have run counter to our good relationship with the Community, are not compatible with that interest. In the short run, it also means our taking account of existing possibilities of cooperation while encouraging longer-range growth of the Community. At the present time, political consultation remains one of the few areas in which the Community has made some recent progress. The American practice of the past few years has been inconsistent, sometimes praising, sometimes resenting, and frequently wishing it would simply go away (as in an earlier phase of the Kissinger initiatives in the Middle East). A more consistent American attitude would require both encouragement of and cooperation with the process of political consultation. The actual practice in the most recent past, involving more or less institutionalized consultations between American representatives and representatives of the Community chairman country, has been good; but there is more that can be done in this area if both sides show imagination and the required degree of flexibility.

To purists the institutionalization of summit meetings three times a year within the Community under the rubric "European Council" has been a mixed blessing. As an expression of residual Gaullism, it might seem to run counter to the supranational thrust of the Rome Treaty. In a stagnant period, however, anything which contributes to the decision-making process within the Community could be considered a gain. It would be hard to maintain that recent summit meetings have demonstrated a propensity for agreement among European Heads of Governments. Here the appropriate American posture, it would seem, is one of tolerance and good wishes, accompanied by close consultation prior to and after Council sessions.

Looking ahead, one can, of course, see a number of potential areas of conflict between the United States and the European Community. In none of these is conflict inevitable, provided that good will and skilful diplomacy are present; but past experience has shown how quickly strains can arise between the Community and the United States when different approaches to troubled areas of the world are followed. For example, it is conceivable that American policy in the Middle East might be considered by the Community, or at least by important members of the Community, as jeopardizing their oil supply and as encouraging the Arab countries to other punitive action in the economic field. In view of Europe's vulnerability to any effective embargo of oil from the Middle East, this could become a sensitive problem involving a real conflict of interests. American policy makers will need to be sensitive to considerations of this kind in calculating the effect of possible actions in the Middle East. Members of the European Community are likely, as in the past, to think that they can make some positive contribution of their own to peace in the area. American petulance and desire for a monopoly role during recent years became a source of strain. In the future we are likely to need all the help we can get, particularly when the difficult phase of economic rehabilitation begins; and American interests would seem to require maximum consultation and cooperation with the Community on the Middle East in the period ahead.

African policy could provide another theoretical bone of contention. Too strong American emphasis on a settlement in South Africa, or in pushing plans for economic development on the African continent in general, might involve moving faster and further than the Community is prepared to go. While there is a broad mutuality of interest between the US and the Community in the whole African area, differing evaluation of economic possibilities and of the need to safeguard minority rights could present a problem. Sensitive diplomacy and frequent consultation is likewise the need here.

Differing approaches to nuclear sales policy or to the achievement of shared objectives in the field of nuclear non-proliferation could also become a source of difficulty, just as they have already led to problems between the Federal Republic and the United States as well as France and the United States. Long-term energy requirements as they are perceived in Europe seem likely to impel members of the Community to put additional stress on the development of nuclear power facilities, both as far as the production of enriched fuel and the manufacturing of power plants are concerned. Differing conceptions of what is required effectively to avoid nuclear proliferation, particularly in terms of the full fuels reprocessing cycle, could lead again to the kind of mutual recrimination that developed recently between the US and the Federal Republic over the latter's large-scale contract with Brazil for the delivery of power plants and technology. There is no simple formula by which these complex issues can easily be resolved. A mutual education process is the necessary beginning. American concerns are legitimate and weighty, but if they are not understood or the motives behind our advocacy are suspect to the Europeans, those concerns will not carry the weight which Washington feels they deserve. There have, from the American point of view, been some encouraging recent signs of growing European understanding of the possible dangers involved in certain aspects of an uninhibited sales policy.

One possible role for the European Community which some have foreseen is as a context for the "Europeanization" of Communist parties in certain Western countries should they come to share power in the governments of those countries. The Italian case is relevant here. One could envisage an American failure to appreciate the Community role in accommodating to possible changes in domestic political configurations, and in attempting to provide an absorptive environment for such changes, should the black and white approach to Eurocommunism continue to be the prevalent mode in the United States. The whole question of Eurocommunism is obviously one that we are going to have very much with us in the years ahead, and this is not the place for a discussion of the phenomenon. The pragmatic approach is the only rational one under the circumstances, and that means a hard-headed appraisal of what is really happening as a necessary basis for judging what is to be done.

Although there is a broad identity of interest between the Community and the US with respect to East-West political relations, economic rivalries in this area could also prove divisive. Just as the European members of the

Community compete among themselves for trade with the Soviet Union and Eastern Europe, with the lion's share so far going to the Federal Republic, so the Community as an aggregate of countries provides strong and effective competition for American efforts at expanded trade with Eastern Europe. The Community as an entity is now negotiating directly on behalf of all member states with Eastern Europe. It naturally seeks to advance the interests of its own constituents rather than those of the US. The at least partial complementariness of American and Western European exports, stemming particularly from American dominance in the agricultural field, should mitigate somewhat the competition for Eastern European markets. In the final analysis, however, since the United States and the countries of the Community both profess adherence to an economic philosophy which stresses the moderating value of competition within markets, neither we nor the Europeans should mourn the advantage which one or the other wins in a fair contest. In real life it is something else again, of course, but the Western world should be able to adjust its differences in an area where the political exigencies clearly require that cooperation be the guiding principle.

Further movement towards enlargement of the European Community, and particularly the possible entry of Greece, Turkey, Portugal and Spain, will in the view of some, fundamentally alter the nature of the Community itself. The growing economic disparity between members, to which reference has been made previously, will be further accentuated, and if the institutions of the Community work as originally contemplated in the Treaty of Rome, a massive transfer of economic resources to the poorer new members will take place. It is doubtful whether any further significant move toward supranationalism could take place under these circumstances; the richer members of the Community will certainly wish to protect themselves as best they can against wasteful transfers and damage to their own economic systems. It may well be, if the trend toward enlargement continues in the way indicated, that the old proposal of Willy Brandt of a two-tier system within the Community (rejected out of hand when he first put it forward a few years ago) may be the only way to save the central core of the Community from institutional stagnation.

Although the legal and political as well as practical problems would be very great, it is not inconceivable that such a two-tier system – a central core of the more prosperous and developed countries and a ring of less prosperous and relatively undeveloped countries – could become the only practical way of permitting the first category of countries to move ahead towards further integration. How the United States would react to such a development within an enlarged Community is far from clear at this point, although one can theoretically see possible areas of conflict. On the other hand, if this would turn out to be the only way in which the forward movement of at least a part of the Community can be assured, it is difficult to imagine that an American government would want actively to oppose it. The internal preferences, particularly in the agricultural field, which would presumably apply to the weaker segment of the Community, would undoubtedly work to the disadvantage of some American farmers, but not on a scale that an American government with some vision could not accept. In any event, the institutional problems which will inevitably come with further enlargement of the Community will require the exercise of real creative imagination by European leaders to which the appropriate American response should be one of sympathetic understanding and, if required, of willingness to help.

One of the few current Community activities which holds some promise of positive institutional development is the decision of member governments to move toward a directly-elected European Parliament. Whether all member countries will accept the originally agreed upon 1978 deadline remains to be seen, nor is it entirely clear what difference direct elections will actually make in practice, since there is no basis of experience from which to draw judgments. It seems likely, however, that those who say it will make a real difference will prove right, for there will probably be a subtle shift in the flow of interests and the allegiance to constituencies from those now prevailing under the current national selection of members to the European Parliament. It is hard to see that the United States would have any interest whatsoever in doing anything but encourage the development of such a European Parliament, observing its activities with sympathy and giving such support as seems relevant, for example through frequent contact with members of the American Congress.

Under the new leadership of Mr. Roy Jenkins as President, the European Commission early this year reconstituted itself, reshuffling some positions and bringing in some new blood. Americans can only wish it well while expressing the hope that Mr. Jenkins will be able to instill a new spirit of achievement while restraining the further growth of those bureaucratic characteristics which have aroused the ire of Euorpean national leaders. The performance of the Commission in the period ahead will be an important factor in determining attitudes towards the Community, and I should hope that the kind of instructions which our Mission to the European Community in Brussels will receive will reflect an awareness of the Commission's role as the only existing embodiment of the supranational principle in Europe.[9]

Many words are written and spoken today about the growing interdependence of the world in which we live, and the word is indeed descriptive of fact.

The problem is that a general concept of this kind is not very helpful in providing specific solutions to problems involving relationships or transfers of assets about which judgments of national interests may vary widely. Certainly, however, the fact of interdependence between the European Community and the United States can provide a basic conceptual framework for future policy. As noted above, the United States has never developed a really comprehensive approach to its relations with Europe. American thinking must logically now move beyond phrase-making. We need to conceptualize our future relations with Europe in terms of this growing interdependence. We may start with the realistic assumption that the United States is not going to join the European Community. Short of that, the interests of the United States will continue strongly to require a healthy, growing, and integrating European Community. No matter how imperfectly the institutions of that Community function in practice, a positive and constructive attitude should remain a constant element of American practice. The kind of carping negativism, or at best passive tolerance, which has characterized certain periods in the past should ideally be replaced by a more active and supportive policy under which the United States, through its representatives in Brussels and through the actions of its government in Washington, can take the initiative to further our basic unity of interests. While this attitude can guarantee nothing in terms of abiding solutions to the very difficult problems which face the Western industrialized world in this last portion of the 20th Century, it can at least assure that opportunities will not be lost, and that the effort that is made to master our problems will be made in a context more likely to arrive at mutually satisfactory and efficacious solutions. If the dream of the "50's" is gone, a piece of reality remains; and it is clearly in the interests of the United States to help nurture and keep it alive, in the hope that, at some point, men of creativity and vision will pick up again the task of building Europe.

Notes

[1] *The Department of State Bulletin.* No. 1204, 23 July 1962, p. 132.

[2] *U.S. foreign policy for the 1970's. A new strategy for Peace.* A Report to the Congress by Richard Nixon. 18 February 1970, Washington: U.S.G.P.O. 1970, p. 32.

[3] See J. Robert Schaetzel. *The Unhinged alliance*, New York: Harper & Row 1975, pp. 50 ff.

[4] In: *The Department of State Bulletin.* No. 1768, 14 May 1973, pp. 593 ff.

[5] See the *Address by Secretary of State Henry A. Kissinger to the Pilgrims of Great Britain*, at the Europa Hotel, London, England, 12 December 1973, in: *Department of State News Release* of same date.

[6] In: *The Times*, 20 June 1974.

[7] *Inaugural Alastair Buchan Memorial Lecture* by Secretary of State Henry A. Kissinger, at the Invitation of the International Institute for Strategic Studies, London, England, 25 June. In: *Department of State Press Release*, 25 June 1976.

[8] *European Union*, Report by Mr. Leo Tindemans, Prime Minister of Belgium, for the European Council, full text contained in: *Bulletin of the European Communities*, Supplement, January 1976.

[9] See Christian Lutz, *The Road to European Union: A Plea for a Constitutional Revolution*, Paris: The Atlantic Institute for International Affairs 1976, pp. 54 ff., for a description, *inter alia*, of the role of the Commission under various possible approaches to the achievement of European union.

The American World Power and the Western European Powers

by PIERRE HASSNER

World power, balance of power, concert of powers . . . There is something inevitable and yet something dubious or at least old-fashioned about these expressions. We cannot help asking what the asymmetries between the United States and the Western European countries (both in terms of perspectives and in terms of influence) do to their mutual relations, yet, in a world where interdependence is balanced by fragmentation, inequality, and unpredictability, we cannot help wondering whether any state, including even the United States, is still a world power, and whether any European state is still a power at all.

Perhaps, then, a good way to start an inquiry into America's relations with its Western European allies is to spend a few moments of hair-splitting reflection about the possible differences and changes in the meaning of the notions "world" and "power."

We know what the term "world" is supposed to indicate, and we know what it is supposed to negate, namely any particularistic, local or regional limitation. But even if we focus on non-limitation to a particular region we encounter two meanings, one which could be called the *pan-regional* and a second the *trans-regional*. The first concept is the more classical one, and is normally associated with the notion of "superpower," i.e., a power which has an interest in every point of the globe and is able to influence it and reach it militarily. The second is more associated with new issues, which transcend geographical divisions and concern the fate of the planet itself and its common problems: oceans, environment (the so-called "global commons") food, non-proliferation, the maintenance of the international system in general.

The United States is certainly a world power in both of these meanings: its military and economic presence is felt around the globe, and, on the other hand, it is a country which feels the greatest responsibility for the fate of the planet and the greatest interest in common problems for which it not only tries to encourage the interest and involvement of other countries but also attempts to actively take the lead itself.

As regards the trans-regional meaning, an additional dimension has become more visible again under President Carter: it concerns interest not only in distant regions or common problems but in universal principles like human rights.

In a certain sense, one might say that the recent evolution of United States policy has been from the first towards the second, and finally to a third meaning. When Henry Kissinger pointed out that the United States had global interests and the Europeans only regional ones, he was basing his stand on the first meaning; yet he was himself aware that the United States could no longer play the direct central role of the past, that its world interest and influence had to be mediated by regional alliances or balances; this was the meaning of the Nixon doctrine.[1] After Kissinger, a trend to the regional limitation of commitments (as evidenced by the attitude of Congress over the Angolan affair) may well reduce America's role as a world power. On the other hand, his critics (for instance, the Trilateral Commission) and himself, after 1973, have shown an increased interest in America's world role taken in the second sense, i.e., in the management of interdependence.

Cynical commentators may well see in this second role a substitute for the first. America would use its economic power to regain or maintain, through the manipulation of interdependence, what it could no longer control by military force. But, in this second role too, dilemmas between the world order or imperial role of providing public goods for the functioning and control of the system, and the national interests of "America as an ordinary country" are inescapable.[2]

Finally the third sense – that of commitment to universal rights and principles – can be seen as a further step towards a more abstract and less physical role. But precisely because of this it raises the question of relations with the other two: influence through moral example and proclamation may ultimately be a most powerful weapon, but in the short- and middle-term dimension of world politics it stands or falls with the ultimate credibility of military or economic sanctions. A decline in global military or economic reach, or a refusal to use them for the implementation of universalistic principles, may make the latter irrelevant as an inspiration for policy. On the other hand, even though America's positive or compellent power may be limited, its negative power or its comparative lack of vulnerability is such that it can afford to try. For Western European countries, the calculation of the risks involved may turn out differently.

An interesting reversal is at work in this case. After Czechoslovakia and at the Helsinki Conference, a difference of emphasis, if not of direction, had seemed to emerge between the American position corresponding to superpower-détente, based on the status quo, and the Western European one, more directly interested in encouraging the evolution of Eastern Europe and a rapprochement between European societies.

This resulted in a more active role of the Nine on the "Third Basket" measures of CSCE, and, conversely, the sphere of influence overtones of some of Henry Kissinger's and Helmut Sonnenfeldt's positions. Today the tables are turned: it is the American superpower that presses the issue of human rights and it is the European powers, in particular France, Germany, and Italy, which counsel caution and apply it themselves, not always in the most creditable way. The paradox is easily explained, particularly if one adds that, among European countries, Holland follows a universalistic moral line on the question of human rights which is distinct from that of the countries mentioned above. France, Germany or Italy have direct interests in relations with the East: they have something to gain and something to fear; this explains both their activity and their caution. The United States and Holland are at the two extremes, which makes it easier for both to apply universal principles: the United States because of its lesser vulnerability, Holland because of its lesser involvement in direct bilateral links and interests.[3]

Here the ambiguities of the terms "world" and "power" both converge and come full circle. Even the United States is no longer quite a world power in the traditional sense, it can be a world power in a new sense precisely because it has remained one to some extent in the old sense. Conversely if, like the European states, you no longer are a world power in the old sense at all, you may, particularly in relations with a superpower like the Soviet Union, lose the capability to defend even your regional or national interests, let alone your universal principles, except under the protection of the other superpower.

And yet, although no European power is a *world* power in the pan-regional sense any longer (except to some extent, commercially, particularly the Federal Republic of Germany), and certainly not a world *power* in a military sense, they have, like everyone else, and more so than relatively self-sufficient superpowers or isolated small powers, a vital interest in global issues in the second sense (who, for instance, is more concerned with the energy problem than Western Europe and Japan?) and an important tradition in the third sense whose loss (i.e., a capitulation concerning universal principles) would be fatal for their self-respect. The problem is whether they can influence global issues and defend universal principles through separate policies or whether only the Community, or even a coordinated policy of the European powers, can, if not become a world power, at least exert significant influence on world issues and in the defense of universal principles and ideas. Obviously this depends both on the ability of the European nations to unite or cooperate, and on the relations between the different forms of power, in particular between power as military strength and power as general influence. From the European point of view, all the Community can aspire to is to become, according to François Duchêne's famous expression, a "civilian power." However, as he would be the first to admit, a civilian power which cannot even envisage with any credibility the acquiring of some autonomous military power ends up without much civilian power either.

Seen from the United States, there is a gap in its favor according to both definitions, but it is more pronounced in the first, the military dimension (where its superiority and protective role are virtually unchallenged) than in the second, the general one where, at least in the economic area, Europe has sometimes appeared as a dangerous competitor. The question then, which has always been central to Atlantic relations, is that of the relationship between issue areas, and of the possibilities it offers for the politics of linkage and leverage. The relations between military protection, economic competition and political influence are the key to the relations between the United States and its European allies.

The Historical Framework : Bilateralism and Multilateralism

Whether on the economic, military, or the less explicit psychological and political level, the combination of bilateralism and multilateralism in American–European relations has been both more complex and more mobile than is usually realized. If one rightly raises the spectre of the alliance being transformed into a network of bilateral relationships, whether on the occasion of de Gaulle's initiatives, of Kissinger's imperial acrobatics and divisive tactics, or, today, of the centrifugal domestic trends in many, particularly the southern European countries, one tends to forget that bilateral concerns have from the very beginning constituted the impulsion and sometimes the reality behind existing multilateral structures. But the point is precisely that even when the motivations, or the "infrastructure," were bilateral, the need for a multilateral framework or "superstructure" was felt as imperative.

The ambiguity is obvious when one looks at NATO's so-called "flanks" where today Greece, Turkey, and perhaps Italy, seem to be drifting towards special situations and special (positive or negative) relations with the United States; they are recreating or publicizing an old state of affairs.

The original conception of NATO was an extension based on the Brussels pact. In 1948, important Americans (like George Kennan) and Italians (like G. Saragat and Manlio Brosio, the future Secretary-General of NATO) while attaching great importance to Italy's ties to the West and to its direct link with the United States, were against its participation in NATO because of its special situation and, in particular, because of excessive fragility. Greece and Turkey, in spite of being the first beneficiaries of American commitment to the containment of communism, were first associated to NATO in 1952, while Spain's link to the United States remained bilateral and was institutionalized by the Madrid treaty of 1953.

More important, although some progress towards integration has been made–even in the South–the bilateral origins have remained predominant. For instance, Italian troops cannot be positioned outside the territory of the Peninsula; conversely the arrangements for the use of American tactical nuclear weapons, while unpublicized, are known to be more favorable to the United States than in any other country of the alliance.

Even before the last round of the Cyprus conflict, cooperation, let alone integration, between the Greek and Turkish forces was minimal.

Essentially, the "southern flank" is based on a series of different bilateral relationships (of which the most important is the use of bases) between the United States and the various countries of the region.

In the North, while no similar bilateral links exist, special situations are indeed the rule – in spite of the collective framework – concerning the various shades of neutrality and participation in NATO with or without foreign troops or nuclear weapons.

Even within the hard core of the alliance, i.e., the relationship of the United States with the three European countries whose role is central both politically and geographically: Britain, France and Germany, it is very hard to disentangle the bilateral and multilateral, especially in the first two cases.

The very idea of the Western postwar multilateral institutions, especially the economic ones, started (as Robert Bowie reminds us in this volume) with bilateral Anglo-American decisions like the Atlantic Charter and the lend-lease agreement. Many of the Atlantic collective undertakings were essentially a generalization of, or substitute for, the cooperation of America and Britain.

Even more importantly, the very backbone of the US–European security relationship since World War II lies in the American concern with Germany. But more precisely, the security structure of the European continent consists of the triangular relationship between the United States, the Soviet Union and Germany. To balance Russian power and provide a Western framework for Germany's energies, to protect Germany both from Russia and from herself, to prevent both from attempting, either jointly or individually, to gain hegemony over the continent; this is the essence of the Atlantic alliance. This is why the presence of American troops in Germany in their double, primarily protective but also, discreetly, controlling function is the one tangible expression of the alliance whose disappearance would directly and fundamentally transform the structure of the continent. It is precisely the ambiguous nature of the German–American relationship that puts it in danger of becoming unacceptable to either of the two partners or to both, and, even more, of provoking fears of joint hegemony in the rest of Europe. Some kind of multilateral or collective framework is then a necessity both as legitimation and as a counterweight.

France has no such historically or structurally based "special relationship" with the United States. It has indeed been pointed out that, alone among the major Western European countries, it has had no significant emigration to the United States and hence no American ethnic minority acting as a link or as a pressure group. The logical conclusion – as understood by statesmen like Robert Schuman (during the Fourth Republic) should have been for France and the Benelux to emphasize the multilateral identity and the role of institutions where, as in Brussels, France long enjoyed a role of *primus inter pares*, because of Britain's and Germany's historical handicaps, stemming from the belief that it had won the war in the one case and from having lost it in the other.

But General de Gaulle's policy, true to a prevailing historical tradition of French diplomacy, was rather an acrobatic attempt to play upon multiple, and often contradictory, bilateral relationships or to rely on France's superior skill and agility to compensate for the superior material weight of Germany and of the superpowers. This has led him and his successors to cultivate first an exclusive bilateral relationship with Adenauer's Germany, then with Heath's Britain. In both cases, it has provoked an American attempt to bring the respective countries into a closer bilateral relationship with the United States; but occasionally, particularly at the beginning of the Nixon–Kissinger administration, some steps towards good relations with France (either out of admiration for de Gaulle or out of tactics aimed at him or at the Federal Republic) have been made by the Americans.

In all these relationships, the psychological element counts as much as any deliberate doctrine or strategy. For years American policy has been to back a United Europe and to put pressure on a reluctant Britain to join it: the high point, of course, was during the Kennedy–Johnson administrations. Henry Kissinger paid little attention to Britain, as compared to France and Germany – and just as little to the European Community as such. The Carter administration seems to have returned to earlier attitudes in this last regard. But it is interesting to note that, whether at a time when it was pushing Britain into Europe or at a time when it was neglecting both, the American administration continued – half-unconsciously – to take a certain special Anglo-American intimacy for granted. Hence Kissinger's irritation at the Franco-British entente under Heath and Pompidou and his particularly violent reaction against the British government's refusal to act as an instrument during the 1973 war.

The interesting point, however, is that the Carter administration seems to have abandoned its predecessor's doctrinal hostility against the Nine enjoying any greater degree of intimacy and of consultation with each other than with the United States. The administration is reported to be using its special relationship with the United Kingdom in order to be directly plugged into the deliberations of the European councils, and thus to be instantly informed and able to make its point of view known before any internal decision is taken.

Concerning Germany, the ambiguity between negative and positive attitudes and between bilateral and multilateral strategies is, of course, even greater. Traditionally, the American attitude has been in close harmony with that of Konrad Adenauer: distrust of Germany's possible future evolution should lead it to being solidly integrated in a wider Western European and/or Atlantic whole: hence an attitude of embracing it in order to control it, both bilaterally and multilaterally. Germany, on the one hand being the most faithful and exposed ally today but potentially the least predictable and most dangerous tomorrow, was given a privileged voice on all American policies in Europe; on the other hand, collective structures were invented to preempt potential German demands, which, if and when they arose in the future, might lead to nationalist adventures, and to give them partial satisfaction within integrated structures: this was the case of the MLF invented by friends of present-day Germany out of fear of the Germany of tomorrow. These friends, inspired by the idea of making their propositions credible to the United States, went so far as to encourage their German associates to express those very aspirations that were so feared but which they did not yet have.

The character – both intense and ambiguous – of the American–German relationship has often led to reactions of exasperation: the Americans have been more than irritated because of having to constantly reassure the Germans that they were not abandoning them; conversely, when the Germans, under Willy Brandt started to take their own eastern initiatives, following the example of the Americans, it was the latter who had to be reassured.

The preeminence of economic issues today and hence of Germany's role within Western Europe, leads to two different attitudes within the American administration. Germany is regarded by some as the competitor to be feared most economically just as the Soviet Union is militarily; others draw the opposite conclusion, at least in terms of tactics, that since only Germany counts in Western Europe, the bilateral American–German link should replace the reliance on cumbersome European institutions. Both views are sometimes held by the same individuals. They may actually be complementary by leading to the same vicious circle of love-hatred inherent in exclusive relationships.

In France, where anti-Americanism is the official creed of a majority of the political elites, the fear of German unpredictability or domination leads to a strong resistance to any reduction of the American military presence in Germany – whereas the Americans are not tolerated in France – or to the acceptance of bilateral economic deals and long-range cooperative projects with the United States rather than with Germany or other European states.

By looking behind the multilateral economic and military structure one discovers a veritable snakepit of ambiguous bilateral relations; but precisely those relations are, however, enveloped by collective myths and organizations. Are these now crumbling today and do they leave bilateral relations exposed in their naked reality? The basis for an answer is partly general, partly specific to the Atlantic relationship.

The Challenge: Old Alliance, New Politics?

In order to describe the general challenges (some of which have been present from the beginning and some of which are fairly new, at least in degree and salience) I must resort to a classification which was presented in an earlier article[4] and distinguish between a new domesticism, a new unilateralism, a new bipolarism, a new globalism, and a new regionalism.

The new domesticism is a catchword for one of the most general trends in the developed Western world, namely, the emphasis on domestic interests and problems. This is probably connected with the historical transformation of values brought about by modernity, from glory and war to work and commerce whose political consequences were well seen by Benjamin Constant or Alexis de Tocqueville. But it acquires an increased relevance in times of economic, social and cultural crisis, when, from students to ethnic minorities, all kinds of groups challenge the legitimacy, authority or efficiency of the nation-state from within. Of course, unsolvable domestic problems can also cause a flight into the realms of foreign policy, in the search either for scapegoats or simply for easier successes. But even in this case, the link to particular interest, – economic or ethnic – due to what Stanley Hoffmann has called the "rooting of foreign policy," is increasing.

Together with other factors this contributes to the *new unilateralism*. Of course, the latter was exaggerated in Europe by de Gaulle and in the United States by Nixon and Kissinger who all made a virtue of secrecy and unpredictability. This is likely to diminish under their successors. But in the case of America, the attempt to impose architectonic structures on a changing world potentially leads to as much unilateralism as acrobatics, out of technocratic or religious righteousness. In all cases, domestic crises and the stagnation of community institutions are likely to make each nation-state continue to insist upon its freedom of action. At most, increasing interdependence may induce, along with reactions of self-protective withdrawal, an increased regard for the consequences of one's own actions upon a fragile environment and hence encourage concentration and coordination, particularly in the field of economic policies. But the relative proportions of ad hoc flexibility and of institutionalization remain to be seen.

Perhaps the most solid ultimate brake on unpredictable unilateralism are certain bilateral ties, and among these superpower *bipolarism* is probably still the most stable one. Each new American administration criticizes its predecessor for emphasizing it excessively, but, although likely to diminish for a while, it is probably inevitable to a considerable degree due to one structural component, the nuclear factor. One of the most important and unresolved questions of the future is whether increasing emphasis on non-proliferation, particularly on the American side, will reinforce "Big-Twoism," which is the philosophy underlying the Non-Proliferation Treaty, or the trend towards oligarchies, oligopolies or cartels, which is the philosophy behind the so-called London Club of nuclear suppliers. The latter hypothesis, which does seem to correspond to the most pervasive trend within the international system, that of a world based on shifting coalitions and inequalities, would emphasize relations between the United States and its allies, both in terms of cooperation and – at least as much – of competition, conflict and pressure, as shown by the tension caused by the German–Brazilian nuclear deal.

In this case, we are back to the *new globalism* we stressed at the beginning, under its double aspect of world issues and of universal principles. But, of course, combined with both is the old irritant of extra-European crises. In the fifties some of the more serious conflicts arose from tensions between the American world power and the European colonial or ex-colonial, imperial or ex-imperial powers, the Suez crisis being the most conspicuous example. With the increasingly global reach of the Soviet Union, confrontations or at least dilemmas are not likely to disappear on the three continents. In the Middle East, in southern Africa, and in Korea, the Europeans are likely to be alternately or simultaneously afraid of American withdrawal symptoms and of American missionary zeal, just as they themselves are likely to appear as selfish, cynical or negative spoilers of Western interests or sinners against universal principles as defined by the United States.

Of course, global issues can produce solidarity as well as conflict, particularly if a common threat to the West is forthcoming from the Soviet Union. The oil producers' power is being felt both by Europeans and Americans, and even divergent situations can produce complementary and coordinated responses. The negative or centrifugal factors are and will be strong enough, however, to encourage a sense of European identity as distinct from American perceptions and interests. But, as seen in the case of the 1973 Middle East War and the oil crisis, this sense of European identity is likely to be combined with an even stronger sense of European impotence.

This may lead us to understand what may be the most important present feature of Euro-American relations. There is no longer any real "gaullist" will of assertion against the United States to create a "European Europe." Even the rather timid attempts of the Heath–Pompidou era have been buried, not by Kissinger's thunder and his "Year of Europe" initiative, but by the energy crisis and the domestic troubles of all European countries. But while the European powers are unable to challenge the United States, the United States is unable to prevent or to channel those very domestic European situations which may avoid a traditional challenge to American primacy but at the same time, pose a more serious threat to the very fabric of the Western world. The problems arise from the weakness of Europe rather than from its strength, from the diversity of situations, both economic and political, in Western Europe, rather than from any common challenge, from Europe's "sick men" rather than from its "strong men." More generally, the problems linked to *new European regionalism* are created on the one hand by the new domesticism and, on the other, by diverging attitudes towards extra-European problems or actors (whether the Soviet Union or the Third World) rather than by direct clashes in leadership or independence.

The Atlantic Relationship: Old Bargain, New Structures?

This does not mean, however, that dissatisfactions or tensions related to the structure of Atlantic relations are absent. But they are caused either by the indirect effect of the factors mentioned above, or by changes in the relations between the various dimensions of the relationship, particularly the economic and the military ones.

The old transatlantic bargain has been analyzed by various authors with great conceptual precision and sophistication.[5] Here we shall only recall it in its crudest and, hence, least accurate form. In short, the United States, through the Marshall Plan and its support of European unification, encouraged a potential economic rival for the sake of political stability; conversely, the Europeans accept an American-dominated international economic (particularly monetary) system for the sake of military protection and, according to some interpretations, for America's services as a world banker. Cracks in that structure appeared in the sixties, with increasing economic rivalries, a decreasing perception of the external military threat due to détente and at the same time an increasing American vulnerability due to nuclear parity. The result is an American tendency to ask for more economic concessions in exchange for less military security.

This was particularly the case during 1973, the year of Europe. As a reaction to this American tendency of transforming a tacit bargain into an explicit linkage, one finds the French position, under Pompidou and Jobert, going to the opposite neo-gaullist, extreme: to treat the United States as an economic (and even, to a great extent, political) adversary or rival while insisting on the maintenance of the American nuclear protection (without acknowledging it) and military presence in Germany.

The more realistic attitude, from this author's viewpoint, is that adopted by the other Western European countries which is distinct both from the American and from the Gaullist position. In a world of complex and asymmetrical interdependence, neither the search for a complete congruence of issues (which is a recurring American tendency from Kennedy to Kissinger and, most probably at least to some extent, to the Carter administration) nor the attempt at achieving their complete separation (as the French would have preferred) are likely to work. Differences in degrees of convergence and competition according to the particular issue-area are inevitable. They may even be beneficial to the relationship as a whole, as long as the intensity of competition and the means employed are moderated by the awareness of common interests.

This does not mean, however, that what is called for is some grand agreement on division of labor or structural reform. Rather the delicate balance between competition and cooperation is likely to have to be redefined from case to case according to variations in several factors. The essential considerations in this respect come under two headings. Firstly, variations in domestic situations: European countries can be seen as rivals to be feared, as victims to be helped, or as associates in the tasks involved. Secondly, variations in the interpretation of the urgency or importance of different issue-areas; this depends upon which threat or crisis (for instance economic collapse or military inferiority) is seen as the more pressing or dangerous. Both sets of considerations would converge in interpreting, for example, the trade-off between the socio-economic advantages and the strategic dangers of a national coalition involving the participation of the Communist party in the Italian government.

With all the wisdom, moderation and mutual tolerance and adaptation conceivable, it would be idle to imagine that agreement will be reached among all partners in all of these cases. There will be divergences of perception and interest between the United States and Europe and among Western European states, more so than in the "golden age" of the late forties and in the already less golden age of the fifties (which saw, in rapid succession, the EDC and the Suez crises). The point is to avoid their degeneration into what, for the author, is the main danger, that of polarization. This could occur along the lines of a division between the United States and Europe, or between the United States plus the remaining atlanticist faithful, or simply, the United States plus West Germany (which would be affected by the Korean or the Israeli symptom) and the other Europeans turned leftist or neutralist, or of northern versus southern Europe. As seen in late 1976 and early 1977, the results of the German and American elections, and even the evolution in southern Europe, where some kind of consensus or at least dialogue between political forces has taken place in Spain, Portugal and Italy, fortunately militate against this polarization. The polarization of the West into right-wing and left-wing regimes would encourage polarization within the various countries. On the one hand, Western organizations would be unable to function; on the other hand, Western societies would lose their main virtue, which is their pluralism and tolerance of diversity.

It is our contention, then, that the answer to the twin dangers of bipolarization and uncontrolled disintegration of the West lies in controlled diversification both of the Atlantic Alliance and of the European Community. On paper, one can distinguish six types of responses to the threats affecting Western organizations. The first three are the more inflexible ones: unity, dissolution, or a combination of both by the separation of a tight hardcore and of excommunicated black sheep. The other three are more flexible, making room for some tolerance of diversity: they are a two-pillar or dumbbell alliance, a network of bilateral relationships, and a combination of the two through a differentiation of roles involving mediating functions for the European Community and for the northern and social-democratic countries. In our view, the first three ought to be rejected, the last three should be adopted in some form or another, the most promising one being the sixth type of response.

Complete unity in the form of an Atlantic Community or Atlantic Union was probably always a pipe-dream but it certainly will remain, like perpetual peace, "not even a beautiful one." Inequalities and national diversities are obviously too important subjectively and objectively for complete unity to be anything but tyrannical, assuming it could be achieved which is more than doubtful. This is why it was surprising to see the rhetoric of "no partial membership" re-emerge in President Ford's 1975 speeches; there is inherent danger as well in the grand cooperative endeavors and architectonics favored by Z. Brzezinski – which probably could not be achieved without a much greater degree of common trilateral purpose than is likely to be possible.

At the other extreme, the perennial advocates of "the end of alliance," of neo-isolationism for America and of some kind of national or regional autarky for the European nation-states can, for the first time, find some support in the trend to domesticism, and the divergent interests and economic nationalism produced by the crisis. But, as we have mentioned, the same crisis clearly shows the Europeans' reliance on America, as well as their inability to agree on a common defense or to weather the energy crisis alone. And while America's increased military vulnerability may work for its military withdrawal, its increasing economic vulnerability works for its economic involvement.

The solution, then, might seem to lie in a narrower but closer cooperation within Western organizations purged or purified of those who do not strive for the same goals or do not join in their common efforts. This undoubtedly would have the advantage of overcoming the paralysis coming from always having to adapt to the lowest (and slowest) common denominator. On the other hand, it would mean encouraging the most negative tendencies among the excluded. The result would be either nationalist self-containment or drift towards the Soviet Union or towards the joint influence of Soviet military power and Arab money (a trend which I have called "maltification" in the case of Italy and of which the symbolic prelude can be seen in the Agnelli–Kadhafi deal concluded under Soviet auspices). Among the elect, it would encourage a siege mentality which would create domestic problems, e.g. in Germany. In the last analysis, no bloc, however united, can escape the twin imperatives of inner diversification and external interdependence.

This is why one should turn to the three other models, which rely on some combination of unity and diversity. Obviously the most desirable would be the old one of Atlantic partnership, based on two autonomous but allied partners, the United States and the European Community with Canada exercising some kind of balancing role. It remains as true as ever that only a European Community capable of defending itself and with its own energy policy could have a stable alliance with the United States, a stable détente with the Soviet Union, a stable cooperation with the Third World, without always falling into the vicious circle of identity and impotence. But it is also certain that firstly, such a united, strong, independent and still cooperative Europe looks less and less likely, and, secondly, that even if it did emerge it would – like its component nation-states and like the Atlantic Community or the developed world – find the problem of diverging interests within and of unavoidable dependencies and bilateral links with the outside world. While the congruence of dimensions or issue-areas might be greater than in the national or in the Atlantic case, it could never be complete; the inner differentiation between strong and weak, stable and unstable, northern and southern, central and peripheral within the Community is growing rather than diminishing and so are the differences in links with the outside world, particularly those with the United States.

Why then not take these differences for granted and, rather than striving to create an artificial entity which would only further distort or constrain diversity, transform Western organization into a network of intersecting bilateral relationships on a functional basis?[6] This solution is perfectly logical but also perfectly abstract. In particular, it abstracts from considerations of power, and from the asymmetrical character of interdependences as well as from the actual historical and geographical background of political tensions within the alliance. The network of relationships is both real and desirable enough; but divorced from a legitimating or countervailing framework, it would place the United States at the center of a gigantic spiderweb, which would freeze present inequalities and make them more visible, thereby encouraging domination and resentment. In particular, the American–German relationship would become central, with all the dangers we have already indicated; on the other hand, in the south, the problem often lies in the deterioration of the bilateral relationship between the United States and countries like Greece and Turkey, or in the danger of head-on confrontation between the United States and left-wing regimes.

This is why the only solution which seems to have a positive and dynamic potential without being unrealistic is one which combines the European idea with that of multiple relationships. One needs a more balanced Western world, and for that one needs a stronger European Community, but this need for more inner balance and diversity also exists within Europe and within the

Community itself. There are limits both to the homogeneity and to the heterogeneity possible and desirable within the Western organization. To achieve the right balance between them, as well as between dimensions and between the most urgent requirements, a diversification of roles is necessary. Here, the two notions, of mediation in the broader sense – involving the role of the Community and its stronger and more moderate member – and the notion of internal re-balancing – involving a greater cooperation between the weaker members to balance the influence of the strongest within the West but also within the Community – are both essential and complementary.

The Community should be able to act as an intermediary between the United States and certain Mediterranean countries, within and outside Europe; an increase in Mediterranean membership and influence within the Community should have a positive effect by making Europe more balanced and, at the same time, serving as a bridge to non-European Mediterranean countries. Conversely, Germany, the Scandinavian countries, the social-democratic parties, could and should, as they have done in the Portuguese case, act as intermediaries between right and left, rich and poor in Europe, and to some extent between European and American allies. Domestic evolutions must – if they are to avoid the dangers of polarization – adapt to the constraints of military security and economic interdependence and hence to Western organizations and structures, but the United States must understand that reliable Western European allies are better able to evaluate trends and possible reactions.

Different tiers, different speeds, different degrees of intimacy and of participation in decision-making are already facts of life and are likely to increase, particularly with the entrance of new members and the progress of political diversity, but it is for precisely this reason that they should be neither stifled nor sanctified in a rigid institutional way. They are best used in a positive way if they are accepted and encouraged on a flexible, usually informal basis, within a collective framework which should be reinforced at the same time.

For Western Europeans, the Atlantic relationship must take priority over any external association, but this priority should not detract from the necessity for the United States to understand the benefits of European autonomy. This involves Western Europeans reaching a preliminary understanding within the Atlantic Alliance before negotiating with the United States, a process which should not be troubled by premature and excessive American interposure. It also involves concerted but independent European initiatives towards the south and the east, which are neither directed against, nor orchestrated by the United States.

The West stands or falls with its ability both to accept diversity and to channel it in directions useful to common structures and purposes.

Notes

[1] See my *Europe and the Contradictions in American Policy*, in: Richard Rosecrance, (ed.), *America as an Ordinary Country*, Ithaca, London: Cornell University Press 1976, p. 60.

[2] cf. Charles Kindleberger, *U.S. Foreign Economic Policy, 1776–1976*, in *Foreign Affairs*, Vol. 55, 1977, No. 2.

[3] For the distinctions between the situations and interests of different European powers in relations with the East see my *The politics of Western Europe and East–West Relations*, in: Nils Andren and Karl E. Birnbaum, (eds.), *Beyond Détente: Prospects for East–West Cooperation and Security in Europe*, Leyden: Sijthoff 1976, pp. 15–36.

[4] *How Troubled a Partnership?*, in: *Beyond NATO* – special issue of *International Journal*, Vol. 29, 1974, No. 2, pp. 166–185.

[5] See in particular Robert Gilpin, *The Politics of Transnational Relations*, in: Robert O. Keohane and Joseph S. Nye, (eds.), *Transnational Relations and World Politics*, Cambridge, Mass.: Harvard University Press 1972, p. 60; and Edward Morse, *The Bargaining Structure of NATO: Multi-issue Negotiations in an Interdependent World*, in: I. William Zartman, (ed.), *The 50% Solution*, Garden City, N.Y.: Anchor 1976, p. 66.

[6] See for instance Seyom Brown, *A World of Multiple Relationships*, in: James Chace and Earl C. Ravenal, (eds.), *Atlantis Lost*, for the Council on Foreign Relations, New York: New York UP 1976, p. 103.

Canada – The Forgotten Partner?

by Peter C. Dobell

Canada emerged suddenly as an important actor on the world stage at the end of the Second World War. Effortlessly it found a comfortable and appropriate role, first as an important member of the wartime alliance and subsequently as an active partner in the Atlantic Alliance. Canada was likewise a keen and respected participant in the formation of the postwar financial and trade institutions and in the United Nations.

What was not clear at the time, however, was that the magnitude of Canada's contribution derived from transitory phenomena: financial strength based on its isolation from the battlefield and on its ability to provide the materials needed by the European nations to rebuild their economies; and the temporary retirement from the world stage of a number of major actors owing to exhaustion or defeat. By the "60s" both situations had altered, and Canada found that it was no longer playing the leading roles to which it had so quickly grown accustomed.

Acceptance of a diminished role is never easy. Moreover first impressions are usually strong and other nations had come to expect active Canadian participation. These persisting international expectations have complicated the problem for Canadians of adapting to the current situation and of developing a new role which is productive and satisfying. For Canada's partners the need is to understand what it is capable of achieving in the circumstances which now prevail.

Not all external perceptions of Canada are identical. But they share a common failing – relating it to another nation or group of nations. Most Americans and many Europeans assume that, because Canada is a North American state, policies which suit the United States will be sufficient for Canada. Some Europeans, conscious of its differences from the United States, look on Canada as "a largely-European country."[1] Both perceptions are misleading because they conceal important and unusual characteristics of the Canadian situation.

Among the developed countries of the world, Canada is set apart from its partners by a number of distinctive factors.

1. Canada is a substantial net exporter of raw materials and food products.

Among industrialized nations, only Australia shares this characteristic. But Canadian resources are not limitless. While it has large reserves, identified and potential, Canadians are aware that increasingly these have to be transported from remote regions or extracted under difficult conditions, so that costs of production for new undertakings will escalate sharply. In an age when attention is being given to the finiteness of the earth's resources, Canadians are increasingly affected by concern, particularly common in developing countries, for the consequences of the widespread export of non-renewable resources. Foreigners are impressed by the sheer size of the Canadian land mass, not realizing how little of the terrain is cultivatable and how marginal the growing season is in many parts of the country. It is not generally known, for instance, that Canada – famous as an exporter of fine quality hard wheat – actually grows less wheat than France.

2. Canada faces severe physical challenges. In their harsh northern climate, snowbound for six months of the year, Canadians are particularly sensitive to their dependence on fuel for sheer survival. Transportation is costly in a country as large as Canada, with developed parts of the country far removed one from another. The climate adds to the cost of transportation, requiring that road and rail beds be constructed to greater depths to withstand frost damage and necessitating continuous snow removal if routes are to be kept open in winter. Construction is also more costly: foundations have to be dug below the frost line and thick insulation is needed to reduce heat loss in winter. These conditions substantially increase the cost of living and working in Canada.

3. Among developed countries, Canada and Australia are likewise unusual in their continuing dependency on imported capital. Due to a very liberal regime on foreign business acquisitions, Canada finds itself with a high proportion of its industry owned and in many instances controlled by foreign companies – over 75 percent of the petroleum and natural gas industry, close to 60 percent of the manufacturing industries and about 50 percent of the mining and smelting industry are controlled by non-Canadian companies. In certain sectors such as chemicals, automobiles, computers, transportation equipment and machinery, foreign control ranges from 80 to over 90 percent. The sense of dependency and unease is the greater since more than 80 percent of these foreign companies are American-owned. While there are undoubted benefits from these connections, there are also costs; and psychologically this heavy involvement of American companies causes Canadians to be highly sensitive on the question of foreign ownership.

This concern is aggravated by Canada's unfavorable trade and payments balances. While the very favorable trade balances of the early 1970s offered some hope that the payments deficit might diminish with time, exports have deteriorated again in recent years and the country faced a massive payments deficit of over $5 billion in 1975. Combined with the growing awareness of the enormous sums of capital needed to develop frontier resources, Canadians have had to recognize that new means will be needed to attract capital while avoiding increasing loss of control of its industrial base.

4. Geography and history have combined to present Canada with the problem identified in the special study issued by the government in 1970 entitled *Foreign Policy for Canadians* "of living distinct from but in harmony with the world's most powerful and dynamic nation, the United States."[2] Two largely English-speaking nations developed side by side. While this caused little problem for Canada until the advent of mass communications, it now represents a pervasive threat to Canadian identity. Lacking the sense of separateness which centuries of conflict have given, say, Austrians from Germans or Belgians from French, Canada is groping for some way of coping with forces pressing toward interdependence in a "situation in relation to the United States . . . unique in two respects: the linkages are probably more numerous and more pervasive than between any two other countries and the affinities between them are also such as to put particular strains on the definition of the Canadian identity."[3]

5. The pre-eminent internal problem is that of maintaining national unity. The new self-awareness of French-Canadians in Canada is the primary factor to be adapted to. The government acknowledged this new situation rather cautiously in *Foreign Policy for Canadians*.

"Canadians of French expression no longer see themselves as a small disadvantaged minority in an English-speaking continent but rather as an essential element in the great international French culture, the most significant group of *francophones* outside metropolitan France."[4]

But in mid-1976 a specific issue – the tension generated throughout the country by the refusal of the association of air controllers to agree to work in French at major airports in Québec – has led Prime Minister Trudeau to speak more candidly. Comparing conditions during internal crises of 1917 and 1942 when "French Canada had nowhere to go in terms of being a different country," he warned that "now perhaps an increasing number of French Canadians think they do have somewhere to go and there's a legal political party which . . . is getting a large percentage of the vote."[5]

English-speaking Canadians have been adjusting to this new sense of awareness in their French-speaking brethren with difficulty and even hostility. In many parts of the country the accommodations necessary to satisfy the new situation in Quebébec have produced a sense of alienation and new demands for recognition of the different needs of other minority groups. Canada has never been an easy country to govern, but the difficulties have grown in recent years. These are problems which have their counterpart in some European countries, notably in Belgium and Ireland. They have had the effect, naturally, of causing Canadians to become more inward looking than they were and the remarkable fact is that the country remains as internationalist in outlook as it is.

The conclusion of this recital of unusual characteristics is that Canada has problems which set it somewhat apart from its partners. The usual practice in such a situation is to leave the country in question alone in the solving of its problems and to ignore it. Canada is too important to be ignored. It is the world's fourth largest exporter, coming after the United States, the European Community, and Japan. The scale of its trade with the United States alone can be judged from the fact that it is larger than the combined trade of France, Germany and Japan with the United States. It is the principal world producer of nickel, silver, zinc and asbestos and a major producer of many other raw materials. Geographically it stands in a strategic position between the USA and USSR and its security is vital to the defense of the United States. Therefore, even apart from its participation in the Atlantic Alliance, the United States and the countries of Western Europe must take an interest in Canada's fate.

In a world becoming increasingly interdependent and moving toward continental or subcontinental integration on the European model, the easy and natural solution for Canada would be to accept closer cooperation with the United States. This has in fact been the trend, even without much governmental encouragement, of the entire century and particularly since the Second World War. But to accept or even more to encourage this outcome is not compatible with the maintenance of a separate economic and cultural identity – at least that is how the prospect is viewed by the majority of Canadians. Even 65 years ago a Liberal government lost a federal election through its advocacy of free trade with the United States. The present government has explicitly rejected any deliberate policy of moving toward closer economic or political union with the United States.

Doing nothing is not a viable alternative. With just over 22 million people, Canada does not provide a large enough market to permit efficient industrial production. World free trade would be the most attractive policy for Canada, but the prospects for such a development are poor. Indeed, Canadian governments have been ambivalent in their pursuit of genuine free trade at international tariff negotiations, since much of Canada's secondary industry is protected and might have trouble competing in a free trade situation.

The dilemma facing Canada has become increasingly clear in the last few years. When Mr. Trudeau replaced Mr. Pearson as Prime Minister in 1968, Canada was still essentially following policies adopted in the immediate postwar years, even though they were no longer effective. Mr. Trudeau commissioned the study entitled *Foreign Policy for Canadians*, the main conclusion of which was the truism that foreign policy should be subject to the test of national interest. One of the first applications of this principle was the decision to reduce Canadian military forces in Europe, the government having concluded that the countries of Western Europe had reached a position where they were capable of defending themselves. At the same time the government announced its intention of extending its relations with Japan, the People's Republic of China and the other countries of the Pacific, with the Soviet Union and with the countries of Latin America. In effect, the government was implying that previously Canadian policy had been overly oriented toward Western Europe.

An unexpected event – the Nixon measures of August, 1971 – undermined the analysis on which the government had determined its new policies and forced it to rethink the whole orientation of Canadian foreign policy. These measures were as much of a shock to Canada as to any country, and owing to the large trade between the two countries, had more serious ramifications. The surprise was the greater when the government discovered that the United States Department of the Treasury, far from being prepared to exempt Canada from the application of the measures as the United States had done twice in the "60s" over hastily introduced control measures, was actually insisting on significant Canadian economic concessions. Canadians suddenly realized the extent of their vulnerability to United States pressures, as a result of the heavy dependency on the United States market. The government stuck to its position that the conditions to which the United States was objecting were temporary and that Canada, by adopting a flexible exchange rate, had already acted so as to relieve pressure on the US dollar. Ultimately the United States removed the surcharge on imports without securing any adjustments of Canadian policy. And Canada benefited from the changes in the exchange rates adopted by Japan and Germany and their tariff changes. The shock of the Nixon measures led the government to commission a study of relations with the United States. The outcome was a decision to adopt what has become known as the "third option," namely,

"over time, to lessen the vulnerability of the Canadian economy to external factors, including, in particular, the impact of the United States and, in the process, to strengthen our capacity to advance basic Canadian goals and develop a more confident sense of national identity."[6]

The practical implication was that Canada had to make strenuous efforts to increase its trade and economic relations with regions other than the United States. Three years of effort in the Pacific region, with the Communist states and in Latin America had produced discouraging results, Japan and a few small countries such as South Korea excepted. This left only Western Europe, where the European Community had just been enlarged with the addition of Britain, Ireland and Denmark. So the Trudeau government found itself, after four years of holding office, very much interested in developing closer ties with the European Community and in strengthening economic links with the member states of the European Community. The truth is that Canadians had largely ignored the development of the Community. No Canadian Minister visited the Commission headquarters in Brussels until November, 1970, and a separate Ambassador to the EC was not appointed until late in 1972.

Fortunately this shift in approach coincided with the awakening of an interest in Canada by EC member countries. For them also the Nixon measures had been an unpleasant surprise and had led them to look for new trading prospects. The strong Canadian resistance to the US measures provided a surprising demonstration to Europeans of the very different character of Canadian trading interests vis-à-vis those of the United States. Far more important, however, as a cause of enhanced European interest in Canada was the Yom Kippur war and the Arab oil embargo, which led Europeans and Japanese to attach new importance to the development of secure supplies of raw materials and energy. Canada was not only a major source of industrial raw materials and food and a large producer of oil, gas and uranium, but was as well a member of the Atlantic Alliance. It assumed a new importance in European eyes.

The effects of this coincidence of interest has been quite remarkable. In the 1960s those in Europe who were working to strengthen the Community were preoccupied with finding a new basis for relations with the United States. Their approach was blatantly continentalist, and for them the dumbbell symbolized the pattern of transatlantic links to which they aspired. That this symbol committed Canada to some form of union with the United States was treated as a development which was historically inevitable. Canada, they argued, should face the facts and make the best terms possible.[7] The United States responded in kind. The Trade Expansion Act of 1962 was designed to provide a basis for negotiating with the Economic Community. As Pierre Uri remarked in commenting on the Act and the subsequent negotiations: "Canada had been forgotten as one of the possible partners in computing the Atlantic share of world exports."[8] Seen against this background, the first problem for Canada in the early "70s" was simply to gain the attention of the Community, preoccupied on the one hand with its own internal developments and still seeking a *modus vivendi* with the United States on the other. Mitchell Sharp, Secretary of State for External Affairs remarked at the time: "We had to rap firmly but politely on the table to get their attention . . . We had, above all, to change their attitude which, for a variety of reasons, had been common in EEC countries, that the view they took of their relations with the United States would do more or less for their relations with Canada."[9]

The first important sign of awakening interest on the European side was the specific reference in the communique of the EC Heads of Government following their summit meeting in Paris in October 1972 to Canada along with the United States and Japan as countries with whom the Community was "determined . . . to maintain a constructive dialogue."

But there remained a hesitancy on both sides. Prime Minister Trudeau was not yet ready to throw his personal prestige into the development of a closer relationship with the Community, partly because his government at the time was in a minority position in the Canadian parliament and partly because difficulties between Canada and France caused by President de Gaulle's espousal in 1967 of Québec separatism had not been resolved to the point where the Prime Minister was welcome in France. On the European side, Canadian interest in the opening of a Community office in Canada and in the development of a more structured relationship through some kind of formal bilateral agreement was resisted on the ground that they would create undesirable precedents.

By 1974 these situations had changed. In the fall of 1973 Premier Bourassa won an overwhelming electoral victory in the Province of Québec and in June, 1974, the Liberal government was returned with a large majority. In April, 1974, Prime Minister Trudeau attended the funeral of President Pompidou of France. Together these events opened the way to President Giscard d'Estaing to invite Prime Minister Trudeau to make a formal visit to France, which he did in October, 1974. Profiting from the opportunity, Mr. Trudeau also visited the Commission headquarters in Brussels, where he spoke strongly in favor of the development of a "contractual link" between Canada and the Community. In this and in a subsequent visit to Europe in March, 1975, he also took this campaign to the capitals of the member states.

In the meantime, the Arab oil embargo had had its impact and the Community's interest in establishing an effective relationship with Canada had grown. The first fruit of this new attitude was the approval in October, 1974, by the Council of Ministers of the Commission's recommendation to open a full scale Community office in Ottawa, the first to be established after Washington and Japan. Only a year and a half earlier Sir Christopher Soames, EC Commissioner for External Relations, had told a Committee of the Canadian Senate visiting Brussels that such a development would not be feasible, indicative of how rapidly perceptions of Canada's importance to the Community had changed. By the end of 1975 the Council of Ministers had authorized the Commission to respond to Canada's proposal to negotiate a "contractual link" and by July, 1976, the agreement was concluded.

This represented an entirely new approach for the Community. "Breaking new ground" was the way Soames put it.[10] Previously the Commission had limited itself in its relations with non-European states to special trade agreements with former colonies – notably the Lomé agreement – and to signing commercial agreements with some developing countries such as Argentina which supplied mainly a single product. With the United States, the Community holds meetings twice a year at the level of Under Secretary and Commissioner, but this formula did not suit the Canadian political structure. What Canada sought and what it finally secured in the Framework Agreement for Commercial and Economic Cooperation was Community recognition of the separate importance of Canada and a structure in the Joint Cooperation Committee which has been established to monitor and promote commercial and economic cooperation.

Parallel with these developments and not unrelated to them has been an interesting shift in Canada's approach to NATO and to the defense of Western Europe. In 1969, when announcing the reduction in Canadian forces in Europe from about 10,000 men to some 5,000, the government had announced that the heavy *Centurion* tank with which Canadian forces were then equipped would not be replaced and that instead a light air-transportable armored vehicle would be acquired. This decision had never been popular with Canada's allies, since it has been judged that only heavy tanks can be effective in Central Europe. For years the government procrastinated. For some time it explored the possibility of buying the British *Scorpion*. All the while it allotted the defense budget a declining share of government revenues. Finally some of Canada's NATO allies spoke privately to the Prime Minister during his European visits. Chancellor Schmidt in particular is reported to have told Mr. Trudeau in March, 1975, that if Canada wanted better economic relations with Europe, it should contribute meaningfully to continental defense. By November, 1975, only a month before the Council of Ministers approved the Community's negotiating position for the Framework Agreement, the Canadian government announced the purchase of the West German *Leopard* tank to replace the almost-derelict *Centurions*. It also decided to acquire 18 Lockheed ASW aircraft to replace the aging Argus for duty over the North Atlantic. By these decisions the government committed itself to an ongoing involvement in the defense of Western Europe, finally recognizing the interaction of military and economic considerations which it had earlier ignored when economic relations with Europe had seemed less important.

Little mention has been made of bilateral relations since these are essentially cordial and likely to remain so. Indeed the campaign for the Framework Agreement had been won largely in the national capitals, where the real resistance lay. Although Denmark had held out against giving its approval to the Agreement, objecting to the absence of a specific obligation for equal access to raw materials by foreigners and Canadians – known in trade jargon as "national treatment" – the Danes maintained privately that they were more concerned about the precedent than future Canadian policy and they eventually did not insist on their point.

The only serious bilateral problem had been with France as a result of President de Gaulle's dramatic espousal in 1967 of the slogan of French-Canadian separatists. While de Gaulle remained President, relations were poor. With his death, and a gradual shift in approach by the French government, relations improved steadily. The invitation to Prime Minister Trudeau to visit France in November, 1974, removed the last impediment to good relations between the two countries.

Canada's campaign to persuade Europeans of its potential importance as an economic partner was not completed with the signature of the Framework Agreement. During the same period President Giscard d'Estaing called the economic summit meeting of industrialized states at Rambouillet, to which he initially invited the United States, Japan, Germany and Britain. Had he stuck to his original intention, Canadian sensitivities would not have been aroused. But when he weakened in the face of Italian importunings and included Italy, Canadians were upset, believing their economic importance to be relatively greater than that of Italy. President Giscard was not to be moved, in spite of United States support for Canada's inclusion. Canada was pleased a year later when Prime Minister Trudeau was invited to join the other participants of Rambouillet at a second summit meeting organized by President Ford in Puerto Rico.

Canadian efforts during the same period to expand economic relations with Japan have also been successful and for many of the same reasons. There were fewer problems to be overcome since only two countries were involved and more attention had been focused on the question earlier. A Joint Ministerial Committee had existed for several years, so no new mechanisms were needed. The main requirement in fact has been to dramatize within each country the potential importance of the other and to help to make this potential better known. The major device for doing this has been prime ministerial visits and this is being done, Mr. Trudeau went to Japan in 1970, Mr. Tanaka came to Canada in 1974, and Mr. Trudeau returned in the autumn of 1976.

In Europe and in Japan, therefore, Canada can no longer be regarded as the forgotten partner. On the contrary, it has recently been the subject of considerable attention – a distinct change from the situation prevailing only two or three years earlier.

With the United States Canada faces a quite different situation. Americans do not really regard Canada as a foreign country. The average visitor to Canada finds the same language and style of life, even the same chains of hotels and restaurants, the same processed foods, the same radio and television programmes, the same cars and gasoline distributors and his money is interchangeable. The reaction of the American tourist can be understood and excused. But similar errors by the United States government are harder to ignore. President Nixon inaugurated with considerable fanfare an annual report on foreign policy. Issued under the title *Foreign Policy for the 1970's*, the first dated February, 1970, and the second made public a year later both failed to make any reference to Canada, and the sections dealing with the Western Hemisphere were dedicated to the "sister republics" of the Americas. This does not mean in fact that Canada is ignored by the US government. Any such concern was diminished by the special demands made upon it as part of the Nixon measures of August, 1971. Canada's difficulty has been to persuade the US authorities that it is a foreign country like any other foreign country.

Events are to a considerable extent removing this problem. Over the years the United States has become dependent on Canada for substantial imports of oil and natural gas. In the pre-Yom Kippur war period, these had amounted to some 8 percent of its oil consumption and 4.5 percent of its gas. Canada with 17 percent of the US oil import market was the largest single supplier and it provided all US imported natural gas. With Canadian reserves declining rapidly, the Canadian government in 1973 felt obliged to introduce export controls and in subsequent years oil exports have been cut back annually and will be phased out entirely in the early 1980s. These conservation measures, added to the recently introduced regulations on foreign ownership and the decision of the Saskatchewan government to nationalize part of the potash industry, which provides about three-quarters of all potash used on American farms, have insured active interest in Canada on the part of the

United States authorities. There is, as a result, no longer any risk of Canada being forgotten in the United States. Moreover the determination of the Canadian government to give some protection to the Canadian mass media against the low cost cultural imports from the United States has caused considerable American irritation and will ensure that Canada remains on the US government's agenda. The problem for the future therefore for Canadians will not be to catch the attention of the United States. Rather it will be to find sufficient understanding of its special problems and to frame its actions with caution and concern for their effect on the United States so that the two nations can continue to live in harmony and cooperate to their mutual benefit. With both sides aware of this over-riding need, there is no reason why this should not happen.

If Canada has caught the attention and aroused the interest of its partners in the last couple of years, this in itself is not sufficient. Canada needs to make its partners aware of some of its particular characteristics – identified earlier in this chapter – so that they will be prepared to consider making an exception in situations where Canadian participation is desired, but where some special treatment is needed to make such participation possible.

There are several examples of such special consideration, a number of them recent, indicating that there is already considerable understanding and respect for Canada's unusual situation. An early and important exception was made in 1961 when Canada joined the enlarged organization of the OECD. The other members agreed to exempt Canada from accepting the obligations of the code on capital movements, acknowledging Canada's argument that as a heavy net importer of capital, it could not agree in all circumstances to allow freer movement.

The most prominent recent example involves obligations arising out of Canada's membership in the International Energy Agency (IEA). Canada, a major producer of oil and gas, was one of the countries originally involved in the formation of the Agency. It participated actively in the elaboration of an emergency sharing plan and a program of long-term cooperation. However, one section of this program obligated participating countries to accord equal access and non-discriminatory treatment as between nationals and non-nationals. Canada took the position that it could not undertake this for constitutional and legislative reasons. Its case was finally accepted and it was granted an exemption from the application of Chapter V of the program which sets out the obligations on equal access. The decision of the Community's member states to sign a Framework Agreement, without requiring, as Denmark wished, a solemn declaration on equality of access to raw materials is further evidence of understanding by Canada's partners of its special characteristics. The same issue of national treatment arose again during the drawing up of the OECD's guidelines for multinational enterprises signed in 1976. In this case Canada finally signed the agreement without modification, since it did not involve a contractual obligation as in the IEA case. The government however sought to increase its latitude for maneuver by making an interpretative statement at the time of signature. A final recent instance of a differing Canadian outlook affecting multilateral negotiations occurred in the fourth UNCTAD conference in Nairobi and in the Conference on International Economic Cooperation (CIEC), where Canada's position as a major exporter of food and raw materials put it more on the side of the developing countries on commodity issues than on the side of the developed countries. This difference in perspective may have helped to moderate the position of the industrialized countries in these negotiations.

At the governmental level it seems clear therefore that Canada's partners no longer ignore its existence. There are explanations, some more obvious than others, for this renewed awareness of Canada. In the past the Community, having achieved a *modus vivendi* with the United States, has been able to look elsewhere. It also reflects, however, a change in the last few years in Canada's relative importance internationally. It is remarkable how rapidly such changes in international standing occur. This chapter opened by noting how Canada's postwar importance quickly diminished as nations defeated or exhausted in the Second World War regained strength and self-confidence. By 1975 however, the pendulum had begun to swing the other way for some of these countries. Economic difficulties during the last few years have reduced the importance of Britain and Italy. The success of the Community as an institution has also to some degree diminished the separate significance of each of its members. While these shifts have been occurring Canada's economy has been growing steadily, supported by a broad and secure resource base. Finally the focus of international economic relations has shifted increasingly toward the exploration of North–South questions. Here Canada's position as both a developed and in a sense a developing country, and one without the liability of a colonial heritage, has given it some natural prominence as a leader in these negotiations, a fact recognized by its election as one of the co-chairmen of CIEC. The increased recognition which Canada has achieved in the last few years reflects to a degree an enhanced importance and relevance.

Canada therefore has no longer the grounds for complaining of neglect it once had. Its partners have shown a growing understanding of unusual elements in its situation and have been willing to make exceptions to accommodate them. What does remain quite uncertain – and this will be a critical consideration over time – is whether the Framework Agreement and the increased interest of the Community countries and Japan in expanding their economic relations with Canada will be sufficient to balance the strong north–south pulls at work across the Canada–United States border. The proportion of Canada's trade with the United States has doubled in little more than a generation to the point where it now represents more than two-thirds of all Canadian trade. Trade with Europe has grown discouragingly slowly. From 1958 to 1972 Canadian exports to the "Six" grew by only 153 percent. During the same period US exports to the EC increased by 204 percent, while those of Japan advanced by a phenomenal 1500 percent. Canadian exports to the United States grew by 733 percent in the same fifteen year period.

If Canadian trade with countries other than the United States is to grow substantially, which it must if the government's intentions are to be realized, a major requirement will be to work out specific cooperative arrangements in which Canadian businesses can and will participate. Unfortunately the trading potential of the Community is still little understood in Canada outside of official circles. The Framework Agreement specifically envisages joint ventures, but these require the active collaboration of business leaders on both sides of the Atlantic Ocean. A major campaign by the federal government at the political and at the bureaucratic levels will be required in order to secure the support of the Canadian business community, which is still sceptical of the value of the Framework Agreement and of the prospects for arresting, let alone reversing, the growing proportion of Canadian exports going to the United States. There is no clear sign that the government has appreciated the size of the public relations problem.

The task is all the greater because public media representatives are surprisingly ignorant of developments in the Community and of their potential significance for Canada. Visits by Community leaders to Canada are sparsely reported in the press and on radio and television. The opening of the Community office in Ottawa should lead to some improvement, since some four members of the staff are to be primarily involved in public education. The same lack of attention is true in the academic world. Only the Centre d'Etude et de Documentation Européenne at the University of Montreal is primarily organized for the study of developments in the Community.

The problem applies in reverse in Community countries. Knowledge of commercial possibilities in Canada is still not widespread in business circles. The most startling fact is that trade between Canada and the Federal Republic of Germany represents less than two percent of their respective trade. More significantly, press coverage has actually declined. There are fewer European correspondents in Canada than there were a decade ago. Even major national British journals which used to have correspondents in Canada such as the London *Times* and the *Economist* no longer are represented, with the result that their coverage of Canada is practically non-existent.

What are the future prospects for Canada's relations with its partners? Much depends on the success of the campaign to give substance to the Framework Agreement. Providing trade with the Community grows at a rate faster than the development of trade with the United States, the government will not feel pressed for this reason to intervene more forcefully in the Canadian economy. But should the trend toward yet further trade dependency on the United States persist, the government can be expected to seek more direct methods for achieving its objective of lessening dependency on the United States. This might involve more stringent controls on foreign ownership, and would certainly include limitations on the free market economy, an economy which compared to the United States already involves more state ownership of industry, public carriers and utilities.

One development with longer term implications for relations with Europe is the shift in immigration streams into Canada. Ninety-five percent of Canadians are of European origin. Close to 15 percent were born in Europe. Most of these Canadians naturally maintain close personal links with their country of birth, and these multiple links represent an important continuing connection with the European continent. But fewer Europeans now seek to emigrate: the percentage of immigrants coming to Canada from European countries has fallen in less than a decade from over 70 percent to under 40 percent. Even among Europeans, the principal countries of origin have shifted from the center to the periphery. Apart from the United Kingdom, which remains a major source of immigrants, Greece and Portugal have replaced countries such as the Netherlands and Italy as the principal source of new Canadians. If these trends towards reduced European entry into Canada continue, the effects in terms of diminished personal links to broaden the connections could be felt in a generation.

The extent to which reliable supplies of raw materials at competitive prices are discovered, exploited and made available for export in Third World countries, the USSR, China and on the ocean floor will significantly affect the degree of interest which Europeans and Japanese feel toward Canada. If supplies become easier and the policy of détente is not disturbed, the interest now being shown in Canada by its industrialized partners would surely diminish. However, if for political or technical reasons supplies become tight, interest in making specific arrangements with Canada should grow rapidly. Similar considerations will also affect US attitudes towards Canada.

Canadian trade policy now involves a heavy emphasis on upgrading raw materials wherever possible rather than exporting them in an unprocessed state. With the Community, however, the problem is less one of upgrading than of preventing downgrading. Several products such as zinc, lead and newsprint, which Canada has traditionally exported to Britain in a finished state face a higher tariff within the Community, where facilities for refining metal concentrates and pulp already exist. The result, unless this situation is modified through negotiation, will be a lower proportion of Canadian exports in a semi-finished state. However Canada's primary need is to increase its exports of fully manufactured goods, which are relatively labor intensive. This is a major reason for some scepticism as to the extent which trade with Community countries can increase substantially as Canada is unlikely to be able to compete easily with the Nine in this area. If it cannot be done, the policy of the Third Option becomes much harder to apply.

Just as uncertainty may exist about the future of France and Italy within the Atlantic Community due to the substantial votes recorded by the Communist parties of these two countries, so in Canada the separatist *Partie Québecois* (PQ) represents a threat and a challenge to the political integrity of Canada. There are commentators who consider it possible that the PQ could form a minority government after the next election. The Party has announced its intention if elected as the government to hold a referendum on Québec's future, the outcome of which would be hard to predict since an uncertain number of PQ voters are opposed to the separation of Québec from Canada and would vote separatist primarily to express opposition to certain policies of the Québec provincial government. What can be stated categorically is that Québec's separation from Canada would cause a whole series of internal problems. Relations with its partners would become a decidedly subordinate question for Canadians. Moreover, it would be impossible to predict the course of political development within Québec, although a shift toward left wing radicalism would be quite possible. If that were to happen, relations between Québec and the United States could become extremely sensitive.

The prospects for Canada's relations with its partners has changed dramatically in the last few years. The deliberate disregard which was characteristic of European attitudes in the "60's" has largely disappeared. It is no longer necessary for Canadians to consider themselves as forgotten. Its special characteristics and needs are increasingly well understood. But the promise of the Framework Agreement awaits realization. Detailed programs attractive to industry must be elaborated and concrete negotiations pressed to successful conclusions if life is to be breathed into the Agreement. If the challenge is faced, there are good prospects for the development of relaxed and productive relations between Canada and all its partners.

Notes

[1] The Assistant Secretary-General of the Council of Europe, Count Sforza as quoted in Jean-Yves Grenon *Canada's Developing Relations with the Europe of "Eighteen"*, in: *International Perspectives*, March/April 1976.

[2] *Foreign Policy for Canadians*, Vol. 1, Ottawa: Department of State for External Affairs 1970, p. 21.

[3] Mitchell Sharp, Secretary of State for External Affairs, *Canada–U.S. Relations: Options for the Future*, in: *International Perspectives*, special issue, Autumn 1972, p. 20.

[4] *Foreign Policy for Canadians*, op. cit., *Europe*, p. 14

[5] *Globe and Mail*, 4 October 1976.

[6] *Canada–U.S. Relations: Options for the Future*, op. cit., p. 17.

[7] Based on conversations reported in: Elliot R. Goodman, *The Fate of the Atlantic Community*, New York: Praeger 1975, pp. 144–145.

[8] Pierre Uri, *Economic Dimensions of Atlantic Partnership*, in: Karl H. Cerny and Henry W. Briefs, (eds.), *NATO in Quest of Cohesion*, New York: Praeger 1965, p. 349.

[9] Department of External Affairs: *Statements and Speeches*, 18 November 1972.

[10] p. 33: quoted in David Humphreys, *Canada's Links with Europe Still not Widely Understood*, in: *International Perspectives*, March/April 1976.

Washington and Bonn
Evolutionary Patterns in the Relations between the United States and the Federal Republic of Germany

by UWE NERLICH

Political Stability in Western Europe: New Dimensions of Atlantic Cooperation

1. The New US Hegemony and its Limits

While Western Europe's dependence upon the United States is greater and more complex than at any time in the last 25 years, social and political processes are unfolding which could fundamentally change the European-American relationship before the end of this century. Such a transformation would hardly lead to greater Western European independence since nothing can abolish the myriad threats from the one superpower or the multiple dependency upon the other. But just as Western Europe's weakness is demonstrated by the fact that no form of emancipation from the major Western power can guarantee the viability of the Western industrial nations, the limits to American hegemony in Europe are demonstrated by the United States' inability to mould and determine Western European relationships as it could in the postwar period: the political weakness of most of the Western European states sets limits to American hegemony.

In the postwar era American policy could be carried out with a considerable degree of indifference to the actual political processes in Western Europe;[1] and, vice versa, political autonomy for Western Europe was only sought under the conservative banner of Gaullism without ever, in the final analysis, forgetting the necessity of American protection. Three basic conditions of this situation no longer exist: Western European political heterogeneity is increasing, the primacy of security has to a great extent lost its previous function in shaping order[2] and the multilateral organizations of the West no longer represent a pre-stabilized harmony.

Under these circumstances political consensus between the United States and Europe becomes more necessary and, at the same time, more difficult than ever. If Europe is to remain European, then as Helmut Schmidt has put it, there can be "no anti-American Europe, nor can the United States today turn away from the old continent without endangering its own identity."[3] But this merely describes an imperative and not a principle of Atlantic policy. In reality, political weakness and increasing heterogeneity amongst Western European countries can make impossible the kind of relations with the United States without which the capacity for economic achievement and military security can no longer be maintained. And, vice versa, given this situation the United States might well lose its willingness and its ability to associate its fate with that of Western Europe, or could even be tempted to employ its military and economic hegemony as a means of political coercion in Western Europe which would only accelerate the deterioration of Atlantic relations. In either case, it would lead not only to an irreversible shift in balance in the relationship between the two world powers, it would also have direct repercussions on the viability of the American republic itself. Whereas the Soviet Union needs the dynamism of politico-ideological confrontation to preserve its inner stability – which appears to the outsider to be a form of expansionism – the United States has always sought the static state of an "environment in which the American system can survive and grow"[4] (which, again to the outsider, seems to be a kind of extensive isolationism), that is, at least since the US was drawn almost reluctantly but inevitably into its unprecedented role as a world power 30 years ago. Such a homogeneous environment for the United States remains impossible to achieve when the existence of a responsive Western Europe is lacking. In the United States today there is a growing awareness of a painful insight: it is not inconceivable that the Western alliance system will lose its stabilizing function which is so important for the United States.[5]

2. Three Crises within the Alliance

In the last thirty years the Western industrial nations have demonstrated a historically unparallelled ability to adapt common organizations to new challenges. To be sure, at times "crisis" seems the best way of describing the basic element of the Western self-image. But in the development of Western institutions crises not only represent disturbances which, in their concrete form can be regarded as the result of accidental circumstances – they also have a necessary catalytic function. From time to time they unexpectedly but nonetheless unavoidably draw attention to those points where incongruities arise between multilateral consensus and the vital interests of the respective partners; integration deficits become apparent which, under extreme conditions, could indeed assume catastrophic proportions, but which, due to such early recognition, can be revised in good time.

   In the Suez Crisis of 1956 limited accord between the three Western powers led to the desperate French suggestion of a directorate, to France's no less desperate withdrawal from NATO as well as to a pragmatic limitation of the functions of the alliance, an alliance which no longer represented the framework for a common foreign policy, but only for military cooperation. Similarly, the Cuban Crisis of 1962 exposed the limited accord between American alliance policy and its relations with the other world power, which in turn, by way of the unnecessary American Multilateral Force proposal and an obstinate American non-proliferation policy led to a practical supplementation of the functions of the alliance: Détente was no longer viewed as a danger to Western security but rather as a means in support of its maintenance.

The repercussions of the Fourth Middle East War and the events which it triggered were not limited to multilateral structures; they demonstrated a limited accord between the internal possibilities and external necessities of all the Western industrial nations. The West is still in the process of adaptation, but three lessons from recent developments are nonetheless clear: first, the Western industrial countries are confronted with threats which are more complex than had as yet been assumed in the previous military cooperation within NATO; second, détente has lost its internal functions within the West, although it remains a useful instrument of security policy;[6] third, the viability of the Western industrial nations will depend decisively upon whether solidarity in cooperation on economic matters can be achieved, a lack of which would endanger the political stability of all Western industrial nations in the long run.

3. Bilateralism from Washington's Point of View

Unlike the practice of the last 25 years, in which partnership was exercised in the framework of multilateral institutions and selective cooperation was avoided for fear of weakening these institutions, Atlantic relations take shape in the present situation primarily at the intergovernmental level. Only in this manner can the vitality of the common institutions of the Western industrial countries be maintained. This requires not only new forms of partnership but a capability for action as well. Innovation is only possible through multiple bilateralism, i.e. through direct cooperation by governments capable of acting. Similarly it is clear that sufficient consensus must be reached in the multilateral framework. Whereas in the last 25 years Atlantic policy was principally conceived in system categories, it is now necessary that it should be understood as a process.

First steps toward new intergovernmental cooperation between the United States and Western Europe have, in fact, been taken in recent years – in

particular at the summit level. On a number of important issues Western
European influence has had its effect in Washington – a phenomenon which
was practically inconceivable in the past. But in the final analysis, it will
depend on Washington's willingness to open new channels of cooperation
with Western Europe. There are four reasons why this could become difficult.
Firstly, the United States could come to the conclusion that, due to its newly
strengthened hegemonial position, it could live with Atlantic relations in
their present form, a conclusion which would be correct in the short run, in
view of America's relatively limited vulnerability, but is insufficient if one
considers its repercussions in the form of Western European alienation from
the United States. Secondly, the United States could consider new forms of
cooperation with Western Europe and Japan to be "important, but important
in connection with other things which are more urgent."[7] This would
unquestionably extenuate the urgency of Atlantic cooperation from the
Western European point of view as well, and without an awareness of this
urgency effective solutions cannot be reached. Thirdly, Washington could in
fact give high priority to cooperation with the industrial nations of Western
Europe and Japan but at the same time remain indifferent to the domestic
situation of its partners or try to push through its own suggestions or strive for
solutions advantageous solely to third parties (as in the case of a framework
for a new global economic order) which would certainly make a viable
political consensus between Washington and Western European governments
impossible. Fourthly, given the present situation in Western Europe, Atlantic
cooperation is only feasible when the few governments which are capable of
action act in the interest of weaker governments as well, in so far as the latter
use such advantages in the interest of a growing capacity for cooperation.
Political disposition either for the one or the other condition is not easily
found in Western Europe.

Washington will proceed pragmatically. In recent years – at least until the
end of 1976 – there has been a growing tendency in American foreign policy
to seek close cooperation above all with the dominant power in a given
region, for example with Brazil in Latin America or with Saudi Arabia in the
Middle East. But the Western European constellation offers no natural
partner for such a policy: it is too complex and unstable a unit. Moreover, it
is inherent in the pragmatic approach that a hegemonial power only seeks a
partner in areas where it is expedient to do so.

4. The Federal Republic as the Scapegoat and Favorite of the United States

The relations between the United States and the Western European nations have historical roots. In this sense, "special relationships" are the only kind of transatlantic relationships that exist. But it is obvious that American interests are oriented (in changing constellations) primarily towards France, Great Britain and the Federal Republic. In recent years the Federal Republic has repeatedly found itself in a special role in its relations with the United States, alternating between being viewed as a "scandalon" because of its lack of cooperation (in Washington's opinion) at one moment and in the next being considered as a potential partner in a "bi-gemony," as if impatience with the institutional deficiency of Western Europe could thus lead to a Western Europe with "one voice."[8]

Recent developments provide a particularly drastic illustration of the evanescence of such notions. The very same advisors who urged President Carter to establish American–German "bigemony" are now pursuing a policy of confrontation in sensitive issues vis-à-vis the Federal Republic. First, high-priority long-term German–American cooperation is recommended as the basis for economic peace,[9] then a full reversal takes place and the Federal Republic is put under American pressure to alter its economic stability policy or even to accept a balance of payments deficit as long as OPEC nations maintain surpluses.[10] This would inevitably throw the viability of the German economy into question. Such vacillations, which can be regularly observed, clearly show that Washington tends to overestimate either the Federal Republic's stability or its compliance. Such a change illustrates the characteristic dynamics of issue formation in American policy; it is perfectly normal in Washington's political system and has seldom been misinterpreted in Bonn.[11]

5. German–American Cooperation: Conditio Sine Qua Non

Looking beyond this current phenomenon, it remains certain that there is no system of Western cooperation in which German–American relations are not of fundamental importance. This follows from the fact that the bulk of American armed forces in Europe is stationed in the Federal Republic, from America's share in the Four-Power responsibility, and from the Federal Republic's economic role in Western Europe. Neither a preferential solidarity, nor an imperative for the Federal Republic to follow the respective guidelines of American policy can be derived from this constellation. But economic performance, military security and political stability in Western Europe are inevitably influenced by decisions in Washington and Bonn regardless of the degree of German–American consensus on such decisions. In this sense special German–American relations exist (which are not intentional) and which do not so much represent a structure of dominance as prove the need for mutual responsibility which either side can fail to live up to. This would also imply that possibilities for political conflict are inherent in the German–American relationship to a high degree.[12]

Thus, it is surprising that in recent years the German–American alliance has been the "only alliance of central importance for American foreign policy which has not been undermined either by the process of détente or through the frictions of the international economy."[13] A whole series of previous difficulties have completely or largely disappeared from the agenda, at least for the moment: the German question, the regulation of relations with the East, the uncertainties over American policy on troop deployment (Mansfield Resolution), the question of the Federal Republic's participation in the nuclear field, the undervaluing of the Mark, the offset issue, etc. Other issues which in the past worked to block consensus have now become the object of cooperation, for example, the strengthening of conventional defense.

Most of these controversial points had in the meantime proven to be points of friction in those multilateral structures which had represented the decisive framework for German–American relations in the fifties and to a large extent in the sixties as well. They could be eliminated or alleviated primarily because the multilateral structures have lost their previous functions (with regard to nuclear participation) or because they have clearly been resolved in recent years (for example, the German question).

The new conflict situations inherent in the German–American relationship do not result, as they did in the past, from the Federal Republic's wish to eliminate the sensitive problems of its integration deficit or from the concern as to whether the special status of the Federal Republic and West Berlin is given sufficient consideration by the West, in particular by the United States. On the contrary, they stem from the increasing absence of the protective conformity of multilateral consensus in German–American relations in situations where both must act in the interest of general stability. German–American cooperation is the *conditio sine qua non* for military security, economic productivity and political stability in Western Europe, but uncertainty arises in all three dimensions of Western European politics because, among other things, the continuity of this cooperation is, in the long run, a question of the art of political leadership. Especially those political tasks which require mutual consensus contain a structural potential for German–American conflict, whether they involve German–American burden-sharing (security and economy) or the coordination of concepts of political stability (for example in relation to the Western European Left).

6. The Contemplation of the Past

Washington and Bonn are facing problems in the last quarter of this century which are without historical precedent. But the definition of these problems and the acknowledged possibilities for solving them as well as the accompanying fears of third parties will probably be more strongly moulded by historical reminiscence than in any of the last few decades.

A historical perspective results from the "view of the society in which we live."[14] One of the effects of the integration of Western institutions in the postwar period was a kind of "historical amnesia."[15] The "screening out" of the world economic crisis was just as important for economic recovery after 1945 as was the "screening out" of the Third Reich for the Western security system.[16]

The result was a Federal Republic of Germany which is viewed even by classic democracies as a model of political, social and economic stability. One could call it a self-fulfilling amnesia. "For the first time, that country is making peace with reality. But at the same time the German idea has lost some of its identity, it is practising empirical techniques, it is willing to adjust and it is concerned with the general welfare."[17] But this has occurred under conditions of considerable political homogeneity and economic prosperity in Western Europe and in a climate where institutionalism dominated the relations between Western industrial countries.

Thus, historical reminiscence can indeed once again become politically effective. This could happen in the Federal Republic, if, for example, political stability should appear threatened by the sort of economic sluggishness which in other industrial nations might still be considered a success. It could also affect the behavior of others, should a political change of power occur in France for example, where the present reality of West Germany could trigger political opposition in the name of the past.

Conceivably such opposition would rally around the flag of political anti-Americanism. More and more signs point in this direction; the fact that the Federal Republic, together with the United States, carries the main burden of a Western policy of stability would provide sufficient motivation. The most difficult dilemma facing Bonn in the coming decade may be that the Federal Republic has no choice but to be partner-in-stability of the United States, whereas the Federal Republic's attempts at political harmonization in Western Europe – so vital to its survival in view of increasing heterogeneity there – may fail to find support particularly from the United States.

But even if historical reminiscence along with increasing political heterogeneity is an unwelcome phenomenon, the structural possibilities for cooperation between western industrial nations are at least more easily recognized as long as they are not simply understood in terms of crisis in a given state of affairs, but rather of the dynamics of structural development. "The law of development" in the system of Western cooperation must find its formulation through the "contemplation of the past."[17a]

Developments during the last decades show that changes in the German–American relationship have always ensued from changes in Europe's political structures in a manner which determined the options both of the United States and of the Federal Republic in Europe. "Not every question can be posed at any given time,"[17b] but given the present situation, an understanding of the dynamics of development within the West is a practical necessity. This is particularly true for the United States whose attitude vis-à-vis Western Europe could undergo profound changes before the end of this century, as well as for the Federal Republic which will discover, particularly in its relationship to the United States, that her identity deficit, made possible by Western institutions in the last few decades, cannot endure.

German–American Relations as a European Structural Problem

There are only few relationships in the modern system of states which have generated movements of global importance; the German–American relationship is, in its own special way, one of them. It is distinguished by a peculiar distance and at the same time by fateful entanglement. Exactly one hundred years ago George Bancroft observed that "our foreign policy interests are almost always parallel to those of Germany."[18] The year 1976 provided ample opportunity to apply the same observation to the present. It was as true then as it is today. But "the experience was bitter enough, that it took two World Wars with their devastation and millions of dead before we came to accept our partnership in fate."[19]

1. The Historical Dimension of German–American Relations

Already in the 19th century many far-sighted thinkers had predicted that "America would transform all global relationships."[20] But whereas political leaders in the United States always believed that in order to do so the United States must keep out of Europe's conflicts, there were Europeans, like Friedrich List, who maintained that a conflict between the United States and Great Britain, the European "world power", was unavoidable. The United States intervened twice, hesitatingly to be sure, in the process of European self-dismemberment, twice on the side of Great Britain.[21] Twice, the European war was decided by the United States, each time with a defeated Germany, each time with a drastic increase in the American as well as the Russian power position, but also accompanied by a decline in the power of Great Britain and France.

While Germany's defeat had twice accelerated the rise of the United States to become a world power unparallelled in history, it was also the United States which twice attempted to save Germany from losing its place in the European state system, once with moderate success, and a second time with the result that the Federal Republic was founded "as a product of American strategy."[22] It was also Germany's defeat in 1945 and the manner in which the US helped Germany preserve its existence as a nation which led to the direct confrontation of the US with the Soviet Union[23] and, as a consequence, the ever-increasing, unparallelled US commitment in Western Europe – in foreign policy as well as in military matters.

This development was unusual. It broke with all US foreign policy traditions and proceeded against the resistance of the Soviet Union as well as of France. Moreover, this course in world politics was set primarily as a result of American decisions and Adenauer's policy, although neither the American nor the German side was aware of the extent of the significance of this German–American cooperation. Both sides saw this development rather in the framework of close collaboration with Great Britain and France: in Washington, in the sense of a "mixture of indecision and deficient historical perspective in a narrow and technocratic approach to the German issue;"[24] while "for Adenauer the United States had not become the global antagonist to the Soviet Union."[25] Both perspectives were perfectly coherent at the time. It is rather astonishing that developments which had such far-reaching repercussions nonetheless occurred. This productive provincialism on both sides is expressed in Acheson's *aperçu*: "All that Adenauer and the German people needed in 1949 was a bit of benign disorder."[26]

This was the point of departure for the development of political structures in Western Europe. Great Britain and France tried to tie the US to Europe and keep Germany out of the Soviet Union's sphere of influence. The US engaged itself reluctantly in Western Europe and was at the same time the most outspoken advocate of a United Europe which would include West Germany. West Germany, on the other hand, sought close ties with its Western European neighbors and viewed the US rather as a peripheral power. Thus, the prerequisites for a close German–American relationship were lacking; neither the US nor West Germany sought such a relationship, and the other European powers strived to prevent it. France and the Soviet

Union in particular soon realized the extent to which the nature of this direct relationship with the US would determine rank and influence in Western Europe.

2. The Federal Republic's Western Ties: Equal Status in Europe through Dependence on the United States

In this situation the basic American policy decision that "Germany is a part of Europe" and must find its place as a strong and equal partner,[27] did not only mark the real birth of the Federal Republic, it made the Federal Republic's relationship with the US the fundamental structural problem in the political development of Western Europe.

In Moscow this not only meant the diminishment of any chance of political expansion in Western Europe; seen in connection with Bonn's revisionism and the strategic potential of the US it could be viewed as a threat as well. The Soviet response was to try to lure the Federal Republic into neutrality – even at the price of concessions on the German issue. In Paris, the hopes of rising from the rubble of World War II as the political hegemonial power in Western Europe dwindled, and at the same time the possibility of an economically and militarily strengthened Federal Republic was considered to implicate the revival of old dangers. The French response was to attempt integration of the Federal Republic into a Western European system; an attempt which excluded Great Britain, and at the same time did not provide for institutionalized relations between the Federal Republic and the US, both measures which would make France the primary partner of the US – even at the price of relinquishing certain aspects of national sovereignty.[28]

Each of these approaches found resonance in Bonn – neutrality on the left and the European Defense Community on the right. Both were thwarted by parliamentary realities, the former in Bonn, the latter in Paris. But although in Bonn the Left mourned (at times still mourns) one of the missed opportunities and the Right the other, both incidents strengthened the Federal Republic's position. The Eastern option, at least in the long-run remained a real alternative in the eyes of the West, despite the *integration* of the Federal Republic, and was thus bound to have a lasting affect on France's willingness to integrate as well as on the United States' European commitment. The failure of the European Defense Community led to the Federal Republic's entry into NATO which, in turn, not only freed the formation of a European community from a discriminatory policy towards the Federal Republic in the military sphere but also opened direct institutional relations between the Federal Republic and the US.

Although it became clear that for the Federal Republic "dependence on the United States meant a march toward equality with other Western powers,"[29] no Atlantic orientation developed in Bonn's foreign policy in the years following despite the Adenauer–Dulles concordance; on the contrary, a persistent distrust of changes in American defense policy (Radford Plan) and of a possible rapprochement of the world powers (the Stassen episode or the agent-theory) developed which was bound to increase exponentially as a result of Bonn's self-induced policy of the linkage between security policy and the German issue.[30]

During the fifties both Moscow and Paris had tried to regulate German–American relations through their respective European strategies before the Federal Republic attained full weight as a state.[31] Yet both failed, even though neither Washington nor Bonn gave the German–American relationship priority.[32]

3. Atlantic Partnership: The Federal Republic's Dilemma in Europe

This mistrust of the United States in Adenauer's entourage increased during the Kennedy era while in Washington, on the other hand, reservations intensified vis-à-vis the Federal Republic to an even greater degree than during the Eisenhower era. Nevertheless, American commitment became highly visible during the Berlin crisis of 1961; at the same time, the Federal Republic was becoming one of the major sectors in the controversy over nuclear sharing in NATO[33] and was one of the central intended participants in Kennedy's concept of Atlantic partnership. A more marked Atlantic orientation developed in Bonn,[34] despite Adenauer, and rather importantly as the result of the growing support for such a policy within the SPD. Moreover, although without deliberately aiming at bilateral relations, the United States' European policy effectively allowed the Federal Republic to grow into a partner role, a situation which, nonetheless, was increasingly interpreted in Moscow and Paris as an American–German axis.

Given this new situation, Moscow sought to isolate the Federal Republic through a détente policy directed towards Bonn's allies rather than to pursue a policy of German neutralization. On the other hand, France no longer endeavored to integrate the Federal Republic in the framework of a Western European system (sanctioned by the United States and acting as an American partner) under French leadership but instead tried to force the Federal Republic to choose between Atlantic orientation and a Western European integration policy directed against the United States. Given the domestic political situation, the Soviet campaign produced an echo in some NATO countries, just as the French campaign was not without effect in the Federal Republic.

The MLF symbolized Washington's willingness to meet the Federal Republic halfway in this phase, and the support which it found in Bonn was aimed primarily at further committing the US in Western Europe. But its artificiality was at the same time the expression of an insufficiently developed intermeshing of American and German interests. In addition, it provided the preventive diplomacy of the Soviet Union or that of France with a welcome point for criticism.

Hence, when the MLF project finally failed, this was seen as a symptom of profound disturbance in the German–American relationship, although the causes lay primarily in the domestic situation in Washington and to an even greater degree in Germany.[35] The 1966 crisis between Bonn and Washington resulted, above all, from the failure on both sides to take advantage of momentary opportunities. However, the failure of the MLF was perceived, especially in Bonn, as being associated with the signing of the Non-Proliferation Treaty which, in turn, was viewed as proof of the long-feared rapprochement of the two super powers, although it could, on the contrary, be best understood as the product of domestic political interests of the American President.

Thus this phase of predominantly Atlantic orientation in the foreign policy of the FRG came to an end. With the MLF it had lost a completely adequate instrument and although the signing of the Non-Proliferation Treaty had no direct consequences for the Western defense system, it was seen as having robbed the Atlantic Alliance of its significance as the main framework of cooperation for Western foreign policy. All this was enhanced as the United States extended involvement in Vietnam, whereas the tendency towards détente increased, in particular in the smaller NATO states. At the same time, although France relinquished its veto rights through its withdrawal from NATO and thus cleared the way for military agreements in that alliance, a situation was thereby created which deprived the FRG of the possibility of finally harmonizing its integration policy in the NATO framework. Throughout the entire "Johnson agony" the United States ceased pursuing a European policy, so that the FRG saw itself doubly robbed of its Atlantic option and without any alternative to this state of affairs.

In the late sixties the US did not, as a consequence of the Non-Proliferation Treaty, give priority to relations with the Soviet Union over Atlantic relations as had often been feared. The US was itself in a state of internal unrest and paralysis regarding its foreign policy; this, in turn aroused increasing indignation in Europe over Vietnam and alarm over the possible repercussions for the Alliance. In Germany, on the other hand, a temporary lack of structural options was accompanied by growing anti-Americanism in the Federal Republic and declining support within the alliance for Bonn's stand on the German issue. It is characteristic of the bizarre nature of this situation that the Alliance conceived MBFR in order to maintain a coordinating function in relations with the Soviet Union and to secure the military presence of the US in Western Europe in negotiations with the Soviet Union.

4. Parallelism in the Ostpolitik: A Capacity for Action Gained by a Decoupling in German–American Relations

The way towards change was paved by the elections in the US and in the FRG in 1969, even though one might rather have expected increasing difficulties due to the victory of the conservative Grand Old Party in Washington and the social–liberal coalition in Bonn. The Federal Republic had not only had to give up its integration concept – which provided for political integration above all within the Western European framework, yet under the primacy of military security incorporated in the Atlantic Alliance – it was also threatened with isolation if it persisted in its policy of non-recognition. Especially the weakness of community policy and particularly of French policy favored the tendency to meet the Soviet Union halfway at the expense of the FRG; similarly, it was the weakness of Atlantic and especially of American policy in this period which stimulated American détente policy vis-à-vis Moscow. Washington, in turn, could only win back domestic support for its foreign policy by attempting to reorganize its relations with the Soviet Union and China. Yet at the same time it was afraid to weaken the alliance with Western Europe and Japan to such an extent that the attempt to create such a new order would be bound to fail.[36]

The FRG was of crucial importance in this context. Out of many possible constellations, the most favorable actually came into being. The FRG sought to reorganize its relations with the East in such a way as to make regulation of its relationship with the GDR feasible; however, Western backing was required in this undertaking. The US wanted to reorganize its relations with the East in such a way that its alliances could take on new, politically viable functions; but to this end it needed disencumbrance of the German question, i.e., it had to act in consensus with the FRG. Without a wide-scale American Ostpolitik into which Bonn's concept could be fitted and without Bonn's willingness to find a *modus vivendi* with the GDR, grave frictions would have developed in the German–American relationship and the two policies would have failed in any case.

Coming from a conservative American administration the former policy was just as surprising as the latter, coming as it did from a social–liberal coalition whose parliamentary majority hung by a thread. Both developments, nonetheless, got under way – not without mutual distrust at first, though eventually with remarkable synchronization between Washington and Bonn regarding their respective Ostpolitiks.[37]

Until the late sixties the FRG tried to block its allies' relations with the East in such a way that reciprocal solidarity became the main criterion of German–American relations – at the price of its own flexibility and growing isolation, indeed of vulnerability to blackmail by third parties (namely France). For varying but equally pressing reasons both Bonn and Washington now strove with a considerable degree of synchronization to attain freedom of maneuver by reorganizing their relations with the East. This German–American accord ensued more out of a parallelism of interests than out of a common strategy. Thus in this phase as well it was not actually political concordance between Bonn and Washington which led to the synchronized moves in German and American foreign policy. On the contrary, it was the result of an accidentally favorable constellation. But both Washington and Bonn did indeed gain considerable freedom of maneuver in foreign policy; Washington in its new global policy, and Bonn in a new margin of maneuver in Europe.

The FRG shook off the burden of its previous stand on the German issue. As a result, Moscow came to regard and accept the FRG as the leading Western European power. Moreover, the FRG is also now immune to French pressure on the German question and has been able to evoke sufficient political confidence to make possible Great Britain's entrance into the European Community, and to give the European Community new momentum as well.[38] At the same time, France, which saw itself robbed of its own options by Bonn's Ostpolitik, and other Western allies, which saw this policy rather as disburdening for the Westpolitik, developed a new image of the FRG with looser ties to the West; this image presumably further enforced their willingness to pursue political integration in this period.[39]

Thus, Ostpolitik had consequences above all for the Western alliance and was in this sense short-term, that is, it was valid up to the point where a modus vivendi was established. As a result, although the Eastern policy may only have been feasible in the framework of considerable collaterality with American foreign policy, it did not provide German–American relations with any lasting priority in the policy of the FRG. Washington certainly did not adhere to such a priority. On the contrary, the Ostpolitik and the Berlin Agreement reduced the compulsion for Washington to always consider

Bonn's special problems in their deliberations – a factor which had determined the character of German-American relations for almost two decades. Hence, the establishment of diplomatic relations between the US and the GDR also symbolizes a kind of normalization in the relations between Washington and Bonn.

One burden in the German–American relationship had been removed. It was no longer susceptible to the diplomatic intervention of third parties as had previously been the case. Moreover, even beyond the period of active Ostpolitik Washington was impressed by Bonn's capacity for action, to such an extent that, as early as 1971, Connally began to advocate close collaboration with Bonn in economic matters as well. However, while the Ostpolitik did open up a new margin of maneuver in German–American relations, it did not establish any lasting role distribution either in the German or in the American foreign policy of those years. An Atlantic orientation in integration policy had in any case been impossible since the mid-sixties.[40]

5. Beyond Multilateralism: The Federal Republic as a Broker and the New US Hegemony

Whereas in the past Bonn was often caught and "immobilized" between Washington and Paris or between Paris and London, it now began, with the support of the other Western European governments, to act increasingly as a mediator. Thus an unexpected revival in the formation of the Community took place which, despite the Jobert episode, left France without any real opportunities to assert a veto.[41] European–American tensions no longer resulted from French obstruction but rather were the outcome of economic competition. To be sure, after gaining momentum for a short period, the goal of the development of a political community in the sense of institutional unity receded into the distant future, but the actual intermeshing progressed steadily. "The European societies are developing a transnationalism of unprecedented intensity and depth."[42] This development opened up new possibilities for harmonious political collaboration, especially inter-party cooperation, which was later to prove valuable in difficult situations, as for example during the Portuguese crisis. In Washington, however, where one still thought primarily in institutional categories, this development evoked a diffuse picture of Western Europe.

Nevertheless, it was Washington in 1973 which tried to bring community building and the revival of the Alliance together under the banner of the Atlantic concept (The Year of Europe). But wherever a joint approach by the

Nine took shape Washington was strangely unprepared to perceive the institutional realities. For example, instead of negotiating over the Atlantic Declaration with the President of the European Council, the US sought its partners, for the most part, in London, Paris and Bonn. This was partly the result of the American evaluation of Western European realities, and partly the result of its new tendency towards bilateralism which paradoxically found its counterpart in France where the conceptual antithesis to Washington was the strongest. It was, above all, the FRG which successfully resisted the bilateralism of both countries. Moreover, by insisting on the observance of multilateral procedures, the FRG increasingly grew into a mediator role.

However, in substantive terms Kissinger's efforts to restore the Alliance – as manifested in the suggestion of a new Atlantic Declaration – coincided with real West German interests; ten years after the failure of Atlanticism, Kissinger once again attempted to find a consensus for that variety of Western integration which assured the protecting power, the US, of its political weight in Western Europe, while at the same time enabling the FRG to reconcile its alliance policy with its Community policy – relieved of the mortgage of the German issue and half a decade after de Gaulle's withdrawal. Miscalculations in Bonn, the impending crisis of authority in Washington, irritation over the San Clemente Agreement and the improvised character of Kissinger's initiative[43] all contributed to the final result: the splitting of the Declaration which once again marked the end of Atlanticism.

In retrospect, none of Bonn's reservations appear sound but the events of 1973/74 did demonstrate that Kissinger's attempt was just as poor a response to the new challenges as was the Western European alternative. It was no longer possible to establish a Community with the regional internal orientation which had been dominant up to that point. Due to external reasons the foundations for economic and monetary cooperation in the European Community were shaken, and, at the same time, the narrow limits to the solidarity between the European Community countries became evident under crisis conditions. The Western European supply of raw materials was visibly dependent upon developments in security policy which had previously not been taken into consideration in the framework of the Alliance (above all developments in the Middle East) and which could, in the final analysis, only be decisively influenced by the US.[44] At the same time it became obvious that the foundations for economic and monetary cooperation in the EC could only be reconstructed in an international framework which likewise extended far beyond the Atlantic Alliance. Here, once again, the US would be the decisive power without itself being as dependent on international regulation and guaranteed raw materials as the European Community.

This development was accompanied by an increasingly marked North–South discrepancy within the Community which not only set narrow limits to a policy of economic stability within the EC framework; even if the process of economic integration were to be maintained or, indeed, to proceed, this discrepancy was bound to call in question the possibility of common political loyalties within the EC. This in turn would tend, at least in the long run, to weaken the willingness of the US to maintain its military presence in Western Europe – let alone its willingness to expand it in view of new threats. American alliance policy has always been oriented on the basis of criteria concerning sufficient political homogeneity.

Paradoxically, it was the Federal Republic which was confronted with this new situation sooner than anyone else. The FRG had supported the US in the Yom Kippur War more than almost any other Western European NATO nation. But when insufficient coordination in the shipping of American military equipment led to discord in the German–American relationship Washington saw the necessity to undertake a "profound reappraisal" of American responsibilities vis-à-vis the Federal Republic.[45]

In the spring of 1974 when the EC opted for their own dialogue with the Arab nations, Bonn tried to mediate between the American course of confrontation in relation to the OPEC countries and French anti-American-ism, with the result that the Euro-Arabian dialogue did indeed get off to a late start. Washington's irritation on the other hand was immediately voiced in a frosty exchange of letters between Nixon and Brandt.[46] A mere three months later Washington and Bonn deemed it nonetheless necessary to counter the impression of a "Bonn–Washington Axis."[47]

This rapid change was not only favored by "the idiosyncrasy of the American mentality."[48] It also corresponded to the novel situation of the FRG which now saw itself robbed of the protective conformity of both institutions in which it had sought to unfold its identity – the European Community and the Atlantic Alliance – according to the stereotype formula "community with France and security through the USA."[49] In a certain sense, an inversion of Atlanticism had taken place.

6. Change in the European Situation

Looking back on the five stages of Western structural development over the last 25 to 30 years, the present state appears as the end-product of a step by step inversion of the European situation. The following were the basic stages of development:

The period of recovery presented Europe as a functional unit with internal hegemonial claims; with hesitant US ties to the continent which were understood by all to be temporary; and with a FRG as the product of American strategy, and opportunities for Soviet political influence as well as for potential clients in Europe.

In the phase of the FRG's integration, Western Europe was still regarded as a functional unit which was to take on its institutional form through the dynamics of economic integration. At the same time Western Europe sought its security through increasing American commitment to Europe in NATO. This had several consequences for its further development: first, it relativized the political nature of the Community in the making; second, it introduced a trend towards equality between the larger nations of the Community through their increasingly equal status in relation to the US; third, it limited the opportunities for Soviet opposition to a multilateral system which was taking form in the West; fourth, it made the regulation of Western Europe's relations with the US relatively uncontroversial, since the new US alliance policy was based on enlightened self-interest and the Community did not yet appear to the US as a competitor. The FRG became the direct partner of the US in this phase and profited considerably from the equalizing effect of these relations in Western Europe although the military integration of the FRG was constrained by the consequences of the American decision.

During the phase of Atlantic partnership, the success of Western European economic integration began to assume a significance in its own right – from both the American and the Soviet perspective. It relativized Western Europe as an economic unit, however, since at this stage regulatory needs within the extended Atlantic framework came into play; problems could not be resolved within the European Community without the participation of the US, being that it was also involved in the mesh of relationships. At the same time Western Europe began to develop a political will of its own, in part as the outcome of the dynamics of economic integration ("spill-over") and in part out of fear both of American dominance and of American disengagement, which in turn demonstrated Western Europe's military dependence on the US. This, in turn, relativized the goal of European unity, which from then on was pursued, above all, at the security policy level. The dollar flow to Western Europe together with the ensuring deterioration of the US balance of payments as well as the American nuclear monopoly and the resulting US overcommitment were problems confronting both the US and Western Europe. The American answer was the "Grand Design" and "Nuclear Sharing," the French answer was the gold standard and proliferation.

As a result, it was no longer possible to harmonize Western European unity with the Atlantic framework; the dynamism of Western European integration had slackened, not only at the security policy level but at the economic level as well. For the first time, the Soviet Union could engage in interference through negotiations with the US, that is, in negotiations which had repercussions for the Alliance. Western Europe's dependency on the US had become an irreversible political reality while at the same time the United States' role as the leading power in the West was rapidly dwindling. The FRG, which had been given preferential treatment by the US in order to counterbalance France once again, was only able to carry out a policy of integration with the support of both France and the US, and thus lost its options at both levels: the Community no longer offered the option of federation, and without an Atlantic regulatory mechanism it became more and more vulnerable to the threat of American protectionism; as concerns the Alliance, the US (whose military indispensability had only recently been acknowledged) became more and more entangled in Southeast Asia, an involvement which began to undermine the political prerequisites for American protection. That is, NATO was unchallenged within Western Europe as the framework for Western European security with the sole exception of Paris while, on the other hand, the US gave priority to security interests outside NATO.

German–American relations were characterized in this phase by the development away from Bonn's immobilizing role as a key figure in Atlantic politics towards an immobilizing lack of options for Bonn.[50] Western Europe's self-sufficiency would have been relativized with or without the development of an Atlantic partnership. But, whereas the FRG was, for the first time, being assigned an active partner role in American policy the phase ended in a climate of considerable intergovernmental indifference with signs of an anti-Americanism not only on the Left but on the Right as well.[51]

During the phase of the Ostpolitik, Western Europe was further relativized as an economic unit by growing internal discrepancies in economic growth as well as the increasing effects of interventions caused by American economic stability measures, while at the same time the role of individual states, particularly the FRG, became more prominent in negotiated adjustment between the Western industrial states. Also, the Ostpolitik helped to remove internal obstacles to integration, in part by building up the confidence of the smaller partners, in part by eliminating possibilities for French obstruction. Moreover, it also diminished the possibilities for Soviet pressure and brought about a remarkably harmonious coordination of American and Western European diplomacy in specific questions. But the political unity of the Community was also relativized by the increasing heterogeneity within the European Community and the increased need for the integration of Western European nonmember states. The dynamics of economic integration almost entirely ceased to open up new possibilities for political unification. On the contrary, it became necessary to find new channels of political harmonization in order to maintain the prerequisites for an economic community.

The Ostpolitik had thus changed the constellations in Western Europe in such a way that different approaches to relations with the East could no longer serve as a vehicle of internal contention or a cause of irritation. But at the same time political forces were growing in Western Europe which could be seen as potential political clients of the Soviet Union. This began to call a fundamental assumption of American European policy into question at a moment when the role of the Alliance in America's endeavor to establish new international peace structures still appeared unclear. Accompanying the advancing bilateralism of the two superpowers was a growing US influence in critical regions such as the Middle East, while the role of Western Europe remained marginal, that is, with the exception of the close and important collaboration between Washington and Bonn on relations with the East.

Watergate, and the fourth Middle East War with its repercussions, kept this development from reaching its culmination. The new situation is distinguished by the following characteristics: Western Europe has ceased to represent a functional unit with a chance of attaining political independence in matters of economy, currency, raw materials supply and military security. In all four realms its dependence on others – above all on the US – has grown. The effort to maintain political homogeneity as far as possible is, nonetheless, an imperative of economic, political and security policy. Consequently, political unification has become an end in itself, but economic and military integration no longer represent solutions; on the contrary they must be maintained through political unification.[52] Such unification need not be conceived in terms of an institutional form,[53] but it must allow for Western European participation in all four realms within a broad international framework in which the US is the dominant power in each sphere.[54] This unification must create and maintain a sufficient capacity for common action in Western Europe – not as an end in itself in the formation of the Community – but, above all, to make possible the management of the foreign affairs of Western Europe in the four realms. Just as the European Community by no means represents the primary framework for the regulation of the international economic relations of its members, in the long run NATO will cease to be a sufficient framework for maintaining Western European security. The integrative framework has become weaker and US dominance stronger at both levels, while the challenges calling for common action have become more complex.

While the Soviet Union is presently more willing than in the past to engage in international multilateralism vis-à-vis Western Europe, and at the same time can hope to acquire direct political influence through the trend to the Left in France and in the Southern European countries, the US is pursuing a policy directed more towards individual partners in Western Europe than towards the EC: increasing political heterogeneity can at the same time lead to a re-examination of the American role in the multilateral organizations of the West. The US needs the cooperation of Western Europe but no longer believes so strongly that it needs a united Western Europe.[55] The bilateralism of the superpowers allowed for a temporary harmonization of Western diplomacy which caused Washington to approach military questions too hesitantly and economic problems too rigorously in Western Europe. An American globalism then followed which strove for solutions which had greater impact on Western European than on American interests, a globalism which could, however, lead Washington to overlook both the necessity of political unification for Western Europe's capacity for external cooperation and the realities of the East–West relationship in Europe – realities which for the first time in 30 years make direct Soviet intervention under conditions of growing Soviet military superiority appear possible.

It could be that American globalism will realize the necessities and realities of political unification in Western Europe in regional categories at that very point in time; in important Western European capitals it has already been recognized more clearly than ever that "partnership with the US is the Archimedean point from which the unification of Europe has first become conceivable and feasible."[56]

Structure and Perspectives in the Development of German –American Relations

1. Analytical Deficits in Political Practice

For a full three decades the relations between industrial nations have been determined by an unprecedented multilateralism in consensus formation and interdependence between national processes. In classic diplomacy, essentially the only multilateralist category was that of the balance of power. International politics consisted ultimately of bilateral processes and the repercussions on third parties. In this perspective the internal dynamics of action of individual states was, as a rule, hardly taken into consideration.[57] In recent years a genuine bilateralism is only to be found in the relationship between the antagonistic superpowers which is primarily determined by the mutual recognition of contrary internal politico-social conditions. It thus still displays the primacy of foreign policy which characterized classic diplomacy. Genuinely bilateral interactions between Western industrial nations (i.e., where outcomes are essentially defined in terms of interests of the two sides) are by definition of secondary importance regardless of how the momentary preferential procedures in important questions may appear.

The postwar system was characterized by stable role differentiation, persistent elites, a regulation of priority conflicts in terms of the primacy of security, by a remarkable absence of upsets in economic relations and thus by levels of action which could be clearly isolated and which allowed the paradigm of the "rational actor" to become the dominant interpretation in practice and research.[58] Here, national governments are "black boxes" and international organizations are ends in themselves. This is particularly true of Washington and Bonn where for different reasons (simplified management in the one and mimicry in the other) the multilateral orientation was particularly predominant. Until a few years ago Bonn's standard interpretation was to identify the interests and positions of the US with explanations offered by American representatives in international organizations like NATO, thus leaving themselves open to be surprised by repercussions of internal changes in Washington.

By and large this system stabilized the roles of the participants in the long run. A state can be thought of as a kind of "monad" with temporarily pre-stabilized harmony. This is true despite the developmental dynamics of the last three decades which did, indeed, alter the distribution of roles from time to time, yet in such a manner that the system was *perceived* in a given situation and remained the basis for decision and action. But the limits of this system necessarily became evident whenever a member state sought independence, as in the case of France, or when in selective decision-making processes mutual misperceptions came into play as illustrated by exceptional cases such as the MLF or the Skybolt affair.[59] In this system it usually made no fundamental difference whether communication channels were well-developed or weak as Washington's graduated indifference to the policy of various partners suggests.[60]

In recent years, such relational structures between Western industrial states have become increasingly weak.[61] Variations in the distribution of roles are more frequent and more pronounced; changes in the political elites have become less controllable and more momentous in their repercussions for third parties; dominating priorities no longer function as unquestionably acknowledged regulators; and the disturbances in international economic relations have reached proportions in which the elimination of national economic failures and the preservation of conditions for international stability have become incongruous. The multilateral aspect of consensus formation has become weaker in this situation whereas the interdependence of internal political economic and social processes has become stronger. Indifference as to the internal state of others has become less tolerable than was previously evident in bilateral relations. At the same time the weakening of multilateral structures has resulted in a far higher number of sensitive interactions and a far less effective communication through permanent representatives. The probability of bilateral frictions thus increases. And in no other case would third parties be as severely affected as in the case of German–American frictions. This makes prudent management of these relations a practical necessity from the point of view of all Western industrial states. Even where such frictions could lead in one case or another to short-term coalitions between third parties and Bonn or Washington as could be observed, for example, in the preparations for the London summit in 1977.

2. Change of Administration in the US

New American administrations in 1953, 1961 and 1969 brought about profound changes in the system of Western cooperation. Since 1969 a transformation of international relations, effected especially through the foreign policy of the US, has taken place. A transformation which, despite increasingly weakened multilateral structures, has enhanced the freedom of action of the US as well as of Western Europe – amongst themselves, in relation to the Soviet Union and in the Third World. Today apprehension is widespread in Western Europe that the foreign policy which survived Watergate will not survive the new change of administration.[62] This is in part a normal Western European reaction to a change of American administration. In part it results from the comparison of the "European" inclination of the old administration with the political idiosyncrasies of the new American leadership, yet it also reflects the increased weakness of the conditions of stability which determined the system of Western cooperation in the past few decades.

In the coming years, it is possible that political change will take place in a number of Western European countries, such as France, which could even more directly impair the willingness for cooperation between the Western industrial countries. But the fact that the American hegemonial position is at its strongest at a time in which multilateral regulatory mechanisms have become weaker coincides with the lesson learned in the Kissinger era in Western European capitals: at the present time a political margin of maneuver does not ensue from the emanation of power potential but is rather the result of diplomacy and the art of leadership. It is not a lack of willingness to cooperate on the part of the new administration which makes Western Europe uneasy; it is the possibility that decisions will be made which for Western Europe would represent wrong decisions at the cost of all involved.

It appears that the present trend in Washington is to sacrifice possibilities for cooperation with the Soviet Union, chances for regulating regional conflicts and relations with precarious allies in favor of a domestically motivated moralism; to pursue a détente policy which abandons the goal of the limitation of Soviet power while at the same time regarding arms controls as the most important level of détente; to relativize the expansion of Soviet influence and the growth of Soviet power in terms of a "One-World" vision;[63] to increase American economic growth at the cost of stability of those partners whose stability has been considered essential in recent years by most Western industrial nations; to acknowledge the demands of the Third World at the cost of Western Europe and Japan instead of looking for common alternatives; to pursue the goal of non-proliferation of nuclear weapons with methods that not only do not promise to be effective in the long run, but also to awaken or enhance the intentions of the recipient nations to proliferate while at the same time making it more difficult for the supplier nations involved to solve their own problems of energy supply, which in the light of new American policies on raw materials and on the Middle East appear more urgent than ever.

These fears exist and they are not unfounded. But they need not necessarily materialize. It is no accident that the FRG is one of the first partners of the US to see itself affected by the repercussions of change in Washington.

3. The FRG as a Partner to the US

As a result of thirty years of European structural development, the German–American relationship cannot be regulated by third parties unless either the US or the FRG offers opportunities to do so. Conversely, decisions made in Bonn and Washington on vital questions concerning economy, monetary matters, security or raw material supply have consequences for third parties regardless of the degree of German–American consensus. As a result of this immediacy, irreversibly detrimental developments are more possible now than in the past. The dwindling stability of political elites as well as the nature of international tasks, which at present lack the preformative influence of multinational organizations, work in favor of such undesirable developments.

But this relationship cannot be based on bilateralism. On the contrary, the US and to an even greater extent the FRG have a vital interest in stability and a politically homogeneous environment; the FRG is concerned because, as a part of a divided Germany, it lies at the dividing line of the two competing industrial society systems and, at the same time, must maintain a sufficient capacity for north–south consensus within Western Europe if it is to avoid fatal instability and polarization.[64] The US is vitally interested because without a complementary political force in Western Europe, it can no longer keep the other superpower in check or maintain the quality of the American politico-social system in the long run.[65] Consensus with partners thus lies in the *raison d'être* of both the US and the FRG. But the relationship is no longer regulated within multilateral structures either. It is thus the task of Washington and Bonn to seek the most suitable form for multilateralization on a case-by-case basis.[66]

The US options for establishing ties obviously differ from those of the FRG; they have – to use a chemical analogy – different valences. The role of the US is more crucial than that of the FRG in all four dimensions – security, economic capacity, monetary stability and raw materials supply. The US would not feel the consequences of political heterogeneity as directly and thus has a greater margin of maneuver. Moreover, Washington is the Archimedean point for the FRG in all important multilateral processes; in the final analysis, without Washington, no structural solutions can be attained. Such structural solutions necessitate consensus which can imply, as recent years have shown, that the FRG has considerable influence on emerging US positions. On the other hand, because the multilateral medium is just as indispensable for the FRG as consensus with the US, the United States can choose between direct cooperation with the Federal Republic on the one hand, and temporary coalitions against the FRG, on the other. The decision to expand the "suppliers club" was the result of such intentions. A similar attitude was observable in the preparation for the London Summit in May 1977, or with regard to UNCTAD IV.

This is enhanced by the fact that the FRG's strengths and weaknesses are but two sides of the same coin. The economic capacity of the FRG is structurally connected with its sensitive dependency on export. As a result of its position in the monetary system, the Federal Republic is confronted simultaneously with the US's pressure towards balance and the irreversible debt of third parties. To be sure, the political stability of the FRG stands out in comparison to that of most of its West European neighbors, but one must still fear that, ultimately, the FRG is politically more vulnerable than others with regard to economic stress (inflation trauma) or to a possible change in the political constellation in Western Europe (a Leftist government in France, for example). The Bundeswehr is the strongest Western European contingent in NATO; the FRG sees itself as the country most directly exposed to the growing military power of the Soviet Union, but has no possibility of meeting this threat alone – and is thus militarily permanently dependent. The FRG is now taking on growing importance for the Third World, above all, in the Middle East, in Africa and in Latin America, however, even in the long run, the FRG will continue to have no capability to project itself as a military power, and yet, as a result of its economic interests, it will be increasingly entangled in regional conflicts (southern Africa) or will appear as a direct competitor to the US (Latin America) – which can, of course, at times well be in the interest of the United States.

On the other hand, in all these dimensions it is also the momentary weakness of third parties which forces the FRG into an active role and which induces Bonn to cooperate directly with the US.[67] It is a paradox that in this situation the active partnership with the US is indispensable for the FRG but at the same time serves the interests of the US more than those of the FRG: just as the strengthening of the FRG's nuclear role in the sixties was not only meant to saturate it but also to balance out third parties (i.e., France). Similarly, Bonn's economic power, which increasingly limits the options of its partners, serves Washington's political power to a greater degree than its own.[68] Perhaps this represents the most stable basis for a German–American community of interest. But it demonstrates at the same time the hegemonial position of the US as well as its political limits.

The efficacy of German–American cooperation structured in the above manner will be seen at four levels: it will crucially affect the development of Western Europe in the next few decades; it will be useful in regions outside Europe (Latin America, Middle East, Southern Africa); it will be selectively important in creating international regimes (e.g., to regulate the spread of civilian nuclear technology) and it will be desirable as a reciprocal learning process in the reform of modern industrial societies.

Western Europe unquestionably has priority in the four dimensions of security, economic capacity, monetary matters and raw materials supply. Yet in all four dimensions solutions cannot be confined to Western Europe or the Atlantic region. Western Europe's security requires that a conventional defense capacity be created without weakening nuclear deterrence, that crises outside NATO territory which could have repercussions for Western Europe can be influenced without weakening the multilateral coherence of NATO,[69] that the political potential of Soviet military power be limited through arms control, without allowing NATO members to be put under domestic pressure to attain successful negotiation outcomes. Western Europe's economic productivity requires, above all, that a compromise be found which does not endanger the FRG's stability and supportive capacity, while at the same time maintaining its export options and promoting the growth of its partners with the goal of alleviating unemployment as a high-priority political goal. Stable monetary relations require not only that the productive capacities of the Western economies be brought into balance, but that this balance be maintained vis-à-vis the surpluses of the OPEC countries and the indebtedness of large sectors of the Third World and COMECON. And lastly, a secured supply of raw material requires measures to decrease dependence, namely in the energy sector (by reducing consumption and through diversification) and measures for securing raw material supply by creating politico-economic incentives in the framework of the efforts to establish a new world economic order and by avoiding crises or making them controllable through preventive diplomacy and an ability to project power.

The political stability of Western Europe, so vitally important for both the US and the FRG, can only be decisively influenced through developments at all four levels. But not even a pragmatic policy on both sides will be able to prevent sensitive political heterogeneity in Western Europe in the long run. The French elections in 1978 could represent a first incisive break. Such a development would confront both the US and the FRG in Western Europe with fundamental conceptual questions for which no adequate answers exist today, either here or there, except perhaps that, even with a strong Communist participation in government, France would still remain in Western Europe and continue to share stability requisites with its neighbors.

In such a situation German–American cooperation will become more necessary and more difficult than ever. It will require a kind of political leadership for which the history of postwar Western Europe offers no parallel – the more so as such a development would tend to reinforce interdependencies with the three other levels of German–American cooperation. This is particularly true of the reciprocal "spill-over"[70] of the reforms of modern industrial societies. The common interest in Western European stability will, in the long run, have to prove itself by maintaining enough common ground through the modernization of Western industrial societies in the coming decades so as not to lose the basis for political consensus in vital questions of stability and security. Given such a perspective, "it is logical that that process which was somewhat bluntly called the Americanization of Europe corresponds to a gentle Europeanization of America."[71] Here lies the hope of Western Europe. It describes the most important imperative of German–American cooperation.

Notes

[1] It is certainly true of the postwar period that "when the American government lost leverage over these (domestic) structures, it tended to forget them ... For the US government Adenauer never died, de Gaulle was a bad dream, the Christian Democrats would rule Italy for ever, and it didn't matter who was in power at Westminster." (Nicholas Wahl: *The Autonomy of "Domestic Structures" in European–American Relations*, in: James Chance and Earl C. Ravenal, (eds.): *Atlantis Lost. U.S.–European Relations after the Cold War*. New York: New York UP 1976, pp. 231 f.).

[2] cf. Uwe Nerlich: *Continuity and Change: The Political Context of Western Europe's Defense*, in: Johan J. Holst and Uwe Nerlich, (eds.): *Beyond Nuclear Deterrence. New Aims, New Arms*. New York: Crane, Russak 1977, pp. 20–29.

[3] Speech by Federal Chancellor Helmut Schmidt in Baltimore, 16 July 1976, in: Bulletin, No. 89, 29 July 1976, p. 844.

[4] As it was put in one of the basic documents of American security policy after 1945, NSC-68, which has just recently been released for publication: *NSC-68. A Report to the National Security Council, April 1950*, in: Naval War College Review, May/June 1975, p. 67f. The static concept of an homogeneous environment corresponded to the concept of the intermediary zone from the dynamic point of view of the Soviet Union.

[5] See Henry Kissinger's Boston speech of 11 March 1976, in: The Department of State Bulletin, No. 1919, 5 April 1976, pp. 425–432, or Zbigniew Brzezinski in: James Chace and Earl C. Ravenal, *Atlantis Lost*, loc. cit., footnote 1, pp. 85ff., or by the same author: *America in a Hostile World*, in: Foreign Policy, No. 24, 1976, pp. 73, 92ff.

[6] cf. Uwe Nerlich: *Détente und Westpolitik. Zum Verhältnis von außenpolitischem Pluralismus und innerer Stabilität Westeuropas*, in: Europa-Archiv, No. 4, 1976, pp. 105–112.

[7] Zbigniew Brzezinski in: Chace and Ravenal, (eds.): *Atlantis Lost*, loc. cit., footnote 1, p. 254.

[8] Klaus Harpprecht very suitably depicted this changing attention in Washington. (*Henry Kissingers liebstes Kind. Wie Wichtig ist Bonn für Washington?* in: Deutsche Zeitung, 15 August 1975, p. 5.) With typical impatience about the complex Western European decision-making mechanisms, Washington often overlooks the multitude of voices with which it often presents itself to its partners on critical questions.

[9] cf. C. Fred Bergsten's plea for bigemony: *The United States and Germany: The Imperative of Economic Bigemony*, in: *Toward a New International Economic Order*, Lexington, Mass.: Heath 1975.

[10] cf. Neue Zürcher Zeitung, 9 February 1977, p. 13.

[11] cf. the interview with Federal Chancellor Helmut Schmidt in: Der Spiegel No. 1–2, 1975, pp. 30–35. Concerning a cause of frequent American misunderstanding of political processes in the Federal Republic cf. Robert Gerald Livingston: "There is little evidence that those who make our policy have fully considered what Germany's rising influence abroad and its self-reliant policies portend," in: *Germany Steps Up*,

Foreign Policy, No. 22, 1976, p. 115. See also Richard E. Neustadt's comments in: *Alliance Politics*, New York and London: Columbia UP 1970, p. 143.

[12] While hopes are attached to German–US cooperation, which was increasingly the case in the Benelux countries and Scandinavia since the Social Democrat/Liberal coalition and Ostpolitik (cf. Livingston, loc. cit., p. 121), at the same time it is also a source of anxiety. But whereas on the other hand such areas of conflict appear to the Soviets partly as an indication of decay, partly as a restriction of exchanges, and already regard capitalist "contradictions" with special interest, particularly in France, the dangers of a German–US stability policy are evoked. This is seen as an interventionism vis-à-vis Western European independence or social change, in such way that Sartre's formula of the "last bulwark against a Europe dominated by a German–American bigemony" (quoted from: Die Welt, 11 February 1977, p. 1) is of relevance to the "socialist militants" (Sartre) and at the same time to the militant Gaullists. In a more moderate form, this also finds current expression in the trilateralism of the United States, the Federal Republic and Japan (cf. for example Alain Vernay, *Le choix de Carter: Europe ou Allemagne?* in: Figaro, 10 February 1977).

[13] Peter Katzenstein: *West Germany's Place in American Foreign Policy: Pivot, Anchor, or Broker?* in: Richard Rosecrance, (ed.): *America as an Ordinary Country. US Foreign Policy and the Future*, Ithaca and London: Cornell UP 1976, p. 111.

[14] Edward Hallett Carr: *What is History?*, New York, London: Macmillan 1961, p. 8.

[15] Daniel J. Boorstin: *The Genius of American Politics*, Chicago: University of Chicago Press 1953, p. 33.

[16] The postwar situation with its selective understanding of history favored the "German disposition for suppression after 1945" (Joachim C. Fest: Hitler. Eine Biographie, Frankfurt/Berlin/Vienna: Propyläen 1973, p. 1039) just as much as did the change in basic American attitudes after 1945 (cf. Gebhard Schweigler: *Politikwissenschaft und Außenpolitik in den USA*, Munich: Oldenbourg 1977, pp. 259 f.). Furthermore, German and American political culture can be characterized through their specific lack of historical thinking, although for fundamentally different reasons: unusual discontinuity in the first, and similar unusual continuity in the second case. In both cases the result was, according to Daniel Boorstin, an "obstinate provincialism" (loc. cit., p. 35).

[17] Fest: *Hitler*, loc. cit., p. 1040.

[17a] Waldemar Besson: *Die Außenpolitik der Bundesrepublik*, Munich: Piper 1970, p. 445.

[17b] Ernst Nolte: *Deutschland und der Kalte Krieg*, Munich: Piper 1974.

[18] Quoted from Alfred Vagts: *Deutschland und die Vereinigten Staaten in der Weltpolitik*, Vol. 2, New York: Macmillan 1935, p. 1914.

[19] Speech by Federal Chancellor Helmut Schmidt in Baltimore, 16 July 1976, loc. cit., footnote 3, p. 844.

[20] Friedrich List: *Die politisch-ökonomische Nationalheinheit der Deutschen*, in: *Schriften, Reden, Briefe*, Vol. 7, Berlin: Hobbing 1931, p. 487.

[21] See Erwin Hölzle's new interpretation of World War I (*Die Selbstentmachtung Europas*, Göttingen: Musterschmidt 1975), with which Hölzle has further developed his previous studies on the entrance of the United States and Russia into world politics (see above all: *Rußland und Amerika. Aufbruch und Begegnung zweier Weltmächte*, Munich: Oldenbourg 1953).

[22] Besson, loc. cit., footnote 17a. See above all Hans-Peter Schwarz: *Vom Reich zur Bundesrepublik*, Neuwied: Luchterhand 1966, pp. 39–146.

[23] If Wilson's peace endeavors in favor of Germany were born out of basic attitudes, then the American endeavors after 1945 ensued from the abrupt end of universalist hopes as expressed in the Stuttgart speech of Secretary of State Byrnes, 6 September 1946 (reprinted in: Department of State: *The United States and Germany 1945–55*. Washington: US Government Printing Office 1955). Compare also Werner Link: *Zum Problem der Kontinuität der amerikanischen Deutschland-Politik im 20. Jahrhundert*, in: Manfred Knapp, (ed.): *Die deutsch-amerikanischen Beziehungen nach 1945*, Frankfurt, New York: Campus Verlag 1975, pp. 86–131.

[24] W. W. Rostow: *The United States in the World Arena. An Essay in Recent History*, New York: Harper 1960, p. 100.

[25] Besson: *Außenpolitik der Bundesrepublik*, loc. cit., footnote 17a, p. 58. According to Besson both Adenauer and Schumacher had "a common purely Euro-centric perspective in 1949, for even Schumacher ignored the United States as a standard for orientation" (op. cit., p. 67). On the further development of Adenauer's relationship to the United States see, above all Kurt Birrenbach: *Adenauer und die Vereinigten Staaten in der Periode seiner Kanzlerschaft*, in: *Konrad Adenauer und seine Zeit*, Vol. 1, Stuttgart: Deutsche Verlags-Anstalt 1976, pp. 477–509.

[26] Dean Acheson: *Present at the Creation*, New York: Norton 1969 (paperback edition), p. 447.

[27] The Stuttgart speech of Secretary of State Byrnes on 6 September 1946, loc. cit., footnote 23, p. 16.

[28] cf. Uwe Nerlich: *Die Dilemmas französischer Sicherheitspolitik in Westeuropa*, in: Europa-Archiv, No. 8, 1974, pp. 238 f.

[29] Stanley Hoffmann: *Gulliver's Troubles, or the Setting of American Foreign Policy*, for the Council on Foreign Relations, New York: McGraw-Hill 1968, p. 398.

[30] This development makes clear that the widespread concept of the "penetrated system" cannot say much about the actual development of the German–American relationship or, indeed, about its repercussions on third parties. Hans-Peter Schwarz has already pointed this out with reference to Adenauer's role. cf. *Konrad Adenauer und seine Zeit*. Vol. 2, Stuttgart: Deutsche Verlags-Anstalt 1976, p. 605.

[31] It hardly came as a surprise that a "coalition of losers" finally came into play in the mid-fifties, i.e. a Franco-Soviet entente, with the goal of preventing at least the material integration of the Federal Republic into the Atlantic Alliance.

[32] The communicative prerequisites simply did not exist. Bonn's ignorance of American policy became evident in 1956 when it was completely surprised by the Radford Plan although it had been discussed in substance ("New Look") for two years. In Washington, a knowledge of Bonn's policy did not even seem necessary: "In the Adenauer era, and thereafter for a time, it scarcely seemed to matter whether we guessed right or wrong about what moved a German player in his own game or how our moves resonated inside his own machine, ... We then possessed a wide latitude for ignorance." (Richard E. Neustadt: *Alliance Politics*, loc. cit., footnote 11, p. 144.)

[33] cf. Uwe Nerlich: *Die nuklearen Dilemmas der Bundesrepublik Deutschland*, in: Europa-Archiv, No. 17, 1965, pp. 637 ff.

[34] "It was above all Gerhard Schröder who sought new foundations for the ties to America in the sixties. He and an overwhelming majority of the Bundestag were convinced that France represented no substitute, since the security of the Federal Republic and West Berlin was still as dependent as ever on the United States." (Waldemar Besson: *Die Außenpolitik der Bundesrepublik*, loc. cit., footnote 17a, p. 446.)

[35] On the circumstances of this failure see Philip Geyelin: *Lyndon B. Johnson and the World*, London: Pall Mall Press 1966, pp. 159–180. Geyelin's description is evidently based on the confidential report made by Richard Neustadt for President Johnson. See also Uwe Nerlich: *Der NV-Vertrag in der Politik der BRD. Zur Struktur eines außenpolitischen Prioritätskonflikts.* SWP-S 217, Ebenhausen: Stiftung Wissenschaft und Politik 1973.

[36] cf. Uwe Nerlich: *Westeuropa und die Entwicklung des amerikanisch-sowjetischen Bilateralismus*, in: Europa-Archiv, No. 20, 1972, pp. 687–702. *Die Anfänge des neuen amerikanisch-sowjetischen Bilateralismus*, in: *Die Internationale Politik 1968–1969. Jahrbücher des Forschungsinstituts der Deutschen Gesellschaft für Auswärtige Politik*, Munich, Vienna: Oldenbourg 1974, pp. 113–137.

[37] cf. Uwe Nerlich: *Die amerikanisch-westeuropäischen Beziehungen 1970–72*, SWP-S 252, Ebenhausen: Stiftung Wissenschaft und Politik 1976.

[38] The other point of political vulnerability was – since the Federal Republic's entrance into NATO, which coincided with NATO's decision to go nuclear – the question of Germany's nuclear participation. This question had disappeared from the considerations of practical politics with the failure of the MLF; but while Bonn's step by step acceptance of the Non-Proliferation Treaty also formally cleared up this question, the consequences for the Westpolitik first took effect in the period of flux in which Bonn's policy of a *modus vivendi* vis-à-vis the GDR led to a recognition of Bonn's role as political leader especially by the smaller Western European countries. The continued fear of Bonn's nuclear ambitions would certainly have hindered such developments in Western policy.

[39] cf. for example Marc Ullmann: *Security Aspects in French Foreign Policy*, in: Survival, No. 6, 1973, pp. 262 ff. (based on extensive interviews with Pompidou and Debreé etc.).

[40] That is, if this is understood to mean the economic integration of the EC to the point of political union: where defense is organized in the framework of NATO, where the economic and monetary relations of the EC and the United States can be harmonized and where the coordination of foreign policy ultimately takes place in the alliance.

[41] cf. Uwe Nerlich: *Die Dilemmas französischer Sicherheitspolitik*, loc. cit., ftn. 28.

[42] Horst Mendershausen: *Who is Leading Whom in the Atlantic Alliance?*, RAND P-5465, Santa Monica: RAND Corporation 1975, p. 4.

[43] cf. Wilfrid L. Kohl: *The Nixon–Kissinger Foreign Policy System and US–European Relations: Patterns of Policy Making*, in: World Politics, Vol. 28, No. 1, 1975, pp. 15 ff.

[44] cf. Robert Ellsworth: *Folgen des Energieproblems für das strategische Gleichgewicht*, in: Europa-Archiv, No. 21, 1975, pp. 653–662: Uwe Nerlich: *Großmachtkonkurrenz und Weltwirtschaftsordnung*, in: Daniel Frey, ed.: *Umstrittene Weltwirtschaftsordnung*, Zürich: Polygraphischer Verlag 1977.

[45] cf. Frankfurter Allgemeine Zeitung, 29 October 1973.

[46] cf. The Times, 19 March 1974.

[47] cf. Frankfurter Allgemeine Zeitung, 26 July 1974.

[48] cf. the intelligent though somewhat exaggerated observations of Klaus Harpprecht: *Henry Kissinger's liebstes Kind. Wie wichtig ist Bonn für Washington?*, loc. cit., footnote 8, p. 5.

[49] "The West German government prefers a multilateral, consensual approach to international politics in which it can fulfill the role of a broker" (Peter Katzenstein: *West Germany's Place in American Foreign Policy: Pivot, Anchor, or Broker?*, loc. cit., footnote 13, p. 127); cf. also the observations in The Economist: "For historical reasons the Germans would rather march in step than rush ahead of its EC partners" (quoted in: *Bonn: Radnabe der Allianz*, in: Der Spiegel, No. 1–2, 1975, p. 22).

[50] cf. Pierre Hassner: *Was wird aus Europa?*, in: Claus Grosser et al., (eds.): *Das 198. Jahrzehnt*. Hamburg: Wegner 1969, pp 62 ff.

[51] cf. Hartmut Wasser: *Die Deutschen und Amerika. Umrisse einer Beziehung*, in: Aus Politik und Zeitgeschichte, supplement to the weekly publication Das Parlament, No. 26, 26 June 1976, pp. 13 ff.

[52] cf. Edward L. Morse: "There appears to be no major issue of immediate concern to the Europeans in which the European region is an appropriate and autonomous unit. This need not at all be the case over the long run." (In: Chace/Ravenal, (eds.): *Atlantis Lost*, loc. cit., footnote 1, p. 179.)

[53] It can proceed jointly but separately from the EC (as in EPC) through intergovernmental or interparty political harmonization or through the support of loyal forces (as in Portugal).

[54] In the sense of Stanley Hoffmann's pointed formulation, the Europeans have two possibilities: ". . . either, through division, they fall into the kind of paralysis and bickering that would compromise whatever has been achieved within the EEC in the past. Or else they cooperate for the solution of the global issues, but under American

leadership, with the EEC playing the role of a subcontractor." (In: Chace Ravenal, (eds.): *Atlantis Lost*, loc. cit., footnote 1, p. 26.)

[55] cf. Zbigniew Brzezinski: "Today the United States needs a united Europe less ... The United States now needs cooperation in the context of global concerns, either with the European Community or through bilateralism. But today Europe needs a united Europe for its own sake, at a time when political and economic developments make unification more important strictly for internal reasons." (In: Chace/Ravenal, (eds.): *Atlantis Lost*, loc. cit., footnote 1, pp. 254 ff.).

[56] Speech by Bundeskanzler Schmidt in Baltimore, loc. cit., footnote 3, p. 884. See also the observations of The Economist: "Mr. Schmidt sees the need for European integration clearly enough, but for him the road to integration lies through Washington. Brussels is, in his opinion, largely irrelevant to the main issues." (*Alone at the Top. West Germany: A Survey*, The Economist, 26 February and 8 March 1977, p. 36.)

[57] A classic exception is the sequel to the works of Charles A. Beard: the monumental work of Alfred Vagts (*Deutschland und die Vereinigten Staaten*, loc. cit., footnote 18) whose insight that foreign policy originates in and ensues from the internal affairs of states has yet to be equalled in neo-marxist research on international relations.

[58] cf. the works of Graham T. Allison, Morton H. Halperin etc. in which this paradigm is compared with the more differentiated model of organizational processes and bureaucratic politics.

[59] The majority of important studies on the German–American relationship either presupposes the multilateral basis or discusses the multilateral conditions for bilateral frictions. The latter applies to studies which, on the basis of an extended historical view, derive everything from a relationship of penetration (Wolfgang F. Hanrieder), or only sort out the bilateral conflict factors (Roger Morgan) or see the German–American relationship as *one* (to be sure important) of 105 bilateral relationships in the Atlantic Alliance (Manfred Knapp).

[60] Amongst the few comprehensive works are Richard Neustadt (Alliance Politics, loc. cit., footnote 11) on the American-British relationship, Nicholas Wahl (in: Chace/Ravenal, loc. cit., footnote 1) on the American-French relationship, and I. M. Destler et al. on the American-Japanese relationship (I. M. Destler, Priscilla Clapp, Hideo Sato, Haruhiro Fukui: *Managing an Alliance. The Politics of US-Japanese Relations*, Washington DC: The Brookings Institution 1976). The methodology of the latter study is particularly useful: 1. Case studies, 2. Description of the decision-making systems in foreign policy, 3. Types of reciprocal misperceptions, 4. Interaction between national systems when problems arise, in the political process and in the solution of the problem, 5. Future management of the relationship. But it is not sufficient for the analysis of German–American relations which take place to a far greater degree in the multilateral medium. Since the early fifties (the studies of the National Planning Association) there have hardly been any American analyses on the role of the Federal Republic in American policy until well into the seventies. Exceptions in recent years have been Livingston (loc. cit., footnote 11) and Katzenstein (loc. cit., footnote 13); cf. Neustadt, loc. cit., footnote 11, p. 139 ff.

[61] The structure of international relations is, as a rule, seen here as the invariable characteristic of such relations vis-à-vis specific changes in the perspectives of the most important actors, i.e. without regard to the preferred permanence of this invariance.

[62] cf. Uwe Nerlich: *Übergang in Washington. Zu den Perspektiven der Carter-Politik und zur deutsch-amerikanischen Agenda.* SWP-LN 2119, Ebenhausen: Stiftung Wissenschaft und Politik 1976.

[63] cf. the interview with Jimmy Carter in: Time Magazine, 15 February 1976, p. 24.

[64] On the importance of the European Community in the case of growing social tensions in the Federal Republic, see for example Alastair Buchan: *The End of the Postwar Era*. London: Weidenfeld & Nicolson 1974, p. 305.

[65] cf. Zbigniew Brzezinski: "Europe is the crossroads for the central choices confronting modern society. Europe is where the two principal alternative concepts of modern society most directly compete; Europe is where the American-Soviet rivalry is played for its highest stakes." (Chace/Ravenal, loc. cit., footnote 1, p. 85.)

[66] cf. Helmut Schmidt: *The Struggle for the World Product. Politics Between Power and Morals*, in: Foreign Affairs, Vol. 52, No. 3, April 1974, p. 449. Moreover, this will cause increasingly high demands on national governmental bureaucracies in Washington and, above all, in Bonn.

[67] cf. Gerald Livingston, loc. cit., footnote 11, p. 117.

[68] Stanley Hoffmann: *No Trumps, No Luck, No Will: Gloomy Thoughts on Europe's Plight*, in: Chace/Ravenal, loc. cit., footnote 1, p. 31.

[69] cf. Uwe Nerlich: *Continuity and Change,* loc. cit., footnote 2, pp. 26–29.

[70] Willy Brandt's comment at the SPD Party convention in Hannover, 10–14 April 1973 has evidently taken on greater significance recently, especially since the change of administration in Washington (from the uncorrected protocols of the convention, as quoted by Peter Christian Ludz: *Deutschlands doppelte Zukunft*, Munich: Hanser 1974, pp. 35 f.).

[71] Speech by Federal Chancellor Schmidt in Baltimore on 16 July 1976, loc. cit., footnote 3, p. 844.

PART FIVE
CONCLUSIONS

Future Tasks of American-European Policy

by HANS-PETER SCHWARZ

A foreign policy agenda can only be related to possibilities, not to probabilities. The science of international relations has not yet been developed far enough so that, as in modern meteorology, it can formulate its predictions with 80 percent probability. In fact the layman will not always believe the meteorologists' assertion that the success quota is that high for their predictions. However, there is no one who is not aware of the fact that the processes in the world community of nations elude exact prediction much more than does the weather.

Yet, the validity of a foreign policy agenda for the industrial democracies of North America and Western Europe is not only affected by the natural difficulties of foreign policy analysis. Such an agenda will have to be drafted in a period of particular uncertainty. The present constellation in Western Europe today, spring 1977, is more unstable than it has been since the end of the "40s". Similarly, no one would dare to offer anything approaching a sure prognosis of future developments in East-West relations. Again everything is in flux and the authors of this volume can only observe once more that we are living in a period of profound and radical change – truly a familiar situation for children of the twentieth century.

Whoever sets out to sketch an agenda will have to emphasize from the start that the capacity of the industrial democracies to realize the tasks mentioned is not especially strong. To be sure, the authors of our volume are not in agreement in their estimation of the foreign policy leeway the United States has. Some feel that Washington will continue to be capable of effective initiatives in the future and, in any case, still maintains an indisputable leadership position, while others show more reserve in this respect. There is, however, far-reaching consensus on the viewpoint that the Western European nations, with the exception of the Federal Republic of Germany, at present more or less resemble crippled Leviathans. (Let it be said by a German observer that the Federal Government's ability to act appears more impressive when viewed from without than from within.) On the other hand, all of the analysts who have cooperated on this volume agree that the tasks facing the Western industrial democracies can only be accomplished by means of a common concerted policy. That there is a contradiction between action required and capacity for action is more than obvious. With these reservations in mind let us attempt to outline four fields in the multitude of problems touched on in which a joint policy by the industrial democracies would have to prove itself in particular. We say joint policy because, despite the difference in views and concepts, there is a conviction of the utility, necessity, and possibility of common policy which reoccurs like a leifmotif in all of the analyses presented here.

One of the authors, Henry Owen, has elsewhere sketched this aim succinctly and quite convincingly: "Our remote and ideal object is to achieve a community of developed nations in which Western Europe, Japan, and the United States will arrange their defenses to deter war in the main areas of potential confrontation, will harmonize their political policies to lessen the prospect of conflict and proliferation, and will coordinate their economic policies to promote steady noninflationary growth in the industrial world and improve economic opportunities for developing countries . . . The means of attaining this long-term goal cannot be defined with precision. At best, it will provide a general direction in which to steer . . ."[1]

The challenges that merit priority attention are:

1. the economic difficulties of the industrial democracies;
2. the disintegrative tendencies in the European Community;
3. the need for self-assertion with respect to the Soviet Union;
4. the restructuring of our relations to the new nations or developing countries.

Joint Action in Overcoming the Economic Crisis

For the industrial democracies in the Atlantic area, and not only for them, the 1970s have been a decade of economic crises. Politicians, scientists, and a major section of the general public are inclined to place economic questions at the top of the agenda. Naturally the problems in the individual areas of economic policy are complex, extremely diverse, and require correspondingly complex solutions. William Diebold goes into considerable detail on this question in his paper. He emphasizes a conviction which has been growing increasingly strongly in transatlantic leadership circles: that the challenges of economic interdependence are best answered in terms of a "trilateral" concept, i.e., in the joint cooperation of the United States, the Western European democracies, and Japan.

In the present volume Henry Owen, Wilhelm Grewe, and François

Duchêne, inter alios, discuss the fundamental ideas, problems, and implications of such an approach. In their papers they visibly attempt to retain the basic concepts of economic liberalism under aggravated conditions of the "70s" and "80s" through more or less strengthened government activity in establishing political frameworks for the functioning of market economy and in coordinating policies. The foremost task appears to be: improvement and maintenance of an international framework of order in which factor mobility and innovation continue to be possible alongside simultaneous harmonization of national economic policies. This alone might prevent internal domestic imbalances and tensions from destroying international economic order.

Yet, it remains uncertain whether or not it will be possible to overcome the danger of renewed economic nationalism through enlightened cooperation of governments open to compromise. This is dependent on a number of factors. In principle, however, the authors of this book are of the opinion that the problem can be solved, however only under certain conditions. Two conditions seem of paramount importance. One of these conditions is cooperative economic policy on the part of the leading Western economic powers. It will be equally important to prevent a breakthrough of socialist concepts of economic order in the Western European area.

The problem of joint economic policies for the industrial democracies would be insoluble firstly, if a Conally-style foreign economic policy were to emerge once again in the United States. Robert J. Schaetzel clearly shows that such an approach would still find a psychological base in American public opinion.

At present the Carter administration has got under control the forces of economic nationalism in the areas of trade and monetary policy. In this respect, however, nothing can be considered of lasting certainty.

There is also cause for concern that any future economic nationalism on the part of the United States and Canada might not be restricted merely to trade with industrial and agricultural products. As François Duchêne and Peter Dobell explain, further turbulence is brewing in the North Atlantic area. Future deterioration of the transatlantic climate might also result from the fact that, in the case of the United States and Canada, two countries rich in natural resources are confronted with a group of Western European states dependent on the import of raw materials. Were the North American nations to make stronger use of their superiority in this field in the future, a series of highly diverse motivations might be combined. Such motivations include: concern about conservation of scarce or limited resources; non-proliferation policy with its effect on uranium exports; the use of oligopolies either in order to make higher profits or to obtain political aims. That today the North American governments are already employing the delivery of uranium as a means of pressure is perhaps a foretaste of things to come. Even if the motives of a policy that does not adhere to contractual agreements and previous pledges may be highly moral, it is obvious that they are viewed in Western Europe as dubious symptoms of a capricious, unpredictable foreign policy on the part of the leading nuclear power. Sooner or later they could be resented as North American economic nationalism.

The problem of jointly mastering the economic crisis would also be insoluble, secondly, if dogmatic socialist economic concepts were to gain ascendancy in key Western European countries.

In Western Europe since the end of the "60s" nationalism has been shifting from right to left on the political spectrum – nationalism in the sense of an atavistic policy that strives to maintain national autonomy in an era of increasing interdependence. It is no longer the old militant nationalism that destroyed Europe in the first half of the century. Neither is it the romantic nationalism of a General de Gaulle which experienced a revival in the "60s". It is the nationalism of debility, ideological doctrinarism, and resentment – debility that has resulted from excessive distribution battles on the domestic front with corresponding inflationary consequences and loss of growth which has already largely immobilized the European Community; ideological doctrinarism such as that of the Tribune group or the Eurocommunists which, in spite of all the European overtures on the part of the Italian communists, could only be realized under the conditions of national autonomy and at the cost of international cooperation; resentment that is directed towards those countries which do not allow themselves the luxury of excessive distribution battles – i.e., against the United States and the Federal Republic of Germany.

This new wave of "national socialism" has not yet come to power in any of the countries of the Atlantic Community; the movement has, however, not yet reached its peak.

It is fortunately true – and both Pierre Hassner and François Duchêne refer to this in their papers – that the new forces of "national socialism" can be externally controlled to a certain degree. Nevertheless, it is still highly improbable that an Atlantic Economic Community can endure in which troubled national economies have to be kept from dropping out of free world trade by means of German, American, or Swiss credits (as well as money from oil-producing countries) in which case a stability policy is imposed on them through the severe conditions laid down by their creditors. An economic policy of "muddling through" cannot, for numerous reasons, be considered a lasting solution. Whether or not this system of emergency aid in one's own interest already in practice today and which the Federal Republic has just begun to engage itself in, would withstand the historical compromise in Italy, a popular front victory in France (with the probability of an ensuing destabilization of the French economy), and the continuing weakness of Great Britain is more than doubtful.

The Community can carry some of its limping members for a time but not the majority. Thus, it cannot be ruled out that any realistic basis for compromise in economic policy will soon become too narrow and that willingness to accommodate concepts of economic policy, widely divergent in the European Community anyway, will weaken. William Diebold correctly states that, at present, there is no intellectual consensus on what commensurate Western economic policy should consist of. The diversity of approaches can be seen in the contributions to this volume by comparing the papers by Norbert Kloten and Andrew Shonfield. Nonetheless, as practice has shown, between enlightened neo-liberals and enlightened Keynesians the kinds of compromises that the future of the Western economic community will be dependent on are possible. It is, however, difficult to believe in the ability of governments to compromise, if the economic ideas of either the Tribune group, the Ceres, the left wing of the German SPD or the Eurocommunists were to play a determining role.

Thus, the success or failure of an interdependently conceived economic policy will, to a considerable degree, depend on domestic developments which can be influenced, but only relatively and not absolutely.

The question of whether or not it will, in fact, be possible in the long run to include Japan in this consensus also remains to be seen.

The institutional arrangements for safeguarding interdependent economic policy will, in the future, have to be as complex and flexible as they have been in the past: summits such as those held at Rambouillet, Puerto Rico, and London; instrumentalization of the IMF, OECD, GATT, and IEA; negotiations by the European Community with Japan or the United States. It is of extreme importance that the existing network of institutions be preserved and, wherever necessary, strengthened and amplified.

Similarly, not just *one* country can be looked to for motivation in the future. Henry Owen rightly points out that leadership will, in the end, continue to lie with the United States as long as Western Europe does not speak with *one* voice and Japan continues to lack self-confidence. The United States, too, would be well advised to share responsibility in proceeding with such initiatives. The history of European unity since the "50s" has shown that joint effort is often better set in motion and makes better progress if the initiatives do not always come from the strongest partners to whom all of the remaining partners tend to attribute hegemonial intentions.

One thing can be predicted with some degree of certainty: whether or not the Western system of economic alliance will be able to successfully cope with the challenges it faces will probably be decided in the present decade. Developments in Western Europe will be especially decisive in this process.

The Disintegrating European Community

At the beginning of the "70s" it was still possible to depart from the assumption that the conflict of interests between an increasingly consolidated European Community and the United States would be a primary cause of future transatlantic tensions. This prognosis, which explains much of the Nixon-Kissinger policy towards Europe, was based on the expectation that the European Community would steadily grow stronger. Despite unmistakable successes in political coordination in the framework of EPC, the process of integration has been stagnating for years and in the future disintegration is more probable than the continuation of economic integration.

The already existing antagonisms and developments which in all probability will become even more critical in the future are frankly discussed in the papers gathered in this volume – with the friendly reserve of the outside observer on the part of Martin J. Hillenbrandt and with self-critical candor by François Duchêne, Pierre Hassner and Uwe Nerlich.

The reasons for this development are known. The gross national products and the economic policies of the EC countries have diverged so strongly in the "70s" that the existence of the Common Market is endangered in the medium term if these trends continue. Joint agricultural policy is under constant pressure as well; it quite probably will not be maintainable with the accession of Spain, Portugal, and Greece.

Thus, stagnation in the area of economic policy has been the order of the day for years. As Pierre Hassner explains, there would be a genuine threat of crisis if the centrist governments of France and Italy were to yield to more or less strongly left-wing governments. Because of the policies that can be expected of them, despite all programmatic declarations to the contrary, not only the chances for maintaining the Common Market will likely be worsened. Such a change in government could also lead to a polarization of the Western European international system, especially in the area of security policy and security-connected East-West relations.

To be sure, this need not be the case. William Griffith's paper shows how differently the directions could be that developments might take – and not necessarily for the worse.

Perhaps it will, in fact, be possible to overcome the still strong Stalinist elements in the Italian Communist Party so that the party will take on the features of an Italian branch of social democracy. Perhaps the popular front in France will lose the elections after all, or Mitterand will prove to be a successful magician able to handle his Communist partners as well as the strong left wing of his own party thereby circumnavigating the danger of a government crisis and economic paralysis. Since the recent rift between Socialists and Communists speculations concerning new combinations of a center-left government in France have arisen. But there are too many "maybes" to provide any kind of reliability. The domestic prospects for joint policy in the EC area as well as in the rest of the industrial democracies are, in any case, not good.

Similarly, there is no way of providing organizational preparation for the eventuality of a political crisis of the Western European international system. For that reason any thought of an American-German axis which would halfway steady its swaying Western European partners is just as theoretical as a division of Western Europe into Mediterranean-Socialist and Central-Northern European groups.

In general, things have developed so negatively that it is no longer admissible to allow ourselves to be deceived about the seriousness of the situation by heart-warming hopes for the miraculous effects of a direct election of the European Parliament. On the contrary, the situation will have to be seen realistically as it is by Uwe Nerlich in his paper: "In questions of economy, currency, raw materials supply, and military security Western Europe has ceased to be a functional unit with prospects of political independence." At the same time, on the other hand, it is true that there continues to be an urgent need for political cooperation at all levels in the framework of Western Europe. This, however, presupposes a capacity for self-assertion on the part of Western European governments that is no longer apparent. This ability to cooperate would be all the more burdened if Western Europeans were to drift still farther apart ideologically.

What might a fragmentation of Western Europe mean for American foreign policy? From the perspective of American balance of power policy, theoretically still possible, the disintegrative tendencies now becoming visible in the European Community might not be viewed only as a disadvantage. Uwe Nerlich quite correctly observes that Western Europe is now much more dependent on the United States than it was in the "60s". But the United States is consciously moving away from the balance of power concept that prevailed under Nixon and Kissinger in its relationship to Western Europe. It seems as if the Carter administration is inspired by the idea of a community of industrial democracies. The crisis of the EC represents a grave hindrance for any such intentions.

This is true of the economic sector where the American administration in its efforts to overcome the recession understandably also has considerable interest in seeing the EC area once again become a growth region. If the Common Market were ever actually to break up the American firms working here would be affected as well.

A political drifting apart of the EC countries would be all the more likely to create just the situation that an administration wants to avoid which is determined to stay on the Continent at any cost: unrest and tensions. Unfortunately, a certain tendency has become evident in the American public, still plagued by the Vietnam trauma, notably in influential groups of the liberal establishment, to turn its back on countries and regions in which difficulties are impending (examples: Angola, Zaire). Of course Europe cannot be compared with the unstable countries of Africa or with South Vietnam. Still, in view of this tendency, it has to be feared that the American public might not react with the cool determination to firm commitment and unconditional staying-put without which the situation in Europe would go completely out of control.

It is relatively easy to imagine the types of difficulties American diplomacy would be up against if, sooner or later, it were forced to take sides in a conflict between Western European countries or groups of countries. What that would mean is best known to those people in Washington who, for years, have desperately been trying to mediate between Greeks and Turks.

However, the main problem at present lies not so much in what the United States might be able to do but rather more in what it might not be able to do. Even though the Western European countries are so strongly dependent on the United States, Washington is not in a position to influence domestic developments in the individual Western European countries decisively, and yet it is precisely in the area of domestic politics that the erosion of the Western European Community has its deepest roots.

As a general strategy the wish might be expressed for the American government to pursue a more active policy than in the past, one which gives more complex consideration to the special circumstances in the individual countries. However, this would signify at the same time that the tendency toward bilateralism would be strengthened. Even finely shaded diplomacy, as desirable and indispensable as it will be, will not be able to work any miracles. The fate of Western Europe, in the final analysis, will not be decided in Washington, but rather in London, Paris, Rome, and Bonn.

The new situation creates difficult questions especially for the Federal Republic of Germany. Paradoxically, this country, which has functioned as a Western European stability factor in the last years, would probably be hit the hardest by a failure of European unification efforts. What would remain of the foreign policy concept of the Federal Republic if both the European Community and the Atlantic Community dissolved into a tangled web of primarily bilateral relations or relations between small groups? The West Germans, totally shaken by the failure of all ambitions to become a superpower and by the division of Germany, had for nearly three decades found psychological support and a kind of substitute for the crushed German Reich in the idea of a community of Western democracies and, above all, in the idea of the European Community. Which direction should Bonn go when this frame of reference is gone?

How nervously the Federal Republic would react to a fundamental change of circumstances in Western Europe is quite unclear. It is relatively certain that dramatic events in Rome and Paris in connection with a dissolution of the European Community would not only effect the economy of this totally export-dependent country, it would also heat up the now relatively relaxed domestic climate and lead to a restless search for new foreign policy options. Since developments in the future defy prediction there has thus far been no way to think the matter through. It is, thus, virtually impossible to make organizational preparations for such a situation.

The European unrest in the first half of this century was in large part German unrest. The stability of the "50s" and "60s" was, by the same token, largely attainable because Germany was relatively stable. In future years one of the most important tasks of Western European and American policy will doubtless be to work tenaciously at keeping the hitherto existing Western European framework of West German foreign policy intact as far as domestic development in the partner countries of the European Community permit this.

It is, incidentally, hard to imagine how a revival of nationalism could be avoided in the case of a Western European community of nations highly charged with elements of socio-political conflict. Socio-political polarization would, of course, lead to a reactivation of nationalisms as it already has in the case of the present well-organized anti-German campaign of radical leftist forces in Western Europe. This, however, would mean jeopardizing the foreign policy results of three decades of peace.

At the moment, we are largely dependent on speculation in assessing these matters, and there may be some consolation in saying, first of all, that it is never so bad that it could not have been worse, and, even if worst should come to worst, Western European and American pragmatism would probably find halfway acceptable solutions since the whole Atlantic world is closely bound together by economic ties. Not even this, however, is certain.

Pierre Hassner is doubtless correct in stating that the relations between the United States and the Western European countries, and also among the European countries themselves, will be increasingly bilateralized. This means that they will be more complex, conceptually as well as procedurally. A principle can be established, as Hassner does, according to which inevitable bilateralism is to be combined with Western European multilateralism (an analogous situation is true for NATO), but whether and how this would be possible is as yet totally uncertain.

The already unstable situation is being further aggravated by the changes presently taking place in the East-West relationship.

The New Soviet Menace

Since the end of the "40s", whenever American and European politicians or analysts have worked out agendas, the question of coexistence with the Soviet Union has always been at the top of the list in the problem catalogue. Today, there is still a pronounced tendency to respond to the universally known problems with traditional strategies and concepts.

Since the middle of the "70s" there has been a growing feeling that the constellation has begun to change fundamentally. In a period of relative Western superiority, lasting from the end of the Cuba crisis to the middle of the "70s", it may have been fitting to respond to given tensions with détente strategies, whatever this may have involved in the individual case: attempts at reaching regional and nuclear strategic arms control arrangements, normalization in Germany, agreeing to the East's request for favorable economic relations, more or less silent acceptance of suppression in the Eastern bloc, extra-European crisis management, or mere symbolic gestures and rhetoric meant either for domestic consumption by left-liberal or socialist groups or to facilitate the consensus between the governments of the Western Alliance. During the past five years the security situation both in Europe and overseas has qualitatively deteriorated.

The Soviet Union has attained nuclear strategic parity and with it has built up an offensive potential in Central and Northern Europe that can be used both for political blackmail and for regionally limited conventional or tactical nuclear warfare. A psychological climate is building up in the general staffs and in the part of the general public that is informed on questions of security policy that is now and again redolent of the atmosphere during the critical years of 1948–1953 and 1959–1962. No war is expected but it must be taken into account that wars or war threats are imaginable in Europe under certain conditions.

The industrial democracies are also in an aggravated situation with respect to global strategy. The Soviet Union is now a world power using its maritime forces to pursue an easily recognizable course of geostrategic expansion all over the world. Above all, Russian Middle East and African policy have been affecting the industrial democracies in such a way as to make them increasingly conscious of their dependence on resources located in these regions. Soviet successes in Angola, Moçambique, and in other African countries stand alongside setbacks (notably in Egypt), but Russian expansionist policy with its as yet unforeseeable consequences for geostrategic and global-economic power shifts is a fact. Here, too, the diagnosis of the problem is easier than designing plans to act upon since the limits in ability to act described in connection with the economic situation and European unification are, of course, just as valid for security.

An attempt to stabilize the situation would have to concentrate especially on the following four points:
1. a political and psychological reorientation of the public in the industrial democracies;
2. development of flexible methods of cooperation in security matters;
3. strengthening of defense capability in the Central European area and in Northern Europe;
4. revision of arms control concepts.

1. More or less all of the authors of our volume are in agreement that public opinion in the industrial democracies is focused on domestic problems and, especially in Western Europe, is beginning to react more and more provincially. In this climate of opinion the governments and foreign policy elites must consider psychological reorientation as one of their most important tasks. In particular, it is imperative that dubious trends in the area of security be stressed as a central problem of future policy. This, however, requires clear language and constant public disclosure of negative developments in Europe that never emerge on a world scale.

In this situation it becomes increasingly problematic when the essence of Western "Ostpolitik" continues to be articulated with the worn and greatly discredited term "détente policy." The governments, which all more or less clearly recognize the new situation, must be willing to redefine their security and Eastern policy. A formula such as *peaceful self-assertion* would imply that the Western industrial democracies continue to value peace as their most treasured possession but that they must define East-West relations today primarily in the light of self-assertion.

2. Of course attempts should not weaken to overcome negative security trends through concerted multilateral policy and, in particular, through the concept of an integrated NATO Alliance. That which was true of the crisis of the European Community is also true here: in future years considerably more flexible combinations of multilateralism and bilateralism will be necessary than has been the case in the past. This is imperative for the Mediterranean area as well as for security policy outside the NATO area.

The new security situation presently emerging overseas has not yet been adequately dealt with either conceptually or organizationally by the NATO Alliance. The fact that dependency on raw materials has turned out to be an Achilles heel for the industrial democracies of Western Europe has given security policy an added dimension. At the same time, the Soviet Union, with the support of its allies, is, for the first time in the postwar period, actually able to directly or, equally problematical, indirectly threaten important overseas sources of raw materials and maritime shipping operations. In doing so it can capitalize on regional tensions in the Middle East and in Southern Africa as well as on the instability of a number of young nations.

The present American administration and the American public view this situation with mixed feelings. Fortunately, there is a deeply rooted, firm determination to counter developments energetically in maritime matters or in Middle East trouble spots. There is a different attitude towards regional developments in Asia and Africa, however. With respect to these regions we are going to have to learn to live for some time with the fact that public opinion in the United States takes to regional involvement like a cat does to water. Securing the existence of the Israeli state is an exception to this rule. Also, concerning Africa, we must not forget that the American president has a large black constituency to think of.

With a view to this partial self-inhibition of American world policy and considering the circumstance that NATO cannot act as an organization in overseas regions, the Western European governments still capable of acting must, in cooperation with friendly overseas countries, take the countering of Soviet expansionism more strongly into their own hands than in the past. The support of Zaire by France and, somewhat more discretely, by the Federal Republic shows that cooperative action is altogether possible when governments do not simply let themselves drift idly in the sea of world events. In the future it will be requisite also in other regions and countries not to wait until the United States has recovered from its Vietnam trauma and moral idiosyncrasies with regard to certain African, Asian, or Latin American regimes.

Western European overseas policy which has had to employ instruments of economic aid and other forms of cooperation more consciously than before will, however, not be entirely susceptible to coordination in the EC area either. Western Europe, after all, also has no lack of governments that are ideologically or by virtue of their weakness inhibited like the United States. This, too, will lead to new forms of bilateral foreign policy and could intensify the process of fragmentation in the Community of industrial democracies. This kind of selective cooperative action would not necessarily be a bad solution; it is not important who acts but rather that someone should act at all in the interest of the entire community.

3. It has been recognized that the conventional and tactical nuclear defense capability of NATO in Central and Northern Europe must be improved rapidly and effectively, an insight that has already led to a whole series of practical measures which must be intensified.

In the process care will have to be taken not to make psychological demands too great on countries like the Federal Republic. François Duchêne notes pointedly that the Western European countries rely on the Federal Republic and America for their defense while they gradually shift their resources to other uses.

If this process continues it will doubtless create dangerous asymmetries in the alliance in the long run and lead to resentments in all concerned – not merely in those countries that today see the Bundeswehr as the strongest Western European army but in the West Germans themselves who, since the Second World War, have never been enthusiastic about assuming the role of British or American doughboys anyway.

It should not be overlooked outside Germany that the security-conscious attitude of the West Germans is not a constant that can be reckoned with permanently when other Western European partners elicit procyclic behavior in their security policy in increasing measure, and reduce their defense spending at a time in which the Warsaw Pact armies are growing dramatically stronger and inflation continues to eat away at the military budget.

4. Finally, there will have to be a more exact recognition in the future that the bilateralism of Soviet-American SALT negotiations will not be a burden for the Atlantic defense community in the long run only if the development of ultramodern weapons for the defense of Western Europe is not impeded.

In this connection the elaboration of a common policy on the cruise missile would appear to be of special importance. France and Great Britain, in addition to requiring more nuclear submarines, will soon need newer, cheaper and highly deterrent delivery systems. Cruise missiles will help to close this gap. Since these new weapons are also suitable for non-nuclear deployment, they could represent a true improvement of deterrent capacity for the Federal Republic as well. The more unfavorable the ratio of military and strategic power in Central Europe becomes, the less Bonn will be able to content itself with being dependent solely on American deterrent potential. If a potential aggressor had the certainty that with a conventional attack he was running the risk of highly effective non-nuclear retaliation against sensitive targets in his own country, equilibrium in Europe could be made more secure and with it peace in general.

The Foundations of the Twenty-first Century

That the industrial democracies will have to grant high priority to reorganizing their relations to developing countries is common knowledge and the authors of this volume clearly emphasize it. However, saying that a problem has high priority is not saying that the problem has been correctly defined. Indeed, the question needs to be asked whether the policy-makers and the public in the industrial democracies have thus far correctly defined the problem of their relationship to the new nations. The humanitarian, liberal ideology that prevails in the West and the image that the poorer and more radical of the developing countries project of their own situation suggests that it is primarily a matter of development.

No one will want to dispute the central importance of development. But development cannot be the sole relevant perspective in the future. It will have to be combined with a vantage point from which the so-called North-South problem and the redistribution wishes of the "Third World" are seen primarily as a game of power-politics. Decolonization led to the formation of a new system of global relations. The countries of Africa, Asia, and the Middle East, freed of European domination, needed time to establish themselves in international politics.

Now, however, many of them, followed by a number of Latin American countries who were in a similar state of relative dependency for a long period, are increasingly beginning to recognize their power potential. Such demands as have been presented by the "group of 77" or at conferences on maritime law during the past years, show that the young nations feel strong enough to propose their own definition of world problems and to impose the acceptance of their ideas. The question arises for the industrial democracies as to whether these concepts are reconcilable with their long-term interests and how far they can go in their willingness to compromise.

In many ways the concepts of radical developing countries today are reminiscent of the strategies with which a lot of people in the nineteenth and early twentieth centuries wanted to resolve the problems of pauperism on national levels. At that time, as well, the situation was defined by radical parties and intellectuals in categories familiar enough in the North-South dialogue: society was seen as a dichotomous class society made up of rich people and poor people; exploitation, progressive pauperization, and mounting tensions seemed ineluctable. On the basis of this view of society plans were devised for revolutionary change or, in other words, an extensive redistribution with total or partial centralized control of production and distribution. Today we know that these definitions, like all macropolitical statements, were only partly correct. In some countries and regions this particular class analysis was, in fact, valid, while in others it was not, and the longer industrial development continued the more clear it became that new, broad classes were emerging that fit neither category, rich nor poor. The theoreticians of redistribution and centralized direction of production and distribution had overlooked the power of individual and collective desire for self-improvement to create prosperity. Likewise, the picture of a dichotomous class society did not correspond to the much more varied social stratification and the considerably divergent interests of the groups competing with each other in individual societies. Solutions suggested by the radical camp frequently proved to be impractical. There were obvious liberal and evolutionary alternatives to revolutionary change and redistribution: expansion of production, raising the purchasing power of the masses, social mobility, political participation of the liberated classes, peaceful change, evolutionary development of new laws, improved organization of those less well off. It is clear, today, that the problems of pauperism and political participation of everyone in the industrial nations of the nineteenth and twentieth centuries were solved faster and more effectively by means of enlightened conservative, liberal, and social democratic policy than with the aid of radical conceptions.

Analogies are always only partly right, yet there is much to be said for the desire to similarly solve the present-day problems of world-wide poverty and fair participation of the younger nations in international decision-making processes, if they are at all solvable, through increased production, improved effectiveness, evolutionary but not too rapid expansion of the rights of political participation, the formation of a kind of new middle class in the international community with optimum encouragement of upward mobility of individual countries and gradual accommodation of legal regulations. If developments are to run in accordance with such positive conceptions of order then it is also necessary to clearly designate wrong radical definitions of problems as such and not to yield to them passively.

The industrial democracies will have to be prepared to devise new conceptions of their own for solving the problem of integrating young countries in the global community of nations, the problem of development, and, also, to solicit the cooperation of those countries that would qualify as priority partners. Previous Western policy approaches to young nations need to be reviewed.

The concept of decolonization as such was not a policy conception in the true sense; instead, it usually only expressed the insight that Europeans were no longer willing and no longer able to control other nations of the world overseas. Inasmuch as revisions were attempted at all, such as with the idea of the Commonwealth of Nations or the Union Française, they have all, especially the former, proved unviable. Experience has also shown that the conception of liberal foreign aid policy, such as prevailed in the "50s" and "60s", did not result in any major improvement. The Pearson Report says all that needs to be said in this respect. Western policy in the bodies created for the North-South dialogue reflect a lack of new ideas, unconvincing negotiations, is more reactive than active, and does not bode well for the future. A global approach and negotiations on the basis of demands, a questionable approach to begin with, do not hold out much hope for new viable structures in relations between the nations of the world.

What new Western policy approaches towards the new nations would have to look like can only be briefly outlined. In the following a few ideas that are presented in the essays of this volume have been singled out and others added that might merit consideration:

1. The industrial democracies should concentrate primarily on supporting the efforts of those developing countries that want to solve the problem of pauperism through increased growth in a system of free markets and fixed systems of rules. This would require a relaxation of Western protectionist attitudes. How fateful a narrow-minded refusal to open up markets soon enough can be, is illustrated by the Japanese example of the "20s" and "30s". Of course, this presupposes in the new partners the insight that the developed countries will only be willing to open their markets without discrimination if their investments in the developing countries are secure. Radical proposals for partial redistribution and creation of international regimes, such as

advocated by the "group of 77" are hardly compatible with this conception.

2. The industrial democracies should not get themselves involved too much in general solutions which can neither overcome the problem of poverty nor be useful to their own specific economic and security interests. Seen in this light, the concept of a general North-South dialogue is a mistaken concept; mercy should be shown as soon as possible by letting it seep into oblivion in the vastly ramified sewers of multilateral conference diplomacy.

A discriminating procedure, one that deals with inequalities in an unequal manner, is much more sensible:

– fair cooperation by the threshold nations which, on the road to industrialization, would have to be included in the club of industrial nations, as François Duchêne suggests. The relatively wealthy industrial democracies will not be able to assert themselves in the long run if they do not consistently accept new members into the club, countries that have successfully gone the way Germany went in the mid-nineteenth century and Japan at the end of the same century. One need only think of countries like Iran, Brazil, Singapore, South Korea, Venezuela, and Greece to name but a few;

– intensified economic cooperation with countries that are important for the industrial democracies for geostrategical reasons (e.g., Egypt, Saudi Arabia, Turkey, Zaire) even if they are not yet among the industrial nations and do not have modern societies;

– preferential treatment of countries that signed the Lomé Convention to which the Western European democracies maintain good relations;

– relief for the especially needy countries that are neither in a position to develop on their own nor are of particular importance from a strategic standpoint.

3. A certain amount of transatlantic cooperation is required. Since the "50s" Africa has been an area for which the industrial democracies of Western Europe feel especially responsible and in which they feel accepted. Let it be respectfully said that the United States has never operated very adroitly there, neither at the beginning of the "60s" in the Congo nor today, concerning the problems of Southern Africa.

Conversely, the Western European nations will have to accept and welcome the fact that the United States has focused its overseas policy on the Middle East and the Indian Ocean, and they should appreciate the fact that in the 1980s America will continue to be in a position to secure the freedom of the seas, determined as it apparently is to follow a policy of establishing and maintaining bases for this purpose.

It is doubtful whether it will benefit the Atlantic Community if the United

States continues to view Latin America as a kind of "chasse gardée." There
is a lot that speaks in favor of the assumption that the overall interests of the
industrial democracies would be served by strengthening the partnership
between Latin America and the Western European countries. Western
Europeans do not encounter the resentments in South Americans that are
provoked in them by North Americans.

4. In addition, it will have to be taken into consideration that the relations
between the industrial democracies and the young nations overseas will
continue to be related to East-West tensions. The Western policy of
supporting allied countries and aiding key nonaligned countries in defending
their independence, developed during the Kennedy administration, still
remains indispensable and thoroughly practicable.

Quite naturally military aid plays a significant role in this connection.
Criticism of the "merchants of death" is, admittedly, an honorable tradition
of liberal humanitarian foreign policy. Unfortunately, however, the good
wishes of Victorian philanthropists and preachers are no longer suitable as
principles in an era in which the Soviet Union continues to push ahead
geostrategic expansion by means of subversive influence, military aid,
establishing military bases, and enlisting the aid of allied peoples.

Here, too, cooperative action is advisable, even if the United States Senate
should have doubts here and there about active commitment.

A viewpoint that does not recognize that the era of decolonization was
accompanied by a new age of imperialism cannot do justice to the situation
in Southeast Asia, the Near East, and Africa. The industrial democracies'
answer to the changed situation cannot consist of opposing the Soviet
Union's expansionist activities with their own expansionism. They must not
back away from the duty of lending energetic support to those countries that
want to resist Eastern penetration, and they should – jointly and cooperatively
– work towards enabling endangered young nations and regions to maintain
their independence in the face of the new imperialism.

A Western policy that looks beyond the immediate present will have to
recognize that the foundations of the twenty-first century are being laid today
at the end of the "70s" and in the "80s". Securing the future of the industrial
democracies overseas is, for that reason, a task that deserves top priority on
the foreign policy agenda.

Note

[1] Henry Owen and Charles L. Schultze: *Setting Priorities for American Foreign Policy*, in: SURVIVAL XIX (1977), p. 75.

Future Tasks of American-European Policy

by KARL KAISER

There have always been problems and turbulence in the American-West European relationship. They have provided continuous subjects for political analysis and political practice, whether they were conflicts in trade policy, debates on troop reductions, Nixon-shocks or differences over export policy in the field of nuclear technology. In such moments the dictates of political reason and a sense of proportion have always reminded us of, or called for the political mobilization of the long-term common interests between North America and Western Europe in the fields of security and economics, as well as in their common political systems which are more important than current political controversies.

To remember the common interests in the American-European relationship is still meaningful today if the problems arising for both sides are to continue to be seen in their proper proportions. This can, however, easily become a welcome escape or a way of avoiding facing the problems of the present. Seen in this respect, traditional "Atlanticism" can result in a highly problematical narrowing of political perspective.

The governments of North America and Western Europe, today, live in a political environment which differs in decisive points from the period in which Atlantic cooperation was developed. A discussion of the tasks to be mastered in the coming years presupposes an understanding of these changes. We will sketch them briefly before addressing ourselves to the tasks facing democracies on both sides of the Atlantic.

Basic Contours of Change: Between Globalization and National Priorities

An attempt to reduce the trends of change in the international politics of recent years to one basic factor would certainly not do justice to a complex reality in which a multitude of forces bring about constant and often rapid change. Nonetheless, many of today's changes reflect a similar conflict of forces. In specific problem areas the dynamics of movement simultaneously tend in opposite directions and, thus, strain the traditional institutions and rules of problem-solving to a high degree: on the one hand, pressure in the direction of national claims, priorities, and approaches to solutions, on the other hand, tendencies toward an expansion of the factual or geographic level of problem solving. Thus the European Community is challenged not only by national demands but also by the inherent logic of concrete supra-regional problems for which the European Community no longer is the adequate framework.

1. Global Change

Three problem areas appear to be of particular importance here: the dilemmas of growing interdependence, the questioning of traditional world economic order, and the increasing relevance of global problems.

The *dilemmas of growing interdependence* arise from the inevitable tension between the modern welfare state on the one hand and the principle of relatively free exchange across national borders on the other hand, as it has become characteristic of the modern, liberal economic system. The rapid growth of international trade, of capital transfer, and of the freedom of movement of persons has considerably increased reciprocal dependency. The increasing proportion of internationally planned and marketed production is a particularly important transnational link between societies. Economic events and decisions in one country spill over to an increasing extent into other countries as a result of the growing degree of intermeshing and have profound effects on economic and social life there. This process takes place in a milieu of welfare states which intervene in economic and social life in response to the increasing demands and expectations of their citizens and in pursuit of far-reaching goals with regard to the standard of living, social security, full employment, old age pensions, etc. The governments' policy increasingly constrains "the invisible hand" of the market, going as far as extensive forms of planning in certain realms of society and economics. This results in the central dilemma of interdependence: The freedom of international exchange is considered to be just as much an indispensable part of our general order as is the social policy in the broadest sense pursued by the welfare state. In the last analysis, the two are only compatible if interdependence is secured by steering mechanisms and coordination of policy between the various governments. Hence, the international coordination of policy becomes necessary to the extent to which transnational interdependence increases between states.[1]

The questioning of the traditional world economic order adds a multitude of wide-ranging problems to these dilemmas. We cannot analyse them in detail here. Essential institutional rules and power relationships of the traditional system have been abandoned or are now being challenged. If in 1971 when several elements of the Bretton Woods system were abandoned it was still basically a question of *reforming* the world economic system, the discussions triggered by the events of 1973 and 1974, indeed, challenged the world economic order *as such*. The developing countries no longer accept the rules and institutions which had, in the past, been defined essentially by the industrialized world, nor do they accept their position which they regard as a purely auxiliary function of the economic system of the industrialized countries. The developing countries want not only a new economic system which would take their interests into full consideration and would set in motion a process of redistribution of wealth in their favor. They also desire a global revision of the market economy from the standpoint of social policy as had been undertaken by the industrial nations in their own realm in the past wherever social and political necessities caused them to move away from a pure market system. The decreasing willingness of the developing countries to accept their poverty and the present distribution of goods in the world heightens their impatience and strengthens tendencies to radicalize the debate between North and South.

Finally we must mention *the growing globalization of issues* as the third tendency for change.[2] In the "50s" and "60s" the threat of the Soviet Union or specific questions of the American-European relationship in the field of industrial trade, the agricultural market, monetary relations, or the Offset Agreement dominated the international discussion. Today, however, the issues are more global in nature; to be sure, their urgency is a function of national considerations, but for substantial reasons the level at which they must be solved or at which the political controversy must be carried out is global. Such problems include the supply of oil and other raw materials, the reform of the world monetary system, the balance-of-payments problems of a multitude of countries, the problems of world nutrition, environmental questions, or the proliferation problems involved with the expanded peaceful use of nuclear energy.

2. Change in the Atlantic Region

Three problem areas appear to be particularly important: the *decline of the primacy of security* in the traditional sense, the strains on the European Community due to global challenges as well as inner nationalism and, lastly, the threat to democracy.

In speaking of the decline of the primacy of security in the traditional sense we do not mean to imply that security has become unimportant. The opposite is true. This means that the traditional institutional structure and orientations which reflected the primacy of security in the past have decreased in importance and thus created difficult tasks for the security policy of the states involved. Two trends are especially important in this connection. First, we should mention the *globalization of American security policy* which Uwe Nerlich has discussed in greater detail in this volume. The concentration on Europe of American foreign policy in the early postwar years has disappeared to a great extent. Of course, postwar American foreign policy saw itself as "global" from the very beginning, but the controversy with the Soviet Union, with Europe as its most important arena, played the central role. The rise of Japan and China, the oil crisis, and the consequently growing role of the oil-producers in world politics, the increased global importance of the Middle East conflict, the developments in Africa as well as the disputes between North and South over the world economic order – to name but a few – have fundamentally changed this picture.

The global involvement of the United States and the conceptualization of its policies in global terms have grown exponentially; one need only think of the Middle East problem, the controversies over a new law of the seas, or the North-South dialogue. President Carter's trilateral concepts, presented as the revival of links with old friends and allies, reduce Europe's position to a certain extent; it becomes one component in a world-wide concept.

The conclusion is obvious: even if Europe's security is still of vital interest for the United States and requires indispensable ties and US presence for many years to come, Western Europe has nonetheless been relegated to the position of a component of a globally conceived American foreign policy. For the same reason the Western alliance has thus, inevitably become but one of several instruments in the framework of a world-wide policy.

A second impetus in the decline of the primacy of security in the traditional sense has been the expansion of the nature of *the security problem*. Today, security policy is rightfully seen in a larger context than in the fifties and sixties, for it is no longer viewed merely as effective military deterrence and defense which only attacks the symptoms but also as a policy of détente which aims at the roots of the security problems by dealing with the origins of the East-West conflict. Détente policy is, therefore, an indispensable element of security policy which attempts not only to stabilize the East-West relationship through common crisis management, the reduction of confrontation as well as through arms control and cooperation but, in the long run, also seeks to change the East-West relationship.

At the same time there has been an *extension of security policy* in that alongside military threats, an increasing number of other developments has come to be considered a threat to security. Amongst these would be domestic developments in several countries of the alliance (e.g., economic deterioration and the rise of Communist parties), conflicts between members of the alliance, economic security (in particular the security of supply), terrorism, or the peaceful use of nuclear energy with its increased risks of proliferation.

As a consequence, security policy is becoming more complex and dependent on an increasing number of factors. The result has been that the Atlantic alliance has suffered a considerable loss of legitimacy and function, since under contemporary circumstances security policy must expand its instrumental base. It is no longer as easily circumscribed and can no longer be easily fitted into the traditional institutional structures. Its manageability and capacity for self-determination decreases. As the case of economic security demonstrates, modern security policy must, therefore, increasingly seek its framework of action in contexts which do not coincide with the traditional alliance.[3]

Today the *European Community stands between global challenge and fragmenting nationalism.* Both forces pull in opposing directions and erode political substance and effectiveness of the Community. Traditional mythical nationalism resulting from the exaltation of the nation, for example the Gaullist type, certainly still plays a role in Europe, though its significance has somewhat diminished. But under contemporary circumstances a nationalism rooted in social policy and the welfare state (already referred to in connection with the dilemmas of interdependence) is of much greater importance. Under pressure from the demands for social security in the broadest sense (e.g., full employment) which arise from domestic policy, this type of nationalism tends to give precedence to the satisfaction of national wishes over the requirements of integration policy. There can be no doubt that under the present circumstances of world-wide recession and structural unemployment throughout Europe this form of nationalism has gained considerably in importance.

The inner heterogeneity of the Community reinforces this tendency. This is true, first, of the increasing economic and social disparity amongst the individual Community members which, contrary to the expectations of the Community's founding fathers, has increased considerably rather than declined. The gap between the economically strongest and weakest regions, e.g., between the Ruhr area and Sicily, is wider than in 1958. Secondly, the specific political and social conditions in the Community countries result in highly diverse approaches to solving their respective social and political problems. For example in France and Italy the inability to carry out the necessary amount of reform in social policy has caused the cooperation of the Communist Party to be viewed increasingly as a necessary condition for undertaking long over-due reforms. However, both tendencies, the economic disparity as well as the diverging political developments, weaken the integrative framework of the Community.

But the pressure of problems coming from "outside" the European Community is no less important. A large proportion of the problems which threaten the functioning of Western Europe's economy and society cannot be solved at the level of the European Community, but only on a larger, supra-regional or, indeed, global level. For example, energy policy lies within the competence of the EC; however, the Community's dependency on imported oil, the type of cooperation necessary between consumers and producers in the case of scarcity, the collaboration required in developing new technologies, or the necessary cooperation in the nuclear energy sector demonstrate that the levels of problem-solving transcend the framework of the Community. This is true of many other areas: the reform of the monetary system, raw material supply, coordination of development aid policy, the establishment of international guidelines concerning multinational corporations, the discussion of a new world economic order, to name but a few. What then remains of the Community's purpose if, for compelling reasons related to concrete problems, countries approach problems at levels beyond that of the EC? The Community cannot escape this fundamental challenge which could have a destructive effect but, as explained below, might possibly provide new impulses towards integration if appropriately handled.

As a third problem area we have mentioned the *threat to democracy*. Here we do not mean the "classic" threat through anti-democratic forces on the extreme right or left, but rather the threat which stems from the economic and social problems of modern industrial states behind which, to be sure, lurks the danger of a breakthrough of anti-democratic forces.

This also applies to what is misleadingly termed "Eurocommunism" (misleading because the concept disguises the heterogeneity of the various directions and national conditions). Certainly, not even the observer in the liberal-democratic camp, well-disposed towards these movements, can guarantee that they will, in fact, respect the rules of Western democracy in the future. This can only be demonstrated through actual participation in and exercise of power and by accepting a lost election. Whether or not this problem will actually present itself depends decisively upon whether economic and social problems facing modern industrialized societies in Western Europe can be alleviated successfully, if not solved.

Where do these problems lie? They have in common that, contrary to the central creed of traditional market economy schools of thought, they do not represent temporary phenomena, but rather stubbornly resist all attempts to solve them; they become structural: inflation, stagnation, unemployment, and, in many countries, balance of payments deficits. Political institutions can only provide short-term solutions, if any, often only postponing the problems to a future date where they will reappear in more intensified form. The high expectations of many societal groups and increasingly uncontrollable disputes on the distribution of wealth under conditions of lower or zero growth rates make far-sighted structural policy more and more difficult. The transmission of these problems across the borders of highly interdependent countries, as analyzed earlier, further accelerates the spiral of problems which modern democratic governments face.

The tasks which pose themselves are becoming inherently more difficult and more complex. To an increasing degree administrations, and parliaments to an even greater degree, are unable to steer or manage social and political processes. The danger of sudden changes and vigorous authoritarian action at both ends of the political spectrum increases in this situation. Due to their mutual dependency Western democracies face this fundamental challenge as a group even if, for the moment, these dangers remain limited primarily to Western Europe. The disappearance of the anti-democratic regimes in Greece, Portugal and Spain which had been an increasingly destructive contradiction within the "free" world, is encouraging but not entirely reassuring since these countries will soon be faced with similar problems.

Tasks of European-American Policy

In sketching the contours of change in Europe and the world we have already outlined the problem areas on which European-American policies must focus in the coming years. Which directions are conceivable here and which of the problems in the various areas are particularly important? We will briefly examine three areas: security in the coming years, problems of a reformed global order and system of management, and the further development of the European Community.

1. Security in the Coming Years

Not only in Europe does security rank high in the list of political priorities,[4] although we concluded earlier that the primacy of security in the traditional sense is declining. In this connection we mentioned the globalization of American security policy. Such a development raises serious problems for American-European policies in the future since it is likely to enhance the probability of diverging political views between the United States and its allies. Three approaches appear particularly relevant in dealing with this problem.

First, it will continue to be the task of European and American policy to maintain awareness of the existing identity of interests and to mobilize this awareness politically. This is all the more necessary when diverging opinions arise in a number of areas. These identities of interest include Western European security, the maintenance of the status quo in West Berlin, and the preservation of an adequate balance of military forces. This presupposes a direct involvement of the United States in Europe and its military presence for many years to come.

A second consequence of the globalization of American foreign policy could be to intensify the American-European consultations on all questions related to Western Europe. It goes without saying that we will have to use as our point of departure a broad security concept (to be briefly discussed below) in which security encompasses the wide range of détente, defense, and deterrence policy, as well as economic security. Two areas appear particularly important here with regard to increased consultations between the United States and Western Europe. The area of arms control and disarmament should be mentioned here. As one important consequence of political developments and the evolution of weapons technology, the scope of topics has shrunk which lend themselves to purely bilateral dealings between the United States and the Soviet Union. This is also true of the SALT talks. A number of its topics are immediately relevant for Western Europe.

Secondly, the necessity for more consultation should be seen against the background of the increased probability of wars. The developments of recent years have shown that war has remained a means of politics outside of Europe and, hence, outside the sphere of nuclear stability created by the two super powers. These are, in part, however, areas from which a military conflict could spread to Europe and which are, therefore, also relevant to the alliance. This is particularly true of the Middle East where a certain coordination of American action with its European allies appears desirable.

Thirdly, the answer to tendencies toward globalization in American policy lies within the Western alliance itself. Precisely because the world-wide involvement of the United States has increased and the individual contribution of a number of alliance members has decreased, the maintenance and strengthening of this framework is decisive. For in this manner the commitment for mutual support, so essential to peace in Europe, is preserved and an institutional framework is retained which ensures all alliance members the opportunity for equal participation in the discussion of central problems of Western security policy.

The inherent expansion of the security problem mentioned above raises particularly difficult problems for the alliance. NATO remains essential and indispensable to carry out an adequate defense and deterrence policy. New kinds of security threats have arisen, however, which can no longer be mastered in the traditional alliance context. In such cases flexible action, suited to the specific problem area, is necessary, whereby bilateral and multilateral approaches are of equal importance; cooperation with non-members can be just as important here as the cooperation with old allies. Only a few examples can be given here to indicate the nature of the challenge to innovation and to point to possible solutions.

As already mentioned, modern security policy does not only consist of an effective military and deterrence policy for which NATO continues to be the only appropriate framework. Détente policy is just as crucial to security, for it tries to diminish the threat at its origins. The reduction of confrontation, arms control, common crisis management, and cooperation with the adversary attempting to change the antagonistic relationship cannot – in contrast to defense policy – be pursued in an "inner-directed" way; this policy requires involvement, negotiation, and cooperation with the opponent, who is at the same time a partner.

Neither politicians nor the public have been prepared by history for mastering such conflicting tasks. This poses difficult problems, above all in democracies: Internally, during periods of détente traditional defense policy is viewed more critically – a development not only unavoidable but inherent in the logic of the détente process; externally, détente reduces the imperative for common policies and alliance discipline. Nevertheless, there is no alternative to détente policy. On the contrary it is hard to imagine that a continuation of the present practically uncontrolled arms race would not sooner or later lead to catastrophe. When the critics of détente policy proclaim it a failure by referring to the absence of fundamental or "systemic" change, they overlooked several factors. First, even a policy conceived for the medium term needs long-term points of orientation. Second, this policy *is* a long-term policy. Finally, it would be unrealistic to expect quick changes given the deep roots of the East-West conflict in the political and economic structures of both systems.

Security has an essential liberal-democratic component. It also always means the "freedom of autonomous societal development of a people."[5] We pointed out earlier that perhaps the most important threat to democracy stems from economic and social problems which the industrial nations of Europe can no longer master. It is obvious that NATO is not the suitable instrument to counteract this kind of threat to Western security. Rather, it is all those measures of international solidarity and those institutions for cooperation which make an effective contribution to solving the difficulties of particularly hard-hit countries. These would include not only measures of financial support and special aid programs but, above all the European Community, which has the decisive function of creating a bond of solidarity for preserving European security in the broadest sense.

A third area is economic security. Its increasing significance represents one of the most predominant changes in the security policy of recent years. The lessons learned in the Suez crisis of 1956 were soon forgotten. The alliance continued to focus its energy on the military components of threat. Moreover, the growing interdependence resulting from the increasing prosperity of Western countries and rising foreign trade was considered to be an advantage rather than a problem.

The oil crisis of 1973–1974 and the ensuing developments suddenly changed this perspective and illustrated the importance of security of supply, above all of essential raw materials, for the continued functioning of the Western economic and political systems. Under the conditions of interdependence and vulnerability of modern industrialized states, economic security has become a vital part of security policy, i.e., governments now are faced with the task of preventing changes in the foreign economic parameters which could result in a breakdown of their social and political system.[6] NATO can, at best, only contribute to such a goal by creating a forum for political coordination. In contrast to the military realm of the alliance, the maintenance of economic security also depends upon non-members of NATO which do, to be sure, have a relationship of economic interdependence with alliance members, but which often pursue completely different foreign policy goals. Hence, the maintenance of economic security is no longer completely in the hands of the alliance, but depends on the cooperation of outside states, in particular producers of raw materials.

Economic security requires collaboration with members and non-members of the alliance and varies in composition according to the concrete problem at hand. Steps in this direction have been taken over the past several years: for example the collaboration of Western industrial states within the OECD, the summit meetings of the most important industrialized states, the International Energy Agency (IEA), the European Community, or the

North-South dialogue in the Conference for International Economic Cooperation (CIEC).

Other relevant problem areas for American and European policy could be added to this list. The cooperation to prevent the proliferation of nuclear weapons through the export of nuclear technology which will be discussed below; the fight against terrorism; the reduction of arms transfer to developing countries which has assumed alarming proportions for regional and global stability; arms control which is becoming increasingly difficult due to new weapons technologies: these are a few of the areas confronting the security policy of Western Europe and North America.

Cooperation in a multilateral alliance framework continues to be decisive for carrying out the security tasks of the coming years. That alone is, however, insufficient. The countries of Western Europe and North America only have a chance of solving future problems if they pursue a flexible security policy with respect to new problems or new partners.

2. A Reformed Order and Management at the Global Level

The countries of North America and Western Europe, for reasons that will be discussed below, are especially called upon to deal with the problems that arise at the global level. In the above we have discussed in detail the dilemma of interdependence, the challenging of the traditional world economic system, as well as the increasing importance of global issues which have resulted from the tensions between the welfare state and the international exchange system. Problems and prospects of European-American policy are to be examined by sketching the possibilities for pragmatic approaches to international management illustrated by two examples: the fight against poverty and the peaceful use of nuclear energy.[7]

In times of rapid change and increasingly urgent economic and social problems at a global level, the question arises whether a suitable approach can be found which may prevent a worsening of the situation and at the same time contribute to creating a better world order which would be more suited to solving the problems at hand than the present system. In this context the thesis is often advanced that global approaches with universal participation of states are required whenever dealing with important issues. Sometimes the possibility of representative bodies such as the International Monetary Fund or the Conference for International Economic Cooperation is mentioned in this context.

Several arguments speak against such an approach. Firstly, the sheer number of 145 or more states impedes the effectiveness of negotiations to an almost paralyzing extent. The various systems of representation share this problem, since those who are to be represented in practice take part as well. Secondly, the minimum degree of trust and experience in cooperation necessary for effective negotiations are low at the global level while mistrust and antagonism are strong. Thirdly, either the interest of many nations in specific questions is minimal or they are unable to make a significant contribution to solving them. Finally, with an increasing number of participants the probability rises that negotiations cannot go beyond the lowest common denominator and will achieve little or nothing.

There are many good reasons to believe that the industrialized democracies of the West – the countries of the trilateral region – should undertake special efforts to contribute to the solution of global problems. Attempts in this direction have been analysed in detail in this volume by Wilhelm Grewe and Henry Owen. Not only the similarity of economic development speaks in favor of such cooperation but also the common bond of democracy, similar values, a strong tradition, and extensive experience in cooperation in a wide variety of fields. These have led to a tradition of intensive interaction between administration, society, economic actors, and other groups.

A trilateral approach does not imply creating an exclusive club, but is rooted in the basic assumption of openness in a double sense: first, the countries of the trilateral region are called upon to internalize, as far as possible, the interests of outsiders in their considerations, thus contributing to the solution of global problems. Of course, such solutions are also in their own enlightened self-interest. Second, this approach should be open to those who, as a result of their position, are able to make a concrete contribution to solving the problems at hand. Hence, a pragmatic and flexible approach to cooperation with other states is essential, which includes different countries to a varying degree depending on the given situation.

Such an approach assumes that possible solutions must be sought according to the specific problem area, since the inclusion of too many issue areas leads again and again either to a standstill or to tedious progress in international negotiations. The mutual adjustment and coordination of policy which is dictated by the interdependence of national economies must, therefore, attempt to keep the individual issue areas separate, and, in addition, extend the group of participants to those countries which are able to effectively contribute to the solution of problems, as for instance the contributions of some OPEC countries to the solution of international monetary problems.

Economic development and the alleviation of poverty in developing countries will be the major task – besides preserving peace – of European-American policy at a global level. Not only our own moral values but also enlightened self-interest require a gradual solution of these problems. Such a policy can only succeed if the risks and benefits of interdependence are more justly distributed – i.e., more in favor of developing countries than at present. Such a policy requires a few basic changes of the previous order, similar to those the industrial countries themselves established in the course of a long development in their own market economy system, when socio-political considerations concerning the welfare of the poor resulted in correction in the market mechanism.

A policy in favor of a more just global distribution of goods presupposes that the industrial countries can themselves maintain a reasonable degree of growth – to be sure, more oriented toward qualitative growth but, nonetheless, a minimum of quantitative growth, since without this growth neither can the exports so necessary to the developing countries be absorbed, nor can the necessary aid be given. Second, an appropriate economic policy will require a system of stabilization of income as well as of price fluctuations of the most important raw materials exports from developing countries without, however, eliminating the market mechanism in its essence. Third, a gradual adaptation of production structures in the industrial countries will be unavoidable, involving the transfer of certain types of production to the developing countries in order to create better possibilities for economic development.

Fourth and finally, the battle against poverty in the developing nations will have to venture onto new paths. Many strategies which have been proposed in this area are simply unrealistic. The goal, occasionally propagated, of reducing the gap between the richest and the poorest tenth of the world population from the present ratio of 13:1 to a 3:1 ratio by the year 2010 cannot be attained in practice, since it would require that growth rates be sustained over decades which have thus far not been maintained over longer periods of time anywhere. What is more, measuring poverty by means of per capita income overlooks the fact that great injustices in internal distribution (indeed even increasing poverty of large sectors of the population as a result of the internal situation) can be disguised by such figures.

A reorientation of the debate on poverty should move away from the globalizing approach and place the satisfaction of minimum human needs in the foreground: nourishment, a minimum of health services, overcoming illiteracy, and, related to it, the creation of enough jobs. Such a policy would require the reorientation of parts of development aid, but could, in return, have a real effect on the lives of many millions of people who no longer can wait or want to wait until the global approaches to development policy have worked their way down far enough to have an effect on the individual and to help improve his fate.

The impetus for such a reorientation of policy can certainly come from various corners, yet the approval of the trilateral countries is not only the prerequisite for successful action, their joint action can be decisive in getting developments moving in this direction.

The peaceful use of nuclear energy is another example of how effective solutions to new problems also require new approaches where the trilateral countries can make a decisive contribution. The postwar policy of non-proliferation, as it was laid down in the Non-Proliferation Treaty and in the founding of the International Atomic Energy Organization, is now confronted with new problems arising from the rapidly growing importance of nuclear energy in the industrial planning of the developing countries.

Although the Non-Proliferation Treaty guarantees the transfer of civilian nuclear technologies (under the usual safeguards and controls), there is increasing doubt as to whether the transfer of sensitive technologies (enrichment and reprocessing of burnt nuclear fuel) does not raise the risks of proliferation to an unacceptable degree. The fear exists that developing countries which are domestically unstable or involved in international conflicts might risk a withdrawal from the control system and produce nuclear arms with the available weapons grade material.

In principle, two basic philosophies towards solving this dilemma can be distinguished which have both played a role in the disputes between the United States and several European countries, in particular the Federal Republic of Germany: first, a strategy of denial which blocks proliferation through a refusal to deliver such technologies; second, a strategy of control through cooperation which is based on the assumption that through the positive incentive of delivery of all technologies – of course, under safeguards – the recipient countries will be kept from going outside the existing control system to buy technologies available on the world market, but then with fatal consequences for non-proliferation policy.

Although we cannot go into greater detail in this context, we should add in summary that long-term solutions to this question can only be found if the corresponding strategies include collaboration with the most important recipients even though there may be cases where a selective denial of specific technologies is called for. The idea that the "Suppliers' Club" of the exporters of nuclear technologies can simply dictate a solution to the developing countries does not do justice to today's realities and is bound to be counter-productive. For these reasons a number of developing countries supported the European governments in their dispute with the United States over the best non-proliferation policy during 1977. An inclusion of the most important recipients by no means excludes the possibility of agreements on additional control measures or the development of different technologies which would lower the risks of proliferation. It is, however, crucial that the important recipients be included in the dialogue.

3. The Further Development of the European Community

The further development of the European Community is the prerequisite for the solution of many of the problems analyzed here – or at least an essential aid. There is no alternative to the Community's further development: it remains an imperative of political reason.

While it is true that the economic and social problems of the member states and the resulting pressure to solve problems at the national level have re-enforced the fragmenting nationalism mentioned earlier, the Community has, at the same time, mobilized forces which counteract this tendency, stressing the Community's function as a political bond which spans its heterogeneous internal structure. Although economic integration has been stalled or slowed down in many areas, political integration has made progress: the Community has succeeded by means of the European Political Cooperation in speaking with one voice on, in part, very important foreign policy issues in the international arena and in articulating a common European will and specific European interests.

The divergence of economic and social developments amongst the member states often makes us overlook the fact that the governments acting here cannot disregard the organic ties which have grown in the course of the last decades as a result of their close economic interdependence without considerable damage to their own interests. The related acts of European political solidarity are, therefore, not only the expression of a common political identity but also of an awareness of constraints which make a European posture a matter of self-interest.

The further development of the political dimension of the Community as expressed in the creation of the European Council, the European Political Cooperation, and a multitude of special acts of mutual aid remains an urgent task for the coming years particularly in view of the internal developments in the individual member states. The direct elections of the European Parliament would point in the same direction, since the process of legitimation which they initiate creates an additional political bond, above all if the Parliament succeeds in securing additional responsibilities for itself and the European Community. The European Community must not only come to terms with the problem of fragmenting nationalism but also faces the dilemma of no longer representing the suitable level for the solution of many problems which must, instead, be sought beyond the Community or even in a global context. Developments in the area of energy supply, world economy, or North-South negotiations illustrate this. However, even in these areas the European Community retains an essential function, since it remains its role to articulate the specifically European interests, to express the mutual solidarity and to contribute as a group to solutions of wider regional or global problems. For example, effective cooperation in the trilateral region requires that Europe speak with one voice as far as possible, even if this often renders the process of cooperation more difficult.

The United States continues to exert considerable influence on the further evolution of the Community. Washington cannot create Europe, but it can certainly prevent it. It will remain an important task and in the self-interest of US policy in the future to promote this process wherever it can. This means, above all, that in negotiating with the Europeans the often easier, bilateral channels – which arouse suspicions of *divide et impera* anyway – should be avoided, whereas means of communication should be favored which treat the Community as a group or a unit, even if it may often be tedious for the United States, and time-consuming for the solution of the problems at hand.

The German-American relationship takes on a particular role in this context. Due to the growing weight of the Federal Republic as a result of its economic resources and its increasing role in European security the temptation of German-American bilateralism exists for both sides. As a result of its present economic position the Federal Republic inevitably has to be the advocate of European interests just as the United States, in turn, should show understanding for this position even if this occasionally means that in fulfilling this European function the Federal Republic differs in opinion from the United States on specific questions. A German-American "bi-gemonial" axis which ignored the requirements of the European Community would have a highly destructive effect and, thus, cannot be in the interest of the United States, the Federal Republic, or Europe.

Although North America and Western Europe continue to share important interests, especially in the field of security policy, differences in interests do exist in some areas, and could further develop in the future. For example, the comparative scarcity of raw materials in Western Europe result in a difference of interests with respect to the United States. It is also conceivable that the domestic political developments in Europe – above all on the southern periphery – will, in the future, be evaluated differently in Washington and European capitals. As mentioned above the European Community is an essential instrument in dealing with those dangers to democracy which arise from their economic and social problems. As concerns the role of the Community in counteracting the threat to democracy, it could play a decisive role in determining where the development of "Eurocommunism" will lead. Only the future will show whether the United States and the European Community will always act in concert on this issue.

The enlargement of the Community to include Greece, Portugal, and Spain should, on the one hand, increase its internal heterogeneity, since this would involve additional countries still in the stage of development and with difficult economic and social problems. On the other hand, the Community would thus be exercising its important role as a political bond uniting Western European states. Such an enlargement, nevertheless, inevitably lowers the effectiveness of its decision-making mechanisms and impedes the articulation of a clear political will of the Community.

These developments make it more necessary than ever to reassess the idea of a graduated integration introduced by Willy Brandt and picked up by Leo Tindemans in order to create a structure for the Community which has a core of states which will advance relatively far on the road of integration and in articulating a common policy and at the same time allow the remaining member states to participate according to their needs and capabilities in an atmosphere of European solidarity.

The European Community is doubtless more dependent than ever on the outside world for its own economic and social survival. And, vice-versa, the important Western and global problems cannot be solved without the specific contribution of the European Community, the further development of which must remain the cardinal goal of far-sighted European and American policy.

Notes

[1] These problems are examined in greater detail in Richard N. Cooper, Karl Kaiser, Masataka Kosaka: *Towards a Renovated International System.* Triangle Papers, No. 14. New York: The Trilateral Commission 1977.

[2] Stanley Hoffmann pursues this point in greater depth in his brilliant essay from which this contribution profited considerably, *Uneven Allies: An Overview,* in: David S. Landes, (ed.), *Western Europe: The Trials of Partnership. Critical Choices for Americans,* Lexington, Mass.: Heath 1977, pp. 55 ff., Vol. 8.

[3] These dimensions have been analyzed in greater detail in a research project of the Research Institute of the German Society for Foreign Affairs. cf. Karl Kaiser and Karl Markus Kries, (eds.), *Sicherheitspolitik vor neuen Aufgaben.* (Schriften des Forschungsinstituts der Deutschen Gesellschaft für Auswärtige Politik, Reihe Rüstungsbeschränkung und Sicherheit, Vol. 13). Frankfurt: Metzner 1977.

[4] The following draws on Karl Kaiser, *Die Sicherheit Europas und die Politik der Bundesrepublik Deutschland*, in: Karl Kaiser/Karl Markus Kreis, (eds.), *Sicherheitspolitik vor neuen Aufgaben*, op. cit., pp. 415 ff.

[5] Richard Löwenthal, *Freiheit der Eigenentwicklung*, in: *Außenpolitische Perspektiven des westdeutschen Staates*, Vol. 1: *Das Ende des Provisoriums*. (Schriften des Forschungs instituts der Deutschen Gesellschaft für Auswärtige Politik, Reihe: Politik und Wirtschaft, Vol. 30/1.) Munich and Vienna: Oldenbourg 1971, pp. 9 ff.

[6] cf. Wolfgang Hager, *Wirtschaftliche Sicherheit*, in: Kaiser/Kreis, (eds.), *Sicherheitspolitik vor neuen Aufgaben*, op. cit., pp. 374 ff.

[7] The following remarks draw on reflections which were discussed in more detail in a paper for the Trilateral Commission, Cooper/Kaiser/Kosaka: *Towards a Renovated International System*, op. cit.

LIST OF AUTHORS

FRANÇOIS BONDY, Journalist, Editor of *Schweizer Monatshefte* and *Die Weltwoche*; former Editor and Editor-in-chief of the monthly *Preuves*, Paris; among other publications author of: *Aus nächster Ferne, Der Rest ist Schreiben, Deutschland-Frankreich*.

ROBERT R. BOWIE, former Dillon Professor of International Affairs and Director of the Center for International Affairs, Harvard University, as well as Director of the Policy Planning Staff and Counselor of the State Department; now Deputy for National Intelligence to the Director of Central Intelligence; among other publications author of: *Studies in Federalism, Shaping the Future, Suez 1956*.

WILLIAM DIEBOLD, Jr., Senior Research Fellow at the Council on Foreign Relations, New York; former member of staff at the Office of Strategic Services and in the State Department; among other publications author of: *The United States and the Industrial World – American Foreign Economic Policy in the 1970s*.

PETER C. DOBELL, Director of the Parliamentary Center for Foreign Affairs and Foreign Trade in Ottawa, Adviser of the Senate and House of Commons Committee on Foreign Affairs and the Senate Committee on National Finance; among other publications author of: *Canada's Search for New Roles*.

FRANÇOIS DUCHÊNE, Director of the Centre for Contemporary European Studies, University of Sussex; former Director of The International Institute for Strategic Studies, London; among other publications author of: *The Case of the Helmeted Airman – A Study of W. H. Auden's Poetry, The Endless Prices*.

WILHELM G. GREWE, Professor emeritus of Constitutional and International Law; various functions in the German Diplomatic Service, Ambassador in Washington, at the NATO-Council, and in Tokyo; among other publications author of: *Gnade und Recht, Ein Besatzungsstatut für Deutschland, Deutsche Außenpolitik der Nachkriegszeit, Spiel der Kräfte in der Weltpolitik*.

WILLIAM E. GRIFFITH, Ford Professor of Political Sciences, Massachusetts Institute of Technology, and Adjunct Professor of Diplomatic History at the Fletcher School of Law and Diplomacy, Tufts University; author of several studies on Soviet foreign policy and world communism.

PIERRE HASSNER, Senior Research Associate at the Centre d'Etudes et de Recherches Internationales of the Fondation Nationale des Sciences Politiques, Paris; Professor of Political Sciences at Johns Hopkins University European Center, Bologna; among other publications author of: *Change and Security in Europe, Europe in the Age of Negotiation.*

MARTIN J. HILLENBRAND, Senior Director, The Atlantic Institute for International Affairs, Paris; former member of the Diplomatic Service of the United States; last posting Ambassador to the Federal Republic of Germany; among other publications author of: *Power and Morals.*

KARL KAISER, Professor of Political Science at Cologne University and Director of the Research Institute of the German Society for Foreign Affairs, Bonn; among other publications author of: *EWG und Freihandelszone, German Foreign Policy in Transition, Europe and the United States – The Future of the Relationship.*

NORBERT KLOTEN, President of the Baden-Württemberg Central Bank; former Professor for Economic Theory, Economic Politics and Political Economy; Head of the Research Institute for Political and Economic Planning Processes, and from 1970–1976 Chairman of the Expert Council for the Appraisal of Economic Development; Joint Editor of *Systeme und Methoden in den Sozialwissenschaften.*

ULRICH LITTMANN, Executive Director of the German–American Fulbright Commission; author of several studies on the US and comparative education theories.

JOHN J. MCCLOY, former Assistant Secretary of War, from 1947–1949 President of the World Bank, from 1949–1952 United States Military Governor and High Commissioner for Germany; among others, Chairman of Chase National Bank, Ford Foundation, and Council on Foreign Relations.

UWE NERLICH, Director of Studies, Research Institute of the Foundation Science and Politics, Ebenhausen; Adviser to the International Institute for Strategic Studies, London; Vice-President of the European–American Institute for Security Research, Los Angeles; author of numerous publications on the issues of East–West relations, American foreign policy, and international security.

HENRY OWEN, Director for Foreign Policy Studies, Brookings Institution; former President's Special Representative for Summit Preparations and Chairman of the State Department's Policy Planning Councils; among other publications author of: *Next Phase of U.S. Foreign Policy, Setting National Priorities.*

WILHELM RALL, Research Assistant at the Department of Economics at Tübingen University and Assistant to an international consulting firm in Düsseldorf; author of various contributions on stabilization policy and economic problems in East–West relations.

KLAUS RITTER, Director, Research Institute of the Foundation Science and Politics, Ebenhausen; Honorary Professor of International Affairs and Security Issues, Munich University; author of several publications on East–West relations and international security issues.

BENJAMIN C. ROBERTS, Head of the Department of International Economic Relations, The London School of Economics and Political Science; former President of the British Universities Industrial Relations Association; Editor of *The British Journal of Industrial Relations.*

J. ROBERT SCHAETZEL, former member of the Diplomatic Service of the United States, 1966–1972 Ambassador to the European Communities; among other publications author of: *The Unhinged Alliance – America and the European Community.*

HANS-PETER SCHWARZ, Professor of Political Science at Cologne University and Member of the Board of Directors of the Federal Institute for Eastern and International Studies, Cologne; among other publications author of: *Vom Reich zur Bundesrepublik, Handbuch der deutschen Außenpolitik* (ed.), *Zwischenbilanz der KSZE.*

ANDREW SHONFIELD, Director, The Royal Institute of International Affairs, London; former Chairman of the British Social Science Research Council and Member of the Royal Commission on Trade Unions and Employer's Association; among other publications author of: *Modern Capitalism, Europe – Journey to an Unknown Destination.*

RAYMOND VERNON, Director, Center for International Affairs, Harvard University, and Herbert F. Johnson Professor for International Business Management, Harvard Business School; among other publications author of: *Storm over the Multinationals – The Real Issues, Sovereignty at Bay – The Multinational Spread of U.S. Enterprises, Big Business and the State – Changing Relations in Western Europe.*

WOLFGANG WAGNER, Editor-in-chief of *Hannoversche Allgemeine Zeitung* and Editor of *Europa-Archiv*; former correspondent of German and foreign daily papers in Bonn, as well as radio and television commentator; among other publications author of: *Die Entstehung der Oder-Neiße-Linie, Die Teilung Europas, Europa zwischen Aufbruch und Restauration, Die Präsidententwahl 1969.*

LIST OF ABBREVIATIONS

AATG	American Association for Teachers of German
AFL	American Federation of Labor
AMF	Allied Command Europe Mobile Force
APSA	American Political Science Association
ASEAN	Association of South-East Asian Nations
ASW	Anti-Submarine Warfare
AWACS	Airborne Warning and Control System
BP	British Petroleum
CBO	Congressional Budget Office
CDU	Christlich Demokratische Union
CERES	Centre de Recherches et d'Etudes Socialistes
CERN	Conseil Européen pour la Recherche Nucléaire
CFDT	Confédération Française Démocratique du Travail
CFP	Compagnie Française du Pétrole
CGIL	Confederazione Generale Italiana del Lavoro
CGT	Confédération Générale du Travail
CIEC	Conference on International Economic Cooperation
CIO	Congress of Industrial Organizations
CIP	Council of International Programs for Youth Leaders and Workers
CCC	Conseil de Coopération Culturelle
CCMSzMP	Central Committee Magyar Szocialista Munkáspart (Hungarian Socialist Worker's Party)
CMEA	Council for Mutual Economic Assistance (COMECON)
CPSU	Communist Party of the Soviet Union
COMECON	Council for Mutual Economic Assistance (CMEA)
CSCE	Conference for Security and Cooperation in Europe
CSU	Christlich Soziale Union
DAAD	German Academic Exchange Service
DAC	Development Assistance Committee (OECD)
DC	Democrazia Cristiana (Italy)
DFG	Deutsche Forschungsgemeinschaft
DGB	Deutscher Gewerkschaftsbund
DKP	Deutsche Kommunistische Partei
EC	European Community
EDC	European Defence Community
EEC	European Economic Community
EFTA	European Free Trade Association
EPC	European Political Cooperation
ETUC	European Trade Union Confederation
Euratom	European Atomic Energy Community

FBIS	Foreign Broadcasting International Service
FBIS/EEU	Foreign Broadcasting International Service East-Europe
FBIS/SOV	Foreign Broadcasting International Service Soviet Union
FBIS/WEU	Foreign Broadcasting International Service West-Europe
FBS	Forward-Based Systems
FDP	Freie Demokratische Partei (FRG)
FGTB	Fédération Générale du Travail de Belgique
FRG	Federal Republic of Germany
GATT	General Agreement on Tariffs and Trade
GDR	German Democratic Republic
GNP	General National Product
HMSO	Her Majesty's Stationery Office
IBRD	International Bank for Reconstruction and Development
ICFTU	International Confederation of Free Trade Unions
ICI	Imperial Chemical Industries
IDA	International Development Association
IEA	International Energy Agency
IIE	Institute of International Education
IISS	International Institute for Strategic Studies (London)
IMF	International Monetary Fund
ITO	International Trade Organisation
ITT	International Telephone and Telegraph
LCY	League of Communists of Yugoslavia
LDC	Less Developed Countries
LO	Landsorganisationen i Sverige (Swedish Trade Unions)
MBFR	Mutual Balanced Force Reductions
MCPL	Military Committee Planning (NATO)
MIT	Massachusetts Institute of Technology
MITI	Ministry of Trade and Industry
MLF	Multilateral Force
MRCA	Multi Role Combat Aircraft
MSI	Movimento Sociale Italiano-Destra-Nazionale
NATO	North Atlantic Treaty Organisation
NDEA	National Defense Education Act
NPG	Nuclear Planning Group (NATO)
NSC	National Security Council
OECD	Organization for Economic Cooperation and Development
OEEC	Organization for European Economic Cooperation
OPEC	Organization of Petroleum Exporting Countries
PCE	Partido Communista de España
PCF	Parti Communiste Français
PCI	Partito Communista Italiano
PGM	Precision Guided Munition
PQ	Parti Québecois
PS	Parti Socialiste (France)
PSDI	Partito Socialista Democratico Italiano
PSI	Partito Socialista Italiano
PSM	Projet Spécial Mobilité
PSOE	Partido Socialista Obrero Español
RFE	Radio Free Europe

SACLANT	Supreme Allied Commander Atlantic
SALT	Strategic Arms Limitation Talks
SED	Sozialistische Einheitspartei Deutschlands (GDR)
SPD	Sozialdemokratische Partei Deutschlands (FRG)
SWP	Stiftung Wissenschaft und Politik, Ebenhausen
TANJUG	Novinsky Agencija Tanjug (Yugoslav News Agency)
TASS	Telegrafnoye Agenstvo Sovietskogo Soyuza (Telegraphic Agency of the Soviet Union)
TUC	Trades Union Congress
UAW	Union of American Workers
UK	United Kingdom
UN	United Nations
UNCTAD	United Nations Conference on Trade and Development
UNESCO	United Nations Educational, Scientific and Cultural Organization
UNRRA	United Nations Relief and Rehabilitation Administration
USIS	United States Information Service
USSR	Union of the Socialist Soviet Republics
VAT	Value-added Tax
WFTU	World Federation of Trade Unions
WRK	West German University Rectors Conference

INDEX OF NAMES

P 8.83